Funding International Development Organizations

AIIB Yearbook of International Law

General Editor

Gerard J. Sanders

Executive Editor

Alberto Ninio

VOLUME 4

The titles published in this series are listed at *brill.com/aiib*

Funding International Development Organizations

Edited by

Christopher Smith
Xuan Gao
Thomas Dollmaier

BRILL
NIJHOFF

LEIDEN | BOSTON

Cover illustration: AIIB, 2020.

Typeface for the Latin, Greek, and Cyrillic scripts: "Brill". See and download: brill.com/brill-typeface.

ISSN 2590-2822
ISBN 978-90-04-46000-3 (hardback)
ISBN 978-90-04-46001-0 (e-book)

This book is printed on acid-free paper and produced in a sustainable manner.

Contents

Appendices

Editors' Note

Figures, Graphs and Tables

Figures

Graphs

Tables

CHAPTER 1

Funding International Development Organizations

Christopher Smith, Xuan Gao**, and Thomas Dollmaier****

1 Introduction

Funding development requires access to financial resources. While this causality is commonsense, the underlying complexity and struggle has accompanied international development organizations ever since they were founded. The objective of the 2020 AIIB Legal Conference and the 4th Volume of the AIIB Yearbook of International Law is to take stock. Taking stock requires us to look back on the history of international development organizations and analyze how their funding models have evolved over time. But taking stock shall also provide answers to how some of the most pressing issues of our time can be addressed and financed, while acknowledging the key role that international development organizations have in this challenge. This introduction seeks to provide a brief historical context of the funding of international development organizations and the significance of law in this process. We then shift the focus toward more current challenges and make brief references to the different chapters of this volume to flag how the contributors address many of them. Finally, we would like to take this opportunity to thank everyone involved in the 2020 AIIB Legal Conference and the production of this yearbook. The motivation behind both the conference and this volume is to create a space for discussion, inspiration and learning among practitioners and academics from a diverse range of institutions. Despite geographical distance and a multifaceted professional expertise, we are united through the "invisible college"[1] of international (development) lawyers. We hope that the 2020 AIIB Legal Conference and this volume contribute to strengthening this bond.

* Chief Counsel, Private Sector Investment & Treasury Operations, at AIIB, christopher.smith@aiib.org.

** Chief Counsel, Institutional and Administrative, at AIIB, xuan.gao@aiib.org.

*** Legal Associate at AIIB, thomas.dollmaier@aiib.org.

1 Schachter, 1977.

2 The Funding Model of Multilateral Development Banks and the Role of Law

If we look back in history, the funding of the International Bank for Reconstruction and Development (IBRD) was unchartered territory. After the conference at Bretton Woods, United States, where the IBRD and the International Monetary Fund were officially founded in 1944, the world was still in the midst of war. At the same time, the founders were explicitly forward-looking and created two institutions designed to contribute to rebuilding war-torn countries and protecting global economic and financial stability. Due to the limited availability of government funds after the war, reliance on resources from capital markets was an early imperative. The final step of the IBRD's success in gaining the trust of financial investors was achieved when it was awarded a AAA rating in 1959.[2]

The law played an important role in this success story. Specifically, the ingenuity of the legal claims for paid-in and callable capital allowed the IBRD to leverage the limited member state subscriptions without the need to actually call in the larger portion of its capital.[3] This way, the law was critical for the development and consolidation of the funding model of multilateral development banks (MDBs) and served as a blueprint for all MDBs subsequently founded. What was thus established in the second half of the 20th century can be called the hybrid character of MDBs. This hybridity describes the dual identity of these institutions as sound financial partners with an explicit development mandate. Hence, the "bank" and the "development institution" are essentially two sides of the same coin.

This connection becomes particularly clear in Chapter 2 and Chapter 3 by Elena Sulima and Purva Chadha, respectively, when describing the experiences of the European Bank for Reconstruction and Development and the International Finance Corporation (IFC) in developing domestic capital markets with a clear development objective. In Chapter 4, Yixin (Christine) Chen provides us with another example of the link between financial markets and economic development when describing the evolution and opening-up of China's debt capital markets supported by MDBs.

Today, the question of funding international development organizations continues to be a fascinating area of legal practice at the intersection of public international law, institutional law, and domestic law. Different elements

2 Kapur et al. 1997, 11–12 and 205–206.

3 Kapur and Raychaudhuri 2014, 2–3.

of these fields are explored by the authors of the Chapters 5, 6 and 7. While Christopher Moore and Paul Kleist in Chapter 5 analyze the status of jurisdictional immunity of MDBs in the United States after the landmark ruling in *Jam v. IFC* by the U.S. Supreme Court in 2019, Paul Dudek in Chapter 6 takes a close look at the regulatory requirements for international financial institutions (IFIs) to issue securities in the United States. In Chapter 7, Minny Siu and James Guan shift the focus toward Chinese domestic law by exploring the legal status of IFIs in China at the intersection of public international law and domestic legislation.

3 Evolution and Current Challenges

At the Asian Infrastructure Investment Bank (AIIB), the AAA rating awarded continuously since 2017 provides the foundation for the growth of the Bank and the expansion in operations. Other milestones include the first bond issuance by AIIB in USD in 2019, as well as subsequent issuances in a host of other currencies, such as GBP, EUR, RMB, TRY and INR. However, the global financial environment has of course changed significantly since the basic funding model of MDBs was first created. Gerd Droesse in Chapter 8 and Ilias Bantekas in Chapter 13 explore some of these developments. In his chapter, Gerd Droesse analyzes the link between the funding models of IFIs and their organizational structures and provides suggestions for how resource mobilization can become more effective. Ilias Bantekas in Chapter 13 describes how MDBs have become agents of private contract despite their public international character.

While the partnership between capital markets and MDBs has grown even stronger, so have the challenges that we are facing today: From the climate crisis, digitalization, the pandemic, to economic downturn and military conflict, to name but a few. In times of crises, the anticyclical investment model of MDBs continues to be an indispensable source of financing for the members of these organizations. Importantly, all of these challenges do not only impact the way international development organizations invest, but also how and through which instruments they raise funds. Today, a close link thus exists between the development solutions these institutions provide, and the funds they raise for that purpose.

A case in point is the unique design of the Green Climate Fund as described by Douglas Leys and Rosanna Anderson in Chapter 9. Further examples of such link between financing and fundraising are social impact bonds or green bonds issued by MDBs. Heikki Cantell in Chapter 10 analyzes the developments and opportunities behind the labelled bond concept. Another example are trust funds established by donor countries for the specific purpose of providing relief in the face of a humanitarian crisis or pandemic.

Finally, the investments of international development organizations increasingly seek to mobilize private capital by providing assurances to private investors about the quality of the project and the high standards traditionally required by multilateral institutions. This may be particularly relevant when it comes to digitalization and smart infrastructure, as Arthur Mitchell argues in Chapter 11. Gayle Girod in Chapter 12 then explains how USAID has engaged the private sector in order to reach its development objectives.

4 The Creative Role of Lawyers and Their Partners in International Development

All of these developments and challenges require and build upon the "creative role of the lawyer", as the former General Counsel of the World Bank, Ibrahim Shihata, has described it.[4] Such creativity most certainly includes striking the right balance between maintaining stability through the law, while developing the law further in view of economic and social progress, as H.E. Judge Xue Hanqin reminds us in Chapter 14. Indeed, we would add that in order to address the challenges of our time and fulfill the development mandate written into the charters, creativity and innovation are required by all partners inside and outside of international development organizations. This volume seeks to contribute some food for thought and clarity on the topic and will hopefully stimulate discussions and innovation going forward.

On a final note, we would like to thank the numerous colleagues who have contributed to making the 2020 AIIB Legal Conference and this volume possible. First, we would like to thank the speakers and contributors to this yearbook as well as all the participants of the Legal Conference. Your expertise and insights made the exchange incredibly stimulating, and we appreciate the valuable time you have taken out of your busy schedules to join us for this discussion. Inside the Legal Department of AIIB, we would like to thank all organizers of the Legal Conference, and in particular the moderators of the panels (Rüdiger Woggon, Tomas Kairys, Ranjini Ramakrishnan and Alex Pauwels) as well as the legal assistants (Yitong Zuo, Bingyi Xu, Yunlu Huang and Yuki Zhang). Without the strong support from colleagues, this event and yearbook would not have been possible. Finally, we would like to thank all reviewers of

4 Shihata 1998.

the contributions for their engagement with the chapters and suggestions to the authors.

5 Conclusion

The unity of the "invisible college"[5] requires dedication, time, and commitment from all legal professionals in order to stay vibrant and innovative, and to find answers to the challenges of our time. Funding international development organizations – and most importantly delivering the development mandate to our clients – are two of these challenges. The task could not be greater, but also could not be more important.

References

Kapur D, Lewis J P, Webb R C, The World Bank: its first half century (Brookings Institution Press 1997).

Kapur D, Raychaudhuri A, 'Rethinking the Financial Design of the World Bank' (2014) Center for Global Development, Working Paper 352 <https://www.cgdev.org/publication/rethinking-financial-design-world-bank-working-paper-352> accessed on 29 June 2022.

Schachter O, 'Invisible college of international lawyers' (1977) 72 Nw. UL Rev., 217.

Shihata I F, 'The Creative Role of the Lawyer-Example: The Office of the World Bank's General Counsel' (1998) 48 Cath. UL Rev., 1041.

5 See note 1.

PART 1

The Role of International Organizations in the Development of Local Capital Markets

CHAPTER 2

Development of Domestic Capital Markets

The EBRD Experience

*Elena Sulima**

Abstract

The European Bank for Reconstruction and Development (EBRD or the Bank) was established in 1991 to help build new, market-based economies in the post-Cold War era in Central and Eastern Europe. The EBRD's regions of operations have since been enlarged significantly to include the Southern and Eastern Mediterranean, Turkey, Mongolia and more. The Bank continues to play a critical role in financing projects and investing in the private and public sectors of its countries of operations and promoting their transition to a market economy. The EBRD's expertise and deep knowledge of the region has allowed it, in cooperation with other international financial institutions (IFIs), to play a crucial role in stabilizing local economies and helping them recover after the shocks of global and regional economic crises. The current global pandemic and related economic slowdown has presented the Bank with a new challenge to provide specific support to local economies in their recovery efforts. The Bank's investment and financing projects are supported by expert policy advice, technical expertise, and training. However, during crises, such as the current pandemic, it becomes especially evident, that financing projects and bringing external investments alone is not sufficient. The Bank's regions need help to build sound local capital markets that will enable countries to channel their resources into domestic, long-term financing and development projects. Many IFIs contribute to the development of local capital markets by being active market participants. The EBRD, additionally, assists with advice and assistance on policy reforms which further help improve the investment climate in its countries of operations. This article focuses on the role of the EBRD in developing domestic capital markets in its countries of operations. It provides examples of the Bank's regulatory reform projects, aimed at creating a legal framework conducive to domestic bond issuances by IFIs. It also provides an overview of the challenges posed by the securities regulatory framework in various countries of the EBRD's regions of

* Associate Director and Senior Counsel, European Bank for Reconstruction and Development, sulimae@ebrd.com.

 | DOI:10.1163/9789004460010_003

operations. The article also considers the regulatory gaps for hedging instruments in the Bank's regions and provides examples of its reform projects, aimed at the development of necessary netting and collateral related legislation in the jurisdictions in question.

1 Introduction

The growth of debt capital markets in emerging economies worldwide, including in the Bank's countries of operations, has shown its potential to become the catalyst for economic growth. This reflects the improvement in private sector credit quality, regulatory and transactional transparency and, in turn, leads to growing domestic liquidity. However, both the financial crises of the past and the economic challenges presented by the current pandemic, underline the need for further development of liquid and self-sufficient local currency capital markets in these economies.

For example, experience shows that resilient and efficient local debt capital markets can help emerging economies reduce their financial vulnerability in times of crises. Local capital markets provide a destination for domestic savings, can facilitate more efficient resource allocation, lower transaction costs, and raise the productivity of resources through invention, innovation and technological progress, all primary factors in stimulating economic growth.[1] Several studies show a direct link between the development of capital markets and economic growth.[2]

Several macroeconomics books and studies have analysed various stages of capital markets development and compared economic growth indicators. They suggest that developed capital markets have a positive correlation to economic growth as they allow easier and more efficient long-term local currency financing, more efficiently channelling domestic savings into the real economy and encouraging local businesses to expand and grow.

The EBRD has been committed to the development of domestic capital markets in the countries of its operations since its establishment. In fact, one of the primary functions of the Bank, under the Agreement Establishing the EBRD, is "to stimulate and encourage the development of capital markets".[3]

1 Todaro and Smith 2011.

2 See, for example, Levine and Zervos 1996; Zhuang et al. 2009.

3 Agreement Establishing the European Bank for Reconstruction and Development (Chapter 1, Article 2. Functions).

Currently, the Banks' countries of operations include 38 countries in Central and Eastern Europe, Central Asia and the Southern and Eastern Mediterranean, plus the West Bank and Gaza. In many of these markets, the Bank has now become the leader among IFIs in this field, especially in respect of policy dialogue efforts relating to capital markets reform, regulatory development, and innovative bond issuances in domestic markets.

2 Rationale for Local Currency Financing

Why is local currency financing such an important part of the Bank's mandate? Except for exporters and companies with foreign currency receivables, borrowers in the Bank's regions are generally not able to efficiently manage currency risks. Hence, foreign currency loans are not an appropriate financing option for them. The Bank's lending in local currency becomes an important tool in mitigating or eliminating the currency exposures of such borrowers.

By providing loans in local currency, the Bank helps to improve the creditworthiness of projects that generate only local currency income, as it reduces foreign exchange risk. The Bank is also able to extend the maturity of local currency financing in the market as it can direct domestic liquidity that is mainly available on a short-term basis, into longer term lending in local currency. In addition, depending on applicable local legislation, projects in certain jurisdictions may be legally required to be funded only in local currency, for example, projects in the municipal sector.

At the same time, by borrowing in local currency, the Bank helps to stimulate the development of local capital markets. Bonds of an issuer with triple-A rating, such as the Bank, provide an alternative and transparent pricing benchmark to the government bond market. For domestic investors, the EBRD bonds serve as an additional investment asset of the highest credit quality, the choice of which is usually quite limited in local markets, and provide an opportunity for credit diversification in their portfolios. They also attract new investors that want to gain exposure to local currency without being exposed to local credit risk. Investing in the Bank's local currency bonds often brings new investors to local markets and encourages them to concurrently invest in the local government and corporate debt market. In addition, this enables the Bank to introduce innovative techniques in local currency financing activities that help foster the overall development of the market.

The EBRD has issued bonds in local currency in a number of domestic markets, including Hungary, Russia, Armenia, Georgia, Serbia, Kazakhstan, and Eurobonds in the currencies of many of its countries of operations. In many markets, the Bank was the first IFI to raise funds in local currency in the domestic market, and the first to offer innovative products that had not been previously available.

3 Developing the Legal Framework for Local Bond Issuance by International Financial Organizations

Issuing the first local currency bond in an IFI's country of operations usually represents the culmination of work of amending or devising local legislation, over months and years, sometimes decades. The Bank's experience has been that developing liquid local bond markets in transition countries is a process that requires a comprehensive reform of financial regulations and institutions, which takes both time and funding.[4]

The changes that are required to achieve a regulatory framework considered acceptable for an IFI bond issuance, encompass a wide range of issues: In addition to favourable issuance and disclosure rules, there needs to be a functioning market infrastructure to mitigate a host of risks, including legal, settlement and regulatory risks. A significant number of changes is usually required in order to achieve a working settlement system, properly functioning depositary services, an appropriate base of investors, clear rules for admission to public trading, a credible money market index, adequate regulation of bondholder rights and representation, etc.

As underlined by the International Monetary Fund, it is widely acknowledged that robust legal and regulatory frameworks are critical building blocks for the structure, development and functioning of local currency bond markets.[5] In this regard, while focusing on the immediate purpose of issuing local currency bonds in a particular country, the Bank aims for the introduction of best international practices and the development of instruments and rules that would benefit all market participants, and not just IFIs.

The approach to regulatory reforms in any particular jurisdiction needs to be individually tailored, as successful policy and structural reform ultimately depends on its specific circumstances, including a country's stage of development and sequencing of other reforms.

4 Local Currency Operations of the EBRD: Considerations on Country and Client Selection, November 2006 available at: <https://www.ebrd.com/cs/Satellite?c=Content&cid=1395239594111&d=&pagename=EBRD%2FContent%2FDownloadDocument> accessed 16 June 2022.

5 Bossu, Hillier and Bergthaler 2020.

Any reform project led by the Bank usually starts with careful analyses of the relevant national regulatory framework and identifying areas for reform and development. Local legislation applicable to the issuance and trading of bonds is usually tailored to the needs of local corporate issuers or national public law entities (governments, central banks, national development institutions, etc.). The regulatory provisions applicable to corporate issuers, even those applicable to foreign issuers, usually do not work for IFIs or address issues relating to their special status.

IFIs are established by, and function under, international treaties between sovereign states and, in many respects, these organisations are very different from corporate entities established under national laws, including in their legal status, especially their immunities and privileges, as reflected in their internal procedures, decision-making processes and documentation. As they are established to achieve positive societal objectives for their members or broader stakeholders, these organizations are designed to adhere to and advocate the highest standards of conduct in the various environments in which they are involved, including local capital markets. Therefore, in order to enable an IFI issuance of securities in a local capital market, applicable legal regulations need to ensure that the specificities of IFIs are recognised, and potential obstacles removed.

With this in mind, various registration, procedural and documentation requirements applicable to the process of securities issuance and placement should be reviewed and amended to adapt them to IFI expectations. It is equally important to make sure that any requirements of information disclosure applicable to the IFIs, both in the form of prospectus disclosure and ongoing disclosure, take into account their special status as international organisations and do not impose restrictions and requirements that are overly burdensome.

3.1 *Issuance Rules*

Bonds issued by IFIs are rarely envisaged by local securities legislation of the Bank's countries of operations. They need to be expressly included in the types of securities authorised under local securities law and IFIs recognised as eligible to issue bonds in the relevant local market(s). This means that, due to their special status and specificities, IFIs should either be entirely exempt from national rules on bonds issuance or, more likely, national laws should provide for specific issuance procedures for IFI bond issuance. In this regard, national law may specify that such exemptions or special rules apply to all international organizations, or only to IFIs of which the particular country is a member or choose to provide a specific list of IFIs eligible for such exemptions.

Typically, the Bank promotes an approach under which IFI bonds are exempt from the requirement of state registration. However, if such an exemption cannot be achieved for any reason, the Bank aims to make the process of the issuance registration suitable for IFIs and compatible with their special status and operational capabilities. The requirements for documents to be filed with a regulator for such issuance registration should be formulated broadly to cater for the IFIs' specific features and should be confined mainly to two points: the proof of their legal status as an international financial institution and the terms and conditions of their bonds.

In short, in formulating reform to encourage IFI issuances, it is important to ensure that national laws governing the issuance of local currency bonds do not pose obstacles or envisage any requirements, which would not be standard from an international debt capital markets perspective.

3.2 *Credit Rating*

Local regulations often require a specific credit rating as a condition for IFI local currency bond issuance and it is not always clear whether such rating relates to the issuer or to each bond issuance. Sometimes there is a requirement to obtain a rating by a local rating agency. Given the generally extensive and well-tested IFI bond issuance programmes, it is reasonable to require that the relevant IFI's credit rating by an internationally recognised rating agency be sufficient for a local bond issuance.

3.3 *Information Disclosure*

The Bank frequently has to persuade local regulators and authorities to exempt IFIs from the local disclosure requirements that are applicable to corporate issuers and allow them to fulfil transparency requirements that apply to them in international markets and that are familiar to them, and in accordance with their special status, constituent documents and standard operating procedures.

IFIs are large organizations, issuing securities in many international and domestic markets. It would not be practical and perhaps not possible for them to disclose material information on their operations and activities in the varied languages, formats, and timelines that would be necessary if the disclosure rules applicable to corporate issuers in each such market were to apply. On the other hand, generally, IFIs' activities and financial position are already made transparent and disclosed to the public in accordance with their treaties, internal by-laws and procedures.

Disclosure regulations that usually apply to public international bodies in connection with their public issuances often recognize such specificities in international markets. For example, public international bodies of which one or more European Union (EU) member state is a member, are exempt from prospectus requirements in the EU, and no disclosure is required by such organisation when issuing non-equity securities.[6] Nevertheless, the EBRD, like many other IFIs, prepares disclosure documentation on a voluntary basis in order to enable potential investors to make informed investment decisions. This is the yardstick that the EBRD applies when opening the dialogue with local jurisdictions on this matter.

IFIs, like the EBRD, are also exempt from on-going disclosure requirements in EU markets. Under the EU Transparency Directive, the rules on disclosure of annual financial reports and half-yearly financial reports do not apply to a state, a regional or local authority of a state, a public international body, of which at least one member state of the EU is a member, the European Central Bank (ECB), the European Financial Stability Facility (EFSF) established by the EFSF Framework Agreement, and member states' national central banks whether or not they issue shares or other securities.[7]

Many countries in the EBRD's regions of operations now follow this approach, allowing IFIs that wish to carry out public offerings, and whose securities are already admitted for trading on one of the recognized international stock exchanges, to disclose information in the same form, at the same time and in respect of the same timeframes. This allows IFIs to disclose information in local markets in the way to which they are accustomed and to carry out only a customary ongoing disclosure. Certain countries in the EBRD's regions have also agreed to allow the disclosure of information by IFI issuers in the English language.

3.4 *Use of Proceeds*

Local regulations may sometimes contain certain restrictions regarding the use of proceeds of bond issuances by international issuers. In certain countries,

6 Article 1.2(b) of Regulation (EU) 2017/1129 of the European Parliament and of the Council of 14 June 2017 on the Prospectus to be published when securities are offered to the public or admitted to trading on a regulated market, and repealing Directive 2003/71/EC.

7 Article 8.1(a) of Directive 2013/50/EU of the European Parliament and of the Council of 22 October 2013 amending Directive 2004/109/EC of the European Parliament and of the Council on the harmonisation of transparency requirements in relation to information about issuers whose securities are admitted to trading on a regulated market, Directive 2003/71/EC of the European Parliament and of the Council on the prospectus to be published when securities are offered to the public or admitted to trading and Commission Directive 2007/14/EC laying down detailed rules for the implementation of certain provisions of Directive 2004/109/EC.

national legislation requires government approval for the use of proceeds or limits the types of potential investment targets. The Bank tries to ensure that such regulations do not contradict any norms of an international treaty in case the particular country is a member state of a specific IFI, and that they do not infringe on the privileges and immunities that such IFI is accorded by such treaty or by international law.

3.5 *Other Regulatory Issues*

In addition to general rules relating to the procedure of bond issuance and information disclosure, issuers often face other issues in emerging markets that can be challenging. These include currency control restrictions, banking restrictions on non-residents, burdensome listing requirements, and many others. For example, certain restrictions may apply to non-nationals opening bank or securities accounts with local banks, registrars, or custodians for the purposes of offering, repurchasing and redeeming bonds or paying interest and other income to investors. There may also be currency control restrictions that adversely affect the ability of foreign investors to invest in local currency debt instruments. In some countries in the EBRD regions, issuers are sometimes faced with rules that require a delay in trading of the issued securities until the issuance report is approved by the relevant regulator.

Additionally, there is a limited potential investor base, as national laws in many countries in the EBRD regions do not allow institutional investors (e.g., pension funds or insurance companies) to invest in securities of foreign issuers, including those issued by IFIs.

The Bank is working with local authorities and regulators with a view to lift such restrictions and bring in best international market practices. The EBRD is also working on the development of the investor base in a number of countries of its region, trying to expand potential pool of local investors and bring in international investors to local markets.

4 Developing Local Capital Markets Operational Infrastructure

In addition to regulatory aspects, issuers in many countries in the Bank's regions also face challenges caused by the insufficient development of the local capital markets' operational infrastructure. These may include fragmented depositary arrangements, a rudimentary and insufficient clearing and settlement system, a lack of credible money market index, and others.

The EBRD frequently provides technical assistance to its countries of operations, aimed at building a sound capital markets infrastructure and achieving a functioning securities market. Depending on the level of the existing infrastructure development, the Bank's experts help with either building or strengthening certain elements thereof or with a complete infrastructure upgrade.

4.1 *Challenges for the Bank's Reform Projects*

Pursuing the task of changing local legislation and infrastructure requires not just technical expertise, for which the Bank has been long praised. It also requires the building of relationships with local authorities and sometimes to be ready to re-start the engagement process from scratch when governments or relevant officials change. It also requires skills to persuade them to follow best international practices. Often, it requires diplomatic skills to promote collaboration between various governmental authorities, in order to achieve the required functionality of the market as a whole.

Communication is, of course, essential for achieving the desired results, and it is important to engage with relevant stakeholders at an early stage. This helps build trust with and obtain the commitment of local authorities, which is a critical element without which no reform project can be successful.

The results of such engagement can be rewarding. Once the necessary regulatory and operational framework is in place, the Bank usually starts with a simple fixed or floating rate note issuance before moving to more complex and innovative structures. For example, following a simple floating rate note offering, the Bank issued index-linked, equity linked and commodity-linked notes in one of its countries of operations. These complex structured bonds may seem relatively usual in the developed capital markets, but they represent significant milestone events for local capital markets, where the choice of financial instruments available to investors is quite narrow and the regulatory environment restrictive, confusing and often in flux. Hence, each debut issuance in a local capital market usually represents a landmark event as it has an important demonstration effect and serves to attract new long-term investors to local markets.

5 The Bank's Reform Projects Aimed at the Development of the Derivatives Market

One of the important pre-requisites for an efficient capital market is the development of financial derivatives and access of local and international participants to domestic hedging instruments. Derivatives are a tool to manage exposures to, amongst others, interest rate and exchange risks, and this is exactly the use that the EBRD promotes across its countries of operations.

However, only a few markets in the EBRD regions provide their participants with access to adequate local hedging instruments, and this is a common issue faced by potential issuers in emerging economies.

According to the recent research published by the Bank for International Settlement, "only 10% of global derivatives turnover is in contracts denominated in the currency of an emerging market economy (EME), much lower than the share of these economies in global GDP or world trade. Derivatives in EME currencies also tend to be less complex and more likely to be traded outside the home economy than those in advanced economy currencies".[8] The reasons for this statistic are several and complex, but the major one is the lack of adequate protections for participants in the local derivatives market. For example, in many emerging markets, the legal and regulatory framework does not provide for the enforceability of derivative transactions or for legal concepts such as close-out netting or financial collateral. In some cases, derivative transactions are even classified as gambling and are therefore considered unenforceable.

Over the years, the Bank has been actively involved in projects aimed at the development of favourable netting and collateral legislation in its countries of operations. As part of the Bank's technical cooperation projects, a package of laws, aimed at the development of netting and collateral structures, has now been passed in each of Armenia, Croatia, Georgia, Latvia, Serbia and Ukraine. New legislative frameworks in each of these countries, established as a result of Bank-led reforms, provide for the enforceability of derivatives transactions, including netting, close-out netting and financial collateral, and reinforce key related concepts, such as settlement finality. Such new legislation allows companies to more safely and efficiently hedge their risk and exposure, including foreign exchange and interest rate risks, and contributes significantly to the development of a local currency financial market. These reforms also provide the green light to cross-border derivatives transactions, which could help attract additional financial resources to each of these countries.

The Bank has been working in these countries in cooperation with, and with the full support of the International Swaps and Derivatives Association (ISDA). In carrying out these technical cooperation projects the Bank has followed the guidance of core international derivatives templates, including the ISDA Model Netting Act and Guide,[9] the UNIDROIT Principles of Operation

8 BIS, Quarterly Review, Emerging Derivatives Markets, 2016.

9 See <https://www.isda.org/a/X2dEE/FINAL_2018-ISDA-Model-Netting-Act-and-Guide_Oct15.pdf> accessed 16 June 2022.

of Close-out Netting Provisions, 2013,[10] the EU Directive 2002/47/EC of the European Parliament and of the Council of 6 June 2002 on financial collateral arrangements,[11] etc.

Needless to say, in order to be implemented efficiently in practice, such international best practices need to be organically adapted to national legal systems, tradition and terminology. While working on each derivatives project, the Bank seeks to weave these concepts into local legal systems, by amending laws and regulations in each such jurisdiction, trying to eliminate the risk of re-characterization of these novel concepts and structures, which may nullify the transparency and assurances sought by market participants. Equally, the Bank aims for the recognition of the contractual documentation and structures used in international markets for documenting derivatives transactions, such as the ISDA Master Agreements.

Following the success of the EBRD reform projects, with the passing of the relevant legislation, the ISDA netting legal opinions for Armenia and Georgia were published in October 2019 and July 2020, respectively. Relevant derivatives legislation was enacted in Ukraine in August 2020, and close-out netting law implemented in Latvia in September 2021. The EBRD is continuing its efforts of developing netting and collateral legislation in its other countries of operations.

6 Conclusion

Over the past thirty years, the EBRD has built a reputation among its member states and beyond as a source of expertise, a trusted counterparty and a partner to local authorities in developing local capital markets. The Bank's involvement, both on the regulatory development level and by way of issuing bonds and entering into financial transactions in local markets, is widely recognised as contributing significantly to the development of capital markets in the countries in its regions to what is, in many ways, a historic transformation of the financial systems of its countries of operations into operational, more liquid and more resilient local financial markets.

10 See <https://www.unidroit.org/instruments/capital-markets/netting> accessed 16 June 2022.

11 See <https://eur-lex.europa.eu/legal-content/EN/TXT/?uri=CELEX%3A32002L0047> accessed 16 June 2022.

References

Bank for International Settlements (BIS), The BIS Quarterly Review for December 2016: A paradigm shift in markets?, (December 2016), <https://www.bis.org/publ/qtrpdf/r_qt1612.htm>, accessed 16 June 2022.

Bossu W; Hillier C and Bergthaler W, IMF Working Paper "Local Currency Bond Markets Law Reform: A Methodology for Emerging Markets and Developing Economies", (20 November 2020), <https://www.imf.org/en/Publications/WP/Issues/2020/11/20/Local-Currency-Bond-Markets-Law-Reform-A-Methodology-for-Emerging-Markets-and-Developing-49905>, accessed 16 June 2022.

European Bank for Reconstruction and Development (EBRD), Agreement Establishing the European Bank for Reconstruction and Development, (28 March 1991), <https://www.ebrd.com/news/publications/institutional-documents/basic-documents-of-the-ebrd.html>, accessed 16 June 2022.

European Bank for Reconstruction and Development (EBRD), Local Currency Operations of the EBRD: Considerations on Country and Client Selection, (November 2006), <https://www.ebrd.com/cs/Satellite?c=Content&cid=1395239594111&d=&pagename=EBRD%2FContent%2FDownloadDocument>, accessed 16 June 2022.

Levine R and Zervos S, Stock Markets, Banks, and Economic Growth, (December 1996). Available at SSRN: <https://ssrn.com/abstract=60141>.

Todaro M P and Smith S C, Economic Development, 11th ed.; Pearson: Harlow, UK, 2011.

Zhuang J et al., Financial Sector Development, Economic Growth, and Poverty Reduction; Economics Working Paper Series Number 173; Asian Development Bank: Manila, Philippines, 2009.

CHAPTER 3

The Role of Development Finance Institutions in Developing and Deepening Local Capital Markets

A Case Study of Masala Bonds and Maharaja Bonds Issued by the International Finance Corporation

*Purva Chadha**

Abstract

Development finance institutions (DFIs) can play a vital role in establishing and deepening local capital markets. Issuing local currency bonds is one of the various ways in which DFIs can achieve this. The International Finance Corporation (IFC) has been a leading player among DFIs in making local currency bond issuances in several countries globally. This chapter seeks to explore the significance of the participation by DFIs in local capital markets by examining the role of the IFC in establishing an offshore market for Indian rupee linked bonds and deepening the local corporate bonds market in India by issuing Indian rupee denominated bonds. In addition, this chapter will also discuss the significance of engaging and having an open dialogue with regulators and to enlist their support in permitting local currency issuances by DFIs, which do not necessarily fit within the existing regulatory framework.

1 Introduction

Why should DFIs participate in local capital markets? Is such participation consistent with their role and mandate? What will their participation in local

* Senior Counsel, International Finance Corporation (IFC), pchadha@ifc.org. The author acknowledges the contributions of Keshav Gaur (Director, Treasury Client Solutions, IFC), Glenn Jessee (Chief Counsel, IFC), and Kannagi Ragunathan (Senior Financial Officer, Treasury Client Solutions Asia, IFC) in sharing their experiences and perspectives from working on the IFC bond issuances referred to in this chapter, and in providing valuable insights and inputs that went into shaping this chapter.

 DOI:10.1163/9789004460010_004

capital markets achieve over and above what they achieve by providing financial assistance to borrowers outside of capital markets? Going to the very heart of these questions is the premise that the development of local capital markets is a valid development objective and an ideal worth striving for.

The author submits that sound capital markets are vital to development as they ensure efficient resource allocation,[1] create jobs, and spur economic growth.[2] Debt capital markets in particular are crucial sources of funds for entities looking to raise financing; they complement the financing available from traditional sources such as banks and financial institutions, and often play an important role in closing large financing gaps in critical sectors that are vital to development, such as infrastructure and housing.[3] In playing this complementary role, capital markets can alleviate some of the stress on the commercial banking system by matching long-term investments with long-term capital. In addition, capital markets also create channels for domestic savings, such as those managed by pension funds, provident funds and other institutional investors, and mobilize those funds for long-term productive uses in the local economy.[4] In such fashion, capital markets foster broader ownership of productive assets by retail savers. They enable individual and household savings to benefit from economic growth and wealth distribution and provide avenues for investment opportunities that encourage a thrift culture, critical in increasing domestic savings and investments that translate into economic growth.[5]

Given the role of local capital markets in economic development, it is natural for DFIs, given their focus and emphasis on development, to be concerned with and interested in the establishment and deepening of local capital markets. Not only is participation by DFIs in capital markets consistent with their role and mandate, but it is in fact imperative that DFIs, with their unique profile, high creditworthiness and credibility, play a role in establishing such markets where none exist and, where already existing, contribute to deepening those markets with their continued participation. When DFIs provide financial assistance to borrowers outside capital markets, their support impacts a project or a corporation or a sector; however, when DFIs provide support to entities through the capital markets, not only does it translate into financial support for the concerned project or entity or sector, but it also sends a strong

1 Andries 2009, 70.
2 Ibid, 74.
3 IFC, 'Debt Capital Markets Solutions' 2017, 21.
4 Cytonn 2019, Section II(b).
5 Ibid.

signal to observers, potential investors, and market participants alike in the market.

There are several ways in which DFIs can support the development of domestic capital markets. DFIs can finance projects or companies using local capital markets instruments – as noted above, this signals to the market that the DFI in question has confidence in the robustness of the local market and the instrument at hand. This can have the effect of attracting other foreign investors and institutional investors to the same market. DFIs can also help borrowers that, owing to their profile, credit rating or other reasons, have not yet been able to access the capital markets to raise financing and diversify their sources of funding. This can be done by having a DFI act as an anchor investor to such borrower's issuance or by such DFI credit enhancing the instrument. This will enable such borrower to raise its profile or the credit rating of its instrument to access the capital markets. DFIs are also uniquely placed, given their status and global experience, to provide policy advice to capital markets regulators, authorities, and market participants. Such advice can range from ways to strengthen the legal and regulatory framework for capital markets to strengthening key market infrastructure, as well as advice in the design of specific instruments, such as infrastructure debt funds or green bonds.[6] Another significant way in which DFIs can support domestic capital markets development is by issuing local currency bonds.[7] This chapter focuses on the issuance of local currency bonds as a tool to establish and deepen local capital markets. It attempts to do this by undertaking a case study of IFC's issuance of Indian rupee (INR) denominated bonds in the local domestic market as well as in the offshore market. For the purposes of simplicity, IFC's issuance of INR denominated bonds in the offshore market will henceforth be referred to as 'Masala Bonds', and IFC's issuance of INR denominated bonds in the local domestic market will henceforth be referred to as 'Maharaja Bonds', consistent with the nomenclature assigned to these instruments by the IFC.

2 Benefits of Local Currency Issuances by Development Finance Institutions

Issuance of local currency bonds by DFIs can promote the development of local capital markets in several ways. The author will lay out five ways in which

6 World Bank Group, 'Capital Markets Development' 2020, 18.

7 IFC, 'Developing Domestic Capital Markets' 2016, 2.

a local currency bond issuance by a DFI can benefit the domestic capital markets and economy at large: Firstly, when a DFI issues local currency bonds, it diversifies its sources of local currency funding for on-lending to entities that wish to borrow in such local currency. Entities with revenues in local currency generally prefer to borrow in their local currency, instead of borrowing in a foreign currency which means taking on currency risk. By matching the currency denomination of their assets and liabilities, borrowers can concentrate on their core businesses rather than focusing on managing exchange rate movements.[8] The most obvious and common tool for DFIs to access local currency funding for on-lending is cross-currency swaps. However, if a DFI makes a local currency bond issuance, it generates a readily accessible pool of local currency that it can then utilize for making local currency loans to companies. The advantage of having such a pool of local currency available compared to cross-currency swaps is that the DFI can then de-link its cost of funding from the swap market, and has the ability to lock-in the pricing of the loan for its borrowers prior to disbursement, thereby giving the borrower certainty when planning and managing its funding options. Secondly, making local currency issuances will involve the DFI testing domestic processes and regulations for bond issuances. Having gained that experience first-hand, the DFI will then be in a position to provide feedback to the market regulators and other relevant authorities on how to improve the existing processes and thereby encourage issuer- and investor-friendly improvements in local regulations.[9] Thirdly, local currency issuances by a DFI can have a catalytic impact on future bond issuances,[10] be it by other DFIs and international institutions or corporate entities operating in the market. A local currency issuance by a DFI demonstrates and signals to the market and other potential entrants into the market that the DFI fundamentally believes in the robustness of the market, including its legal, operational and market infrastructure. Further, it signals to the market an endorsement of and belief in the stability of the local currency, which can go a long way in attracting and facilitating other institutions and corporates to make similar issuances. Fourthly, through a local currency bond issuance, a DFI may introduce new investors to the local capital market, particularly international investors.[11] Such issuance by DFIs, which typically have a better credit rating than many sovereigns, will invariably attract strong demand from a wide variety of international investors which may otherwise not have participated.

8 IFC, 'Local Currency and Hedging Solutions' 2017, 19.
9 Ibid.
10 Ibid.
11 Ibid.

For instance, there may be investors who are interested in taking exposure to the underlying market, for reasons of diversification or otherwise, but have thus far not found the right credit to invest with. An issuance in the market by a DFI with a superior credit rating will attract this type of investors to the local capital market at hand. Fifthly, a local currency bond issuance by a DFI can introduce a new high quality asset class for local investors who are active in the domestic capital markets.[12] An issuance by a DFI in the local capital markets will provide local investors with an additional avenue for investment that was previously not available to them, and give them the opportunity to diversify their portfolio by investing in an instrument issued by an entity with high creditworthiness and credibility. All of these benefits will be observed in action in the subsequent parts of this chapter when delving into IFC's issuances of Masala and Maharaja Bonds.

3 IFC's Masala Bond Issuance

In 2013, the IFC held a series of discussions with the Government of India to develop solutions to deepen Indian capital markets. The objective was to expand the participation of foreign institutional investors in Indian markets, both onshore and offshore, as well as to allow a larger base of Indian corporate borrowers to access diverse funding options, beyond what was then available in the market.[13] These discussions took place in the context of the Indian economy's growing investment needs, and a challenging economic backdrop. India's investment requirements at the time were estimated at USD 4.7 trillion over a five-year period, to achieve average growth of 7 percent per annum. The public banking sector was expected to be constrained in respect of long term financing due to applicable prudential regulations.[14] The Indian Rupee had fallen to a record low against the USD due to capital flights spurred by a severe current account deficit and the tapering of quantitative easing by the US Federal Reserve.[15] In response, the IFC worked with the Government of India to develop offshore and onshore INR bond programs to support the development of capital markets in INR.[16]

12 Ibid.
13 'Mobilization of Private Finance by MDBs and DFIs' 2018, 73.
14 Ibid.
15 IFC, 'Masala Bond Program' 2017, 1.
16 'Mobilization of Private Finance by MDBs and DFIs' 2018, 73.

The issuance of Masala Bonds by the IFC was announced in October 2013 by the Indian government and IFC for an amount of up to USD 1 billion equivalent. This amount was increased more than two-fold subsequently in light of the success of the program.[17] The Masala Bond was issued outside India and listed on the London Stock Exchange.[18] The unique feature of this instrument was that it was denominated in INR but settled in USD (since INR cannot be delivered overseas).[19] To take an example, if IFC wanted to raise INR 1 billion, and there was an investor willing to lend the IFC INR 1 billion rupees by buying the Masala Bond, the investor would pay IFC the USD equivalent of INR 1 billion based on the current INR-USD exchange rate. At maturity, the IFC would repay the investor the USD equivalent of INR 1 billion, at the then prevailing INR-USD exchange rate. Therefore, all cash flows associated with Masala Bonds were settled in USD, but the investors received a return explicitly linked to the INR-USD exchange rate. In other words, the investors were taking the INR-USD currency risk. Hence, economically, a Masala Bond was equivalent to an INR bond.

This was an excellent instrument for investors seeking exposure to the INR. But what made it more attractive than other INR instruments was that it did not come with any of the restrictions of investing directly in India. Ordinarily, if a foreign investor wishes to invest in India, it must navigate through a complex maze of Indian rules and regulations. In many cases, the investor needs to register with local regulatory authorities to invest in INR instruments in India. What this instrument offered international investors was the ability to get INR exposure without needing to invest in India and therefore be subject to Indian rules and regulations. Masala Bonds gave investors the ability to benefit from India's strong economic fundamentals while avoiding the cumbersome onshore rules, regulations, registration procedures, and currency convertibility issues.[20] In addition, if you take into account IFC's AAA rating, this instrument not only gave investors exposure to INR, but also gave them that exposure without taking much credit risk at all.

Under its Masala Bond program, the IFC issued bonds of several maturities ranging from 3-year bonds, 5-year bonds and 7-year bonds, to 10-year bonds and 15-year bonds.[21] The 15-year tranche marked the longest-dated bonds in the offshore rupee market at the time.[22] The IFC also issued the first green

17 IFC, 'IFC Capital Market Solutions in Asia', 15.
18 LSE, 'Accessing the Global Markets through London', 25.
19 IFC, 'Masala Bond Program' 2017, 1.
20 IFC, 'Masala Bond Program' 2017, 2.
21 Ibid.
22 Ibid.

Masala Bond, the proceeds of which were earmarked for specific climate and environmental sustainability purposes.[23] Given the wide range of maturities, IFC's Masala Bond program created an Indian Rupee yield curve in the offshore market.[24] IFC's Vice President and Treasurer, Jingdong Hua, was quoted saying: "Lasting prosperity depends on strong and efficient capital markets. With our latest Masala Bond issuance, IFC has created an offshore rupee-market yield curve that stretches from three to fifteen years, deepening the market and making it more resilient. This sends a clear signal that investor demand for high-quality assets in India remains strong, despite global financial uncertainties".[25] All issuances under the Masala Bond program attracted a diverse investor base and received very strong interest from global investors and were oversubscribed.[26] The yields of the Masala Bonds were approximately 100 to 190 basis points below yields of Indian government bonds for corresponding maturities.[27]

The Masala Bond helped IFC diversify its sources of INR funding and created an alternative source of INR, ultimately with a view to optimizing the funding cost of local currency loans for borrowers in India. IFC had and continues to have large exposures in India – in fact, India is the country where IFC has its largest exposure globally.[28] IFC provides both dollar funding and local currency funding to companies in India. Before the Masala Bond, IFC would provide local currency funding to Indian corporates by entering into cross currency swaps with a swap counterparty. However, the Masala Bond provided IFC with a readily available pool of INR, which was very attractively priced and could, in turn, be used to make local currency loans in India at favorable pricing levels for borrowers. In other words, IFC was not only able to raise resources that could be invested into India, but it also raised them at pricing levels that were attractive for Indian borrowers. Indian borrowers benefited not just from the improved pricing of IFC loans, but also from the certainty of pricing that IFC was now able to provide. In the past, whenever IFC had funded local currency loans in India, it had done so relying on cross-currency swaps to obtain INR for on-lending. By its very nature, this necessarily had to be done at the time of funding the deal, leaving the pricing of the ultimate loan uncertain

23 Ibid.
24 IFC, 'IFC Capital Market Solutions in Asia', 15.
25 LSE, 'London Stock Exchange Welcomes IFC', 1.
26 IFC, 'IFC Capital Market Solutions in Asia', 15.
27 IFC, 'Masala Bond Program' 2017, 2.
28 Standard & Poor's 2020, 7 (IFC's India exposure accounts for 12% of its committed portfolio).

for Indian borrowers as it would be dependent on last-minute movements in the swap market. Since the Masala Bond issuance provided IFC with a pool of INR, the cost of which was known, IFC was able to provide borrowers in India certainty on how IFC local currency loans to them would be priced. This further helped the borrowers plan their fund-raising activities better, as they could compare their funding options in real time with concrete data. Tarun Bajaj, Joint Secretary, Department of Economic Affairs of India was quoted as saying: "The IFC Masala bonds [...] pave the way for more foreign investment to help meet India's private sector development needs".[29]

The impact of IFC's issuance of Masala Bonds, however, went beyond the volume of financing in local currency that IFC generated for investment in projects in India or the price at which such investments were made. The Masala Bond issuance had a very significant signaling effect. Following the success of the Masala Bonds issuance by IFC, the Reserve Bank of India, in 2015, amended its overseas borrowing regulations and allowed Indian corporates to issue masala bonds or offshore INR denominated bonds,[30] opening a new avenue for Indian companies to access foreign capital without bearing the currency risk of borrowing in foreign currency. Following this liberalization of regulations, several Indian corporates as well as state-owned firms have accessed the offshore market to raise financing by issuing INR denominated bonds. These issuers include Housing and Development Finance Corporation, which is one of India's leading housing finance company, Axis Bank Limited, which is India's third largest bank, NTPC Limited which is India's largest power utility company[31] and several others. A factsheet released by the London Stock Exchange on 14 July 2021 notes that there are 26 masala bonds listed on the London Stock Exchange with a combined outstanding value of over INR330 billion (approximately USD 5.1 billion equivalent).[32] For Indian entities which have accessed this market as issuers, the market provides access to a large global investor base looking for high-quality, INR denominated assets, which in turn allows for a larger potential program size to be executed in offshore markets.[33] Issuers who have accessed this market include not only Indian corporates, but also other DFIs such as the Asian Development Bank (ADB)[34] and the European Bank for Reconstruction and Development (EBRD)[35] which have raised funds,

29 IFC, 'IFC issued first Masala Bonds in London', 1.
30 RBI, 'Issuance of Rupee denominated bonds overseas' 2015, 1.
31 LSE, 'Accessing the Global Markets through London' 2017, 32.
32 LSE, 'Indian Rupee Bonds on London Stock Exchange' 2021, 1.
33 IFC, 'Masala Bond Program' 2017, 2.
34 Gong 2017, 1.
35 LSE, 'Accessing the Global Markets through London' 2017, 32.

like IFC, to support the financing of projects in India. This demonstrates that the Masala Bond issued by the IFC had a profound signaling and demonstrative impact that prompted changes in legislation, additional issuances and created an offshore rupee bond market.[36] It was a step towards the internationalization of the Indian rupee.[37] It made Indian rupee exposure accessible to global investors who had not been able to easily access it thus far. It is possible that over the long-term, investors willing to invest in offshore INR issuances may also start participating in INR issuances in India as their familiarity with the Indian rupee and financial system grows, which will also go a long way in deepening India's domestic capital markets. To quote Jin-Yong Cai, who was at that time the IFC Executive Vice President and CEO: "This bond issue demonstrates the powerful role that capital markets can play in linking international savings to infrastructure investment".[38]

4 IFC's Maharaja Bond Issuance

In addition to the Masala Bond, in August 2014, IFC also announced the launch of an INR bond to be issued by IFC in India for USD 2.5 billion equivalent.[39] This INR bond was later termed as a "Maharaja Bond" and was listed on the National Stock Exchange India (NSE).[40] The primary objective of the Maharaja Bond was to create a source of very long-term financing for IFC's infrastructure lending program in India,[41] and at the same time extend the maximum maturity of corporate bonds in the domestic bond market, in order to deepen the market.

The Maharaja Bonds had an innovative structure designed to attract different types of investors to India's capital markets.[42] The novel feature of the Maharaja Bond was that IFC created two separate classes of bonds to cater to different market segments. Four inaugural tranches worth USD 100 million equivalent were launched in September 2014. Tranches 1 and 2, which were constituted of bonds with 5-year bullet and 10-year bullet features, respectively, were targeted towards international investors active in the Indian

36 IFC, 'Masala Bond Program' 2017, 2.
37 Banerjee 2016, 5.
38 IFC, 'IFC issued first Masala Bonds in London', 1.
39 IFC, 'IFC Capital Market Solutions in Asia', 16.
40 IFC, 'IFC Debuts Maharaja Bonds', 1.
41 IFC, 'IFC Capital Market Solutions in Asia', 16.
42 IFC, 'IFC Debuts Maharaja Bonds', 1.

market,[43] *i.e.*, structured as traditional bonds with a bullet repayment upon maturity. These bonds were priced using the offshore Masala Bond pricing as benchmark and were priced lower than Indian government bonds. This was the first bond issuance to pierce the Indian sovereign bond curve.[44] Up until IFC issued the Maharaja Bond, the main option for these international investors was to buy Indian rupee bonds in the local market. Foreign investors value IFC's global triple A rating more than domestic investors, and therefore these foreign investors were willing to accept a lower coupon for IFC compared to a coupon from the Government of India. The tranches issued to such investors were priced at 50 basis points below the Indian Government Bond (IGB) yields of comparable maturities. IFC's Vice President and Treasurer, Jingdong Hua was quoted as saying: "Normally the Indian government would be the best benchmark. But investors recognize we are an international AAA-rated issuer, so they are willing to buy our bond at a lower yield".[45]

Domestic investors, on the other hand, consider the country's sovereign government issues to be the risk-free benchmarks. Therefore, they would not necessarily be attracted to a bond priced lower than Indian sovereign bonds. Further, the domestic investors' base largely comprised insurance companies, pension funds, and provident funds[46] that were "buy and hold" investors and therefore required very long-term investment assets to match their long-term liabilities. In order to tap the demand from such domestic investors, IFC issued Tranches 3 and 4 bonds with tenors of 13–18 years and 19–20 years respectively. These bonds were priced in the range of 20 to 30 basis points above the relevant maturity IGB benchmark yields.[47] Tranches 3 and 4 were issued as separately tradeable redeemable principal parts (STRPPS), which essentially meant that the coupon and the principal were separate parts that could be detached and traded separately.[48] In addition to the extremely long tenors of these bonds and the detachability of the principal and coupon parts, there were two other unique features of these tranches 3 and 4: First, IFC issued the bonds for the full amount but did not receive all of the cash immediately. Instead, IFC structured the bonds so that IFC could call for the remainder of the cash from investors, as required to be deployed for infrastructure projects in India over a period of up to two years. This was done to avoid negative carry in parking

---

43 IFC, 'IFC Debuts Maharaja Bonds', 1.
44 IFC, 'IFC Capital Market Solutions in Asia', 16.
45 Crabtree 2014, 1.
46 Roy 2014, 1.
47 IFC, 'IFC Debuts Maharaja Bonds', 1.
48 Roy 2014, 1.

the funds until needed for deployment. This feature, affording the issuer the flexibility to draw down over a period of time at a fixed spread, had not been seen previously in the domestic bond markets.[49] Secondly, IFC designed these tranches 3 and 4 to replicate an amortizing bond structure. While all bonds were bullet bonds, these were issued with different maturities to replicate an amortizing bond structure. This is because IFC's deployment needs were also for long term amortizing loans in the infrastructure space. By issuing differently structured bonds aimed at different investor groups, IFC was able to optimize the pricing as well as tenors of its Maharaja Bonds, which ultimately benefited the infrastructure sector in India where they were deployed. IFC's Vice President and Treasurer, Jingdong Hua was quoted as saying: "Deep, efficient capital markets are the foundations of long-term growth because they create access to finance for the private sector. The innovative structure of IFC's Maharaja bonds enables us to efficiently connect savings from international and domestic investors to investments in infrastructure, while setting a triple-A pricing benchmark in the domestic capital markets that will pave the way for other high-credit issuers".[50] Chitra Ramkrishna, chief executive officer of the NSE stated that "[t]he bonds will help create an ecosystem for more such bond sales in the country, which will deepen the Indian corporate bond market".[51]

5 Role of the Indian Government

The author would like to briefly touch upon another facet of the development of the Masala Bond and Maharaja Bond programs that may be of interest to legal practitioners. The bond issuances under these programs did not fit into any existing regulatory framework for INR bonds at the time. Indian regulations did not envisage an issuer with a profile like the IFC, that is, a foreign issuer making INR or INR-linked bond issuances either in the onshore or offshore markets. The launch and operationalization of these programs required intense interactions and dialogue with several regulators in India and were made possible by special approvals from the Government of India and the various Indian regulators involved. If one were to conjecture, it is possible that in a different economic setting, background and context, or given a different government, such approvals may not have been forthcoming, irrespective of the profile of the DFI seeking such approvals. It is important therefore to

49 Ibid.

50 IFC, 'IFC Capital Market Solutions in Asia', 16.

51 Roy 2014, 1.

acknowledge that while a DFI can certainly play an important role in developing and deepening local capital markets, a successful outcome is equally dependent on several external factors, including the appropriate regulatory framework or the support of the local government in enabling participation by such DFI in the local capital markets.

6 Conclusion

The author submits that IFC's Masala Bond issuance went a long way in achieving the goals that IFC and the Government of India had set out. First and foremost, it established an offshore market for INR instruments, in particular by encouraging the liberalization of local regulations which then allowed Indian corporates to tap this market to address their funding needs. It essentially resulted in the introduction of a new source of financing for Indian corporates that did not previously exist. The fact that the Reserve Bank of India allowed Indian corporates to issue other masala bonds highlights the catalytic impact and signaling effect of the program beyond IFC's balance sheet. It ensured that any future use of the instrument will lead to inflows of institutional investments to the economy, without direct or indirect IFC involvement as issuer or anchor investor.[52]

The issuance also attracted a class of investors to India that had not previously invested in India and helped in raising funds that would directly be invested in Indian projects as loans to Indian borrowers. For the IFC, the issuance of Masala Bonds helped to diversify the sources of funding and optimize the cost of INR funding, with the ultimate goal of improving IFC's product offerings for Indian companies.

It appears that the Maharaja Bond, though very innovatively structured and executed, did not have the same magnitude of impact on India's domestic debt capital markets, and did not by itself, result in invigorating the debt capital markets. While India has a strong and vibrant equity capital market, the debt capital markets continue to be tepid. In 2020, India stood out with USD 13.7 billion worth of outflows from its bond market even as most of its Asian peers saw record inflows.[53] The country's equity market continues to see record dollar inflows but foreign investors are still exiting bonds. There could be a number of reasons for this, including the legal and regulatory framework for debt capital

52 'Mobilization of Private Finance by MDBs and DFIs' 2018, 77.

53 Iyer 2021, 1.

markets in India, the high cost of raising funds in the public bond markets, the inability of foreign institutional investors to provide credit enhancement to local bond issuances owing to regulations, or the overlap among various regulators and the lack of delineation among the various regulatory roles.[54] While the Maharaja Bond issuance may not have resulted in a long-term impact in terms of deepening the bond market in India, what it demonstrated at the time was the IFC's belief in and commitment to the Indian growth story and India's strategic long-term importance for the IFC as an investor.

To conclude, the author would like to re-emphasize that in talking about local currency bond issuances by DFIs, the role of the relevant government in making such an issuance possible cannot be overlooked. Often such issuances are needed in jurisdictions where the regulatory framework may not yet have evolved enough to envisage or support such issuances. However, a government that has positive intent, and that recognizes the value of such issuances to the domestic capital markets, can partner with a DFI or possibly multiple DFIs to put in place an enabling framework within which such issuances can take place.

References

Andries, Alin Marius The Importance of Capital Market in Economy, (2009), Vol. 1(2), Issue 2, CES Working Papers, ISSN 2067-7693, Centre for European Studies, Alexandru Ioan Cuza University of Iasi, 69–75 <https://ceswp.uaic.ro/articles/CESWP2009_I2_AND.pdf> accessed 19 July 2021.

Banerjee, Ashok Masala Bonds: An Innovative Financial Instrument (2016), Artha, Indian Institute of Management, Calcutta, Volume 3, Issue 3 (2016), <http://indiafa.org/wp-content/uploads/2016/02/1454043542.pdf> accessed 22 July 2021.

Crabtree, James IFC launches India's first Maharaja Bond, Financial Times, 23 September 2014, <https://www.ft.com/content/c19ba334-42cf-11e4-847d-00144feabdc0> accessed 24 July 2021.

Cytonn, The Role of Capital Markets in Economic Development (2019), <https://cytonn.com/topicals/the-role-of-the-capital-markets-in-economic-development> accessed 19 July 2021.

Gong, Addison ADB issues Rp3bn Masala to fund renewable projects, Global Capital Asia (2017) <https://www.globalcapital.com/article/b131k2fmjx99vs/adb-issues-rp3bn-masala-to-fund-renewable-projects> accessed 22 July 2021.

54 World Bank, 'Developing India's Corporate Bond Market', 33.

International Finance Corporation, Developing Domestic Capital Markets (2016), <https://www.un.org/esa/ffd/wp-content/uploads/2016/01/Developing-domestic-capital-markets_IFC-World-Bank-Group_IATF-Issue-Brief.pdf> accessed 19 July 2021.

International Finance Corporation, IFC Capital Market Solutions in Asia, <https://www.ifc.org/wps/wcm/connect/60f9f172-2a8f-49f3-bd4e-c1506f3fdaac/Capital+Market+Solutions+in+Asia+-+OCTOBER+2017.pdf?MOD=AJPERES&CVID=marVCzO> accessed 20 July 2021.

International Finance Corporation, IFC Debt Capital Markets Solutions (2017), <https://www.ifc.org/wps/wcm/connect/bbfb288e-263f-473f-a329-75ca8c200191/IFC_DebtCapitalMarkets+-+Apr2018.pdf?MOD=AJPERES&CVID=marUJA5> accessed 19 July 2020.

International Finance Corporation, IFC Debuts Maharaja Bonds, Attracting Foreign Investment and Setting Triple-A Benchmark for India's Domestic Capital Markets (2014), <https://pressroom.ifc.org/all/pages/PressDetail.aspx?ID=17926> accessed 23 July 2021.

International Finance Corporation, IFC Issued First Masala Bonds in London to Attract International Investment for Infrastructure in India, <https://www.ifc.org/wps/wcm/connect/news_ext_content/ifc_external_corporate_site/news+and+events/news/ifc+issued+first+masala+bonds+in+london+to+attract+international+investment+for+infrastructure+in+india> accessed 22 July 2021.

International Finance Corporation, Local Currency and Hedging Solutions (2017), <https://www.ifc.org/wps/wcm/connect/d3850eb8-601c-41a5-9b0a-a74e6f88009c/IFC_LocalCurrency+and+Hedging+Solutions+Pitchbook+-+Updated+10-2017.pdf?MOD=AJPERES&CVID=marVqgH> accessed 19 July 2021.

International Finance Corporation, Masala Bond Program – Nurturing a Local Currency Bond Market (2017), <https://www.ifc.org/wps/wcm/connect/be6c1b09-9e08-4fc4-9630-45ecc078cc88/EMCompass+Note+28+Masala+Bond+Program+FINAL.pdf?MOD=AJPERES&CVID=lDmkW5e> accessed 20 July 2021.

Iyer, Aparna Why India's bond market sticks out like a sore thumb, Mint, 13 January 2021, <https://www.livemint.com/mutual-fund/mf-news/why-india-s-bond-market-sticks-out-like-a-sore-thumb-11610557084253.html> accessed 28 July 2021.

London Stock Exchange, Accessing the Global Markets through London (2017), <https://www.lseg.com/sites/default/files/content/documents/20170105%20Masala%20Bonds%20Presentation_1.pdf > accessed 20 July 2021.

London Stock Exchange, Indian Rupee Bonds on London Stock Exchange (2021), <https://docs.londonstockexchange.com/sites/default/files/documents/masalabonds-pdf.pdf> accessed 23 July 2021.

London Stock Exchange, London Stock Exchange Welcomes IFC, <https://www.lseg.com/markets-products-and-services/our-markets/london-stock-exchange/equities-markets/raising-equity-finance/market-open-ceremony/london-stock-exchange-welcomes-ifc> accessed 20 July 2021.

Mobilization of Private Finance by Multilateral Development Banks and Development Finance Institutions (2018), <https://www.ifc.org/wps/wcm/connect/4366950e-b757-4190-8074-7db86e2860a7/201806_Mobilization-of-Private-Finance_v2.pdf?MOD=AJPERES&CVID=mfmjKJZ> accessed 28 July 2021.

Reserve Bank of India, External Commercial Borrowings (ECB) Policy – Issuance of Rupee denominated bonds overseas, RBI/2015-16/193 September 29, 2015 A.P. (DIR Series) Circular No.17, <https://rbidocs.rbi.org.in/rdocs/notification/PDFs/APDIR17F3216FECE3F0441C8E1107F5E2BA1927.PDF> accessed 22 July 2021.

Roy, Anup IFC Concludes First Tranche of Rupee Bond Programme, Mint, 24 September 2014, <https://www.livemint.com/Money/nIRZap8KQalaYdWqByz2bN/IFC-concludes-first-tranche-of-rupee-bond-programme.html> accessed 24 July 2021.

Standard & Poor's Financial Services LLC, Ratings Direct: International Finance Corp. (2020), <https://www.ifc.org/wps/wcm/connect/204b9131-c04d-4a37-bdee-1b140f1630c6/RatingsDirect_InternationalFinanceCorp_43828038_Feb-25-2020.pdf?MOD=AJPERES&CVID=n2wKCJI> accessed 22 July 2021.

The World Bank Group, Capital Markets Development: A Primer for Policy Makers (2020), <https://www.ifc.org/wps/wcm/connect/a1bcbfc3-a203-4d5b-b64a-b82a80df11a5/PrimerforPolicymakers-PublicRelease.pdf?MOD=AJPERES&CVID=no.kJ3u> accessed 19 July 2021.

The World Bank, Developing India's Corporate Bond Market (2006), <https://openknowledge.worldbank.org/bitstream/handle/10986/19625/391970IN0P09061Bond0Market01PUBLIC1.pdf?sequence=1&isAllowed=y> accessed 28 July 2021.

CHAPTER 4

Inspiring Opening-Up, Innovation and Transparency

International Organizations in the Development of China's Debt Capital Market

*Yixin (Christine) Chen**

Abstract

International organizations have played an important role in propelling opening-up and innovation on China's debt capital market. The continued development and internationalisation of China's debt capital market will offer increasing opportunities for the expansion and diversification of funding sources and investment options for international organizations. This chapter, through an empirical study of the history of the development and internationalisation of China's debt capital market, illustrates that international organizations have been a pioneer in (I) pushing China's debt capital market to open up to the international issuer community and investor base, (II) driving the relaxation of China's foreign exchange control to allow global investors to access China's debt capital market and manage related foreign exchange risks, (III) promoting innovation to broaden product offerings on China's debt capital market, and (IV) advocating transparency in China's debt capital market, particularly in building up a more transparent regulatory regime and increasing the availability of market information. The policy and regulatory evolution in China's debt capital market in the past two decades demonstrates the value of the early experience of international organizations to the gradual opening-up and expansion of this market. This chapter also discusses the benefits brought by the development and internationalisation of China's debt capital market to international organizations. China's debt capital market has become one of the major investment destinations of international organizations. The deepening debt capital market in China will also provide an increasingly important funding source to international organizations. This chapter concludes that the increased participation of international organizations in China's debt capital market is not only mutually beneficial, but also will help to make the global market more inclusive and dynamic.

* Yixin (Christine) Chen is a partner at Fangda Partners, christine.chen@fangdalaw.com.

 | DOI:10.1163/9789004460010_005

1 Introduction

The debt capital market in the People's Republic of China (China or the PRC) has become the second-largest in the world after two decades' rapid expansion and development.[1] International organizations have played an important role in propelling opening-up and innovation on China's debt capital market. The continued development and internationalisation of China's debt capital market will offer increasing opportunities for the expansion and diversification of funding sources and investment options for international organizations. This chapter, through an empirical study of the history of the development and internationalisation of China's debt capital market, examines the role of international organizations in the development and opening up of China's debt capital market, and concludes that the increased participation of international organizations in China's debt capital market will help to make the global market more inclusive and dynamic.

2 International Organizations Are Pioneers in Accessing China's Debt Capital Market

International organizations are pioneers in pushing China's debt capital market to open up to the international issuer community and investor base. The early experience with international organization issuers and investors has proven valuable to China's gradual opening up of its debt capital market.

2.1 *International Organizations Are First International Issuers on China's Debt Capital Market*

For many years China's debt capital market was not available to international issuers. The first issuers granted access to this market were international organizations. In October 2005, International Finance Corporation (IFC) and Asian

1 Before the Shanghai Stock Exchange and the Shenzhen Stock Exchange commenced operation in December 1990, China's debt capital market was in its infancy. Only China government bonds (CGBs) were issued, and they were only tradable over the counter at the banks. Since 1991, CGBs have been traded on the stock exchanges. China's interbank bond market (CIBM) was established in June 1997. The trading volume on the CIBM exceeded that on the stock exchange market in 2001. Since then, China's debt capital market has experienced significant growth and now becomes the second-largest in the world. The CIBM accounts for 90 percent of bond financing in China and is complemented by the exchange market. Schipke et al. 2019, 7; International Capital Markets Association 2021, 6; China Foreign Exchange Trade System and National Interbank Funding Center 2019, 1.

Development Bank (ADB) issued their first ever RMB-denominated bonds (so-called “Panda Bonds”) on the CIBM, thus becoming the first non-Chinese issuers tapping China’s debt capital market.[2]

IFC and ADB were the only Panda Bonds issuers for nearly a decade.[3] The strict issuer qualification requirements, the cumbersome regulatory approval process, the onerous requirements on offering documents as well as the rigid restrictions on the use of proceeds effectively deterred other potential issuers from issuing bonds in China.[4]

In December 2013, Daimler registered its first Panda Bonds program for private placements on the CIBM.[5] Since 2015 China has gradually opened its debt capital market to a variety of international issuers, including international organizations, foreign sovereigns and agencies, financial institutions and corporates. In the meantime, China has relaxed certain regulatory requirements for Panda Bonds issuers and streamlined the regulatory consent process.[6] The volume of Panda Bonds issuances has increased significantly since then. As of the end of 2019, more than 50 international issuers had obtained regulatory approval or registration for issuing up to an aggregate of RMB 797.6 billion Panda Bonds, of which RMB 375.1 billion bonds had been issued.[7] The earlier offerings by IFC and ADB have provided precedential value to the revamp of the Panda Bonds market. In particular, the experience and lessons learned from regulating international organizations offering Panda Bonds in China have inspired the streamlining of the regulatory regime governing Panda

2 Both IFC and ADB issued their first Panda Bonds in China on 14 October 2005. The issuance size of the bonds issued by IFC and ADB was RMB 1.13 billion and RMB 1 billion, respectively. Both bonds had a 10-year tenor and bear interest at fixed rates. For details of the bonds issued by IFC and ADB, see <https://www.chinabond.com.cn/jsp/include/EJB/queryResultSingle.jsp?zqdm=053001> and <https://www.chinabond.com.cn/jsp/include/EJB/queryResultSingle.jsp?zqdm=053101>, respectively, accessed 16 June 2022. Also see Schipke et al. 2019, 393.

3 Following their debut Panda Bonds offerings, IFC issued RMB 870 million 7-year fixed-rate bonds on the CIBM on 15 November 2006, and ADB issued RMB 1 billion 10-year fixed-rate bonds on the CIBM on 4 December 2009. For details of these bonds, see <https://www.chinabond.com.cn/jsp/include/EJB/queryResultSingle.jsp?zqdm=063001> and <https://www.chinabond.com.cn/jsp/include/EJB/queryResultSingle.jsp?zqdm=093101>, respectively, accessed 16 June 2022.

4 Schipke et al. 2019, 198.

5 Daimler AG registered its first Panda Bonds issuance program of RMB 5 billion with the National Association of Financial Market Institutional Investors (NAFMII) in December 2013. See ICMA-NAFMII Working Group 2017, 17.

6 People’s Bank of China 2020, 68–69; Schipke et al. 2019, 198.

7 People’s Bank of China 2020, 68. Also, see the webpage of the Shanghai Clearing House (SHCH) listing the Panda Bonds issuers who have issued Panda Bonds on the CIBM and their offering documents: <https://www.shclearing.com/xxpl/fxpl/rmb1/>.

Bonds, which is believed to have contributed to the rapid expansion of the Panda Bonds market.[8]

2.2 *International Organizations Investing in CIBM Heralds China's Opening-Up of Its Debt Capital Market to International Investors*

China's capital markets started to open to international investors through a qualified foreign institutional investors (QFIIs) regime, which was first introduced in 2002.[9] For many years QFIIs were subject to strict quota limits in terms of the overall investment size[10] and only permitted to invest in the stock, CGBs, convertible bonds, and corporate bonds traded on China's stock exchanges.[11] Given that the initial QFIIs were focused on investing in shares listed on China's stock exchanges and the exchange market represents a small portion of China's debt capital market, QFIIs' holding of debt securities was negligible. In 2010, foreign central banks, the RMB clearing banks in Hong Kong, China, and Macau, and overseas participating banks were allowed to invest in the CIBM, subject to a quota limit.[12] The volume of debt securities held by international investors remained insignificant.

International investors became visible on China's debt capital market after international organizations, foreign central banks, and sovereign wealth funds (so-called "three types of organizations") were given full and more convenient access to the CIBM, without a quota limitation, in 2015.[13] These "three types of organizations" have since been permitted to trade cash bonds and repos, and enter into bond lending, forwards, interest rate swaps, and certain other types of trades on the CIBM.[14] Since then, China's debt capital market has gradually opened to a wide range of international institutional investors, and the trading volume of international investors on the CIBM has increased significantly.

---

8 People's Bank of China 2020, 68; Schipke et al. 2019, 16. Also, see Section 4.2.

9 On 5 November 2002, the China Securities Regulatory Commission (CSRC) and the People's Bank of China (PBoC) jointly issued the *Provisional Measures on Administration of Domestic Securities Investment of Qualified Foreign Institutional Investors* (the Provisional QFII Rule), launching the QFII regime on a pilot basis, allowing international investors to invest in China's capital markets.

10 Art. 10 of the Provisional QFII Rule required international investors to apply to the State Administration of Foreign Exchange (SAFE) for investment quota; Ch. 5 of the Provisional QFII Rule imposed stringent regulation on remittance by QFIIs of funds in and out of China and special RMB accounts opened by QFIIs for holding funds.

11 Art. 18 of the Provisional QFII Rule.

12 PBoC Circular [2010] 217.

13 PBoC Circular [2015] 220. See also Schipke et al. 2019, 198.

14 Art. 2 of PBoC Circular [2015] 220.

After seven months of the successful pilot run of granting "three types of organizations" full access to the CIBM, eligible investors on the CIBM were expanded to include foreign financial institutions (including banks, insurance companies, securities firms, fund management companies, asset management companies, and their investment products) as well as pension funds, charity funds, endowment funds and other approved long-term institutional investors.[15] The CIBM has effectively opened to almost all types of foreign institutional investors.[16] International investors are allowed to invest in all types of fixed income securities traded on the CIBM and enter into bond lending, bond forwards, interest rate forwards, interest rate swaps, and foreign exchange (FX) derivatives trades for hedging purposes.[17]

In July 2017, a new regime called "Bond Connect" was launched, allowing international investors to access the CIBM through an infrastructure linkage between mainland China and Hong Kong, China.[18] Under this regime, foreign investors can submit requests for quotes through electronic trading platforms in Hong Kong, China, and execute trades with onshore dealers on the CIBM without opening onshore accounts in mainland China to hold bonds or trading through onshore settlement agents.[19]

By the end of 2020, there were 468 international institutional investors,[20] including 10 international organizations,[21] approved by PBoC to invest in the CIBM directly, and 625 international institutional investors investing through Bond Connect, of which 188 also invested directly in the CIBM.[22] As of the end of 2020, international investors' holding of debt securities on the CIBM amounted to RMB 3.25 trillion, representing 3.2% of the total size of the CIBM.[23]

With the increased participation of foreign investors, China's debt capital market or the bond products traded on this market have been included in the world's major debt indices. For example, CGBs and policy bank bonds became part of Bloomberg Barclays Global Aggregate Index in April 2019,[24] and CGBs

15 Art. 1 of PBoC Announcement [2016] 3.

16 Schipke et al. 2019, 198–199.

17 International Capital Market Association 2021, 11.

18 PBoC [2017]1.

19 International Capital Market Association 2021, 11.

20 People's Bank of China's Shanghai Headquarters 2021, 1.

21 A list of the three types of organizations approved to invest directly in the CIBM is available at PBoC SH HQ's website <http://shanghai.pbc.gov.cn/fzhshanghai/113595/4162207/index.html> accessed 16 June 2022.

22 People's Bank of China's Shanghai Headquarters 2021, 1.

23 *Ibid.*

24 Schipke et al. 2019, 4, 17.

have also been included in FTSE World Government Bond Index (WGBI) and the JPMorgan Government Bond Index-Emerging Markets (GBI-EM).[25] The inclusion of such bonds in these indices is expected to increase investment from international investors, further enlarging the global investor base of China's debt capital market and their holding of debt securities in this market.

3 International Organizations Have Contributed to the Relaxation of China's FX Control to Allow International Investors to Access China's Debt Capital Market and Manage Related FX Risks

Given that the RMB is not a convertible currency and China has historically imposed stringent control on investment-related FX transactions, for investing in China's debt capital market, it is critically important for international investors to be able to remit foreign currency funds into China, convert such funds into RMB and repatriate funds in the relevant foreign currencies out of China.

China has always been cautious in opening up its FX market, taking a step-by-step approach to gradually relax the FX control connected with investment by international investors in China's debt capital market. The first step of opening up China's domestic FX market started with "three types of organizations", including international organizations. In November 2015, PBoC started to approve "three types of organizations" to enter China's interbank FX market to trade FX spot, forwards, swaps and options.[26] Seven such organizations, including three international organizations, namely, the International Bank for Reconstruction and Development (IBRD), the International Development Association, and the World Bank's Trust Fund, were granted access to China's interbank FX market to become trading members of the China Foreign Exchange Trade System (CFETS).[27]

In 2016, after foreign institutional investors (primarily financial institutions) were allowed to trade on the CIBM,[28] SAFE issued a notice setting forth the procedures for foreign institutional investors to complete FX registration,

25 Schipke et al. 2019, 17; People's Bank of China 2020, 71.

26 Q&As on Foreign Central Banks and Similar Institutions Entering China's Interbank FX Market, released by PBoC on 6 November 2015 <http://www.pbc.gov.cn/goutongjiaoliu/113456/113469/2973750/index.html> accessed 16 June 2022.

27 News release *First Batch of Foreign Central Banks and Similar Institutions Entering China's Interbank FX Market*, released by PBoC on 25 November 2015 <http://www.pbc.gov.cn/goutongjiaoliu/113456/113469/2981891/index.html> accessed 16 June 2022..

28 See Section 2.2.

currency conversion, and funds remittance and repatriation to facilitate their trading on the CIBM.[29] In 2017, SAFE issued another notice to allow foreign institutional investors to hedge their FX risks from their investment in the CIBM by entering into FX derivatives trades on China's interbank FX market.[30]

In connection with the launch of the Bond Connect regime in July 2017,[31] foreign investors have been allowed to convert foreign currency funds into RMB through RMB settlement banks in Hong Kong, China.[32]

In September 2019, China removed the FX quota limit for QFIIs and RMB-QFIIs (RQFIIs).[33] On 1 November 2020, China's new QFIIs/RQFIIs rule became effective, expanding the scope of permitted investments.[34] Trading on China's FX market and repatriation of FX funds have also been relaxed.[35] This development represents a significant step to enable international investors to manage their FX risks in China and facilitates their investment in China's capital markets.

China's gradualism approach to open its debt capital market and relax the related FX restrictions is in line with China's overall strategy of its economic reform and opening-up process. It is a practical approach described as "crossing the river by touching the stones".[36] When opening up China's debt capital market and FX market, it is important to conduct a pilot run with international organizations because they are generally viewed as the safest group of issuers and investors. International organizations are typically long-term investors not aiming to seek short-term gains from speculating the market. Many international organizations are frequent issuers possessing in-depth experience in issuing debt securities in various local markets. The pilot run with international organizations provides the PRC government with valuable experience in testing the effectiveness of the opening-up policies and, where necessary, to make adjustments before opening up the market to a wider international issuer and investor community.

---

29 Hui Fa [2016] 12.

30 Circular of the State Administration of Foreign Exchange on Foreign Exchange Risk Management of Overseas Institutional Investors in the Interbank Bond Market (Hui Fa [2017] 5), issued by SAFE on 24 February 2017, which has been repealed and replaced by Hui Fa [2020] 2.

31 See Section 2.2.

32 Art. 10 of PBoC Order [2017] 1.

33 News release *To Further Facilitate Overseas Institutional Investors Investing in the Interbank Bond Market*, released by PBoC and SAFE on 16 October 2019; also see Yin Fa [2019] 240.

34 CSRC, PBoC, and SAFE Order (176).

35 *Ibid.*

36 Schipke et al. 2019, 18.

4 International Organizations Have Been Driving Innovation and Transparency on China's Debt Capital Market

International organizations are not only among the first issuers and investors on China's debt capital market, they have also been vigorously driving innovation and transparency on this market. Their efforts have yielded landmark transactions with innovative product features. More importantly, they have been instrumental in increasing the transparency of China's debt capital market.

4.1 *International Organizations Have Been Promoting Product Innovation on China's Debt Capital Market*

International organizations have pursued product innovation through issuing new types of debt securities in China. In recent years, most debut Panda Bonds offered by international organizations are innovative products on China's debt capital market.

In 2016, IBRD issued 500 million special drawing rights (SDR)-denominated bonds on the CIBM. This is the first SDR bond offering in China, and the bonds are the first SDR-denominated bonds settled in RMB in history.[37] The transaction expanded the use of SDR and promoted the internationalisation of the RMB.[38]

International organizations are the first international issuers of thematic Panda Bonds. They have contributed to green finance and sustainable development through bond issuances in China. New Development Bank (NDB) issued the first green Panda Bonds in 2016[39] and the first COVID-19 combating Panda Bonds in 2020.[40] In June 2020, the Asian Infrastructure

37 See the World Bank's press release, *World Bank Successfully Prices Oversubscribed Landmark SDR Denominated Bond in China*, on 31 August 2016 <https://www.worldbank.org/en/news/press-release/2016/08/31/world-bank-successfully-prices-oversubscribed-landmark-sdr-denominated-bond-in-china> accessed 16 June 2022.

38 See the remarks by Arunma Oteh, World Bank Vice President and Treasurer, in the World Bank's press release, *World Bank Successfully Prices Oversubscribed Landmark SDR Denominated Bond in China*, on 31 August 2016. *Ibid.*

39 See NDB's press release, *NDB Successfully Issued First RMB-Denominated Green Financial Bond*, on 19 July 2016 <https://www.ndb.int/press_release/ndb-successfully-issued-first-rmb-denominated-green-financial-bond/> accessed 16 June 2022.

40 See NDB's press release, *New Development Bank issues Coronavirus Combating Bond raising RMB 5 bln*, on 3 April 2020 <https://www.ndb.int/press_release/new-development-bank-issues-coronavirus-combating-bond-raising-rmb-5-bln/> accessed 16 June 2022.

Investment Bank (AIIB) issued the first ever sustainable development bonds in China.[41]

Recently, PBoC has reiterated China's commitment to strengthening international cooperation to promote green finance, sustainable development and the 'belt and road' coordination, and PBoC will focus on the development of green bond criteria and information disclosure standards for climate change to facilitate international investors to participate in China's green finance market.[42] It is anticipated that international organizations will make further contributions to these initiatives.

4.2 *International Organizations Have Been Promoting Transparency of the PRC Regulatory Regime*

China has long been criticised for lacking transparency in its legal and regulatory systems. Many laws, rules and regulations are broadly worded and sufficiently vague, and detailed interpretations are critical to their implementation. In providing interpretations to the market, the PRC regulators often give "window guidance" (direct, verbal guidance to specific regulated entities, on most occasions without written records) rather than publishing official interpretations. The international community has urged China to increase the transparency of relevant policies to reduce uncertainty and stabilise market expectations, thus enhancing investors' confidence in China's debt capital market.[43]

However, given that China's regulatory regime is ever-evolving, the premature release of official rules and regulations may impede the market's development. In 2010, four regulatory authorities jointly issued a rule regulating Panda Bonds issued by international development organizations.[44] Due to the stringent requirements (including those on accounting standards for financial statements, auditor qualifications, and cross-border remittance of bond proceeds) and onerous regulatory approval process imposed by this rule,[45] no

41 See AIIB's press release, *AIIB Prices RMB3 Billion Inaugural Panda Bond,* on 11 June 2020 <https://www.aiib.org/en/news-events/news/2020/AIIB-Prices-RMB3-Billion-Inaugural-Panda-Bond.html> accessed 16 June 2022.

42 See the meeting minutes of the press conference organised by the State Council Information Office on 9 February 2021 <http://www.pbc.gov.cn/goutongjiaoliu/113456/113469/4191657/index.html> accessed 16 June 2022.

43 Schipke et al. 2019, 208.

44 The Interim Administrative Rules on Issuances of RMB Bonds by International Development Institutions jointly issued by PBoC, the Ministry of Finance (MoF), the National Development and Reform Commission (NDRC) and CSRC on 16 September 2010 (2010 IDI Panda Bonds Rule).

45 Arts. 4, 5, 8, 11 and 17 of the 2010 IDI Panda Bonds Rule.

international organization issued any Panda Bonds under this rule, and the Panda Bonds market was almost dormant for half a decade. It is not surprising that around three dozens of Panda Bonds offerings were completed before the new Panda Bonds rule was officially released,[46] and the 2010 IDI Panda Bonds Rule was repealed in September 2018.[47] Detailed guidelines on Panda Bonds issued by corporate issuers as well as supranational, sovereign and agency issuers were released throughout 2019 and 2020.[48] The new Panda Bonds rule and these NAFMII guidelines were released after PBoC and NAFMII solicited multiple rounds of comments from various market participants on the draft rules. The early experience with international organization issuers and the lessons learned from the 2010 IDI Panda Bonds Rule have proven highly valuable to the rule-making process for these recent Panda Bonds rules and guidelines.

For international investors investing in China's debt capital market, the PRC regulators took a different approach to address the transparency of relevant guidelines, which avoided the pitfalls of the 2010 IDI Panda Bonds Rule. In connection with permitting the 'three types of organizations' to invest in the CIBM, PBoC released operational manuals and Q&As, rather than officially promulgated rules, on the detailed procedures for these organizations to access the CIBM and the interbank FX market as well as on issues relating to, among other things, account opening, execution of master agreements, trade confirms, settlement of funds and market data services.[49] These operational

---

46 See the Interim Measures for the Administration of Bonds Issued by Overseas Issuers on the National Interbank Bond Market issued by PBoC and MoF on 8 September 2018 (PBoC and MoF 2018, 16) <http://www.pbc.gov.cn/tiaofasi/144941/3581332/3730127/index.html> (the new Panda Bonds rule) accessed 16 June 2022.

47 See PBoC, MoF, NDRC and CSRC Announcement 2018, 15 issued on 8 September 2018 <http://www.pbc.gov.cn/tiaofasi/144941/3581332/3730114/index.html> accessed 16 June 2022.

48 These Panda Bonds guidelines consist primarily of (I) the Guidelines on Debt Financing Instruments of Overseas Non-Financial Enterprises, which NAFMII initially issued on 17 January 2019 and amended and reissued on 25 December 2020, (II) the Detailed Rules for the Administration of Tiered Management of Debt Financing Instruments of Overseas Non-Financial Enterprises, the Form Requirements for Registration Documents for Debt Financing Instruments of Overseas Non-Financial Enterprises and the related notice on the promulgation and implementation of such rules and form requirements issued by NAFMII on 30 September 2020, and (III) the Guidelines on Bond Issuance by Foreign Governmental Agency and International Development Institution Issuers (for Trial Implementation) issued by NAFMII on 25 December 2020 (SSA Panda Bonds Guidelines). See <http://nafmii.org.cn//english/lawsandregulations/selfregulatory_e/index.html> accessed 16 June 2022.

49 See the Procedures & FAQ for Foreign Central Banks and Similar Institutions to Enter China's Interbank Bond Market and Interbank FX Market released by PBoC on 14 April

manuals and Q&As provided clear and practical guidance on a timely basis, which enhanced the transparency of the regulatory regime for "three types of organizations" to access the China market and maintained the flexibility for quick adjustments where necessary.

Whether refraining from promulgating official rules until they have been tested with market participants or publishing practical operational manuals instead of official rules, the objective is to ensure that the official rules, once promulgated, will function to help to develop and open up China's debt capital market. This is equally important to, if not more important than, the transparency of the regulatory regimes.

4.3 *International Organizations Have Contributed to the Increased Availability of Market Information*

Historically, when China's financial markets were not open to the international community, and the pricing on many financial products was not determined by the market, the availability of product, pricing and trading information on China's debt capital market and FX market was limited. As China has gradually opened its financial markets, the international community demands the transparency of market information. In the meantime, as China moves to a more market-based economy and price-based monetary policy framework, more market-based information has become available. International organizations have contributed to the increased availability of China's debt capital market and FX market information.

For example, IBRD's SDR bond offering directly led to China's publication of certain FX reference rates. Pursuant to the terms of IBRD's SDR bonds, the subscription price for the bonds, the interest amount payable on each interest payment date and redemption amount payable upon maturity are determined based on the reference rates for CNY to other SDR basket currencies published by CFETS on China's interbank FX market.[50] Before this offering, CFETS only published USD/CNY reference rates on an hourly basis. To facilitate this transaction, CFETS has since been publishing the reference rates for new currency pairs, namely, EUR/CNY, 100JPY/CNY and GBP/CNY, at the specified hours on each trading day.

2016<http://www.pbc.gov.cn/goutongjiaoliu/113456/113469/3048164/index.html>accessed 16 June 2022.

50 See the offering circular for IBRD's SDR bond offering published on 26 August 2016, available at <https://www.shclearing.com/xxpl/fxpl/sdr1/201608/t20160826_178854.html> accessed 16 June 2022.

Additionally, to respond to international investors' requests for more market information, over the years, CFETS and the two clearing and depositary institutions on the CIBM, China Central Depository and Clearing Co., Ltd. (CCDC) and the SHCH, have made more market and trading information available on their websites and provided more services to market participants. For example, data relating to various bond indices, valuation, yield curves and VaR as well as interest, FX, credit and commodities derivatives are readily available on the websites of CCDC and SHCH.[51]

4.4 *International Organizations, as Panda Bonds Issuers, Have Set High Standards for Disclosure*

Most international organization issuers have issued debt securities on the international markets as seasoned issuers before issuing Panda Bonds in China. They have generally maintained updated disclosure on their business, management, financial condition and operations across different markets. In particular, most of such issuers have set high standards for discussing and analysing their financial information, meeting the disclosure requirements and investors' expectations in the developed markets with robust securities regulation, such as in the U.S.[52] Their disclosure not only provides helpful information to investors on China's debt capital market, but also offers precedential and educational value to the PRC regulators in the process of improving disclosure requirements and modernising its regulatory framework on information disclosure.

Furthermore, most international organizations adhere to the fair disclosure principle, treating investors in different markets equally and releasing the same material information across different markets at or around the same time. This is highly aligned with the PRC regulators' overall requirements on information disclosure and helps foster the transparency in China's debt capital market and reduce information asymmetry among different markets.

51 See CCDC's website <https://www.chinabond.com.cn/> and SHCH's website <https://www.shclearing.com/> accessed 16 June 2022.

52 Four (IFC, ADB, IBRD and AIIB) of the five international organizations that have issued Panda Bonds (the above four and NDB) are frequent issuers having maintained shelf registration programs in the U.S.

5 The Development of China's Debt Capital Market Helps International Organizations to Diversify Investment Portfolios and Funding Sources

As China's debt capital market continues to grow and open up, it is becoming an increasingly important market for international organizations to make investments and raise funds. The continued development and internationalisation of China's debt capital market are expected to increase opportunities for the expansion and diversification of investment options and funding sources for international organizations.

5.1 *China's Debt Capital Market Has Become a Major Investment Destination for International Organizations*

Given the rapid growth and increasing importance of China's debt capital market, and in light of the recent opening-up policies,[53] as well as the inclusion of China's bond products in major global bond indices,[54] China's debt capital market has become a major destination for foreign investments. In addition, it is believed that PRC sovereign and quasi-sovereign bonds offer higher returns compared to advanced economies such as the U.S. and Japan, and the relatively stable FX rates of the RMB have also contributed to the increased foreign holding.[55] As China's debt capital market is increasingly being viewed as an international asset class,[56] it will offer attractive investment options to international organizations and help to diversify their investment portfolios further.

5.2 *China's Debt Capital Market Will Have an Increasing Role in Diversifying Funding Sources of International Organizations*

While Panda Bonds remain a tiny segment of China's debt capital market,[57] its importance is growing for international issuers, including international organizations, as they look to diversify their funding sources or fund their CNY liabilities. The newly released SSA Panda Bonds Guidelines provides certain regulatory clarity and can help potential issuers planning for Panda Bonds issuances. The recently announced policy priority on green finance, sustainable

53 See Sections 2.2 and 3 for details of China's opening-up policies in recent years.

54 See Section 2.2 for details.

55 Asian Development Bank 2020, 22.

56 International Capital Market Association 2021, 17.

57 As of the end of 2020, the outstanding aggregate principal amount of Panda Bonds was RMB253 billion, representing 0.22% of the total bond volume in China. China Chengxin International Credit Rating Co., Ltd. 2021, 1.

development and the "Belt and Road Initiative"[58] may offer further funding opportunities to international organizations. It is anticipated that more international organizations will be encouraged to issue green, social and sustainable Panda Bonds, given their exemplary role in promoting green and sustainable development.[59] Many international organizations seek to maintain diversified borrowing programs in terms of product, tenor and currency and issue debt securities on both global and local markets. Issuing Panda Bonds could provide them with access to a new market and help to expand their investor base. In the long run, China is expected to become an important funding market for international organizations.

6 Conclusion

International organizations have made significant contributions to the opening-up and development of China's debt capital market. As the first movers on this market, they have been instrumental to China's opening-up process. Their experience and efforts are conducive to the modernisation and internationalisation of the market. The increased participation of international organizations in China's debt capital market is mutually beneficial and will help to make the global market more inclusive and dynamic.

References

PRC Regulatory Sources

Circular of the People's Bank of China on Issues Relating to RMB Investments in Interbank Bond Market by Three Types of Institutions Including Overseas RMB Clearing Banks on a Pilot Basis (PBoC Circular [2010] 217), issued by the PBoC on 17 August 2010 <http://www.pbc.gov.cn/goutongjiaoliu/113456/113469/2888287/index.html> accessed 16 June 2022.

Circular on Issues Concerning Investment of Foreign Central Banks, International Financial Institutions and Sovereign Wealth Funds with RMB Funds in the Interbank Market (PBoC Circular [2015] 220), issued by PBoC on 14 July 2015 <http://www.pbc.gov.cn/en/3688110/3688181/3712712/index.html>.

58 See the meeting minutes of the press conference organised by the State Council Information Office on 9 February 2021 <http://www.pbc.gov.cn/goutongjiaoliu/113456/113469/4191657/index.html> accessed 16 June 2022.

59 China Chengxin International Credit Rating Co., Ltd. 2021, 17.

Q&As on Foreign Central Banks and Similar Institutions Entering China's Interbank FX Market, released by PBoC on 6 November 2015 <http://www.pbc.gov.cn/goutongjiaoliu/113456/113469/2973750/index.html> accessed 16 June 2022.

People's Bank of China Announcement [2016] 3 (PBoC Announcement [2016] 3), issued by PBoC on 24 February 2016 <http://www.pbc.gov.cn/jinrongshichangsi/147160/147171/147358/147400/3021203/index.html> accessed 16 June 2022.

Procedures & FAQ for Foreign Central Banks and Similar Institutions to Enter China's Interbank Bond Market and Interbank FX Market issued by PBoC on 14 April 2016 <http://www.pbc.gov.cn/goutongjiaoliu/113456/113469/3048164/index.html> accessed 16 June 2022.

Circular of the State Administration of Foreign Exchange on Certain Issues Concerning Foreign Exchange Administration of Foreign Institutional Investors Investing in the Interbank Bond Market (Hui Fa [2016] 12), issued by SAFE on 27 May 2016 <http://www.safe.gov.cn/safe/2016/0527/5587.html> accessed 16 June 2022.

Interim Measures for the Administration of Mutual Bond Market Access between Mainland China and Hong Kong SAR (PBoC Order [2017] 1), issued by PBoC on 21 June 2017 <http://www.pbc.gov.cn/goutongjiaoliu/113456/113469/3330621/index.html> accessed 16 June 2022.

Circular of the People's Bank of China and the State Administration of Foreign Exchange on Certain Issues Concerning Facilitating Overseas Institutional Investors Investing in the Interbank Bond Market (Yin Fa [2019] 240), issued by PBoC and SAFE on 16 October 2019 < http://www.safe.gov.cn/safe/2019/1015/14366.html> accessed 16 June 2022.

Circular of the State Administration of Foreign Exchange on Relevant Issues concerning Improving the Foreign Exchange Risk Management of Foreign Institutional Investors in the Interbank Bond Market (Hui Fa [2020] 2), issued by SAFE on 13 January 2020 <http://www.safe.gov.cn/safe/2020/0113/15143.html> accessed 16 June 2022.

Administrative Measures for Securities and Futures Investment Made in China by Qualified Foreign Institutional Investors and RMB Qualified Foreign Institutional Investors (CSRC, PBoC, and SAFE Order (176)), issued by CSRC, PBoC and SAFE on 25 September 2020, effective 1 November 2020 <http://www.csrc.gov.cn/zjhpublic/zjh/202009/t20200925_383650.htm> accessed 16 June 2022.

Books and Reports

Asian Development Bank (ed), *The Asia Bond Monitor—September 2020* (Manila, Philippines, November 2020) <https://www.adb.org/sites/default/files/publication/655141/asia-bond-monitor-november-2020.pdf> accessed 16 June 2022.

China Chengxin International Credit Rating Co., Ltd. (CCXI), *Panda Bonds in 5 Years: Finding its Way out* (Beijing, January 2021).

China Foreign Exchange Trade System and National Interbank Funding Center (ed), *China Interbank Bond Market Overview* (January 2019).

ICMA-NAFMII Working Group (ed), *The Panda Bond Market and Perspectives of Foreign Issuers* (Zurich, Beijing, November 2017).

International Capital Market Association (ed), *The Internationalization of the China Corporate Bond Market* (Zurich, January 2021).

People's Republic of China (ed), *2020 RMB Internationalization Report* (August 2020).

People's Republic of China Shanghai Headquarters, *Briefing on Financial Markets Trading Reports, Issue 1 of 2021* (January 2021) <http://shanghai.pbc.gov.cn/fzhshanghai/113595/4159922/index.html> accessed 16 June 2022.

Schipke, Alfred, Markus Rodlauer, and Zhang Longmei (ed), *The Future of China's Bond Market* (Washington, DC: International Monetary Fund, 2019).

PART 2

The Legal Status of International Organizations

CHAPTER 5

Immunity for Multilateral Development Banks in the United States

Assessing Litigation Exposure Following the U.S. Supreme Court's Decision in Jam v. International Finance Corporation

Christopher P. Moore and Paul C. Kleist***

Abstract

In *Jam v. International Finance Corporation*, the U.S. Supreme Court held that the immunity to which international organizations (IOs) are entitled under the International Organization Immunities Act tracks the law of foreign sovereign immunity as it exists in the United States today, not as it existed when the statute was enacted in 1945, meaning that IOs relying on the statute are not entitled to absolute immunity, as the U.S. Court of Appeals for the D.C. Circuit had held, but rather restrictive immunity, which is subject to an oft-litigated exception for commercial activity. This chapter examines the impact of the Supreme Court's decision on immunity for multilateral development banks in connection with both their funding and fundraising activities and provides a framework for assessing potential litigation exposure in the United States based on those activities.

1 Introduction

Under the International Organizations Immunities Act (IOIA), designated international organizations (IOs) "enjoy the same immunity from suit and every form of judicial process [in the United States] as is enjoyed by foreign governments".[1] Interpreting this provision, the U.S. Supreme Court held in *Jam v. International Finance Corporation* that the IOIA tracks the law of foreign sovereign immunity as it exists today, not as it existed when the IOIA was enacted

* Partner, Cleary Gottlieb Steen & Hamilton LLP, cmoore@cgsh.com.

** Associate, Cleary Gottlieb Steen & Hamilton LLP, pkleist@cgsh.com. The authors would like to thank Katie Gonzalez, Associate, Cleary Gottlieb Steen & Hamilton LLP, kgonzalez@cgsh.com, for her assistance preparing this chapter.

1 IOIA, 22 U.S.C. § 288a(b).

in 1945—and thus, IOs are not entitled to absolute immunity, as the U.S. Court of Appeals for the D.C. Circuit had held, but rather "the limited or 'restrictive' immunity that foreign governments currently enjoy" under the Foreign Sovereign Immunities Act (FSIA).[2]

Jam concerned the funding activities of the International Finance Corporation (IFC), a prominent multilateral development bank (MDB). This chapter examines the impact of the Supreme Court's decision on immunity for IOs in connection with both their funding and fundraising activities and provides a framework for assessing potential litigation exposure in the United States.

Section 2 of this chapter describes the conceptual basis and scope of immunity for foreign governments as compared to IOs. Section 3 summarizes the Supreme Court's decision in *Jam* and the rulings of the District Court and D.C. Circuit on remand, as well as a more recent case applying *Jam*, *Rodriguez v. Pan American Health Organization*. Section 4 considers the application of the FSIA's commercial activity exception to IOs and highlights two issues that are likely to be litigated post-*Jam*: the gravamen analysis and the FSIA definition of "commercial activity". Section 5 describes potential sources of immunity for IOs in the United States other than the IOIA, including the position under customary international law. Finally, Section 6 provides a framework for IOs to assess their potential litigation exposure in the United States, including guidance for determining the source and scope of their immunity.

2 The Conceptual Basis and Scope of Immunity for Foreign Governments as Compared to International Organizations

The IOIA defines immunity from suit for IOs by reference to the immunity enjoyed by foreign governments.[3] But the conceptual basis of immunity for foreign governments is different than for IOs, and the scope of immunity for foreign governments in the United States has evolved since 1945, when the IOIA was enacted.

2 139 S. Ct. 759, 765 (2019).

3 IOIA, 22 U.S.C. § 288a(b); see also *Jam*, 139 S. Ct. at 765 ("The IOIA defines certain privileges and immunities by reference to comparable privileges and immunities enjoyed by foreign governments").

2.1 *Foreign Sovereign Immunity*

The conceptual basis of immunity for foreign governments, or foreign sovereign immunity, is equality: "the domestic courts of a State must not adjudicate upon the rights and obligations of another State because [...] equals do not have authority over one another".[4]

Historically, the United States granted foreign governments immunity "as a matter of grace and comity", in an effort to promote and maintain good international relations.[5] First established as a common law doctrine by the Supreme Court in 1812, by the early 20th century U.S. courts had ceded primary responsibility for determining questions of immunity to the U.S. Department of State, and would defer to the State Department's recommendation whether to grant immunity on a case-by-case basis.[6]

"Until 1952, the State Department ordinarily requested immunity in all actions against friendly sovereigns", such that they enjoyed "virtually absolute immunity" in the United States, as the Supreme Court has recognized.[7] That year, in response to the increasing involvement of States and State enterprises in cross-border commerce, the State Department issued what has come to be known as the "Tate Letter" announcing the adoption of a "restrictive" rather than "absolute" approach to foreign sovereign immunity. Under the restrictive approach, "immunity is confined to suits involving the foreign sovereign's public acts, and does not extend to cases arising out of a foreign state's strictly commercial acts".[8]

The FSIA, enacted in 1976, codifies the restrictive approach to sovereign immunity and confirms that it is for the courts, rather than the State Department, to decide "[c]laims of foreign states to immunity".[9] Under the FSIA, States and State instrumentalities are presumptively immune from suit in the United States, however several exceptions apply, including an oft-litigated exception for commercial activity. In this regard, the FSIA provides that a foreign State shall not be immune from suit in any case in which the action is:

> based upon [1] a commercial activity carried on in the United States by the foreign state; or upon [2] an act performed in the United States in

4 Bordin 2020, 11.

5 *Verlinden B.V. v. Central Bank of Nigeria*, 461 U.S. 480, 486 (1983).

6 See *Samantar v. Yousuf*, 560 U.S. 305, 311 (2010).

7 *Verlinden*, 461 U.S. at 486.

8 Ibid, 487.

9 FSIA, 28 U.S.C. § 1602.

> connection with a commercial activity of the foreign state elsewhere; or upon [3] an act outside the territory of the United States in connection with a commercial activity of the foreign state elsewhere and that act causes a direct effect in the United States[.][10]

2.2 *International Organization Immunity*

Unlike foreign sovereign immunity, IO immunity is not rooted in notions of equality, grace or comity, but rather operational necessity, and in particular the need to protect IO independence and avoid State interference in IO activities. As the International Bank for Reconstruction and Development (IBRD) and other IOs explained in their amicus brief in *Jam*:

> International organizations have no territory of their own, and are dependent on countries to exercise restraint to ensure their independent operations. They lack the co-equal standing with sovereigns that would hypothetically entitle them to certain inherent rights or comity under the law of nations. The immunities provided to international organizations—in particular, immunity from suit and legal process—thus protect international organizations from unilateral control by a member nation over the activities of the international organization within its territory.[11]

IOs may also operate with limited financial resources, and it has been argued that IO immunity provides the added benefit of enabling IOs to avoid or minimize certain litigation costs, thereby allowing IOs to more effectively "mobilize their resources and live up to expectations of Member States".[12]

Because IO immunity is based on operational necessity, it is often described as 'functional' immunity. This is epitomized by the UN Charter, which provides that the UN "shall enjoy in the territory of each of its Members such privileges and immunities as are necessary for the fulfillment of its purposes".[13]

Although, as one scholar has recognized, "the theory of functionalism has long pervaded legal thinking about IOs",[14] the immunity claimed by them in their constituent instruments varies and may resemble absolute immunity

10 FSIA, 28 U.S.C. § 1605(a)(2).

11 Brief for the International Bank for Reconstruction and Development et al. as Amici Curiae Supporting Respondent (IBRD Amicus Brief) at 10, *Jam v. International Finance Corporation*, 139 S. Ct. 759 (2019).

12 See Tesfagabir 2011, 110–111.

13 UN Charter, art. 105, paragraph 1.

14 Bordin 2020, 16.

or restrictive immunity. For example, the Convention on the Privileges and Immunities of the United Nations (General Convention) provides that the UN "shall enjoy immunity from every form of legal process except insofar as in any particular case it has expressly waived its immunity".[15] This suggests that UN immunity is "not merely functional but downright absolute".[16] In contrast, the IFC's Articles of Agreement define the IFC's immunity restrictively, and include a carve out for claims against the IFC "in a court of competent jurisdiction in the territories of a member in which [the IFC] has an office, has appointed an agent for the purpose of accepting service of process, or has issued or guaranteed securities".[17]

3 Summarizing *Jam v. International Finance Corporation*

This section sets out the key facts and procedural background of *Jam* and summarizes both the Supreme Court's decision and the decisions of the District Court and D.C. Circuit on remand, as well as more recent District Court and D.C. Circuit decisions applying *Jam*, *Rodriguez v. Pan American Health Organization.*

3.1 *Key Facts and Procedural Background*

Jam is a case involving an MDB's funding rather than fundraising activities. The plaintiffs in *Jam* were Indian fisherman and farmers. They brought tort claims against the IFC in federal court in Washington, D.C. related to a loan made by the IFC for the construction and operation of a coal-fired power plant in India. The plaintiffs alleged that the IFC failed to ensure that the project, over which the IFC retained supervisory authority, was carried out in accordance with the IFC's social and environmental standards, and that the project caused damage to fishing stocks, agricultural yields and public health for which the IFC should be held liable.

15 Convention on the Privileges and Immunities of the United Nations, art. 2, § 2. As noted in the text, the UN Charter provides that the UN shall enjoy what amounts to functional immunity. The UN Charter also empowers the General Assembly to "make recommendations with a view to determining the details of the application" of the functional immunity provision, UN Charter, art. 105, paragraph 3, and less than one year after the execution of the UN Charter in 1945, the General Assembly proposed the General Convention to define the organization's immunity in more detail.

16 Bordin 2020, 17.

17 IFC Articles of Agreement, Art. VI, § 3.

As explained in Section 5, IOs may be entitled to immunity from suit in the United States on the basis of their constituent instruments and/or international agreements, in addition to the IOIA. But as noted above, the IFC's Articles of Agreement permit claims against it in the territories in which the IFC has an office, including the United States. For this reason, the IFC could not rely on its Articles of Agreement for immunity in the *Jam* case, and turned to the IOIA instead.

The IOIA extends immunity to IOs "which shall have been designated by the President through appropriate Executive order as being entitled to enjoy" IOIA immunity.[18] This includes the IFC and many other—but not all—IOs.[19]

In *Atkinson v. Inter-American Development Bank*, a decision issued in 1998 by the D.C. Circuit, the court held that when Congress enacted the IOIA in 1945, it had intended to adopt for IOs the law of foreign sovereign immunity as it existed more than 70 years ago, "when immunity of foreign sovereigns was absolute".[20] Relying on this decision, the IFC argued that it was entitled to absolute immunity under the statute and thus the claims against it should be dismissed for lack of jurisdiction.[21]

In response, the plaintiffs argued that *Atkinson* had been wrongly decided, and that "even assuming foreign sovereigns enjoyed absolute immunity in 1945, if that immunity diminished, as it has with the codification of the commercial activity exception, Congress intended that international organizations fare no better".[22] The plaintiffs also argued that the IFC had waived any IOIA immunity it might have via its Articles of Agreement.[23]

18 The IOIA seemingly limits immunity to those IOs in which the United States participates. See IOIA, 22 U.S.C. § 288 (defining "international organization" for purposes of the statute). However, a number of IOs have been designated as entitled to enjoy IOIA immunity even though the United States does not directly participate in and is not a member of the organization, including the African Union and the European Central Bank. Ibid, Editorial Notes, 'Public International Organizations Designated by Statute'.

19 In addition to the IFC, the African Development Bank, Asian Development Bank, Inter-American Development Bank and IBRD are designated IOs. Conversely, the Asia Infrastructure Investment Bank, New Development Bank and Nordic Investment Bank, among others, are not. See ibid.

20 156 F. 3d 1335, 1341 (D.C. Cir. 1998).

21 *Jam v. International Finance Corporation*, 860 F.3d 703, 705 (D.C. Cir. 2017).

22 Ibid.

23 Ibid, 706.

Both the District Court and D.C. Circuit sided with the IFC, concluding that they were bound by *Atkinson* and that the IFC had not waived its IOIA immunity.[24]

Addressing the latter issue, the D.C. Circuit acknowledged that the IFC's Articles of Agreement, "read literally, would seem to include a categorical waiver", but declined to read them this way.[25] In an earlier case, *Mendaro v. World Bank*, the D.C. Circuit took the position that waiver language contained in the constituent instruments of IOs should be read narrowly, on the theory that it is "logically less probable" that an IO intends to waive its immunity "when the benefits accruing to the organization as a result of the waiver would be substantially outweighed by the burdens".[26] Citing this case, the D.C. Circuit in *Jam* held that the IFC did not waive its immunity from suit notwithstanding the plain language of the Articles of Agreement because the plaintiffs' claims arose out of the IFC's core business operations, and litigation related to those operations "would threaten the policy discretion of the organization".[27]

In a concurring opinion, Judge Pillard acknowledged that the court was bound by precedent but suggested that it was time to revisit *Atkinson* and *Mendaro*, explaining that the court had taken "a wrong turn" when it "read the IOIA to grant international organizations a static, absolute immunity" substantially broader than what is currently enjoyed by foreign governments, and that the language contained in the constituent instruments of IOs should control whether immunity is waived—not the court's view whether waiver in a particular case would ultimately benefit the organization.[28]

3.2 *The Supreme Court's Decision*

The plaintiffs sought review of the D.C. Circuit's decision in the Supreme Court, challenging the D.C. Circuit's interpretation of the IOIA but not the *Mendaro* waiver doctrine.[29]

Analyzing the text of the IOIA, a 7–1 majority of the Supreme Court reversed the decision of the D.C. Circuit, concluding that Congress had intended to "link the law of international organization immunity to the law of foreign sovereign

24 See ibid, 706, 708; *Jam v. International Finance Corporation*, 172 F. Supp. 3d 104, 112 (D.D.C. 2016).

25 *Jam*, 860 F.3d at 706.

26 717 F.2d 610, 617 (D.C. Cir. 1983).

27 *Jam*, 860 F.3d at 70.

28 Ibid, 708, 711 (Pillard, J., concurring).

29 See Petition for a Writ of Certiorari at 11, *Jam v. International Finance Corporation*, 139 S. Ct. 759 (2019).

immunity, so that one develops in tandem with the other".[30] Accordingly, the majority held, "the Foreign Sovereign Immunities Act governs the immunity of international organizations", and the IFC "is therefore not absolutely immune from suit".[31]

In reaching this holding, the majority downplayed the concerns of the IFC and other IOs that anything less than absolute immunity under the IOIA would lead to a flood of litigation against them in the United States.

First, the majority confirmed that the "privileges and immunities of the IOIA are only default rules", and suggested that "[i]f the work of a given international organization would be impaired by restricted immunity, the organization's charter can always specify a different level of immunity".[32] The majority noted that "[t]he charters of many international organizations do just that", citing the General Convention as an example.[33]

Second, the majority suggested that the funding activities of IOs may not fall within the FSIA's commercial activity exception. According to the majority, "it is not clear that the lending activity of all development banks qualifies as commercial activity within the meaning of the FSIA".[34] The majority also suggested that even if the activity at issue is deemed to be commercial under the FSIA, there may not be a sufficient nexus or link between the activity and the United States, or the case may not be "based upon" that activity but rather "tortious activity abroad".[35]

Justice Breyer was less optimistic, pointing out in dissent that the constituent instruments of many IOs do not have the force of law in the United States, and thus these organizations "continue to rely upon [the IOIA] to secure immunity", rather than their charters or articles of agreement.[36] Justice Breyer also explained that the definition of "commercial activity" under the FSIA is broad, and this will "at the very least create uncertainty for organizations involved in finance", given the core functions of these organizations "are at least arguably 'commercial' in nature".[37]

30 *Jam*, 139 S. Ct. at 769.
31 Ibid, 772.
32 Ibid, 771–772.
33 Ibid, 771.
34 *Jam*, 139 S. Ct. at 772.
35 Ibid.
36 Ibid, 778 (Breyer, J., dissenting).
37 Ibid (Breyer, J., dissenting).

3.3 *The Decisions on Remand*

The Supreme Court remanded the case to the District Court to decide whether the IFC was entitled to immunity under the IOIA and in turn the FSIA or, as the plaintiffs argued, the FSIA's commercial activity exception applied.

The District Court did not consider whether the IFC's funding activities were commercial in nature, but focused instead on whether the plaintiffs' claims were based upon activity, commercial or otherwise, carried on or performed in the United States.[38] The District Court concluded that they were not.

Undertaking a holistic assessment of the plaintiffs' claims, the District Court found that the main focus, or "gravamen" of the complaint was the IFC's alleged failure to ensure that the design, construction and operation of the power plant complied with relevant environmental and social sustainability standards, and that this occurred in India, not the United States.[39] Notably, the mere fact that the IFC approved the financing of the power plant in the United States, at the IFC's headquarters there, and also disbursed funds from the United States, was not sufficient to satisfy the U.S. nexus requirement, given the misconduct alleged occurred primarily in India, where the plant is located and the harm occurred.[40] Accordingly, the IFC's immunity "remain[ed] intact", and the District Court dismissed the plaintiffs' claims.[41]

The D.C. Circuit affirmed the decision of the District Court and upheld the dismissal of the plaintiffs' claims, concluding, like the District Court, that "all of [the plaintiffs'] claims turn on alleged wrongful conduct in India, which has led to injuries suffered in India", and "[t]he gravamen of [the plaintiffs'] lawsuit is therefore conduct that occurred in India, not the United States".[42]

3.4 *Applying Jam in Rodriguez v. Pan American Health Organization*

In a more recent decision applying *Jam*, the District Court in *Rodriguez v. Pan American Health Organization* reached a different result, holding that one of the plaintiffs' claims in that case, which relates to the role of the Pan American

---

38 *Jam v. International Finance Corporation*, 442 F. Supp. 3d 162, 171 (D.D.C. 2020). Because the plaintiffs did not allege that the IFC's conduct caused a direct effect in the United States, the District Court did not consider the third prong of the commercial activity exception. See ibid, footnote 1.

39 See generally ibid, 175–177.

40 Ibid, 177–179.

41 Ibid, 179.

42 *Jam v. International Finance Corporation*, 3 F.4th 405, 409 (D.C. Cir. 2021). On April 25, 2022, the U.S. Supreme Court denied a *certiorari* petition to review the *Jam* decisions before the District Court and D.C. Circuit on remand. See *Jam v. International Finance Corporation*, --- S.Ct. ----, 2022 WL 1205953 (Mem.) (2022).

Health Organization (PAHO) as a financial intermediary, *does* trigger the FSIA's commercial activity exception, and, accordingly, that PAHO was not immune from suit under the IOIA in connection with that claim.[43]

The *Rodriguez* plaintiffs are Cuban doctors. They allege that they were coerced by the Cuban government into participating in a medical mission in Brazil and that the Cuban government restricted their movement and withheld most of their wages while they were abroad. The plaintiffs allege further that PAHO facilitated this misconduct, including by arranging payment by Brazil for the work performed by the plaintiffs, most of which PAHO remitted to Cuba and some of which it kept for itself.

Accepting these allegations as true solely for purposes of addressing PAHO's motion to dismiss,[44] the District Court concluded that the gravamen of one of the plaintiffs' claims—that PAHO knowingly profited from forced labor—was based on the allegation that PAHO "mov[ed] [...] money, for a fee, between Cuba and Brazil", and that this qualified as commercial activity under the FSIA "and thus the IOIA".[45] The District Court also concluded that there was a sufficient nexus between PAHO's commercial activity and the United States, given that the Director-General approved the agreements committing PAHO to its role as a financial intermediary at PAHO's headquarters in Washington, D.C., and the money passed through PAHO's bank account there.[46]

The D.C. Circuit affirmed the District Court's decision, permitting certain claims against PAHO to proceed. The D.C. Circuit concluded that when considering the gravamen of the suit, the conduct underlying plaintiffs' claims was not simply the alleged human trafficking and forced labor that resulted in plaintiffs' injury, but also PAHO's "financial intermediary" activity that gave rise to plaintiffs' claims under the U.S. Trafficking Victims Protection Act.[47] Because this conduct involved PAHO's receipt, remittance, and retention of certain funds through its Washington, D.C. bank account, the D.C. Circuit

43 2020 WL 6561448, No. 20–928, at *9 (D.D.C. Nov. 9, 2020).

44 U.S. courts are required to accept a plaintiff's allegations as true for purposes of addressing a motion to dismiss. See ibid, *4. PAHO has expressly denied any wrongdoing. See Memorandum of Law in Support of Pan American Health Organization's Motion to Dismiss, *Rodriguez v. Pan American Health Organization*, No. 20-cv-00928, ECF No. 54–1, 2–3 (June 26, 2020).

45 Ibid, *7.

46 Ibid. The plaintiffs in *Rodriguez* asserted two other claims against PAHO, however the District Court concluded that these did not trigger the commercial activity exception.

47 *Rodriguez v. Pan American Health Organization*, 29 F.4th 706, 708–09, 711–15 (D.C. Cir. 2022). On May 26, 2022, the D.C. Circuit denied PAHO's request for rehearing en banc. PAHO may file a petition for *certiorari* requesting Supreme Court review.

agreed with the District Court's previous conclusion and found that there was sufficient nexus to the United States, such that the commercial activity exception applied and PAHO was not immune from suit.[48] In relation to a claim made by PAHO to immunity not under the IOIA but the WHO Constitution (as the constituent document of PAHO's parent entity), the D.C. Circuit additionally found—as did the District Court—that the WHO Constitution did not confer broader immunity than the restrictive immunity that the IOIA provides, because the WHO Constitution was not self-executing nor had it been enacted into U.S. law by subsequent legislation.[49]

4 Applying the FSIA's Commercial Activity Exception to IOs

As noted by the Supreme Court in *Jam* and discussed below, IOs may be able to claim immunity in the Unites States on the basis of their constituent instruments, to the extent these provide more robust protections than the IOIA.[50] But for IOs relying on the IOIA—particularly in cases related to funding or fundraising activities—whether the statute provides immunity is likely to turn on the application of the FSIA's commercial activity exception.

Analyzing whether the commercial activity exception applies involves a two-step analysis for each claim alleged.[51] As *Jam* and *Rodriguez* demonstrate, the first step is to identify the conduct on which the claim is based, i.e., the gravamen of the claim.[52] The second step is to determine whether the conduct

48 Ibid, 716–17.

49 Ibid, 718. The question of whether the WHO Constitution is a self-executing treaty in the United States that can confer greater immunity than the default baseline of immunity provided by the IOIA was also raised before the District Court for the Southern District of New York in *Kling v. World Health Organization*. The District Court ultimately declined to make any ruling regarding the nature of the WHO Constitution, finding such a determination "not necessary", because "[r]egardless of whether the WHO [C]onstitution is a self-executing treaty, the WHO is independently immune from suit under the [IOIA]", which the court found to be "concurrent with and separate from any treaty-based immunity the WHO may have". *Kling v. World Health Organization*, 532 F. Supp. 3d 141, 148 (S.D.N.Y. 2021) (citation omitted).

50 As discussed in Section 5.1 below, an IO may be able to rely on its constituent instruments for more robust immunity protections than the IOIA, but importantly, this applies only to the extent that the constituent instruments are part of or referenced in a treaty of which the United States is a member, and the relevant treaty provisions are self-executing, or else the constituent instruments have been enacted into law by Congress.

51 See *Rodriguez*, 2020 WL 6561448, at *5 (describing the two-step analysis).

52 Ibid.

identified as the gravamen of the claim constitutes commercial activity under the FSIA and, if so, whether there is a sufficient nexus between that conduct and the United States.[53] Both of these requirements must be satisfied for the commercial activity exception to apply.[54]

In relation to the commercial activity exception, at least two issues are likely to be litigated in disputes in which an IO asserts immunity under the IOIA: (1) how courts identify the gravamen of a claim in funding-related cases involving a third party outside of the United States, and the related issue of whether there is a sufficient nexus between the gravamen identified and the United States; and (2) how courts interpret and apply the FSIA definition of "commercial activity" in the IO context.

Identifying the gravamen of a claim is important: whether the "commercial" element of the commercial activity exception is satisfied, and whether there is a sufficient nexus between the conduct alleged and the United States, turns on how the court understands and frames the conduct at issue. To identify the gravamen of a claim, the court must "zero in on the core".[55] While there is no bright line rule, Supreme Court precedent suggests that the gravamen of a claim is typically the conduct that "actually injured" the plaintiff.[56]

Applying this test is simple in theory but more complicated in practice, particularly in circumstances where the conduct that actually injured the plaintiff, or at least caused the most direct injury, was performed not by the named defendant but by a third party outside of the United States. This may occur, as in *Jam*, when an international development project is funded by an MDB but carried out by a local partner, and the alleged harm occurs 'on the ground', where the project is being implemented.

Both *Jam* and *Rodriguez* grapple with this issue. In the former case, the IFC argued that the conduct that actually injured the plaintiffs, and thus the gravamen of the plaintiffs' claims, was not the loan it had authorized in the United States, but mismanagement of the power plant in India by the Indian power company that had undertaken the project. The District Court did not fully endorse this argument—it was wary of "effective[ly] immunizing" IOs from claims with an intervening cause, so long as the "last act" in the causal chain that led to injury occurred outside the United States[57]—but it did ultimately agree, in a subsequent decision denying the plaintiffs' motion to amend their

53 Ibid.

54 See FSIA, 28 U.S.C. § 1605(a)(2).

55 *OBB Personenverkehr AG v. Sachs*, 577 U.S. 27, 35 (2015).

56 See ibid; *Saudi Arabia v. Nelson*, 507 U.S. 349, 358 (1993).

57 *Jam*, 442 F. Supp. 3d at 173.

complaint, that "for purposes of the FSIA, a suit can be based primarily upon the conduct of a third party" abroad, and courts should consider this as part of the gravamen analysis—and should not permit plaintiffs to "manufacture jurisdiction under the FSIA by choosing not to name a defendant".[58]

The D.C. Circuit, on appeal, adopted a similar approach, making clear that the gravamen analysis is not limited to the IO defendant's conduct, as the plaintiffs had argued, and neither Supreme Court Precedent, nor the text of the FSIA, "require[s] courts to ignore the importance of third parties' conduct".[59]

Making a similar argument to the IFC in *Jam*, PAHO in *Rodriguez* argued that the core of the plaintiffs' claim in that case was not any injury traceable to its financial activities, but the alleged forced labor itself, which was directed by the Cuban government and occurred outside the United States. As compared to the District Court and D.C. Circuit in *Jam*, the *Rodriguez* District Court and D.C. Circuit on appeal were less receptive to this argument. The District Court concluded, and the D.C. Circuit agreed, that the gravamen of the claim was not Cuba's "separate malfeasance" but rather PAHO's alleged role as a "knowing money middleman", because this activity was not "minor or ancillary" and, if proven, would itself violate a U.S. anti-trafficking statute.[60] The *Rodriguez* District Court and D.C. Circuit also concluded that this conduct "easily" met the nexus requirement, because the key administrative decisions were made at PAHO's headquarters in Washington, D.C., and PAHO used a U.S. bank account.[61]

In their approach to the gravamen analysis, the *Jam* decisions and the *Rodriguez* decisions are not directly at odds: all acknowledge that plaintiffs should not be able to trigger application of the FSIA's commercial activity exception through artful pleading. But the focus by the *Jam* courts on the conduct of third parties, as compared to the *Rodriguez* District Court's and D.C. Circuit's reluctance to do so, suggests that the extent to which the conduct of third parties will influence the gravamen analysis is subject to further clarification and change in the future.

Likewise unsettled, or at least uncertain, is how courts will interpret and apply the FSIA definition of "commercial activity" in the IO context. The FSIA

58 *Jam v. International Finance Corporation*, 2020 WL 4933618, No. 15–612, at *5-*6 (D.D.C. Aug. 24, 2020).

59 *Jam*, 3 F.4th at 410.

60 *Rodriguez*, 2020 WL 6561448, at *7-*9.

61 Ibid, *7. See *Rodriguez*, 29 F.4th at 716–17 (finding that because "PAHO received, forwarded and retained the [...] money through its Washington, D.C. bank account", this alleged wrongful conduct occurred in the United States).

definition of "commercial activity" is comprised of two elements. First, the statute itself specifies that "[t]he commercial character of an activity shall be determined by reference to the nature of the course of conduct or particular transaction or act, rather than by reference to its purpose".[62] Second, there is a "core doctrinal dichotomy" in the case law between private parties and foreign States, such that a foreign State engages in commercial activity "where it exercises only those powers that can also be exercised by private citizens, as distinct from those powers peculiar to sovereigns".[63] Combining these elements, the relevant question for courts is:

> [N]ot whether the foreign government is acting with a profit motive or instead with the aim of fulfilling uniquely sovereign objectives, but rather whether the particular actions that the foreign state performs (whatever the motive behind them) are the type of actions by which a private party engages in trade and traffic or commerce[.][64]

This definition, insofar as it relies on the distinction between the type of actions undertaken by private parties as compared to "powers peculiar to sovereigns", can be awkward when applied to IOs, which are obviously not sovereigns and do not have the same powers. In addition, as the IBRD and other IOs have pointed out, "IOs do not act as mere private players [...] in the market", but are "mission bound to pursue economic development and support investments that may not be possible in the private market".[65]

The Supreme Court did not directly address this issue in *Jam*, but the majority did suggest that not all MDB funding activities qualify as "commercial activity" within the meaning of the FSIA—or at least, this was "not clear", as noted above.[66] By way of example, the majority cited loans made to governments on the condition that they change their laws or enact certain restrictions.[67]

Citing this passage, PAHO argued in *Rodriguez* that there should be a different doctrinal dichotomy for IOs, between conduct that falls within an IO's mission, which would be non-commercial, and conduct outside of its mission, which may not be.[68] Addressing this argument, the District Court acknowledged

62 FSIA, 22 U.S.C. § 1603(d).
63 *Rodriguez*, 2020 WL 6561448, at *5 (quotations omitted).
64 Ibid (quoting *Republic of Argentina v. Weltover, Inc.*, 504 U.S. 607, 614 (1992)).
65 IBRD Amicus Brief, 21.
66 *Jam*, 139 S. Ct. at 772.
67 Ibid; see also *Rodriguez*, 2020 WL 6561448, at *6.
68 *Rodriguez*, 2020 WL 6561448, at *5.

that the existing dichotomy—"acting as a sovereign versus as a market participant"—"cannot easily be applied to an entity like PAHO, which is, of course, not a nation state".[69] But it declined to adopt PAHO's position, reasoning that an approach linking the definition of "commercial activity" to an IO's mission would conflict with the statutory rule that the nature of the activity at issue is what matters, not its purpose, and that the Supreme Court did not discard this rule in *Jam*—in fact, "it retained it", since the Court's "apparent point" was that conditional loans to governments "may not be commercial activity precisely because they may not be the type of activity by which a private party engages in trade or commerce".[70] On appeal, the D.C. Circuit endorsed this position, accepting that plaintiffs "sufficiently alleged that PAHO's conduct of 'moving money for a fee' constituted 'commercial activity'".[71]

5 Potential Sources of IO Immunity in the United States Other than the IOIA

As noted above, many but not all IOs are entitled to IOIA immunity. For IOs not covered by the statute, or those seeking more robust immunity than the statute provides post-*Jam*, there are other potential sources of IO immunity in the United States: constituent instruments and international agreements, such as headquarters agreements, as well as customary international law. While constituent instruments and international agreements may provide greater protection than the IOIA, as discussed below, these may not have binding legal force in the United States, while customary international law, on closer inspection, may not be a reliable source of IO immunity there.

5.1 *Constituent Instruments and International Agreements*

As noted above, the Supreme Court majority in *Jam* confirmed that the IOIA provides "only default" immunity and suggested that "[i]f the work of a given international organization would be impaired by restricted immunity, the organization's charter can always specify a different level of immunity".[72] A different level of immunity may also be specified in an international agreement, such as a headquarters agreement.

69 Ibid.

70 Ibid, *5-*6.

71 *Rodriguez*, 29 F.4th at 717.

72 *Jam*, 139 S. Ct. at 771.

Importantly, however, these potential sources of immunity only have binding legal force in the United States if they are part of or referenced in a treaty of which the United States is a member, *and* the relevant treaty provisions are self-executing, or else the constituent instrument or international agreement (as the case may be) has been enacted into law by Congress.[73] Thus, as Justice Breyer recognized in dissent, many IOs will "continue to rely upon [the IOIA] to secure immunity, for the United States has never ratified treaties nor enacted statutes that might extend the necessary immunity".[74]

Rodriguez is instructive in this regard. In that case, PAHO claimed immunity on the basis of the UN Charter and WHO Constitution, in addition to the IOIA. But looking to the text and drafting history of the immunity provisions of these documents, the District Court, and later the D.C. Circuit, concluded that they were not self-executing, and thus did not have domestic legal effect.[75] As a result, neither immunity provision rendered PAHO immune from suit.[76] Given that few constituent documents are likely to be considered self-executing treaties or subsequently implemented through U.S. legislation, the D.C. Circuit's decision in *Rodriguez* raises questions regarding IOs' ability to rely on their founding documents to provide for broader immunity than is afforded under the IOIA.

5.2 *Customary International Law*

For IOs unable to rely on their constituent instruments, international agreements or the IOIA for immunity, the question becomes whether they are entitled to immunity in the United States under customary international law.[77]

---

73 See Restatement (Fourth) of the Foreign Relations Law of the United States § 310 (explaining the distinction between self-executing and non-self-executing treaties). The Asian Development Bank is an example of an organization entitled to rely on the immunity provisions of its Articles of Agreement because Congress has enacted these into law. See Acceptance of membership by United States in Asian Development Bank, 22 U.S.C. § 285g. The Organization of American States is an example of an organization entitled to absolute immunity through a headquarters agreement with the United States, which was self-executing. See Headquarters Agreement Between the Government of the United States of America and the Organization of American States, art. IV, § 1.

74 *Jam*, 139 S. Ct. at 778 (Breyer, J., dissenting).

75 *Rodriguez*, 2020 WL 6561448, at *16-*18.

76 Ibid, *18. *Rodriguez*, 29 F.4th at 717–19.

77 See Xu and Gu 2018, 62 ("Customary international law is largely a gap-filling resource for immunities when there is no applicable international treaty or domestic legislation".); Restatement (Third) of Foreign Relations Law § 467, comment (f) ("Organizations of which the United States is not a member, and that have not been designated under the [IOIA], do not enjoy privileges and immunities in the United States except insofar as a particular organization might be entitled to them by customary law".).

IO immunity is recognized in a number of treaties and other international agreements, and some commentators have suggested that IO immunity has become part of customary international law.[78] Others disagree, noting that "many domestic courts do not seem to recognize the immunities of international organizations in the absence of relevant treaty law".[79] The status of IO immunity is thus a "controversial subject",[80] and whether IOs are entitled to immunity under customary international law—and the scope of any such immunity—remains unsettled.[81]

As a result, some U.S. courts may be reluctant to recognize IO immunity on the basis of customary international law.[82] Also complicating the analysis from a U.S. perspective is the status of customary international law in U.S. courts: while U.S. courts will endeavor to interpret U.S. statutes to avoid a conflict with customary international law "[w]here fairly possible",[83] there is much debate regarding whether and to what extent customary international law is applicable and binding in U.S. courts absent authorization by self-executing treaty or statute.[84] For both of these reasons—the unsettled status of IO immunity under customary international law, and of customary international law in U.S. courts—customary international law may not be a reliable source of immunity for IOs in the United States.

6 Assessing Litigation Exposure in the United States

Post-*Jam*, IOs relying on the IOIA are not entitled to absolute immunity and may be exposed to litigation based on their commercial activities. This section

78 See Wood 2014, 308–309 (surveying the scholarship on the issue of IO immunity under customary international law).

79 Ryngaert 2010, 124. As Michael Wood concluded, following a review of court practice in several countries including Austria, France, Italy, and the United Kingdom, "[i]t is [...] difficult to discern a general practice accepted as law, to the effect that international organizations enjoy immunity under customary international law". Wood 2014, 313.

80 Tesfagabir 2011, 107.

81 See Wood 2014, 310–312; Bordin 2020, 10.

82 See Restatement (Third) of the Foreign Relations Law of the United States § 102(2) (explaining that customary international law results from "a general and consistent practice" of States). The D.C. Circuit in *Mendaro* did suggest that IO immunity is "an accepted doctrine of customary international law", 717 F.2d at 615, however this statement was dicta and as Wood has pointed out, the court relied on outdated cases from Italy and France. Wood 2014, 307–308.

83 Restatement (Third) of the Foreign Relations Law of the United States § 114.

84 See generally Born 2017.

draws on the foregoing discussion of the Supreme Court's decision and the sources of IO immunity in the United States to provide a framework for IOs to assess potential litigation exposure in the United States, with a focus on funding and fundraising activities.

6.1 *Assessing Litigation Exposure*

To assess litigation exposure in the United States, an MDB should first determine the source of its immunity. The MDB should then consider the scope of that immunity, including any applicable waivers.

6.1.1 Step One: Determining the Source of Immunity

In determining the source of its immunity, the MDB should, at the outset, confirm whether its charter, articles of agreement or other constituent instruments, or an international agreement, like a headquarters agreement, provide it with some level of immunity. If the answer is 'no', then the MDB should next consider whether it has been designated by the President as entitled to IOIA immunity. If the answer is 'yes', then the MDB should look to the IOIA for immunity, cognizant that the FSIA's commercial activity exception will apply post-*Jam*. If the answer is 'no', then the MDB is limited to customary international law—and as noted above, it remains unsettled whether this would provide robust immunity or indeed any immunity at all in U.S. courts.

If, as is more likely, an MDB's constituent instruments do provide it with some level of immunity, or this is recognized in an international agreement, then there are a series of questions to consider, as set out in the diagram below:

As reflected in the diagram, among the questions to consider are whether the treaty's immunity provisions are self-executing. This is a matter of treaty interpretation—do the treaty terms "reflect a determination by the President who negotiated it and the Senate that confirmed it that the treaty has domestic effect", or was the treaty not intended to be legally binding in the United States absent implementing legislation?[85] The starting point for the analysis is the text of the treaty, but U.S. courts will also look to the treaty's negotiation and drafting history, the understanding of the Executive Branch when the President agreed to the treaty and the post-ratification understanding of signatory nations.[86]

85 *Rodriguez*, 2020 WL 6561448, at *15.

86 Ibid.

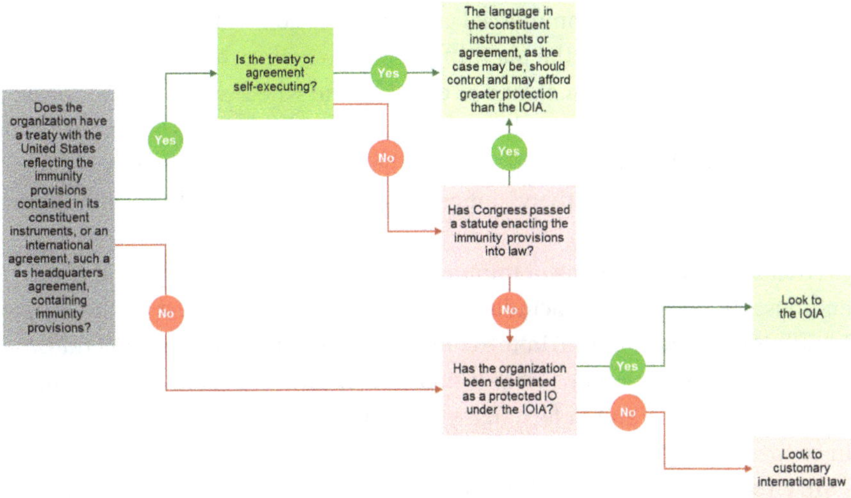

FIGURE 5.1 Determining the source of an IO's immunity

6.1.2 Step Two: Assessing the Scope of Immunity

Once the MDB has determined the source of its immunity, it should next assess the scope of that immunity.

If the MDB is relying on its charter, articles of agreement or other constituent instruments for immunity, or an international agreement with binding force in the United States, this will involve consideration of the operative immunity language and how this applies to the claims at issue. For example, as discussed above, the General Convention provides that the UN is immune from every form of legal process, absent waiver, suggesting that the UN enjoys immunity in most circumstances. The constituent instruments of many IOs extend more limited immunity, however.[87] This includes the IFC, as discussed above, as well as the Asian Development Bank, which "shall enjoy immunity from every form of legal process" except in certain cases—including, notably, "cases arising out of or in connection with the exercise of its powers to borrow money, to guarantee obligations, or to buy and sell or underwrite the sale of securities".[88]

If the MDB is relying on the IOIA for immunity, the scope of immunity is restrictive post-*Jam*. The question then becomes whether any of the FSIA's exceptions to immunity apply to the activities upon which any claims might

87 See Okada 2020, 34.

88 Asian Development Bank, Agreement Establishing the Asian Development Bank, art. 50, paragraph 1.

be based, including the commercial activity exception. This involves consideration of the gravamen of the plaintiff's claims, whether the activity at issue is "commercial" within the meaning of the FSIA and whether there is a sufficient nexus between the activity and the United States. This analysis is complex and fact specific, and as discussed in Section 4 both the gravamen analysis and definition of "commercial activity", among other issues, are likely to be litigated further.

After assessing the scope of immunity, the existence of any applicable waivers must be considered, including any waivers that may exist in the MDB's constituent instruments or, in the context of a funding or fundraising transaction, in the transaction documents themselves. A waiver of immunity can be express or implied, and in fact, many IOs expressly waive immunity from suit in connection with their fundraising activities.[89]

In circumstances where it is unclear whether an MDB has impliedly waived its immunity in connection with the claims alleged, or the MDB disputes an alleged waiver, courts within the D.C. Circuit—where many cases involving IOs are heard—are likely to continue to apply the *Mendaro* waiver doctrine and construe the alleged waiver "narrowly to allow only the type of suit by the type of plaintiff that would benefit the organization over the long term".[90] Notwithstanding the criticism this doctrine has received—from members of the D.C. Circuit[91] as well as commentators[92]—the Supreme Court did not address it in *Jam*, and it remains good law, at least for now.[93]

The impact of *Mendaro* on IOs may be minimal, however, particularly in relation to their funding and fundraising activities. The rule that waiver language should be read narrowly contains its own carve-out: "suits by debtors, creditors, [and] bondholders", on the theory that those parties "would not enter into negotiations or contract with the organization absent waiver".[94]

89 See IBRD Amicus Brief, 13–14 (nothing that the IBRD includes waiver language in its constituent instruments "in order to effect and enhance the marketability of IBRD's securities and the credibility of its activities in the lending markets" and that many other MDBs have adopted similar language) (internal quotations marks and citation omitted).

90 *Jam*, 860 F.3d at 706 (internal quotation marks and citation omitted).

91 As noted above, Judge Pillard suggested in her concurring opinion in *Jam* that the court should revisit the *Mendaro* waiver doctrine. Even Judge Silberman, writing for the panel, acknowledged that "it is a bit strange that it is the judiciary that determines when a claim 'benefits' the international organization". Ibid, 707.

92 See Herz 2008, 519–524 (criticizing the D.C. Circuit's treatment of the waiver issue as "not persuasive").

93 See *Jam*, 3 F.4th at 411 (noting that *Mendaro* "remains the law of the circuit" following the Supreme Court's decision).

94 *Jam*, 860 F.3d at 707.

Thus, as a practical matter, IOs may not be able to rely on the *Mendaro* waiver doctrine to protect against the waiver of immunity in connection with commercial transactions, at least when facing claims by contractual counterparties related to loan agreements or bond offerings.[95]

6.2 *Potential Means to Manage Litigation Exposure*

IOs may seek to manage litigation exposure in the United States by taking certain steps, including the following.

Avoid express waivers: As noted above, many IOs expressly waive immunity from suit in connection with their fundraising activities, which could expose them to suit in the event of a dispute related to bond offerings or other capital markets transactions regardless of the source of their immunity. Avoiding such waivers would preserve any existing immunity in this context, however this may be easier said than done.

From a commercial perspective, it may be difficult to attract investment absent a waiver of immunity in relation to the fundraising sought. Indeed, this is the reason why many IOs agree to limited waivers of immunity in the first place.[96] From a practical perspective, if an MDB's waiver is built into its constituent instruments, the waiver may be difficult to amend. For example, the IFC Articles of Agreement may be amended only by a vote of three-fifths of the member State representatives exercising 85% of the organization's total voting power.[97]

Adopt an arbitration clause: If an MDB accepts that its contractual counterparties should have some recourse to binding dispute resolution but is seeking to avoid litigation, it may consider adopting an arbitration clause in its funding

95 The *Mendaro* waiver doctrine may still be effective in cases related to funding activities when the claim is not directly related to the commercial transaction or brought by the contractual counterparty, as the D.C. Circuit concluded in *Jam* in relation to the Indian plaintiffs' claims against the IFC.

96 See *Osseiran v. International Finance Corporation*, 552 F.3d 836, 840 (D.C. Cir. 2009) (recognizing that "immunity from suits based on commercial transactions with the outside world can hinder an organization's ability to operate in the marketplace", because "parties hesitate to do business with an entity insulated from judicial process") (internal quotation marks and citation omitted).

97 IFC Articles of Agreement, art. 7(a). For the same reason, it may be difficult for an IO to amend its constituent instruments to provide more robust immunity protections, and even if an IO accomplished this, these protections would likely not be effective in the United States unless they were reflected in a self-executing treaty or had been enacted into law by Congress, as discussed above.

or fundraising documents.[98] Courts in the United States typically enforce such clauses, and if a contractual counterparty attempted to litigate a claim that the parties had agreed to arbitrate, the court would likely dismiss the claim in favor of arbitration.[99]

Minimize or avoid U.S. contacts: Some IOs may also seek to limit litigation exposure in the United States by taking steps to minimize or avoid U.S. contacts in connection with their funding and fundraising activities, including structuring transactions to avoid soliciting and obtaining investments from U.S. investors and processing the payment of funds through non-U.S. bank accounts. Although it will be a fact-specific issue determined on a case-by-case basis, taking such steps could support potential defenses including lack of personal jurisdiction and forum non conveniens, and may also mitigate the risk of being found to have triggered the FSIA's commercial activity exception, which requires a sufficient nexus with the United States. This may be difficult to accomplish, however, given that many IOs are based in or have offices in the United States and the United States is often a significant source of investors.

Strengthen internal review and accountability mechanisms: Many IOs have internal review and accountability mechanisms to address complaints by third parties in a non-judicial forum. For example, the World Bank has established a Compliance Advisor Ombudsman (CAO) to respond to issues raised by local communities. The CAO can provide mediation services, "but does not make judgment about the merits of a complaint".[100]

The CAO mechanism was triggered in the *Jam* case. Following an internal audit, the CAO determined that the power plant failed to comply with the environmental requirements set out in the loan documents, but did not compel the IFC or the loan recipient to remedy this.[101] Where IOs are able to provide more robust dispute resolution options, this may help to avoid or discourage proceedings in the U.S. or other national courts.

---

98 Many MDBs have adopted arbitration clauses in their fundraising documents, including, for example, the Asia Infrastructure Investment Bank. See Asia Infrastructure Investment Bank, Form of Fiscal Agency Agreement, § 16(a).

99 See, e.g., *Paramedics Electromedicina Comercial, LTDA v. GE Medical Systems Information Technologies, Inc.*, 369 F.3d 645, 653–655 (2d Cir. 2004) (affirming district court ruling compelling defendant to arbitrate and enjoining foreign litigation and noting that "[f]ederal policy strongly favors the enforcement of arbitration agreements").

100 International Finance Corporation, Office of the Compliance Advisor Ombudsman, 'How We Work: Ombudsman'.

101 See *Jam*, 442 F. Supp. 3d at 169.

7 Conclusion

Post-*Jam*, IOs cannot claim absolute immunity from suit under the IOIA and may be exposed to U.S. litigation related to their commercial activities provided there is a sufficient nexus between those activities and the United States. It remains to be seen whether this will result in an increase in the number of cases against IOs in the United States, but there is reason to doubt that *Jam* will significantly alter the litigation landscape in relation to fundraising: many IOs, in an effort to enhance the marketability of their securities, already waive immunity in this context.

Funding may be a different story. The Supreme Court's decision arguably opens the door for aggrieved third parties to bring claims against IOs if the development projects they have funded go wrong, and may inspire "enterprising plaintiff's counsel to fashion new and creative arguments as to why the actions of the international organizations fall within any of the enumerated FSIA exceptions".[102] IOs are far from defenseless, however. They can continue to rely on the immunity provisions contained in their constituent instruments or relevant international agreements, provided these are reflected in a self-executing treaty and/or have been enacted into law by Congress, and for those covered by the IOIA, the statute will continue to provide presumptive immunity.[103] IOs may also be able to take steps to limit their litigation exposure in the United States, including minimizing or avoiding U.S. contacts.

References

Acceptance of membership by United States in Asian Development Bank (1966), 22 U.S.C. § 285 et seq.

Asia Infrastructure Investment Bank, Form of Fiscal Agency Agreement <https://www.sec.gov/Archives/edgar/data/1733112/000119312518339616/d644843dex99d.htm> accessed 21 January 2021.

Asian Development Bank, Agreement Establishing the Asian Development Bank <https://www.adb.org/sites/default/files/institutional-document/32120/charter.pdf> accessed 26 January 2021.

Atkinson v. Inter-American Development Bank, 156 F. 3d 1335 (D.C. Cir. 1998).

102 IBRD Amicus Brief, 15.

103 As *Jam* and *Rodriguez* demonstrate, plaintiffs may face an uphill battle to overcome presumptive immunity and establish that the commercial activity exception applies: in those cases, only one of nine claims was found to satisfy the relevant standard.

Bordin F L, 'To what immunities are international organizations entitled under general international law? Thoughts on *Jam v IFC* and the 'default rules' of IO immunity' (2020) 72 Questions of International Law 5.

Born G, 'Customary International Law in United States Courts' (2017) 92 Washington Law Review 1641.

Brief for the International Bank for Reconstruction and Development et al. as Amici Curiae Supporting Respondent, *Jam v. International Finance Corporation*, 139 S. Ct. 759 (2019).

Foreign Sovereign Immunities Act (1976), 28 U.S.C. § 1602 et seq.

Headquarters Agreement Between the Government of the United States of America and the Organization of American States <http://www.oas.org/legal/english/docs/bilateralagree/us/sedeusa.htm> accessed 5 September 2021.

Herz S, 'International Organizations in U.S. Courts: Reconsidering the Anachronism of Absolute Immunity' (2008) 31 Suffolk Transnational Law Review 471.

International Finance Corporation, Articles of Agreement <https://www.ifc.org/wps/wcm/connect/d057dbd5-4b02-40f8-8065-9e6315c5a9aa/2020-IFC-AoA-English.pdf?MOD=AJPERES&CVID=n7H2n-h> accessed 26 January 2021.

International Finance Corporation, Office of the Compliance Advisor Ombudsman, 'How We Work: Ombudsman' <http://www.cao-ombudsman.org/howwework/ombudsman/> accessed 21 January 2021.

International Organizations Immunities Act (1945), 22 U.S.C. § 288 et seq.

Jam v. International Finance Corporation, 172 F. Supp. 3d 104 (D.D.C. 2016).

Jam v. International Finance Corporation, 860 F.3d 703 (D.C. Cir. 2017).

Jam v. International Finance Corporation, 139 S. Ct. 759 (2019).

Jam v. International Finance Corporation, 442 F. Supp. 3d 162 (D.D.C. 2020).

Jam v. International Finance Corporation, 2020 WL 4933618, No. 15-612 (D.D.C. Aug. 24, 2020).

Jam v. International Finance Corporation, 3 F.4th 405 (D.C. Cir. 2021).

Jam v. International Finance Corporation, --- S.Ct. ----, 2022 WL 1205953 (Mem.) (2022).

Kling v. World Health Organization, 532 F. Supp. 3d 141 (S.D.N.Y. 2021).

Memorandum of Law in Support of Pan American Health Organization's Motion to Dismiss, *Rodriguez v. Pan American Health Organization*, No. 20-cv-00928, ECF No. 54-1 (June 26, 2020).

Mendaro v. World Bank, 717 F.2d 610 (D.C. Cir. 1983).

OBB Personenverkehr AG v. Sachs, 577 U.S. 27 (2015).

Okada Y, 'The immunity of international organizations before and after Jam v. IFC: Is the functional necessity rationale still relevant?' (2020) 72 Questions of International Law 29.

Osseiran v. International Finance Corporation, 552 F.3d 836 (D.C. Cir. 2009).

Paramedics Electromedicina Comercial, LTDA *v.* GE *Medical Systems Information Technologies, Inc.*, 369 F.3d 645 (2d Cir. 2004).

Petition for a Writ of Certiorari, *Jam v. International Finance Corporation*, 139 S. Ct. 759 (2019).

Restatement (Fourth) of the Foreign Relations Law of the United States § 310.

Restatement (Third) of the Foreign Relations Law of the United States §§ 102, 114, 467.

Rodriguez v. Pan American Health Organization, 2020 WL 6561448, No. 20-928 (D.D.C. Nov. 9, 2020).

Rodriguez v. Pan American Health Organization, 29 F.4th 706 (D.C. Cir. 2022).

Ryngaert C, 'The Immunity of International Organizations before Domestic Courts: Recent Trends' (2010) 7 International Organizations Law Review 121.

Samantar v. Yousuf, 560 U.S. 305 (2010).

Saudi Arabia v. Nelson, 507 U.S. 349 (1993).

Tesfagabir K, 'The State of Functional Immunity of International Organizations and Their Officials and Why it Should be Streamlined' (2011) 10 Chinese Journal of International Law 97.

United Nations, Charter of the United Nations (1945) 1 UNTS XVI.

United Nations General Assembly, Convention on the Privileges and Immunities of the United Nations (1946) <https://treaties.un.org/doc/Treaties/1946/12/19461214%20 10-17%20PM/Ch_III_1p.pdf> accessed 26 January 2021.

Verlinden B.V. v. Central Bank of Nigeria, 461 U.S. 480 (1983).

Wood M, 'Do International Organizations Enjoy Immunity under Customary International Law' (2014) 10 International Organizations Law Review 287.

Xu C and Gu B, 'A Critique of Immunity for Multilateral Development Banks in National Courts' (2018) 4 The Chinese Journal of Global Governance 49.

CHAPTER 6

Regulation of Offerings by International Financial Institutions under the U.S. Federal Securities Laws

*Paul Dudek**

Abstract

International financial institutions (IFIs) face large funding needs to fulfill their missions. These funding needs are often met through the issuance of debt securities to global investors. US investors have historically shown a strong interest in debt securities of IFIs. Offerings of securities in the United States must comply with applicable US laws, in particular the US federal securities laws administered by the US Securities and Exchange Commission (SEC). This article discusses the US federal securities laws and regulations that are applicable to IFIs that offer debt securities in the United States.

1 Introduction

1.1 *Investment Trends*

National governments frequently join together with other national governments to sponsor and support supranational and multilateral development banks (broadly referred to as international financial institutions or IFIs) for the purpose of promoting and funding economic and social progress in specific countries or regions of the world. These IFIs face large funding needs to fulfill their missions. These funding needs are often met through the issuance of debt securities to global investors. Investors in the United States have historically shown a strong interest in debt securities of IFIs, as evidenced by reports from the US Department of the Treasury. These reports indicate steadily increasing holdings by US investors of debt securities issued by "international organizations".

* Partner, Latham & Watkins, LLP, Washington, D.C., paul.dudek@lw.com. Chief, Office of International Corporate Finance, Division of Corporation Finance, US Securities and Exchange Commission, 1993 – 2016.

DOI:10.1163/9789004460010_007

TABLE 6.1 US holdings of debt securities of international organizations as of December 31, 1994–2020[a] (in billions of USD)

Year	Total	Long-term debt	Short-term debt
1994	9.6	9.6	*n.a.*
1997	17.0	17.0	*n.a.*
2001	12.2	11.7	0.5
2003	18.3	17.2	1.1
2004	20.0	17.8	2.2
2005	24.0	19.0	3.0
2006	21.5	19.0	2.5
2007	23.7	22.2	1.5
2008	25.2	20.3	4.9
2009	48.3	40.2	8.1
2010	54.7	41.4	13.3
2011	52.4	45.9	6.5
2012	57.0	50.3	6.7
2013	61.8	53.9	7.9
2014	64.4	58.2	6.2
2015	65.8	54.6	11.2
2016	75.2	70.6	4.6
2017	90.4	81.7	8.7
2018	85.6	75.7	9.9
2019	100.8	86.7	14.1
2020	119.2	108.4	10.8

a US Portfolio Holdings of Foreign Securities, US Department of the Treasury, Federal Reserve Bank of New York, Board of Governors of the Federal Reserve System, reports from April 2000 through October 2021. This report does not specifically define the entities included within this category, although from context it appears to closely track IFIs.

1.2 *US Statutory Framework*

Offerings of securities in the United States must comply with applicable US laws, in particular the US federal securities laws administered by the SEC. These laws provide a comprehensive set of regulations that all issuers must address when they raise funds in the United States.

Two Depression-era US federal statutes form the center of the US regulatory regime relating to the issuance and trading of securities in the United

States: the Securities Act of 1933[1] (Securities Act), and the Securities Exchange Act of 1934[2] (Exchange Act). The Securities Act generally governs the initial offer and sale of securities in the United States, while the Exchange Act generally regulates the post-issuance trading of securities, reporting obligations of entities with publicly traded securities, and the activities of financial intermediaries such as broker-dealers, transfer agents, and stock exchanges.

The Securities Act requires registration with the SEC of any transaction involving the offer or sale of a security, unless the security is of a type that is exempt from registration or the transaction is structured to take advantage of an available exemption from registration. The terms "offer", "sale", and "security" are broadly defined.

The registration requirement applies to all entities that issue securities, although some entities, such as US banks and state and local governments in the United States, benefit from an exemption. Sovereign governments, and by extension IFIs, must comply with the registration requirement. In 2001, the SEC settled an enforcement action against a foreign sovereign bank that had offered and sold securities in the United States without complying with the registration requirements.[3] The SEC found that the bank had promoted an offering of debt securities through activities such as a mass mailing to 30,000 to 40,000 Indian nationals residing in the United States, full page advertisements in Indian newspapers published in the United States, and television advertisements on Indian broadcast channels. In this instance, the SEC did not seek a penalty or fine. Rather, the bank agreed with the SEC that it would cease and desist from committing future violations of the registration provisions of the Securities Act.

2 Registered Offerings under the Securities Act

2.1 *General Process for Registration*

In order to register securities under the Securities Act, an issuer of securities must file a registration statement with the SEC that meets the detailed disclosure requirements prescribed by the SEC under the Securities Act. The Securities Act delineates two types of issuers: foreign governments and political subdivisions thereof; and all other issuers.[4] The Securities Act also sets out

1 15 U.S. Code, Section 77a et seq.

2 15 U.S. Code, Section 78a et seq.

3 U.S. Securities and Exchange Commission 2001.

4 See Section 7(a)(1) of the Securities Act of 1933. For ease of reference, this article refers to issuers that are not foreign governments or political subdivisions as "corporate issuers".

the information to be included in a registration statement: Schedule A to the Securities Act specifies 32 items of information that corporate issuers must provide in a registration statement; and Schedule B to the Securities Act specifies 14 items of information that foreign governments must provide.

In the Securities Act, the US Congress gave the SEC the authority to supplement the information that must be provided in registration statements. Over the decades, the SEC has used this authority broadly with respect to corporate issuers, and has adopted numerous forms and many additional detailed disclosure requirements beyond the matters enumerated under Schedule A. For foreign governmental issuers however, the SEC has taken a more limited approach, adopting minimal rules relating to disclosures that must be provided in a registration statement.

Schedule B requires disclosure of the following matters: (1) the name of the borrowing government; (2) the use of proceeds of the offering; (3) the amount of funded debt of the government, and a brief description of outstanding indebtedness, addressing such matters as interest rate and maturity date of such indebtedness; (4) whether the government or its predecessor has, within the prior 20 years, defaulted on the principal or interest of any external indebtedness, and if so, the details of such default; (5) receipts (classified by source) and expenditures (classified by purpose) for the latest fiscal year and the two preceding fiscal years on a year-by-year basis; (6) the names and addresses of the underwriters; (7) the name and address of the government's authorized agent in the United States, if any; (8) the estimated net proceeds from the offering of securities; (9) the price at which the securities will be offered to the public or the method by which such price will be computed; (10) commissions paid or to be paid to the underwriters in connection with the offering; (11) the estimated expenses of the offering; (12) the names and addresses of the government's counsel who provide an opinion on the legality of the securities; (13) a copy of the underwriting agreement for the offering; and (14) an agreement to furnish a copy of the legal opinion relating to the securities being offered.

Although the SEC has not adopted additional detailed disclosure requirements for foreign governments as it has for corporate issuers, by course of practice the registration statements of foreign governmental issuers will generally include much more information than strictly required under Schedule B and cover a standard set of topics for investors, providing extensive information relating to the foreign country's economy and financial system and additional information about the political, social, and governance environment in the foreign country.

As discussed below, disclosures in registration statements are subject to the antifraud provisions under the US federal securities laws, which impose liability for material misstatements and omissions in the offer or sale of securities. The fundamental test for "materiality" is whether there is a substantial likelihood that a reasonable investor would consider the misstatement or omission important in deciding whether to purchase or sell a security. The US Supreme Court has explained that "there must be a substantial likelihood that the disclosure of the omitted fact would have been viewed by the reasonable investor as having significantly altered the 'total mix' of information made available".[5] Thus, the determination of materiality is a mixed question of law and fact, with no bright-line quantitative test for materiality.

Registration statements under the Securities Act are subject to review and comment by SEC staff. The purpose of the review process is to enhance compliance with applicable disclosure requirements by issuers. The SEC staff does not evaluate the merits of offerings or issuers and does not determine whether an investment is appropriate for investors. The SEC review process is not an in-depth on-site evaluation of the veracity of the information in the registration statement. Rather, it is more like a desk review, and the staff's comments on the disclosures are based on publicly available information and the staff's assessment of the importance of the information to investors. The SEC staff process results in a registration statement being declared "effective", a statutory term of art under the Securities Act indicating that the securities have been registered with the SEC and that sales of securities under the registration statement can occur.

The US securities laws contain several overlapping provisions which impose so-called antifraud liability if certain disclosure documents, or in some cases oral statements, contain an untrue statement of a material fact or omitted to state a material fact required to be stated therein or necessary to make the statements therein not misleading. Cases may be brought by private litigants as well as governmental authorities such as the SEC and the US Department of Justice. Registered securities offerings are subject to specific antifraud provisions that are not applicable to unregistered offerings such as under Rule 144A, as discussed below.

2.2 *Registration under the Securities Act by International Financial Institutions*

As noted above, the registration provisions of the Securities Act draw a distinction between issuers of securities that qualify as foreign governments and all other issuers. For an IFI considering a registered offering of debt securities

5 TSC Industries, Inc. v Northway, Inc., (1976).

in the United States, a key factor is determining whether the SEC would treat the IFI like a foreign government. If the SEC would not treat the IFI like a foreign government, then the IFI would be required to comply with the extensive financial statement and other disclosure requirements that apply to corporate issuers, rather than those outlined under Schedule B.

That said, the SEC has permitted a number of entities that are not strictly foreign governments (or political subdivisions) to register securities on Schedule B. Examples include financial institutions that are owned by a foreign government, whose activities carry out a social purpose for that foreign government and whose debt securities are guaranteed by, or which benefit from a form of credit support from, that foreign government.

In the past, the SEC staff would provide written advice to a requesting entity advising as to the SEC staff's view on whether the use of Schedule B was permitted for the entity. The requesting letter to the SEC staff would generally describe the legal status of the entity under local law, the ownership structure, the public purpose, governmental control, and any guarantee or the credit support provided by the foreign government, including whether the government's taxing power was available to support any debt securities. In response, the SEC staff would generally not raise an issue to the use of Schedule B.[6]

IFIs can have a more difficult time establishing the appropriateness of using the Schedule B registration regime rather than the registration regime for corporate issuers. IFIs are not owned by a single foreign government and are frequently created under a multilateral treaty rather than a specified law. Also, their financial obligations are generally not guaranteed by the foreign governments that are members of the IFI, although the IFI may be entitled to effect capital calls upon its members.

Nonetheless, the SEC has long recognized that the use of Schedule B is appropriate for some IFIs with relevant characteristics. For example, in 1973, the Central American Bank for Economic Integration (CABEI) requested permission to register its debt securities on Schedule B.[7] In its request letter, the CABEI explained its formation as an international institution with five Central American countries as members and its purpose of promoting economic integration and balanced economic development of member states. The CABEI was administered by a board of governors consisting of ministerial officials from the member states, and officers employed by the bank. Its capital structure consisted of ordinary capital and guarantee capital subscribed to by

6 See U.S. Securities and Exchange Commission 1987, and ibid. 1993.

7 See ibid. 1973.

member states. The SEC staff responded favorably to the CABEI's request to use Schedule B.[8]

In the absence of formal SEC rules describing the disclosures required to be provided beyond the minimum requirements described in Schedule B, IFIs have adapted their registration statement disclosures to provide relevant information to investors. This information generally includes disclosures relating to the administration of the IFI, as well as its capital structure, funding, governance and operations. Disclosures may also relate to projects funded and/or loans extended by the IFI, providing details on the countries involved and the specific borrowing entities in those countries. When appropriate, disclosures relating to the potential impact of economic sanctions may also be provided. Financial statements of the IFI are included as part of the registration statement, but unlike for corporate issuers, such financial statements are not required to be audited under SEC-prescribed standards or prepared in accordance with SEC-recognized accounting standards.

2.3 *Periodic Reporting under the Exchange Act*

When a corporate issuer sells securities in an offering that is registered under the Securities Act, it becomes obligated under Section 15(d) of the Exchange Act to file with the SEC periodic reports for the remainder of the fiscal year in which the offering takes place, and on a continuous basis thereafter, unless the securities are held by fewer than 300 holders of record or the securities mature or are redeemed and are no longer outstanding. This filing obligation helps assure that purchasers in the secondary market shortly after the offering have access to current information about the issuer. Foreign governments and political subdivisions are exempted from this requirement.[9] By course of practice, this exemption is also extended to IFIs that are permitted to register their securities on Schedule B.

Even when foreign governments choose to register securities under the Securities Act for sale to the public in the United States, the large majority of such securities are not listed on a US stock exchange. Instead, such securities will trade in the broad over-the-counter market in the United States, an unorganized trading venue among US broker-dealers and financial institutions.

Should a foreign government decide to list its securities on a US stock exchange, then under Section 12(a) of the Exchange Act, the foreign government must file a separate registration statement for the purpose of such listing.

8 For similar correspondence, see ibid. 1982 (I).

9 The last sentence of Exchange Act , Section 15(d) reads: "Nothing in this subsection shall apply to securities issued by a foreign government or political subdivision thereof".

The SEC has adopted a registration statement form for this purpose: Form 18. As noted, foreign government debt securities are rarely listed on a US stock exchange and, as a result, Form 18 is used very infrequently.

Additionally, the SEC has adopted an annual report form to be used by foreign governments: Form 18-K. As explained in the next section, many foreign governments, as well as foreign governmental banks and IFIs that are permitted to register securities on Schedule B, file Form 18-K annual reports with the SEC on a voluntary basis for the purpose of maintaining a shelf registration statement current and keeping their disclosures up-to-date. There is no specific SEC form type for a foreign government to file materials other than an annual report. As a result, when a foreign government, including an IFI that has registered securities on Schedule B, seeks to file with the SEC a semi-annual or quarterly report or other information, the filing must be made as an amendment to the Form 18-K annual report.[10]

2.4 *Shelf Registration*

The Securities Act contemplates a registration regime that applies on an offering, by offering basis: each discrete registered offering of securities should be the subject of a separate registration statement. Over time, this approach produced delays associated with preparing long-form disclosure documents, which detracted from issuers' ability to quickly access market windows for favorable financings. The SEC addressed this problem in 1982 by creating a system for corporate issuers known as shelf registration, under which companies could register a large dollar amount of generic unspecified securities on an up-front basis. When financing opportunities arose, companies could take securities "off the shelf" for immediate sale, with specified terms for the securities provided in updated offering documents without any prior SEC review. The shelf registration system also allowed for short-form prospectuses, under which information already on file with the SEC was deemed to be incorporated by reference into a short prospectus, so that information need not be repeated.

The shelf registration system for corporate issuers has been enhanced and improved over the years through a number of formal rule changes. The most recent enhancements were adopted in 2005 under an initiative referred to as Securities Offering Reform, which permits certain SEC-reporting corporate issuers to undertake registered offerings without any regulatory delays associated with registering securities.

10 On the SEC's EDGAR filing system, these amendments are styled as a "Form 18-K/A".

For IFIs and foreign governmental issuers that register securities on Schedule B, the shelf registration system has been implemented through two statements of policy (not formal rules) published by the SEC in 1980 and 1982.[11] The statements provide for a procedure under which an issuer can file a base prospectus disclosing standard political, economic and statistical information with regard to the IFI or foreign government that is appropriate for a Schedule B registration statement, in addition to a generic description of the debt securities to be offered. When an offering of specific securities is planned, the issuer will prepare a prospectus supplement that describes the use of proceeds, the complete description of the securities offered (such as the interest rate and interest payment and maturity dates), the plan of distribution (typically this is a firm commitment underwriting), the underwriters' names and their compensation, and any recent material developments not disclosed in the earlier base prospectus.

The SEC's shelf registration procedure for IFIs and foreign governments does not contemplate the availability of an incorporation-by-reference approach. By its terms, the SEC's procedure set out in its policy statements requires an IFI or foreign government to prepare and update a long-form prospectus annually. Through an informal process, however, the SEC has permitted Schedule B filers to use an incorporation-by-reference procedure. In this informal process, the IFI or foreign government makes a written request explaining to the SEC that it is setting up a shelf registration for its debt securities and that the IFI or foreign government will disclose in a Form 18-K annual report, and in amendments to that annual report, the same type of information that would be contained in a Schedule B registration statement. Then when the IFI or foreign government files a Schedule B shelf registration statement, it will incorporate by reference the most current Form 18-K and any recent amendments. The SEC staff will generally respond to this written request that it will not object to the use of this procedure. Numerous IFIs and foreign governments have taken advantage of this informal process.

11 Interpretative Release relating to Delayed Offerings by Foreign Governments or Political Subdivisions Thereof, U.S. Securities and Exchange Commission 1980; Interpretative Release relating to Continuous and Delayed Offerings by Foreign Governments or Political Subdivisions Thereof, U.S. Securities and Exchange Commission 1982 (II).

3 Exempt Offerings under the Securities Act

Offerings of debt securities by IFIs are often structured as global offerings that are simultaneously offered to investors inside and outside the United States. When these offerings are not registered with the SEC, they are typically structured to take advantage of a combination of exemptions from registration under the Securities Act. Most typically, the portion of the transaction sold to investors outside the United States will be designed to comply with the safe harbor for offshore offerings provided by Regulation S under the Securities Act. At the same time, the portion sold to US investors will be structured to comply with the safe harbor from registration under Rule 144A under the Securities Act, which allows for resales of offered securities to certain large US institutional investors known as "qualified institutional buyers" or QIBs. Some exempt offerings in the United States (generally smaller transactions) may be structured as private placements under Section 4(a)(2) of the Securities Act or Regulation D under the Securities Act.

Even though an offering may qualify for an exemption from registration with the SEC, any offering of securities that involves a US domestic transaction in securities, conduct within the United States or that has effects in the United States may be subject to the broad antifraud liability provisions under Exchange Act Section 10(b) and Rule 10b-5 under the Exchange Act, under which claims may be brought by parties to a transaction as well as by the SEC and the US Department of Justice. As a result, offering participants pay particular attention, especially in Rule 144A offerings in which securities are sold to US institutional investors, to prepare an offering document that contains information that meets high standards.

3.1 *Regulation S*

By the express terms of the statute, the registration requirements under the Securities Act apply to any offer or sale of a security involving interstate commerce or use of the US mail system, unless an exemption is available. The Securities Act defines "interstate commerce" to include "trade or commerce in securities or any transaction or communication relating thereto [...] between any foreign country and any State, Territory or the District of Columbia".[12]

Upon initial consideration, an offering of securities by an IFI located outside the United States to investors also located outside the United States would not appear to involve interstate commerce under the Securities Act. However,

12 Securities Act Section 2(a)(7).

as a practical matter, widely distributed offerings of debt securities in global offerings frequently involve US-headquartered broker-dealers, even if the transaction is mainly executed through a non-US office. In light of this involvement and the resultant potential for e-mail messages and telephonic communications into the United States – coupled with the breadth of how the US interstate commerce threshold is interpreted and applied – an IFI could face difficulty establishing that its offering did not use US interstate commerce.

Fortunately, the SEC has historically recognized that registration of securities offerings with only incidental contacts with the United States should not be required. This approach is codified in Regulation S, which adopts what the SEC refers to as a territorial approach to the registration provisions of the Securities Act.

Regulation S provides a safe harbor from the Securities Act's registration requirements for certain offerings outside the United States. If the conditions of Regulation S are met, the transaction is deemed to take place outside the United States and hence does not trigger the registration requirements of the Securities Act.

All Regulation S transactions start with the same basic requirements, which are set out in Rule 903 under the Securities Act. Regulation S then layers on additional restrictions depending on the nature of the issuer and the securities being offered. The basic requirements under Regulation S, referred to as general conditions, are that:

(1) The offer or sale must be made in an "offshore transaction"; and
(2) There must be no "directed selling efforts" in the United States in connection with the offering.

An "offshore transaction" is defined as an offer that is (1) not made to a person in the United States and (2) at the time the buy order is originated, the buyer is outside the United States, or the seller (and any person acting on the seller's behalf, such as an underwriter) reasonably believes that the buyer is outside the United States.[13]

The term "directed selling efforts" is broadly defined to include any activities that have, or can reasonably be expected to have, the effect of conditioning the market in the United States for the securities being offered in reliance

13 Regulation S, Rule 903(h). An "offshore transaction" also includes a transaction that is executed in, on or through the physical trading floor of an established foreign securities exchange located outside the United States. This aspect of Regulation S is less relevant because most securities exchanges have migrated to fully electronic trading.

on Regulation S. Prohibited efforts include mailing offering materials into the United States, conducting promotional seminars in the United States, granting interviews about the offering in the United States (including by telephone), or placing advertisements with radio or television stations broadcasting in the United States. Importantly, selling activities in the United States in concurrent US offerings – whether registered or exempt – do not constitute directed selling efforts. In addition, offshore transactions that are carried out in compliance with Regulation S are not integrated with registered or exempt US domestic offerings.

In the context of offerings by issuers, Regulation S provides a safe harbor for sales by any issuer, "distributors" employed by an issuer (essentially, broker-dealers who act as underwriters or placement agents for the issuer) and entities and individuals who are considered affiliates of the issuer or a distributor. This safe harbor distinguishes among three classes (or "categories") of securities, with varying procedural safeguards imposed. Such safeguards are designed to have the securities come to rest outside the United States. The criteria used to designate securities into a particular group were chosen because the criteria reflect the likelihood that the securities may be resold into the United States after their initial sale.

The first issuer safe harbor category, known as Category 1, has no requirements other than the two general conditions discussed above. Of most relevance for offerings of debt securities by IFIs, offerings included in Category 1 include:

(1) Securities backed by the full faith and credit of a foreign government;
(2) Securities offered by non-US issuers who reasonably believe at the commencement of the offering that there is no "substantial US market interest"[14] in the securities offered; and
(3) Securities offered in an "overseas directed offering".[15]

---

14 A substantial US market interest in debt securities is measured at the commencement of the offering and is defined as (a) the issuer's debt securities being held of record by 300 or more US persons, (b) USD 1 billion or more of principal amount of debt securities being held of record by US persons, and (c) 20% or more of the principal amount of outstanding debt securities being held of record by US persons. In light of the increasing US investor interest in IFI debt securities as discussed above, some IFIs may find that there is a substantial US market interest in their debt securities.

15 For an IFI, an overseas directed offering is one that is directed to residents of a single foreign country other than the United States made in accordance with local laws and customary practices and documentation in that country. Given the typical practice of IFIs selling securities in multiple jurisdictions, this aspect of Regulation S is of limited utility.

As discussed above, there is a lack of clarity as to whether an IFI would be considered a foreign government for the purposes of being able to utilize the Category 1 safe harbor as a matter of right without having to undertake further analysis on the extent of US market interest in the IFI's debt securities or the type of offering being undertaken. The SEC offers no formal or informal guidance on whether IFIs can be treated as foreign governments under the Regulation S safe harbor.

If an IFI was not considered a foreign government, it would be treated in the same fashion as a foreign corporation for purposes of determining the appropriate safe harbor category under Regulation S. When an IFI has made several debt offerings under Reg S and Rule 144A, it may find that its debt is held by a large number of US investors and that it would fall under Category 2 under Regulation S because it is considered to have a substantial US market interest in its debt securities.[16] IFIs in Category 2 may take advantage of the safe harbor if various additional conditions are satisfied along with the two general conditions discussed above. These additional conditions include a 40-day compliance period during which offers and sales of newly issued debt securities cannot be made to a US person (as defined under Regulation S), an agreement by the underwriters not to so offer and sell the securities, and legends on offering documents and other materials relating to the selling restrictions.[17]

3.2 *Rule 144A*

By its terms, Rule 144A under the Securities Act is not available for an offering of securities by the issuer of the security; Rule 144A is only available for resale transactions. Although market participants often refer to financings involving the use of this rule as "Rule 144A offerings", as a technical matter most Rule 144A offerings involve two distinct steps: (1) there is a sale to one or more initial purchasers under an exemption, which is followed by (2) resales to QIBs under Rule 144A. The initial purchasers are typically US broker-dealers and serve much the same function as underwriters in connection with registered offerings. The requirements for a valid Rule 144A offering include:

16 See footnote 13 for the thresholds to determine whether there is a substantial US market interest in debt securities.

17 A further Category 3 under Regulation S provides for additional restrictions, such as the use of a temporary global certificate to initially represent the offered securities, and a required certification as to non-US status in order to obtain definitive certificates. It is unlikely that an IFI, if it is formed under the laws of a non-US jurisdiction and is owned by foreign governments or foreign governmental entities, would need to comply with the Category 3 safe harbor procedures.

(1) Resale to QIBS: the securities must be offered and sold only to QIBS or to a person who the seller (and any person acting on its behalf) reasonably believes is a QIB;

(2) Notice to buyers: the seller and any person acting on its behalf must take reasonable steps to ensure that the buyer is aware that the seller may be relying on Rule 144A;[18]

(3) Fungibility: the securities must not be, when issued, of the same class as securities listed on a US stock exchange;[19] and

(4) Information delivery: a holder or the purchaser must have the right to obtain from the seller or the issuer, upon request, certain minimal reasonably current information concerning the business of the issuer and its financial statements.

Rule 144A contains an exemption from the information delivery condition for "foreign governments [...] that are eligible to register securities on Schedule B".[20] For an IFI, the question of Schedule B eligibility surfaces again in the context of an unregistered offering conducted under Rule 144A.

3.3 *Certain US-Supported International Financial Institutions*

There are six IFIS that benefit from an exemption from the registration requirements under the Securities Act and reporting requirements under the Exchange Act: the International Bank for Reconstruction and Development (better known as the World Bank), the Inter-American Development Bank, the Asian Development Bank, the African Development Bank, the International Finance Corporation and the European Bank for Reconstruction and Development. The enabling legislation enacted by the US Congress for each of these IFIS contains an express exemption from such registration requirements.[21] Each of these IFIS files reports and offering documents with the SEC pursuant to separate rules adopted by the SEC specific for each of these IFIS.

---

18 This notice is generally made through disclosure in an offering memorandum or a trade confirmation.

19 An IFI is unlikely to have debt listed in the United States.

20 Rule 144A(d)(4)(i).

21 For example, Section 15(a) of the Bretton Woods Agreements Act, 1945, which established the World Bank, provides that "any securities issued by International Bank for Reconstruction and Development (including any guaranty by the bank, whether or not limited in scope), [...] shall be deemed to be exempted securities" under the Securities Act and the Exchange Act.

4 Conclusion

IFIs have many regulatory options from which to choose when considering undertaking a financing in the United States, including registering on Schedule B or making a Rule 144A offering. More broadly, IFIs can utilize Regulation S in a global offering. The SEC has provided helpful procedures and guidance for IFIs in each area, although interpretive questions continue to arise.

References

U.S. Congress, Securities Act of 1933, (1933), Periodical. Retrieved from the Library of Congress, <www.loc.gov/item/uscode1934-001015002a/>, accessed 20 June 2022.

U.S. Congress, Securities Exchange Act of 1934, (1934), <https://www.govinfo.gov/content/pkg/COMPS-1885/pdf/COMPS-1885.pdf>, accessed 20 June 2022.

U.S. Congress, Bretton Woods Agreements Act, Chapter 339 of the 79th Congress, (31 July 1945), <https://www.govinfo.gov/content/pkg/COMPS-10334/pdf/COMPS-10334.pdf>, accessed 20 June 2022.

U.S. Securities and Exchange Commission, Central American Bank for Economic Integration, SEC staff no-action letter, (14 March 1973).

U.S. Securities and Exchange Commission, SEC Release No. 33-6240, (10 September 1980).

U.S. Securities and Exchange Commission, Nordiska Investingsbanken, SEC staff no-action letter, (1 February 1982), (I).

U.S. Securities and Exchange Commission, SEC Release No. 33-6424, (2 September 1982) (II).

U.S. Securities and Exchange Commission, Kreditanstalt für Wiederanfbau, SEC staff no-action letter, (20 August 1987).

U.S. Securities and Exchange Commission, Bank of Greece, SEC staff no-action letter, (2 June 1993).

U.S. Securities and Exchange Commission, In the Matter of The State Bank of India, SEC Administrative Proceeding No. 3-10643, Release No. 33-8036, (19 November 2001), <https://www.sec.gov/litigation/admin/33-8036.htm>, accessed 20 June 2022.

U.S. Supreme Court, TSC Industries, Inc. v Northway, Inc., 426 US 438, 449, (1976).

CHAPTER 7

International Financial Institutions and China

The Legal Status of International Financial Institutions and the Asian Infrastructure Investment Bank under the Law of the People's Republic of China

Minny Siu and James Guan***

Abstract

There is no domestic law or regulation in the People's Republic of China (the PRC or China) which specifically applies to, or regulates, international financial institutions (IFIs) or their establishment. The legal status of an IFI under PRC law depends on three key threshold issues, namely: (I) any immunity and/or privilege enjoyed by it, (II) whether it can be a party to civil proceedings in the PRC, and (III) whether it has legal capacity under PRC law.

1 Introduction

There is no domestic law or regulation in the People's Republic of China (the PRC or China)[1] which specifically applies to or regulates international financial institutions[2] (IFIs) or their establishment.

This chapter considers how a PRC court would assess the legal classification and legal capacity of an IFI under PRC law with reference to the following:

* Minny Siu (a partner in the King & Wood Mallesons Hong Kong, China, office, minny.siu@hk.kwm.com) specializes in derivatives, structured products, financial regulatory and Fin Tech and is qualified to advise on matters under Hong Kong and English law.

** James Guan (a partner in the King & Wood Mallesons Shanghai office, guanfeng@cn.kwm.com) specializes in cross-border litigation and arbitration, especially cases pertaining to finance, asset management, equity, insurance, product liability and commercial contracts.

1 For the purposes of this chapter, references to PRC or China excludes Hong Kong, China, as well as Macau Special Administrative Region and Taiwan.

2 For the purposes of this chapter, IFI refers to any intergovernmental organization (i.e., an organization established by treaty, whose members comprise primarily sovereign states), constituted under public international law, of which China is a member (such as AIIB).

DOI:10.1163/9789004460010_008

(I) The constitutional documents of the IFI in question and the related relevant international treaty(ies) to which the PRC has acceded, in particular, how these documents describe such IFI's legal status and whether these documents confer legal capacity on it; and
(II) The general principles of law in the PRC.

2 Key Threshold Issues

The following section provides an overview and addresses each of the key threshold issues.

2.1 *Overview*

For the purpose of determining the legal capacity of parties, with respect to civil proceedings under PRC law, it is necessary to examine the issue from (I) a procedural law perspective and (II) a substantive law perspective.

(I) Procedural law aspect in the context of civil proceedings: The *legal classification* of parties to civil proceedings in the PRC is primarily determined pursuant to the PRC's procedural law.
(II) Substantive law aspect in the context of capacity issues for civil rights and obligations: The *legal capacity* of parties to civil proceedings in the PRC is determined pursuant to the PRC's substantive law, where such law applies.

Therefore, as a matter of judicial practice in the PRC, a court would assess the legal status of an IFI by considering the following three threshold issues from the perspective of PRC law:

(I) A PRC court will first determine whether an IFI (which has a claim to immunity from legal process) has waived its immunity, such that the court may exercise jurisdiction over it;
(II) If a PRC court determines that it has jurisdiction over an IFI, it will proceed to assess whether, as a matter of PRC procedural law, the IFI can be a party to civil proceedings in the PRC; and
(III) The PRC court will then assess whether, as a matter of PRC substantive law, the IFI has legal capacity to enter into the relevant contract and perform its obligations under such contract.

The following sections examine each of these three threshold issues.

2.2 *Immunities of IFIs*

The following section will provide an overview of state immunity under PRC law before discussing the immunity of IFIs. We then explore the determination of a PRC court's jurisdiction over an IFI.

2.2.1 Overview of State Immunity under PRC Law

There is no special immunity law in the PRC, but the legal stance can be inferred from other PRC laws and representations made by the Central People's Government (the CPG) in foreign courts and in notices to Hong Kong, China.

The CPG applies an 'absolute' foreign state immunity rule to the PRC, whereby both China and other foreign states are immune from being sued, and state assets are immune from court orders, in the PRC, unless the immunity is waived.[3]

"Absolute immunity" refers to a form of legal immunity for a foreign state or international organization that confers total immunity from criminal prosecution and lawsuits so long as they are acting within the scope of their duties. Absolute immunity contrasts with "qualified immunity". The United Nations Convention on Jurisdictional Immunities of States and their Properties (2004 NY Convention) was adopted by the General Assembly of the United Nations in New York on 2 December 2004. The 2004 NY Convention holds a position of qualified immunity according to which a state cannot invoke immunity from the jurisdiction of the court of other states arising out of commercial transactions and certain other activities. The 2004 NY Convention is yet to come into force in the PRC. China signed the 2004 NY Convention on 14 September 2005 but has not ratified it. Therefore, it has no effect in China in respect of international law or practice.

In foreign courts, the CPG has consistently argued for absolute immunity of states. In 1986, the US Court of Appeals for the Eleventh Circuit heard the CPG's declaration of its adherence to the doctrine of absolute immunity in the case of *Russell Jackson et al. v People's Republic of China*,[4] where the US plaintiffs had sued the CPG for payments on bonds issued in 1911. However, the CPG prefers extrajudicial and diplomatic means in asserting its absolutist position. For example, during the US case of *Morris v. People's Republic of China*, the Chinese Embassy in Washington, D.C. sent a memorandum to the US Department of State, reaffirming the PRC's position on absolute immunity but the memorandum was not reviewed by the court nor referred to in the judgment.[5]

---

3 For the purposes of this chapter, we exclude Chinese State-Owned Enterprises (which require a separate analysis).

4 794 F.2d 1490, 1494 (11th Cir. 1986).

5 478 F. Supp. 2d 561 (S.D.N.Y. 2007).

The PRC's views on absolute immunity were reiterated in the Hong Kong, China, case of *FG Hemisphere Associates LLC v Democratic Republic of the Congo* (the Congo case).[6] In the first-instance trial of the Congo case, a letter from the Ministry of Foreign Affairs of the PRC was introduced by the Hong Kong, China, Government as evidence. The thrust of it is that the PRC has always taken the position that sovereign states enjoy absolute immunity from suit in foreign courts.[7] The Ministry of Foreign Affairs sent two more letters to reiterate the PRC's adherence to the doctrine of absolute immunity, and that its signature on the 2004 UN Convention does not render a change in this position.[8]

2.2.2 Immunity of IFIs

In many states, the national constitution determines the status of international law in the domestic legal system. The Chinese Constitution, however, is silent about international law.[9] Nevertheless, the general principles of PRC civil law stipulate that, if any international treaty, concluded or acceded to by the PRC, contains provisions differing from those of the civil laws of the PRC, the provisions of the international treaty shall apply, unless the provisions are such on which the PRC has announced reservations. Therefore, as a matter of PRC law, PRC courts will generally respect the privileges and immunities enjoyed by IFIs pursuant to the international treaty(ies) to which China has acceded.

Additionally, the PRC applies its "absolute" foreign state immunity doctrine also to IFIs. The Supreme People's Court (SPC) has indicated that:

(I) "[O]nly where the international organization or foreign country clearly indicates its waiver of jurisdictional immunity in civil cases can the PRC courts exercise jurisdiction over them.";[10] and

(II) [T]he PRC people's court shall not seal, seize or freeze "properties immune from being sealed up, distrained or frozen, as prescribed in a treaty, agreement, or other document having the nature of a treaty or agreement, which is concluded in the name of the PRC, the PRC government or a governmental department of the PRC with a foreign country or IFI in accordance with the Law of the

6 [2009] 1 HKLRD 410; [2010] 2 HKLRD 66; (2011) 14 HKCFAR 95.

7 [2009] 1 HKLRD 410.

8 (2011) 14 HKCFAR 95 [46] – [47].

9 Cai 2016, 269.

10 Responses to a reporter's questions on the "Interpretations of the Supreme People's Court on Several Issues Concerning Application of the Law of the People's Republic of China on Choice of Law for Foreign-Related Civil Relationships (I)" issued by the Fourth Chamber of the People's Supreme Court issued by the SPC on 6 January 2013.

> People's Republic of China on the Procedures for Conclusion of Treaties".[11]

Therefore, where the international treaty(ies) of an IFI (to which China has acceded) confers immunity on it, the IFI is absolutely immune from the jurisdiction of the PRC courts, and the enforcement of court orders. A PRC court can only exercise jurisdiction over the IFI where the IFI has clearly indicated its waiver of jurisdictional immunity in the relevant civil proceedings. The specific waiver of immunity by an IFI is necessary even where the IFI is itself a plaintiff, initiating a court proceeding in the PRC.

As a matter of judicial practice in the PRC, a court generally respects and gives effect to the waiver of immunity expressly made by an IFI.[12]

2.2.3 Determining a PRC Court's Jurisdiction over an IFI

The procedure by which a PRC court determines whether it has jurisdiction over an IFI that has waived its immunity is set out in the Notice of the Supreme People's Court on the Relevant Issues concerning the People's Courts to Accept Civil Cases Involving Privilege and Immunity, issued by the SPC on, and effective as of, 22 May 2007 (SPC Notice). The SPC Notice is binding on the lower courts and is intended to provide a clear standard to them when they encounter a case involving issues of state immunity. The English translation of the key provision of the SPC Notice is extracted below, as follows:

> To strictly enforce the provisions of the Civil Procedure Law of the People's Republic of China and the relevant international conventions that China has acceded to and ensure the correct acceptance of civil cases involving

11 Provisions of the Supreme People's Court for the People's Courts to Seal up, Distrain and Freeze Properties in Civil Enforcement (2020 Amendment) issued by the SPC on 29 December 2020.

12 (2014) 三中民终字第06823号. In this PRC court case involving a lawsuit filed by a PRC citizen against the International Committee of the Red Cross Regional Representative Office in East Asia (ICRC) relating to a lease contract (ICRC Case) available at http://wenshu.court.gov.cn/website/wenshu/181107ANFZ0BXSK4/index.html?docId=958220a8945349189e30e27e5984946e, accessed 12 September 2022, the court of first instance held that: (I) the ICRC enjoyed judicial immunity in accordance with the relevant provisions of the agreement entered into between the PRC and the ICRC for the establishment of a regional representative office in China; and \ (II) therefore, the court did not have jurisdiction over the claim brought against the ICRC. On appeal, the court requested ICRC to confirm whether it wishes to claim immunity against the lawsuit and the ICRC confirmed in writing to the court that it waived its jurisdictional immunity. The PRC appeal court therefore accepted ICRC's waiver and exercised its jurisdiction.

> privileges and immunities, this court has decided to establish a reporting system for cases involving privilege and immunity accepted by the people's courts, and a notice is hereby issued as follows:
>
> For a civil case filed with the people's court where the defendant or third party is any of the following subjects that enjoys privilege or immunity in China, before deciding to accept it, the people's court shall submit it to the higher people's court with jurisdiction for examination; the higher people's court agreeing on the acceptance shall submit its examination opinions to the Supreme People's Court. Before the Supreme People's Court responds, no acceptance shall be made.

The SPC Notice lists various "subjects that enjoy privilege or immunity in China" and includes foreign countries, any representative body in China of an organization within the United Nations system and any other subject enjoying privilege or immunity in China (such as IFIs, as explained above).

Therefore, before a PRC court decides to accept a civil case involving a party entitled to privileges and immunities (such as an IFI), it must file an application for review with the higher court.

Generally speaking, PRC courts are divided into four levels in accordance with the descending order of powers, i.e. the SPC, higher people's courts, intermediate people's courts and primary people's courts (the latter three levels are collectively referred to herein as the "lower courts"). The SPC Notice requires lower courts to refer any case involving an IFI defendant or third party to higher-level courts in order to be able to *accept* the case, but not in order to *reject* it. Therefore, before a lower court can accept a case involving an IFI, the primary people's court must refer the case to the higher people's court. Similarly, before the relevant higher people's court wishes to accept the case, it must file an application for approval with the SPC. The relevant PRC courts may not accept such a case unless and until the SPC grants its approval.[13]

According to other SPC guidance, the judicial committee of the higher court must discuss the issue before it is reported to the SPC.[14] In a PRC court case involving a lawsuit filed by a PRC citizen, against the International Committee of the Red Cross Regional Representative Office in East Asia (ICRC), relating

13 This practice is known as the "SPC reporting system".

14 This is illustrated in a reply by the SPC's in a 2009 case, the Reply of the Supreme People's Court to the Request for Instructions on Issues concerning Immunities in the Case of Disputes over a House Lease Contract between Li Xiaobo and the Regional Delegation for East Asia of the International Committee of the Red Cross.

to a lease contract, as the ICRC enjoyed judicial immunity in accordance with the relevant provisions of its agreement with China, for the establishment of a regional representative office in China, the Beijing Higher People's Court referred the case to the SPC, who determined that the PRC courts do not have jurisdiction over the claim brought against the ICRC.

2.3 *Legal Classification of IFIs: IFIs as a Party to Civil Proceedings in the PRC*

Where an IFI (which has a claim to immunity) has waived its immunities, and upon acceptance of a civil case involving the IFI by the PRC court pursuant to the SPC reporting procedure described above, the PRC court will proceed to determine the IFI's legal classification during the civil proceedings, in accordance with the Civil Procedure Law of the PRC (PRC Civil Procedure Law).[15]

2.3.1 Legal Classification of Parties to Civil Proceedings under PRC Law

Under the PRC Civil Procedure Law, parties to civil proceedings in the PRC are categorised into the following types:[16] (I) PRC citizens;[17] (II) legal persons[18] and (III) other organizations[19] (Other Organizations).

2.3.2 Legal Classification of an IFI under PRC Law

A PRC court is likely to recognise that an IFI can be a party to civil proceedings in the PRC (and can therefore exercise jurisdiction over it) for the two reasons set out below.

International organizations (including IFIs) are normally categorized as Other Organizations. The PRC Civil Procedure Law and the Interpretation of the Supreme People's Court on the Application of the Civil Procedure Law of the People's Republic of China (2022 Amendment), issued by the SPC on 1 April 2022 (Civil Procedure Law Interpretation), clarify that the concept of Other Organizations refers to organizations that are not "legal persons" but are lawfully established, have an organizational structure and own property.[20] Other Organizations can be a party to civil proceedings in the PRC. In a court ruling issued by the Zhejiang High People's Court in 2010, the court stated that:

15 Article 51 of the Civil Procedure Law of the People's Republic of China (2021 Amendment).

16 Article 51 of the PRC Civil Procedure Law.

17 Referred to as '自然人' or '公民' in Chinese.

18 Referred to as '法人' in Chinese. A legal person is defined as "an organization that has the capacity for civil rights and the capacity for civil conduct, which independently enjoys civil rights and assumes civil obligations" in accordance with PRC law.

19 Referred to as '其他组织' in Chinese.

20 Article 52 of the Civil Procedure Law Interpretation.

> According to international practice, the legal personality[21] of the International Fund for Compensation for Oil Pollution Damage, being an international organization, can be determined in accordance with the relevant international treaty or domestic laws [...] an international organization that has the characteristics of Other Organizations under PRC law can, pursuant to Article 48[22] of the PRC Civil Procedure Law, be a party to civil proceedings in the PRC.[23]

Alternatively, a PRC court may apply Article 268 of the PRC Civil Procedure Law (as set out below) and consider the international treaty(ies) entered into between the relevant IFI and the PRC (such as its constitutional documents) to assess the IFI's ability to be a party to civil proceedings in the PRC.[24] If the applicable treaty(ies) clearly provide for the IFI's ability to be a party to civil proceedings, the PRC courts will respect and uphold such provisions. Article 268 of the PRC Civil Procedure Law provides that:

> Civil actions instituted against foreigners, foreign organizations or international organizations that enjoy diplomatic privileges and immunities shall be handled in accordance with the relevant laws of the People's Republic of China and the relevant international treaties concluded or acceded to by the People's Republic of China.[25]

2.4 *Determining the Legal Capacity of IFIs*

The PRC courts assess the legal capacity of an IFI by determining, firstly, the applicable law to assess the IFI's legal capacity and, second, the legal capacity of the IFI under such applicable law. Under PRC law, the capacity of a person generally refers to the legal ability of the person to enter into a legally binding contract.

2.4.1 Applicable Law to Determine the Legal Capacity of IFIs

In identifying the applicable law that should be used to determine an IFI's legal capacity, a PRC court would first consider whether a "foreign element" is involved.

---

21 It is referred to as '法律人格' in Chinese.

22 The PRC Civil Procedure Law was amended in 2021, with Article 48 of the previous version renumbered as Article 51 under the 2021 amended version.

23 (2010) 浙辖终字第136号.

24 Article 268 of the PRC Civil Procedure Law.

25 Ibid.

A contract has a foreign element if:

(I) at least one of the parties is a foreign citizen, foreign legal person or stateless person;

(II) the subject matter of the contract is located outside of the PRC (for example, if the contract concerns land or goods outside the PRC);

(III) the legal factor that led to the establishment of, any change in, or termination of, the contract occurs outside of the PRC (for example, where a sale and purchase agreement provides for delivery of goods outside of the PRC);

(IV) the habitual residence of any of the parties is outside the PRC; or

(V) there are any other circumstances which may deem the contract as having a foreign element.[26]

For instance, an ISDA Master Agreement[27] and Transfer Annex[28] entered into by an IFI is generally considered to involve a "foreign element" enabling a PRC court to apply the Foreign Relationships Application Law[29], and the judicial interpretation thereof, for determination of the IFI's legal capacity.

2.4.2 Determining the Legal Capacity of IFIs

Pursuant to the SPC Response to Foreign Relationships Application Law[30] the PRC courts are required to apply and respect international treaty(ies) which have been concluded or acceded to by China to determine, amongst other things, the legal capacity of the IFI. And in respect of an IFI (such as the Asian Infrastructure Investment Bank), the PRC courts will determine the IFI's capacity in accordance with the provisions of the international treaty(ies) concluded or acceded to by China (unless the provisions are such, on which

26 Article 1 of the Interpretation (I) of the SPC on Several Issues concerning the Application of the PRC Law on Application of Laws for Foreign Related Civil Relationships (2020 Amendment) issued by the SPC on 29 December 2020.

27 The standard form agreement published by the International Swaps and Derivatives Association, Inc. (ISDA), which is used to document over-the-counter (OTC) derivatives trades.

28 The title transfer collateral arrangements in connection with an ISDA Master Agreement, governed by English law, under annexed terms, in the form of an ISDA Credit Support Annex (Transfer Annex).

29 Law of the PRC on the Laws Applicable to Foreign-Related Civil Relations issued by the Standing Committee of the National People's Congress (NPCSC) on 28 October 2010.

30 Responses to reporter's questions on the "Interpretations of the Supreme People's Court on Several Issues Concerning Application of the Law of the People's Republic of China on Choice of Law for Foreign-Related Civil Relationships (I)" issued by the Fourth Chamber of the People's Supreme Court issued by the SPC on 6 January 2013.

the PRC has announced reservations), which usually means the constitutional documents of the IFI (such as the relevant international treaty that stipulates the capacity of the IFI).

3 The Asian Infrastructure Investment Bank (AIIB)

As an international organization established pursuant to an international multilateral treaty (being the Articles of Agreement which were opened for signature on 29 June 2015 and entered into force on 25 December 2015 (AIIB Articles)) to which the PRC is a signatory, the analysis above regarding IFIs also applies *mutatis mutandis* to AIIB.

3.1 *No Specific Domestic Law Regulating AIIB*

There is no domestic law or regulation in the PRC which specifically applies to AIIB or its establishment. As such, a PRC court would assess the legal classification and legal capacity of AIIB under PRC law by reference to the international treaties of AIIB to which China has acceded to (including the AIIB Articles and the headquarters agreement concluded on 16 January 2016 between AIIB and the Government of the PRC (the Headquarters Agreement)) and the general principles of PRC law.

3.2 *Privileges and Immunities of AIIB and Jurisdiction of PRC Courts over AIIB*

We note the AIIB Articles specifically provide as follows:[31]

> Article 46 Immunity from Judicial Proceedings
>
> 1. [AIIB] shall enjoy immunity from every form of legal process, *except* (emphasis added) in cases arising out of or in connection with the *exercise of its powers to raise funds, through borrowings or other means, to guarantee obligations, or to buy and sell or underwrite the sale of securities* (emphasis added), in which cases actions *may be brought against [AIIB] only in a court of competent jurisdiction (emphasis added)* in the territory of a country *in which [AIIB] has an office, or has appointed an agent for the purpose of accepting service* (emphasis added) or notice of process, or has issued or guaranteed securities.

31 Article 46 and 47 of the AIIB Articles.

2. Notwithstanding the provisions of paragraph 1 of this Article, no action shall be brought against [AIIB] by any member, or by any agency or instrumentality of a member, or by any entity or person directly or indirectly acting for or deriving claims from a member or from any agency or instrumentality of a member. Members shall have recourse to such special procedures for the settlement of controversies between [AIIB] and its members as may be prescribed in this Agreement, in the by-laws and regulations of [AIIB], or in the contracts entered into with [AIIB].
3. Property and assets of [AIIB] shall, wheresoever located and by whomsoever held, be immune from all forms of seizure, attachment or execution before the delivery of final judgment against [AIIB].

Article 47 Immunity of Assets and Archives
1. Property and assets of [AIIB], wheresoever located and by whomsoever held, shall be immune from search, requisition, confiscation, expropriation or any other form of taking or foreclosure by executive or legislative action.
2. The archives of [AIIB], and, in general, all documents belonging to it, or held by it, shall be inviolable, wheresoever located and by whomsoever held.

The Headquarters Agreement further provides as follows:[32]

Article 4 Immunity from Judicial Proceedings
1. [AIIB] shall *enjoy immunity from every form of legal process, except that the immunity of [AIIB] shall not apply* (emphasis added):
   (a) to the extent that Bank shall have *expressly waived* (emphasis added) any such immunity in any particular case or in any written document;
   (b) in respect of a civil action arising out of or in connection with its powers to raise funds, through borrowings or other means, to guarantee obligations, or to buy and sell or underwrite the sale of *securities*;

32 Article 4 of the Headquarters Agreement.

(c) in respect of the enforcement of an arbitration award made against [AIIB] as a result of an *express submission to arbitration* (emphasis added) by or on behalf of [AIIB];
(d) in respect of a civil action brought by a third party for damages arising from an accident in the People's Republic of China caused by a vehicle belonging to [AIIB] or operated on its behalf; or
(e) in respect of any counter-claim directly connected with court proceedings initiated by [AIIB].

2. Notwithstanding the provisions of paragraph 1 of this Article, no action shall be brought against [AIIB] by the Government, or by any agency or instrumentality of the Government, or by any entity or person directly or indirectly acting for or deriving claims from the Government or from any agency or instrumentality of the Government. The Government shall have recourse to such special procedures for the settlement of controversies between [AIIB] and its members as may be prescribed in the Articles of Agreement of [AIIB], in the by-Laws and regulations of [AIIB] or in contracts entered into with [AIIB].
3. The property and assets of [AIIB], wheresoever located and by whomsoever held, shall be immune from all forms of restraint, seizure, attachment or execution except upon the delivery of final judgment against [AIIB].

Therefore, the AIIB Articles and Headquarters Agreement confer on AIIB qualified immunity. Hence, AIIB will not enjoy immunity in those cases that are specified as exceptions (for example, those arising out of or in connection with the exercise of its powers to raise funds, through borrowings or other means, to guarantee obligations, or to buy and sell or underwrite the sale of securities). As set out above, since the PRC adopts the principle of absolute immunity, a PRC court will only accept jurisdiction over AIIB in respect of these exceptions, where it has expressly waived immunity.

In this respect, we note that the AIIB Articles authorize AIIB to waive immunity by providing as follows:

Article 52 Waivers

1. [AIIB] at its discretion may waive any of the privileges, immunities and exemptions conferred under this Chapter in any case or instance, in such manner and upon such conditions as it may determine to be appropriate in the best interests of [AIIB].

3.3 *AIIB's Legal Capacity From the PRC Law Perspective*

Assuming that AIIB's privileges and immunities do not bar a PRC court from exercising its jurisdiction over AIIB, a PRC court will give effect to the AIIB Articles and Headquarters Agreement and recognise AIIB's legal capacity to enter into a contract from a PRC law perspective. We believe a PRC court is likely to conclude that a contract entered by AIIB will have a foreign element from a PRC law perspective (given that AIIB is an IFI whose members comprise primarily sovereign states) and will therefore apply the Foreign Relationships Application Law, and relevant judicial interpretation, to determine AIIB's legal capacity.

Pursuant to the relevant laws, (I) international treaty(ies) which have been concluded or acceded to by China to determine, amongst other things, the legal capacity of an IFI will be applied and respected; and (II) the IFI's capacity will be determined in accordance with the provisions of the international treaty(ies) concluded or acceded to by China (unless the provisions are such, on which the PRC has announced reservations), which usually means the constitutional documents of the IFI, i.e., the international treaty that establishes the IFI.

Therefore, the PRC courts will determine AIIB's legal capacity on the basis of the AIIB Articles and the Headquarters Agreement, as the international treaties to which China is a party, which confer on AIIB, amongst other things, "full juridical personality" and "full legal capacity" to contract; acquire and dispose of, immovable and movable property; institute and respond to legal proceedings; and take such other action as may be necessary or useful for its purpose, activities and functions.[33]

4 Conclusion

Provided an IFI has clearly waived its immunity, a PRC court is likely to agree to exercise jurisdiction over such IFI. Thereafter, in determining the legal capacity of the IFI, and provided there is a foreign element involved, a PRC court would determine the legal capacity of the IFI by reference to the provisions of the international treaty/ies, which China has concluded or acceded to, taking into account, for example, how these documents describe the IFI's legal status and whether such documents confer legal capacity on it.

33 Article 45 of the AIIB Articles and Article 3 of the Headquarters Agreement.

References

Asian Infrastructure Investment Bank, 'Articles of Agreement of the Asian Infrastructure Investment Bank' (effective since 25 December 2015).

Asian Infrastructure Investment Bank, 'Headquarters Agreement Between the Government of the People's Republic of China and the Asian Infrastructure Investment Bank' (effective since 16 January 2016).

Cai C, 'International Law in Chinese Courts during the Rise of China' (2016) 110 Am J Int'l L 269.

Democratic Republic of the Congo v FG Hemisphere Associates LLC (No 1) (2011) 14 HKCFAR 95 [46] – [47].

FG Hemisphere Associates LLC v Democratic Republic of the Congo [2009] 1 HKLRD 410.

FG Hemisphere Associates LLC v Democratic Republic of the Congo [2010] 2 HKLRD 66.

International Swaps and Derivatives Association, Inc, '1992 ISDA Master Agreement'.

International Swaps and Derivatives Association, Inc, '2002 ISDA Master Agreement'.

Jackson v. People's Republic of China 794 F.2d 1490 (11th Cir. 1986).

Morris v. People's Republic of China 478 F. Supp. 2d 561 (S.D.N.Y. 2007).

The National People's Congress of the People's Republic of China, 'Civil Procedure Law of the People's Republic of China' (2021 Amendment) (issued on 24 December 2021, effective from 1 January 2022) <http://www.ssf.gov.cn/portal/rootfiles/2022/01/07/1643159469539952-1643159469560439.pdf > accessed 12 September 2022.

The Supreme People's Court of the People's Republic of China, 'Interpretation (I) of the Supreme People's Court on Several Issues concerning the Application of the PRC Law on Application of Laws for Foreign Related Civil Relationships (2020 Amendment)' (issued on 29 December 2020, effective from 1 January 2021) <http://gongbao.court.gov.cn/Details/cd2e8428c4de894455038e760c6472.html> accessed 12 September 2022.

上诉人三星重工业株式会社、三星物产株式会社因与1992年国××油××金船舶污染损害追偿纠纷一案. (2010) 浙辖终字第136号.

朱珠劳动争议二审民事裁定书 (2014) 三中民终字第06823号.

PART 3

Innovations in Resource Mobilization

CHAPTER 8

International Financial Institutions

Paradigms of Organizational Structures, Funding Structures and Innovative Funding Modalities

*Gerd Droesse**

Abstract

This article analyses the connections between organizational structures and funding structures for three different kinds of organizational paradigms: (I) organizational groups (e.g. the World Bank Group) composed of organizations with proper legal personality under international law and legal capacity under national law, (II) organizations administering various resources and providing various financing modalities under one legal personality (e.g. the Asian Development Bank), and (III) organizations established by a treaty which were not designed to leverage resources through callable capital (e.g. the International Fund for Agricultural Development or the OPEC Fund). Specifically, this article explores to what extent organizational structures and institutional and legal frameworks constrain the ability of institutions to enhance their impact, realize synergies, mobilize resources, and have access to capital markets. With reference to the exponential increases of capital and borrowings of multilateral development banks (MDBs), it is argued that these have become too big to fail. This finding is discussed in light of proposals that MDBs should substantially further expand their borrowings and lending without increase of their paid-in capital ratios. As shown, the solution cannot be that MDBs and rating agencies should weaken their criteria or that MDBs participate in advanced financial engineering. Also, the G20 should not be involved in determining the capital adequacy of MDBs as they are intrinsically conflicted in dealing with this matter. Rather, MDBs and other international financial institutions (IFIs) should open themselves to the participation of non-state actors (like export credit agencies and reinsurance companies), and explore new sources of funding which are not linked to an institution's capitalization (like securitization and the subordinated, hybrid debt recognized as equity, sponsoring schemes

* Gerd Droesse is a Senior Advisor to Governments and International Organizations and a Visiting Professor at Tashkent State University of Law, gdroesse@gmail.com. The author wishes to thank Christopher W. MacCormac and Oliver Burnage for their valuable comments.

 | DOI:10.1163/9789004460010_009

and match-making mechanisms). This would embrace innovation and offer new ways to enhance the overall impact of IFIs.

1 Introduction

MDBs and other IFIs may be considered from three different perspectives: as international organizations, as development institutions and as financial intermediaries. With a membership that "is for the most part reserved to States", they were conceived as "financial intermediaries between private or official lenders or investors in capital exporting countries and private or public parties in countries who are importers of capital" for the common purpose of assisting "member countries in their development efforts".[1] They generally have a "dual character".[2] While as "subjects of international law, their rights and obligations arise from the applicable international law principles", "they engage in financial transactions, which, despite their public purpose, are, by nature similar to market-based transactions" and "share many characteristics with the private-sector's contracts".[3]

IFIs need to be looked at in a holistic perspective as has been shown by this author in his book "Funds for Development".[4] In the following, the relationships between organizations organizational structures and their funding structures will be explored.

The paper will analyse three paradigms of organizational structures and related funding structures, both market-based and concessional, which have evolved over four generations.[5]

1. Organizational Groups (e.g., World Bank Group, African Development Bank Group, Inter-American Development Bank Group, Nordic Development Bank Group, Islamic Development Group) composed of financial institutions, generally established by a treaty with proper legal personality under international law and legal capacity under national law.
2. Financial institutions established by a treaty providing various types of financing and financing modalities under one legal personality (e.g. Asian Development Bank).

1 Sureda 2005, 25.
2 Bradlow 2010, 1.
3 Ibid.
4 Droesse 2011a.
5 See Droesse 2011b, 6–33; See also Blokker and Schermers 2001.

3. Organizations established by a treaty that were initially designed as revolving funds and do not have the capacity to leverage resources through callable capital, such as the International Fund for Agricultural Development (IFAD) and the OPEC Fund.

The main thrust of this paper is to highlight the legal, financial and policy implications of organizational structure and its implications for the ability of IFIs to enhance their impact, realize synergies, mobilize resources and have access to capital markets.

There is wide-spread agreement in IFIs that revolving funds are no longer efficient mechanisms for funding (concessional) loans and need to be restructured or terminated for this reason. Such restructuring or termination may be achieved as a matter of policy in organizations which follow the second paradigm and administer a wide range of resources under one legal personality. However, a similar course of action entails particular challenges for institutions designed as revolving funds (e.g., concessional windows) that belong to organizational groups (i.e., the first paradigm) and for self-standing organizations which follow the third paradigm. The reason is that these organizations are international organizations with treaty foundation in their own right. Hence, any termination of such organizations or fundamental changes to their funding structures are matters of great complexity, given vested interests and the qualified majorities and quorum provisions required for their termination or amendment to their constituent agreements. Nevertheless, while these organizations are precluded by their constituent agreements to mobilize resources on capital markets against callable capital, their legal personality and high capitalization may still be the basis for them to have access to capital markets.

However, there are also fundamental challenges for IFIs following the first or second paradigm and providing financing on market-based terms as the ability of these organizations to mobilize resources on capital markets is intrinsically linked to the willingness of their members to provide the necessary paid-in capital. States are facing increasingly problems in providing the resources that are necessary for IFIs to substantially expand their financing. The solution to this predicament cannot be to substantially further erode the paid-in capital ratios of IFIs, or to weaken the standards of rating agencies, or for IFIs to engage in advanced financial engineering. Rather, IFIs should join forces with export credit agencies, reinsurance companies and other reputable private-sector entities by admitting them to full or partial membership. This will enhance their financial situation and risk-bearing capacity and enable them to engage in advanced financial transactions. In addition, they need to find innovative solutions for maximizing their existing resources through changes to their operational and transactional profiles and explore new sources of funding which do not require the infusion of paid-in capital. The implications of securitization for increasing the headroom are being explored in this context. Moreover, the fact that rating agencies have recognized sub-ordinated hybrid capital as equity may offer entirely new funding opportunities for IFIs. However, even such mechanisms will not be sufficient to fund the transition of countries to a green economy or for facilitating the transition to the Fourth Industrial Revolution (4IR), as the required resources are so enormous that they can never be funded by public sources alone. Hence, for these and similar pursuits other funding mechanisms which are not linked to the infusion of paid-in capital are required.

2 Organizational Groups and Organizations Providing Various Financing Modalities

To be able to analyse the three paradigms of organizational structure highlighted above, it is essential to understand the intrinsic rationale for their creation.

2.1 *Organizational Groups*

The organizations belonging to organizational groups are mostly, but not necessarily, organizations with treaty foundation and international legal personality. There may be different reasons why organizational groups are established. In particular, this may be due to legal constraints in the constituent agreement of the organization sponsoring the establishment of the group or be done to supplement the activities of such organization, or for both reasons.

2.1.1 The World Bank Group

The rationale for the evolution of the World Bank Group is clearly one of legal constraint and exclusion. This relates to the establishment of the International Development Association (IDA), the International Finance Corporation (IFC) and the Multilateral Investment Guaranty Agency (MIGA) alike.

As regards IDA, the concessional arm of the World Bank Group, an amendment of its Articles of Agreement that would have enabled IBRD to make soft loans was deemed "just 'too hazardous a procedure,' because it might have opened discussions on the IBRD Articles and invited more amendments. Moreover, there was the fear of contagion expressed by IBRD at the time of the creation of IDA to be associated with a 'soft lender' in a single institution. Thus, IBRD and IDA were established as legally separate organizations under separate intergovernmental agreements 'to keep some distance between the two'."[6]

Also, the creation of IFC was due to constraints resulting from the wording of the IBRD Articles of Agreement which did not allow the IBRD to provide financing without a sovereign guarantee. As IDA, also IFC "could have been created by relatively simple amendments to the Bank's Articles of Agreement, but this procedure might have opened the floodgates to more controversial amendments [....]".[7] Instead, IBRD President Black pursued the establishment of IFC,[8] which emerged in 1956 as the private-sector arm of the World Bank Group. However, also the IFC Articles contained constraints which were included to accommodate the concerns of the U.S., which was opposed to the IFC conducting equity investments.[9] Thus, the IFC Articles had to be amended the first time already in 1961 to remove that prohibition.[10]

While in the case of MIGA, earlier proposals envisaged an agency closely linked to the IBRD, MIGA was "designed to be an autonomous institution which will operate on its own account and within its own responsibility while maintaining a symbolic, but significant, link with the Bank".[11] MIGA is providing "political risk insurance (guarantees) for projects in a broad range of sectors in developing member countries, covering all regions of the world".[12] The "main differences between the IBRD/IDA guarantee products and the MIGA guarantees[13] are that (I) the IBRD/IDA guarantees require a counter-guarantee of the host government, creating a direct contractual link with the host country relating to the project, while MIGA requires host country approval before

6 See Droesse 2011c, 63 with further references.

7 Mason 2010, 79.

8 Ibid, 345–350.

9 Glazer 1957.

10 The IFC Board of Governors then adopted an amendment to Section 2 of Article III of the Articles of Agreement of the Corporation allowing IFC "make investments of its funds in such form or forms as it may deem appropriate in the circumstances". See IFC Board of Governors resolution No. 21 (1961).

11 Shihata 1986, 488. See also Shihata 1987 and Shihata 1988, Chapter 1: The Making of MIGA – A historical Account.

12 The World Bank. MIGA, https://inquiries.worldbank.org/knowledgebase/articles/931722-miga, accessed 21 April 2022.

13 The MIGA Convention provides for coverage of three generally accepted categories of commercial risk: "the currency transfer risk resulting from host government restrictions and delays in converting and transferring local currency earned by an investor, expropriation, and the risk of war and civil disturbance. The Convention adds to these traditionally covered risks the risk of breach or repudiation of a contractual commitment by the host government towards an investor [....]". See Commentary on the Convention Establishing the MIGA 1985, 8.

issuing a guarantee"; also "(II) MIGA pricing is tailored to the specific transaction, and (III) MIGA may reinsure, while the World Bank does not sell down or syndicate its guarantee" and "the IBRD/IDA guarantees only directly cover debt instruments, while MIGA covers equity as well as debt instruments".[14]

2.1.2 Inter-American Development Bank Group

As the IBRD, also the IADB sponsored the establishment of a group of organizations, but there are fundamental differences between the World Bank Group and the IADB Group as regards the rationale of their creation.

IADB was "designed as a bank of regional cooperation and solidarity", as is evident in its "principle that less developed or economically vulnerable borrowing countries would receive more favorable terms than the more developed countries".[15] Consistent with the above, the IADB Charter incorporates provisions on the Fund for Special Operations (FSO) that "was set up to service loan applications that absolutely required resources under concessional conditions".[16]

IADB evolved to an organizational group through the establishment of the Inter-American Investment Corporation (IIC) in 1989 and the Multilateral Investment Fund (MIF) in 1993, however, again the situation is very different from that of the World Bank Group.

IADB does not have a competence under its Charter to take equity. Given that its charter prevented the IADB "from engaging in venture capital investments with its own resources, there was no other alternative than to create an entity for this purpose".[17] Hence, following the failed initiative to create a regional finance corporation (COFIAL) in 1970s and the creation of a Venezuelan trust fund piloting support to medium-sized industry,[18] President Ortiz Mena proposed in the early 1980s a scheme for a new entity providing "small amounts of seed capital that would be quickly recycled by selling shares in small and medium-size businesses to private investment funds".[19] In line with this proposal, the IIC was created in 1984.

14 World Bank Group Guidance Note 2016, 11.

15 IADB 2001, 21.

16 Ibid., 31. See Art. IV of the Agreement Establishing the Inter-American Development Bank which became effective in 1959, as amended.

17 IADB 2001, 136.

18 Ibid. 137.

19 Ibid.

Unlike IBRD, IADB is not prevented, however, from providing loans and guarantees of loans without a sovereign counter-guarantee[20] and effectively has conducted private sector operations ever since its establishment, with particular emphasis since its Ninth General Capital Increase in 2010.[21] Thus, inasmuch as IIC provides financing to private-sector entities, it is supplementing[22] the activities of the IADB rather than substituting for it.

As regards the MIF established in 1993, it "was conceived within the framework of the 'Enterprise for the Americas Initiative'" to provide support "for innovative mechanisms designed to improve the climate for private investment, promote training for the labor force, and foster the development of small businesses".[23]

An evaluation carried out by the Office of Evaluation and Oversight of IADB (OVE) in 2012 showed that the various private-sector windows of IADB and the IIC and MIF had partially overlapping functions and were poorly coordinated[24]

20 In accordance with Art. II, Section 8 of the IADB Charter, it is for IADB to decide whether to require such a guarantee.

21 IADB conducted its private-sector activities initially through financial intermediaries and since 1994 through direct lending to private-sector entities. In 1994, IADB, "faced with a dearth of long-term fiancé avenues" relating to infrastructure investments, in particular, opened the door to private participation by authorizing direct lending to the private sector (IADB 2004, 3). IADB initially made little use of this additional operational capacity. Things only changed after the IADB Board of Governors raised in 2001 "the ceiling on private sector loans and guarantees to 10% of the amount of loans and guarantees outstanding" (IADB Board of Governors Resolution AG-09/01 "Lending to the Private Sector") and, in particular, during the period covering the years 2004 to 2011(IADB 2011b, 8). Moreover, consistent with the Cancun Declaration adopted by the IADB Board of Governors in 2010 (IADB 2011a, 5), the Ninth General Capital Increase of IADB (GCI-9) triggered a further expansion of IADB's private-sector activities. Private Sector development was one of the core elements of the GCI-9 Agreement, which tied the capital increase to a series of reforms. In particular, the Report on GCI-9 (IADB 2010, 14) mandated IADB to adopt an integrated approach and adopt a strategy "to increase the development impact of private sector activities by capitalizing on the IDB's comparative advantages in a manner consistent with its institutional goals". (IADB 2010, 15) The Report further mandated IADB to gradually increase the ceiling for IADB's private-sector activities from 10 to 20 percent of total equity (Ibid.).

22 The Agreement establishing IIC is called "Agreement Establishing, for the Purpose of Encouraging Private Enterprises to *Supplement* Activities of the Inter-American Development Bank" (emphasis added).

23 IADB 2001,166.

24 See IADB 2013. While noting that IADB had taken action to implement the GCI-9 commitments, OVE concluded that IADB needed "a framework on which to base its strategy" and that the absence of such a framework had been "the major conceptual obstacle to IDB's responding to the IDB-9 mandate to promote PSD as an instrument for development" (IADB 2013, 14). OVE made various suggestions for going forward, among which

Consistent with the recommendations of OVE, the Board of Governors of IADB and IIC, each separately in accordance with their constituent agreement, authorized on 30 March 2015 "the transfer of operational and administrative functions and nonfinancial resources associated with [non-sovereign guaranteed] NSG activities from the [IADB] to the IIC" and instructed "the Boards of Executive Directors and Management of the IDB and of the IIC to take all steps necessary to complete such transfer by January 1, 2016 or such later date as may be approved by the Boards of Executive Directors of the [IADB] and the IIC".[25] "The merge-out was undertaken to deliver on a renewed vision to foster development through the private sector, aiming at improving the development effectiveness of [IADB Group's] intervention in the region [....]".[26]

In 2016, IADB went "through a self-described 'startup' year" as the merge-out pooled together "all private sector lending under the IIC umbrella to serve as a single-entry point for clients in the region wanting to access institutional financing and services".[27] In the context of the merge-out, IIC was rebranded as "IDB Invest".[28]

As regards the MIF, its mandates evolved and underwent substantial changes, as highlighted in a recent report of OVE.[29] It became the innovation laboratory of IADB, offering "the rest of the [IADB] Group a platform for proof of concepts, experimentation, early-stage investments, and market solutions that can later be scaled by [IADB], 'IDB Invest' or external partners".[30] It is an important development that an MDB has incorporated such a laboratory in its organizational structure.

---

the one to "to fully integrate the private sector windows" and "collapse them into the sectoral departments [of IADB]" and the other proposing to "merge the private sector windows into a single entity (inside or outside the Bank)." (IADB 2013, 25). Discussions subsequently focused on the latter option.

25 Resolution AG-9/15 and CII/AG-2/15 "Delivering the Renewed Vision: Organizational and Capitalization Proposal for the IDB Group Private Sector Merge-out", para. 1.

26 "Though the key documents related to the merge-out contain a wide range of objectives, three were highlighted throughout the process leading up to the merge-out:
- strengthening development effectiveness, development impact and additionality;
- maximizing the efficient use of resources; and
- maximizing the synergies between public and private sector activities". IADB 2017, 2.

27 Mendoza 2016, 1–4.

28 As part of the consolidation process of its private-sector development activities, IDB Invest "created value-added products and solutions" and "made its portfolio available to new sectors. As the focal point of IADB for all private-sector operations, IDB Invest provides multiple financial products, such as loans, guarantees, equity investments and debt securities, as well as advisory services". See IADB Invest 2017, 28 and IADB Invest 2018, 131.

29 See IADB 2020.

30 IDB LAB, About.

2.1.3 African Development Bank Group

One major difference between the African Development Bank (AfDB) and the IADB is that AfDB may engage in equity investments that "include both direct participations in private and/or public-enterprises, and national and/or regional DFIs,[31] and indirect participations through subscriptions to private equity funds and other funds and portfolio vehicles. They also include quasi-equity financing such as preferred stock, mezzanine financing, and convertible debt".[32] As the AfDB is able to take equity, it was not necessary to establish a separate organization for the purpose of providing such financing. However, the AfDB sponsored the establishment of the African Development Fund (AfDF) for the purpose of providing financing on concessional terms to the poorest African countries. The rationale for the establishment of the AfDF is related to the mobilization of resources and needs to be seen in the context of the AfDB's opening itself for membership on non-regional countries.[33] Thus, the relation of AfDB and AfDF membership is the reverse of what is applicable to IDA. While IBRD (and by implication) IMF membership is a requirement for IDA membership, in the AfDB Group, AfDF membership is for all non-regional countries a prerequisite for AfDB membership.[34] In that sense, AfDF membership had for non-regional countries to a certain extent the character of an entrance fee. Unlike ADB, the AfDB also has admitted non-regional developing countries willing to pay that entrance fee (e.g. China and Korea).[35]

31 Development finance institutions.

32 AfDB. 2015, 25.

33 For the background on the establishment of the AfDF, see: Akin-Olugbade and Flory 2011, 402–403.

34 Art. 3 para. 3 of the Agreement establishing the African Development Bank provides: "Non-regional countries which are, or become, members of the African Development Fund, or which have made, or are making, contributions to the African Development Fund under terms and conditions similar to the terms and conditions of the Agreement Establishing the African Development Fund, may also be admitted to the Bank, at such times and under such general rules as the Board of Governors shall have established". [....] See Droesse 2011c, 92–96.

35 The AfDB group also comprises the Nigeria Trust Fund which was created in 1976 by agreement between the AfDB Group and the Nigerian Government. Its objective is to assist the development efforts of the Bank's low-income regional member countries whose economic and social conditions and prospects require concessional financing. It is a self-sustaining revolving fund that only provides concessional loans. Its objective is to assist the development efforts of the Bank's low-income regional member countries whose economic and social conditions and prospects require concessional financing. Its initial capital of USD 80 million was replenished in 1981 with USD 71 million. In 2008, the Federal Republic of Nigeria and the Bank agreed to a ten-year extension of the NTF. (See Nigeria Trust Fund. https://www.AfDB.org/en/about-us/corporate-information/nigeria-trust-fund-ntf, accessed 21 April 2022).

2.1.4 Nordic Finance Group

As the history of the Nordic Finance Group shows, the fact that organizations belong to a group does not imply that the various organizations of the group have coordinated governance structures or actually cooperate. The Nordic Investment Bank (NIB) and the Nordic Development Fund (NDF), which both have a treaty foundation, previously belonged to the Nordic Investment Bank Group. As has been shown by Haralz,[36] while the NDF initially was meant to cooperate closely with the NIB, it "acquired the profile of a separate entity maintaining its own outside relations and conducting its own operations"[37] and there was very limited cooperation, if any, between the NIB and the NDF.[38]

The situation only changed to a limited extent after the NDF emerged in 2009 from the coma in which it had been placed in 2005 by the decision of the Nordic Finance Ministers to cancel the negotiation for a replenishment of the NDF and focus instead on concluding the operations of the Fund. However, the aforementioned decision effectively was never implemented as the NDF was resuscitated in 2009 and given a new set of functions relating to environmental protection.[39]

The NIB, NDF and Nordic Environment Financing Corporation currently belong to the Nordic Finance Group.[40] All three entities are established by a treaty which defines their governance structure. While each organization has its own institutional framework with its own executive head and its own board members and there are no institutionalized coordination mechanisms between the three institutions based on their establishing agreements, a Cooperation Council dealing with employment matters has been created based on executive action.[41] A potential point for synergies is that that all three

---

36 Haralz 1999, 17.

37 Droesse 2011c, 65–66.

38 As far as the relations between the Organization of Petroleum Exporting Countries (OPEC) and the OPEC Fund for International Development (OPEC Fund) are concerned, it cannot even be said that these form an organizational group. While OPEC members provide the core funding for the OPEC Fund both evolved as entirely separate organizations without any relevant interaction between these organizations.

39 Droesse 2011c, 66.

40 Nordic Finance Group, https://www.nefco.int/wp-content/uploads/2019/10/Nordic-Finance-Group.pdf, accessed 21 April 2022.

41 The Cooperation Council was created according to decision by NIB's President on 5 June 2001, as amended by NIB's President's decision 17 November 2006, following submission of statements by Managing Directors of NDF and NEFCO. See NIB 2006 and NIB 2009.

institutions are located under one roof and have a strong environmental focus, but they have different functions and funding mechanisms.[42]

2.1.5 Islamic Development Bank Group

The Islamic Development Bank Group (IsDB), while much smaller than other MDBs (e.g., the World Bank, IADB, ADB and AfDB), is another example of institutional diversification.

Unlike in the case of the IBRD, the rationale of such diversification was generally not related to legal constraints on the part of the IsDB to provide certain activities. This can be derived from Article 2 of the IsDB Articles of Agreement which defines the functions and powers of the IsDB in rather wide terms, referring to equity and infrastructure investments, loans to public and private-sector entities, promotion of foreign trade and provision of technical assistance and training facilities. While IsDB, when financing sovereign entities "requires a full sovereign guarantee or the equivalent", it is also exposed to non-sovereign credit risk arising "from financing operations extended to projects, corporates, and financial institutions without explicit guarantees of concerned governments".[43]

The organizations of the IsDB Group mostly supplement the activities performed by the IsDB. This is also true for the IsDB Institute.[44] Moreover, also the creation of the other three organizations of the IsDB Group is intrinsically related to the fact that IsDB has supported since its inception private-sector development and the "importance of private sector as an engine of growth and its key role in eradicating poverty and fostering an inclusive society".[45]

---

42 NIB is offering long term financing to projects that improve productivity and benefit the environment of the Nordic and Baltic countries, while NEFCO finances sustainable green growth and climate projects globally, focusing on small and medium-sized projects with demonstration value and the NDF provides concessional financing (loans, grants, equity) for climate change and development projects primarily in low-income countries (Nordic Finance Group 2010, 1).The NIB is structured like as other market-based windows with intermediary functions and mobilizes money on capital markets against its equity base of approximately 8, 369 million consisting of about 10.10 % paid-in and the remaining callable capital. NEFCO which has an equity of EUR113, 4 million and accumulated reserves, income consists of their net interest income (on loans, debt securities and placements), their lending fees and other income, such as trust fund management fees. As regards the NDF, it was replenished on five occasions; the last two replenishments after its restructuring were in the amounts of EUR 330 and 350 million, respectively (NDF Governing bodies and capital 1971, 1–12).

43 IsDB 2019 Financial Statements (2020), 43.

44 On the establishment of the IsDB Institute in 1981 (then known as Islamic Research and Training Institute or IRTI), see Meenai 1989, 191–194 and IRTI 2019, 1–44.

45 IsDB 2016, 16.

The Islamic Corporation for the Insurance of Investment and Export Credit (ICIEC) was established in 1994 "to boost intra-trade among OIC member countries by providing exporters, banks, trade financiers and export credit agencies with Shari'ah-compliant export credit insurance and reinsurance facilities".[46]

The ICIEC, which is referred to in Art. 1 of the ICIEC Articles of Agreement as a "subsidiary company", enjoys autonomy and possesses international legal personality and legal capacity under national law. Under Art. 6 of the ICIEC Articles of Agreement, members are the listed original members and other OIC members admitted by the governors (member states may authorize any entity or agency to represent them). The IsDB owns half of the ICIEC's shares.[47] ICEIC provides Shariah-compliant export credit and investment insurance[48] and does not require a sovereign guarantee.[49]

The Islamic Corporation for the Development of the Private Sector (ICD) is an international specialized institution established pursuant its Articles of Agreement[50] and commenced its operations on 8 July 2000.[51] While

46 Ibid. IDB Group Entities: Summary. The idea to establish ICIEC originated from an agreement between members of the Organization of Islamic Cooperation (OIC), mandating the OIC through IsDB to establish "an Islamic Insurance Company operating under Shari'ah principles, to provide insurance products for investments and export credits". Hence, "[f]ollowing the Agreement, the Board of Governors of IsDB Group, at its 16th Annual Meeting held in Tripoli, Libya, in Sha'ban 1412H (February 1992), approved the Articles of Agreement of the Islamic Corporation for the Insurance of Investment and Export Credit (ICIEC), declaring its establishment." see ICIEC Who we are, https://iciec.IsDB.org/who-we-are/, accessed 21 April 2022. As regards the Articles of Agreement, see ICIEC 2016.

47 Upon the establishment of ICIEC, the IsDB subscribed to 50,000 of the 100,000 share then available for subscription. See Art. 9 (1) of the ICIEC Articles of Agreement.

48 See ICIEC 2019 Annual Report, 9 with further details.

49 The business model is well summarized in the IEICE financial statements as follows: "In accordance with the Articles of Agreement", the Corporation is required to maintain and administer two separate funds: I. A Policyholders' fund" \ II. A Shareholders' fund. As an Islamic Insurance entity, the Corporation manages the Policyholders' fund. According to the Islamic model of Wakala, whereby the Corporation acts as an agent for managing the technical insurance accounts on behalf of the Policyholders', and investing the income from the insurance operations according to Mudaraba model. No wakala fee is charged to Policyholders' fund by Shareholders' fund. All expenses to run the Islamic insurance business are charged to the Policyholders' fund at cost, without any administration fee levied by the Shareholders' fund. The Shareholders' fund is not entitled to a share in any surplus accruing to the Policyholders' fund; any deficit in the Policyholders' fund is covered from the Shareholders' fund capital by way of a qard (loan) to be repaid from future surplus accruing to the Policyholders' fund." See ICIEC Financial Statements 2019, 9.

50 ICD Articles of Agreement: Establishing the Islamic Corporation for the Development of the Private Sector 2012a. See ICD 2018.

51 ICD Articles of Agreement 2012, Annex A.

ICD[52] was created primarily to conduct "direct investments in small and medium-scale enterprises located in [ICD] member countries",[53] it adopted a wider focus which led to an overlap of ICD's activities with those of IsDB.

The last member of the IsDB Group to be effectively established in 2008 was the Islamic Trade Finance Corporation (ITFC), which was created "with the primary objective of advancing trade among OIC Member Countries, which would ultimately contribute to the overarching goal of improving socioeconomic conditions of the people across the world".[54]

The ITFC was established for the specific purpose of consolidating the various trade financing activities which had previously performed by ISDB since its early days through various channels, inter alia through IsDB's "Trade Financing Operations Programme (ITFO)".[55] Such consolidation was to "to increase the trade volume" in addition to "consolidating all of IDB's trade finance activities under a single umbrella thus eliminating the overlapping and bringing greater efficiency to the delivery of trade finance services", using "financial instruments that are Shariah compliant".[56]

ICIEC has a special position and special functions within the IsDB Group. Moreover, while also the IsDB is mandated to provide trade-financing, ITFC has since consolidated all trade finance businesses that used to be handled by various windows within the IsDB Group.[57] However, in the past, there was in the ISDB Group substantial functional overlap and duplication of functions, in particular between the IsDB and ICD, which both are mandated to provide private-sector financing. ICD also had to battle with the fact that its credit rating was downgraded by Fitch from AA to AA-, "following material financial losses (totaling USD 107 million) incurred in 2017 as a result of

52 In accordance with Article 4 (a) of the ICD Articles of Agreement, the Corporation shall "assist, alone or in cooperation with other sources of finance, in the financing of the establishment, expansion and modernization of private enterprises, utilizing such financial instruments and mechanisms as the Corporation deems appropriate in each instance". In accordance with Article 4 (b)–(e) of the said Articles of Agreement, the Corporation is to support enterprises by facilitating "their access to private and public capital, domestic and foreign including access to capital markets", "stimulate the development of investment opportunities conducive to the flow of private capital, domestic and foreign", "contribute to the development and diversification of financial products" and "provide technical assistance for the preparation, financing and execution of projects, including the transfer of appropriate technology". See ICD Articles of Agreement 2012b.

53 ICD Articles of Agreement, Art. 5, 2(b).

54 ITFC: What is ITFC? 2018.

55 IsDB 2007, 1.

56 Ibid.

57 Ibid.

significant write-downs in the valuation of the bank's equity investments".[58] Nevertheless, there were recently positive developments as ICD was able to return to the Sukuk markets after four years absence in October 2020.[59] IsDB and ICD undertook to redefine and reset their relationships in response to the vision of the IsDB President and in accordance with their recent inter-agency agreement to the terms that had originally been envisioned for ICD.[60]

In addition, there are other examples of organizational groups.[61] As shown above, organizational groups vary greatly as regards their legal and governance and financial structures. These structures are intrinsically related to the funding mechanisms which can be used by each organization belonging to a group.

2.2 *Organizations Providing a Wide Range of Different Financing Modalities under One Legal Personality*

There is a number of IFIs which provide a wide range of modalities of financing under one legal personality. The ADB is the epitome of the above paradigm as it is mandated to provide both concessional and non-concessional financing, and in the latter category both sovereign and private-sector loans, as well as guarantee and equity investments.

There is a number of organizations which fall into this category, ranging from the Asian Infrastructure Investment Bank (AIIB)[62] and the New Development

58 FitchRatings 2018.

59 DDCAP Group 2020, 1.

60 As stressed by the IsDB President, the signature of this agreement entailed agreement on a "clear accountability framework assigning roles and responsibilities between IsDB and ICD" under which "ICD will continue to make important contributions to the development of small and medium enterprises (SMEs) sector." IsDB 2021.

61 Also the European Investment Bank forms a group with the European Investment Fund (which is very small in financial terms if compared with the EIB). The European Investment Bank established in 1958 has a special status as an organ of the European Community. It has been an important player in the European Project and is currently covered by the Treaty on the Functioning of the European Union which confers to the EIB international legal personality within the context of the EU. The EIB has a clear focus on market-based financing. The EIB evolved to a Group in 2000 when it acquired majority shareholding of the European Investment Fund which had been established in 1994. EIF is the EIB Group's specialist provider of integrated risk finance to SMEs across the EU, EFTA and Candidate Countries, offering a spectrum of financing solutions to public and private sector intermediaries with the objective of enhancing SME finance and addressing market gaps. EIF fosters EU objectives in support of innovation, regional development, entrepreneurship, growth, and employment. See EIF. Supporting entrepreneurship and innovation in Europe and EIF. The Governance of the European Investment Fund.

62 Asian Infrastructure Investment Bank, https://www.aiib.org/en/index.html, accessed 21 April 2022.

Bank (NDB)[63] to the Council of Europe Development Bank[64] and various sub-regional development banks. Under this paradigm, also organizations such as the Inter-American Development Bank (IADB), the African Development Bank (AfDB), the Islamic Development Bank (ISDB) and the European Investment Bank (EIB) may be comprised, which are legally entitled to administer a wide range of financial modalities, including private sector financing, but have for policy reasons sponsored the establishment of organizations which supplement their financing.

While it is common for financial institutions to provide both sovereign and private-sector financing, as well as guarantees, the capacity to conduct equity investments is a distinguishing feature among organizations in this category. As has been shown above, some organizations do not have the capacity to provide such financing. Moreover, only in some cases an express or implied authority is provided to organizations to provide trade-financing.

However, the most important difference between institutions in this category relates to their ability to provide financing on concessional terms. In this context, various cases can be distinguished.[65] The establishment of concessional windows gives organizations the opportunity to engage with states and entities that are unable to borrow on market-based terms. However, there are IFIs which do not have concessional windows or provide concessional financing not from their own recourses but under mandates from another organization. As the different arrangements have been analyzed in detail by this author in his book "Funds for Development", it would not serve any useful purpose to repeat in this occasion the detailed analysis provided by that book.

2.3 *Financial Institutions Without Formal Equity Base Established by a Treaty for Specific Purposes*

IFAD and the OPEC Fund for International Development (OPEC Fund) were both designed and conceived as revolving funds. Hence, unlike other IFIs,

---

63 New Development Bank, https://www.ndb.int/, accessed 21 April 2022.

64 Council of Europe Development Bank. https://coebank.org/en/, accessed 21 April 2022.

65 (I) In some cases (e.g., the IADB and Caribbean Development Bank), express provision on a concessional financing window has been incorporated in the constituent agreement of an IFI (Droesse 2011c, 66–69). In some cases, only general provision for the establishment of special funds has been made (Ibid, 69–78. See also Droesse 2011e) (III) In some cases, concessional financing is provided through funds which are not deemed to part of an organization's resources (Droesse 2011c, 78–79). (IV) In other cases, financing is provided exclusively or predominantly through external resources, including trust funds and funds under administration or other external arrangements (Droesse 2011c, 79–89).

their constituent agreements do not allow them to mobilize resources on capital markets against an equity base consisting of paid-in and callable capital. As this entailed for both organizations constraints to their effectiveness, they pursued institutional reforms allowing them to have access to capital markets.

2.3.1 IFAD

The establishment of IFAD was one of the major outcomes of the 1974 World Food Conference held in 1974.[66] IFAD is, with the organizations of the World Bank Group, the only IFI which has the status of a specialized agency of the United Nations. Considering the special role of the OPEC countries in the establishment of IFAD, IFAD has classified its membership in three categories: lists A, B and C.[67]

Prior to the fourth IFAD replenishment, there was no link between IFAD contributions and voting rights. As this was not conducive to mobilizing resources, a new vote allocation system was introduced in 1995 through an amendment to the IFAD Articles.[68]

Consistent with Art. 4 of the Agreement Establishing IFAD (AEI),[69] which predominantly covers contributions from states, traditionally "IFAD's financial architecture has been centred on replenishment contributions and other non-reimbursable sources of funding (e.g., reflows from loans, income from treasury investments, and supplementary and complementary funding)", based on the embedded assumption that "over the long term, IFAD Members would be able and willing to continue providing financial support in grant form and at

66 The Conference resolved (Resolution XIII) that: "1. An International Fund for Agricultural Development should be established immediately to finance agricultural development projects primarily for food production in the developing countries; 2. All developed countries and all those developing countries that are in a position to contribute to this Fund should do so on a voluntary basis; 3. The Fund should be administered by a Governing Board consisting of representatives of contributing developed countries, and potential recipient countries, taking into consideration the need for ensuring equitable distribution of representation amongst these three categories and regional balance amongst the potential recipient representation." See: World Food Conference 1974, 12–13.

67 See Weill-Hallé, Licul, and García Villanueva, 457–458.

68 Ibid., 464–466.

69 As may be seen from Art. 4 Sections 1 and 2 AEI, the resources of IFAD shall consist of: (I) initial contributions (of original and non-original members); (II) additional contributions (which the Governing Council may, based on a review of adequacy of resources, invite members to make to ensure continuity of the operations of IFAD); (III) special contributions from non-member States and from other sources; (IV) funds derived or to be derived from operations or otherwise accruing to the Fund.

a level allowing the Fund to maintain or increase its programme of loans and grants [....]".[70]

Nevertheless, it has been discussed at length already after the second replenishment of IFAD whether IFAD can mobilize resources other than those set forth Art. 4, Section 1 AEI. As shown by Kamau and Colaiacomo, "IFAD began its operations in 1977 after a very constrained process of raising the initial contributions that had been pledged", most from its OPEC member states.[71] The first IFAD replenishment was "difficult and protracted" and the "second replenishment negotiations went on for almost two and a half years and by the time these negotiations were completed, the initial agreed level of USD 1 billion had shrunk to USD 460 million".[72] This prompted IFAD's General Counsel to constitute "a high-level committee of experts (HLEG) to assess alternative approaches to the 'long term financial structure of IFAD'" that "should aim at making IFAD more 'self-supportive financially' and ensure that the future replenishments are conducted on a more predictable basis".[73]

In accordance with Art. 2 AEI, IFAD is only authorized to provide financing on concessional terms. However, as "resource mobilization is a broad concept that entails borrowing and raising funds from other sources outside the replenishment process",[74] the HLEG concluded that Art. 4 Section 1 is not exclusive and considered other sources of financing, such as special programs, trust funds and borrowing, for IFAD to close the financing gap and enable IFAD to fulfil its mandate.[75]

Notwithstanding the above, initially IFAD relied on the funding of its operations on the contributions of its members.[76] As since IFAD9, the traditional funding sources (replenishment contributions, loan reflows and treasury income) "have not been sufficient to finance the desired PoLG [program

70 IFAD 2018, para 6.

71 Kamau and Colaicomo 2012, 477.

72 Ibid., 477–478.

73 Ibid., 478.

74 Ibid., 481.

75 Ibid. 481. HLEG committee further concluded that: "IFAD could be authorized to borrow capital from member governments, international financial organizations, commercial banks and capital markets. However, like other international financial institutions, borrowing from the capital market may require member governments' guarantees in the form of callable capital". To the extent that borrowing would require member states guarantees, the HLEG committee of experts felt that an "amendment to the Agreement Establishing IFAD would be necessary". (Ibid., 481).

76 There was a "steep rise in total core contribution pledges between the Seventh Replenishment of IFAD's Resources (IFAD7) and IFAD8"; however, afterwards, contributions stabilized in IFAD9 and slightly decreased in IFAD10. See IFAD 2018, para. 8.

of loans and grants]",[77] additional sources of finance needed to be explored. Hence, IFAD has begun using debt to leverage its equity and narrow the gap, and has recently pursued a credit rating which gives IFAD access to capital markets (see below).

2.3.2 OPEC Fund

The origins of the OPEC Fund can be traced to the "Agreement establishing the OPEC Special Fund" in 1976[78] which reflected a concern "for flexibility, swift decision-making, maximization of use of existing resources, and a receptivity to innovation".[79] Created in January 1976 as a collective aid facility of OPEC member countries, in the form of an international account jointly owned by these countries and jointly administered by a 'Governing Committee' of which they were all members, the OPEC Special Fund was transformed to the OPEC Fund for International Development (OFID or OPEC Fund) based on a number of successive amendments culminating in the revision of the Agreement Establishing the Fund.[80]

In comparison with IDA and IFAD, the aforementioned constituent agreement is more succinct and it affords additional flexibility. This relates to the fact that the functions of OFID are defined in wide terms,[81] which enabled OFID in broad terms to "do all that its Board deemed necessary in assisting other developing countries. As a result, the OFID was the first international institution of its kind to combine balance of payments (BOP) support with project lending and to add to its direct assistance to governments the financing of other development agencies [....]".[82] Moreover, it is special as it is only providing financial support to non-member countries.

Currently, the OPEC Fund is providing a range of services comprising public-sector lending, private-sector and trade financing and grants[83] in support of

77 Ibid., para. 11.

78 United Nations Treaties Series: Agreement establishing the OPEC Special Fund 1976, 12–14.

79 Shihata 1983, 29.

80 Shihata 1980, 19. See Shihata 1983, 23-28

81 Art. 2.02 of the OFID Agreement states: "The Fund is empowered to engage in all functions necessary or incidental to the carrying out of its objectives according to the guidelines to be issued for this purpose by the Ministerial Council and the Governing Board. It is, in particular, empowered to: a) provide concessional loans for balance of payments support; b) provide concessional loans for the implementation of development projects and programs; c) make contributions and/or provide loans to eligible international agencies; and d) finance technical assistance activities".

82 Shihata 1982, 107.

83 OFID 2017: Financial Statements and Report of the Independent Auditors for the Years ended December 31, 2016 and 2015, 1.

operations in agriculture, education, energy, the financial sector, health, water and sanitation, transport, as well as multi-sector projects.[84]

The resources of the OPEC Fund, which previously was structured as a revolving fund,[85] were increased in four replenishments.[86] However, as in the case of IFAD, such structure constrained its effectiveness. Hence, also the OPEC Fund sought a credit rating and access to capital markets (see below).

3 Implications of Organizational and Institutional Structures and Legal Personality

While not necessarily all organizations belonging to an organizational group are established by a treaty,[87] in many cases they have a treaty foundation. One of the implications of the separate legal personality of the organizations belonging to a group is that these may have different membership structures and capital structures; relative shareholdings and voting rights of members and resource-mobilization mechanisms of the various organizations which form the group may differ as well. The governance structures of the organizations belonging to a group, may or may not be coordinated.[88]

In organizational groups, the legal personality of each organization of a group shields all other organizations belonging to the group from legal claims against that organization. This is an effective mechanism for limiting the exposure to higher-risk transactions to the balance sheet of one organization of the group alone. Thus, regularly no material liabilities result, for example, for IBRD from IFC's operations.

84 See OPEC Fund. 2020. More Impact where it matters most. Annual Report 2019. Pp. 22–53, https://content.yudu.com/web/435ju/0A430b9/AnnualReport2019-EN/html/index.html?origin=reader, accessed 21 April 2022.

85 Art. 4.1 of the OFID Agreement provides: "The resources of the Fund shall consist of: I) Contributions by Member Countries; II) Funds received from operations or otherwise accruing to the Fund".

86 As set out in OPEC Fund's 2017 Financial Statements: "OFID commenced operations with a pledged and confirmed contribution of USD 391 from member countries. There were further replenishments in 1977 (USD391.5), 1980 (USD 655.5) and 1981 (USD 664.7) from member countries. [....] On June 16, 2011, the Ministerial Council approved the fourth replenishment in the amount of USD 1 billion (MC Decision No. 4(XXXII)) [....]". OPEC Fund, 2017, 26.

87 E.g., the revised statute of the IsDB Institute (previously known as IRTI) was adopted by the IsDB Board of Governors. See: IsDB 2021. Statute of IsDBI.

88 See in detail Droesse. 2011c, 117–147.

However, the situation is different for organizations following the second paradigm which administer various operational modalities, including private sector financing and concessional financing, under one legal personality. In such a case, any exposure from concessional financing, private-sector financing, equity investments or guarantees, and any exposure from trust funds without legal personality[89] administered by the organization concerned may entail, as a matter of principle, a material liability for the balance sheet of the organization administering such funds and activities under one legal personality. This may induce the organization concerned to adopt more conservative and risk-averse practices. On the other hand, the fact that the various financing windows of an organization (e.g., for sovereign and non-sovereign loans and market-based and concessional financing) are not isolated through a separate legal personality, potentially opens a wide field of synergies as coordination does not require agreements between different organizations but can be achieved based on executive action or as a matter of policy.

It is regrettable that many opportunities for exploiting synergies which the latter paradigm offers have not been adequately pursued. While MDBs and other IFIs have made some progress in mainstreaming public-private partnerships and scaling-up financing through private-sector participation,[90] the core problem has not been addressed. It relates to the fact that institutional frameworks geared to the administration of different resources (public and private sector, concessional finance, trust funds, co-financing), which are currently still widely used, are more likely to support silo thinking than result in the exploration of synergies. Institutional frameworks should focus instead from

89 While in principle, legal claims relating to a trust fund without legal personality are directed against the trustee, the liability of the trustee may be limited to the resources of the trust fund as a matter of practice. This approach was followed in the case of the Credit Guarantee and Investment Facility (CGIF) which provides "guarantees to local currency denominated bonds issued by corporations in the Region which paves the way for corporations to issue local currency bonds with longer maturities". (CGIF. About US) While the CGIF was established as an ADB trust fund without international legal personality and legal capacity under local law (ADB 2010), it is stressed in all CGIF legal documentation that CGIF resources are separate and distinct from those of ADB. On that basis, CGIF was given by rating agencies a credit rating that is different from that of ADB and legal claims against the CGIF are not considered a material liability of ADB. See Standard and Poor's Global, 2017.

90 For example, in the ADB, the termination of the ADF concessional loan window (see below) has created opportunities for enhanced cooperation. Synergies may be created inter alia through blended concessional finance that "can be used to unlock investment into sustainable development, especially from the private sector." DFI Working Group on Blended Concessional Finance for Private Sector Projects 2020.

a holistic perspective on outcomes rather than on resources and on facilitating synergies between different types of resources and operational modalities. One effective mechanism for enhancing synergies is the creation of umbrella operational frameworks for specific countries and sectors which comprise all resources and are administered to the extent possible on the same terms and conditions.[91]

In organizational groups, achieving synergies is more difficult, as a matter of principle, but not impossible. The World Bank Group stands for an organization that has created, with the One Bank initiative launched by President Zoellick, a conceptional framework for generating substantial synergies. The private-sector window created in IDA, which allows IFC and MIGA to leverage IDA's resources and help mobilize sustainable private sector investment in the poorest and most fragile markets,[92] may serve as an example.[93] The importance of synergies is increasingly also realized by other MDBs and IFIs. Thus, IsDB, ICIEC and ICD recently signed in 2019 a cooperation agreement aimed at "mainstreaming group synergies".[94] Nevertheless, examples such as the private-sector window of IDA are so far still sporadic in nature and there is much room for further enhancement and amplification of such approaches.

It can be derived from the above that for the first and second paradigms both liability profiles of organizations and their potential for creating synergies are intrinsically related to their legal personality. As regards the organizations following the third paradigm, these are constrained by the parameters defined by their constituent agreements which do not allow them to mobilize resources against callable capital, but their legal personality and high capitalization may still allow them to have access to capital markets.

91 See Droesse 2011c, 165–167.

92 IDA: IDA-IFC-MIGA Private Sector Window.

93 Moreover, while in the case of IDA, a specific provision was included into the Articles of Agreement precluding that IDA may borrow from IBRD, loans from the IBRD are one of the regular funding modalities of MIGA. Moreover, to afford cost savings, administrative, legal and other services may be provided by one organization to other organizations of a group.

94 Given ICIEC mandate to support the exports of its member countries and to encourage the inflow of foreign direct investments, ICIEC anticipates great potential for complementarity with the product offering of ICD & ITFC. This agreement will support ICIEC to extend its Shariah Compliant Insurance Solutions and Services to back ICD and ITFC financing activities. ICIEC will also benefit from ICD and ITFC proven track record and experience in trade and project finance to customize and develop new products for beneficiaries in member countries. See IsDB 2019c.

4 Hard and Soft Windows

4.1 *Differences between Hard and Soft Windows*

MDBs provide financing under hard and soft windows. Under hard windows, MDBs generally perform functions of financial intermediaries that resemble those of commercial banks in certain aspects. They borrow on capital markets against a capital base comprising paid-in capital and reserves, as well as callable capital subscribed by their member countries. Hard windows "are constrained in the amount of loans they can make only to the extent that their outstanding borrowings have reached nearly the same level as that of their existing capital resources [....]".[95] Soft windows, on the other hand, require funding arrangements to cover the cost of concessional financing granted below market-rates and/or the cost of grants. Traditionally, they were structured as revolving funds irrespective of their legal structure.

4.2 *New Dimensions of Discussion on Hard and Soft Windows*

The traditional concepts regarding a distinction between hard and soft windows are challenged, in particular, on two grounds. While there are still many cases where the revolving-fund model is used,[96] in the case of IFIs, this model is often no longer seen as an efficient financial instrument. Second, the traditionally rigid distinction between the market-based funding structures of hard windows and the revolving fund structures of concessional windows is increasingly seen as outdated.

In IFIs, the revolving-fund model has traditionally been used as the funding mechanism of choice for concessional windows. While the legal status of the concessional arm of the World Bank Group, IDA, is different from that of an organization like IFAD providing concessional financing, or a special fund like the Asian Development Fund of the ADB (ADF), the financial structures of these windows were similar in the past to the extent that they were based on the revolving fund model. Hence, in all three cases funding was obtained from members in the context of replenishments that were either conducted through external mechanisms (e.g., meetings of deputies or donors) or, like in the case of IFAD, conducted through the plenary body.[97]

---

95 Mistry, 18.

96 It is currently still largely used for grant giving organizations, as well as in the case of the climate funds (e.g. the Multilateral Fund for the Montreal Protocol, the Adaptation Fund and the Green Climate Fund) and for trust funds (like the Global Environment Facility) and for various other purposes.

97 Droesse 2011d, 280–283. For ADB, see Droesse 2012, for AfDB, see Akin-Olugbade and Flory and for IFAD Weill-Hallé, Licul, and García Villanueva.

Erquiaga has well explained the deficiencies of the revolving fund model in his financial history of ADB by comparing the financial structure of the Asian Development Fund (ADF) with that of ADB's ordinary capital resources (OCR).[98]

It is a core problem of concessional windows structured as revolving funds that they can only pass monies received from donors to recipients at a rate of 1:1 or less (after deduction of administrative expenses and with some enhancement of commitment authority). Such funding structure is neither effective from a financial point of view as shown by Erquiaga, nor is it sustainable, as it does not allow organizations to have access to capital markets or to mobilize resources as and when and to the extent these are required. Furthermore, at times the so-called concessional loans turned out to be quite expensive for borrowers. While they carried low interest rates, the amount disbursed in convertible currency sometimes had to be repaid by the borrower under loan regulations in a different currency, i.e., in the currency of the donor contribution funding that loan. Where such currency substantially appreciated, repayment of the so-called "concessional loan" could involve very substantial costs for the borrowers. Finally, the whole system was led *ad absurdum* when for a certain period the rates of the now defunct LIBOR were lower that the interest rates on the so-called concessional loans.

Hence, as will be shown in further detail below, several organizations recently have taken action to terminate or restructure their concessional loan windows to be able to leverage resources on capital markets. Furthermore, the revolving fund model is particularly unsuitable for funding any loans on market-based terms. The recent changes to the financial structure of the OPEC Fund, which is providing financing on both concessional and non-concessional terms, need to be seen in this context.

---

98 "While ADF equity capital is about double the size of the equity capital of OCR, ADF outstanding loans of D 29.1 billion were only about 54% the size of OCR outstanding loans (D 54.2 billion). This translated into a mobilization (leverage) ratio of loans and guarantees to equity capital of 3.1 for OCR, but only 0.9 for the ADF. The divergence in mobilization ratios was attributable to the fact that the ADF, which does not have a separate legal identity as a structured special window of ADB, is not able to issue bonds to support its lending". Erquiaga 2016, 69. As further indicated by Erquiaga: "When the ADF was created, this inability to issue debt was not considered problematic as the low creditworthiness of ADF borrowers would have proved to be a constraint in convincing capital market investors to purchase bonds issued by a new entity for lending to these borrowers. This absence of financial leverage was now deemed suboptimal, particularly given the strong track record of regular ADF loan service payments. A leveraged approach was considered more efficient and effective in optimizing the management of concessional financing". Ibid.

Finally, the approach to treat concessional and non-concessional windows as entirely separate and distinct is questionable on conceptual grounds. There is a "large middle ground between organizations' concessional and non-concessional windows, which has not been sufficiently explored thus far".[99] Moreover, there is much room for realizing synergies between concessional and non-concessional windows as has been shown above.

5 Restructuring of Soft Windows

Due to the deficiencies of the revolving fund structure and consistent with the G20 sponsored Action Plan aiming at the optimization of MDB balance sheets (see below), ADB pursued with the "Project Galaxy" a merger between ADF and OCR. Such merger combined (effective from January 2017) the ADF lending operations with the OCR balance sheet, thus retaining the ADF as a grant-only operation. This important innovation increased OCR equity from USD 18.3 billion to USD 53 billion. ADB continued to offer ADF countries concessional financing on the same terms and conditions as previously provided but through its OCR window, while the ADF would provide only grant assistance.[100] This merger enhanced the efficiency of ADB's concessional operations but it also entails certain legal risks. While previously under Art. 10.1 of the ADB Charter, ADF resources (i.e., special funds resources) were "held, used, committed, invested or otherwise disposed of entirely separate from" OCR resources, such strict separation between OCR and special funds resources no longer applies. As concessional loans are now funded from OCR equity, any arrears or defaults regarding such loans may have implications for ADB's OCR balance sheet and, potentially, for the credit rating of ADB. Given the deterioration of the debt situation of many countries, the implications of this matter need to be carefully assessed.

IADB followed a similar approach as ADB and in "September 2016 the Governors approved a proposal to transfer the net assets of the former Fund for Special Operations (FSO) to the Ordinary Capital (OC) and to create a concessional lending instrument in the form of a blended loan where both legs of the blended operation would be financed from the OC. The proposal became effective on January 1, 2017".[101]

---

99 Droesse 2011c, 165. See also ibid. 211 and 296.

100 Project Galaxy has been described in detail by Erquiaga. This paragraph draws on Erquiaga's description. See Erquiaga 2016, 68.

101 IADB. Concessional Resources: With further references.

From a purely financial perspective, a similar approach like that adopted by ADB and IADB, i.e., involving a merger of IDA and IBRD and the use of IDA resources, mostly in the form of loans, for increasing the IBRD equity, would have been the "most cost-effective solution"[102] for the World Bank Group.

In the past, Shihata had reflected on a possible merger of IBRD, IFC, and MIGA "while restructuring IDA as an international trust fund administered by the resulting mega institution".[103] The reason why a merger of IBRD and IDA or any approach to restructure or terminate IDA has never realistically been considered is related on the one hand to the fact that IDA is an international organization in its own right which possesses international legal personality and legal capacity under national law. Generally, any termination of an international organization or any merger of two organizations is a daunting task, given the resilience of international organizations against annihilation and the applicable qualified majorities which are a formidable obstacle to institutional reform.[104] Furthermore, any proposed merger of IDA and IBRD would meet tremendous obstacles due to vested interests of IDA members.[105]

Thus, rather than merging IBRD and IDA, IDA opted pursuing the issuance of a credit rating in preparation of bond issuances. While unlike IBRD, IDA

102 As indicated by Humphrey in 2017: "The World Bank's IDA has the most financial potential from a balance sheet merger, based on its D 154.7 billion in equity (most of it in loans). A merger would boost IBRD equity from D 39.4 billion to D 194.1 billion, resulting in space for several hundred billion dollars more in potential loan portfolio size." See Humphrey 2017, 11. In comparison to 2017, IDA's equity has substantially further increased, given the successful conclusion of the IDA 19 Replenishment negotiations.

103 Shihata 2001, 119.

104 In accordance with Art. VII Section 5 (a) of the IDA Articles of Agreement, the permanent suspension of IDA requires a "vote of a majority of the Governors exercising a majority of the total voting power". In accordance with (c) of Section 5 mentioned above and subject to special arrangements which may be made for supplementary contributions of members, the assets of IDA would be distributed in such a case to members "pro rata in proportion to amounts paid in by them on account of their subscriptions". Hence, it any different disposition would require the approval of all IDA members. Moreover, for using the assets of IDA for an infusion of equity in the IBRD and IBRD to commence to operate on concessional terms, an amendment to the IBRD Articles of Agreement would be necessary, which, in accordance with Art. VIII (a) of IBRD Articles of Agreement, requires approval by the IBRD Board of Governor and acceptance by "three-fifth of the members, having eighty-five percent of the total voting power".

105 As stated by Humphrey: "Wealthy countries have a much higher ownership stake in IDA equity than at IBRD, due to their donations over the years. Merging the two windows would mean either increasing the voting share of wealthy countries at the new merged bank relative to borrower shareholders, or asking the wealthy countries to give up their ownership stake in IDA – both technically feasible options, but politically difficult". Humphrey 2017, 11.

has no callable capital, Standard & Poors (S & P) gave IDA a AAA rating, i.e., the highest credit rating also given to the IBRD, based on its "strong business profile and extremely strong financial profile".[106] A similar rating was given to IDA also by Moody's[107] which greatly increased IDA's leverage to mobilize additional resources.[108]

The first bond issued by IDA was sold within hours to institutional investors,[109] which suggests a strong interest of capital markets in IDA bonds. Since then, IDA has issued various bonds, initially with a maturity of 5 years, and in 2000 IDA first priced its first "10-year USD benchmark" bond[110] with a maturity of 10 years. As IDA was able to enhance its efficiency and impact by leveraging monies on capital markets, it was able to exceed its IDA 19 target despite the fact that U.S. had reduced its IDA contribution.[111]

As regards the African Development Fund, the "High Level Panel convened by the AfDB president in 2006 recommended eliminating the division between AfDB and the AfDF in its January 2008 report, suggesting a merger of the two institutions and their boards".[112] Nevertheless, also in the AfDB Group,

106 S&P Global Ratings 2018a.

107 Fitch gave IDA an AAA-rating. See Moody's 2020c.

108 Ibid. The IDA Deputies stressed in this context in their Report that "the transformation of IDA's financing framework through capital market access will help deliver on the Billions to Trillions agenda necessary to achieve the SDGs and match the ambitions, and challenges, of the 2030 agenda. In this context, IDA's triple-A ratings – the highest credit rating possible – represent a landmark in private sector capital mobilization for development finance, allowing IDA to leverage its significant capital base. Augmenting IDA finances through capital markets represents one of the most radical transformations in IDA's 55-year history". IDA Executive Directors Report to the BOGs – Additions to IDA Resources: Eighteenth Replenishment 2017, 57.

109 IDA 2018.

110 IDA 2020a.

111 Edwards 2019, 3. The IDA Deputies stressed in 2017 that "IDA's hybrid financial model presents unmatched value for money, by optimizing IDA's financial capacity and putting it to work for the world's poorest and most vulnerable countries". Moreover, the IDA 19 Deputies highlighted: "IDA leverages its Partner contributions and its equity to access financial markets, so that every USD 1 in Partner contributions supports more than USD 3 of financing for programs in IDA19 compared to only USD 2 in IDA17 [....]. Furthermore, the hybrid financial model dramatically increases IDA's grant financing capacity: in IDA17, less than one-third of Partner contributions financed grants; but now IDA can utilize nearly all new Partner contributions to finance grants [....]. Administrative costs are fully covered by revenues, ensuring that all of donor contributions are used for financing of programs for IDA clients"., IDA Executive Directors Report to the BOGs – Additions to IDA Resources: Nineteenth Replenishment, 2020b, 25.

112 AfDB 2007, 27. It was indicated by the Panel: "The [AfDB] must better integrate its operations and develop an appropriate array of instruments. And to be more responsive to the needs of the diverse clients, the [AfDB] and the [AfDF] should be brought together

neither a termination of the AfDF nor a merger of the AfDB and AfDF proved to be a realistic option in the past, for very similar reasons as highlighted for IDA above.

In 2016, the African Development Bank Group launched analytical work to assess the costs and benefits of either leveraging the African Development Fund, as done by the World Bank Group, or merging the Fund's loan portfolio into the African Development Bank, as done by the Asian and Inter-American Development Banks. While so far, the AfDB Group has not yet received a credit rating for the AfDB, the AfDB Group is seeking "new and creative ways of mobilizing resources to support Africa's transformation, especially by leveraging its own resources",[113] and the AfDB is engaged in a process of institutional reform and confirmed its "commitment to implementation of the One Bank vision in 2019" which emphasized "quality, delivery, and joint accountability".[114]

Nevertheless, as indicated by Birdsall in 2018, the AfDF was then "six to seven times smaller than the World Bank's IDA in Africa"[115] and it adds to its challenges that its reflows and equity bases are lower than for IDA. While AfDF donors committed in 2019 USD 7.6 billion for the fifteenth replenishment of the AfDF,[116] it is necessary to seek new ways for "reinvigorating African concessional finance", e.g. through the issuance of a "Big Bond" implemented through a new financing facility.[117]

---

to tailor lending accordingly, operating as a single bank with a single board". [....] "In line with our belief that there should be a single bank, we also believe there should be a single board. [....]."

Ibid, 4.

113 AfDB Financing Strategy. Also see AfDB's Strategy for 2013–2022.

114 AfDB Annual Report 2019.

115 "First, IDA will continue to receive higher reflows to relend in each of the next several three-year replenishment periods. In the current period, reflows are projected to be almost D 20 billion to IDA and perhaps D 600 million to the AfDF; one reason is that IDA continues to receive reflows from China, India and other countries outside Africa that no longer borrow from IDA or borrow only limited amounts. Second, IDA now has its own AAA credit rating, separate from that of the IBRD, and for the first time has borrowed on the capital market. Its own borrowing of as much as D 25 billion will not necessarily increase every three years (the number of countries eligible for highly concessional lending should continue to decline), but other demands for concessional resources, for refugees, for natural disaster relief, possibly for debt relief could rise. But even if the amounts decline, they will be large compared to any possible borrowing by the AfDF, given that the 'equity' of the AfDF in terms of expected future reflows is so much smaller". Birdsall 2018, 16.

116 AfDB Group 2019.

117 See AfDB 2017. The "High- Level Panel on Transforming Trust in the AfDB Group into Influence" reviewed "market borrowing" as planned in IDA and ADB's merger of ADF and OCR, but concluded that based on both approaches only a "modest increase" in the size

6 Transformation of the Funding Structures of IFAD and the OPEC Fund

It is an important development that IFAD and the OPEC Fund, while not designed to mobilize resources against callable capital, have both transformed their funding structures by seeking a credit rating and access to capital markets.

6.1 *IFAD*

In IFAD, a precursor to sovereign loans was the Spanish Food Security Co-Financing Facility Trust Fund approved by the Executive Board in 2010.[118] In 2015, following a first borrowing from KfW,[119] a "Sovereign Borrowing Framework" was put in place "setting out the parameters within which IFAD may borrow from sovereign states and state-supported institutions" which, however, did not "address the subject of IFAD borrowing from the financial markets through the issuance of bonds".[120]

The corporate evaluation of IFAD's financial architecture prepared in 2018 concluded that IFAD's financial architecture had failed "the test of financial sustainability" as it had "incurred financial losses every year since 2010" (except in 2017), resulting in an erosion of its retained earnings and capital base.[121]

---

of the AfDF can be secured (Ibid., 19). The Panel proposed instead frontloading of ODA through the issuance of a "Big Bond" to be implemented through a new financing facility within the Bank Group (Ibid., 1, 23). "The target investors for the bond would be financial institutions looking for stable long-term returns, such as pension funds, insurance companies, and sovereign wealth funds"; since "MCLs [Moderately concessional loans] need to be repaid, the projects financed would need to generate revenues. It [was] therefore expected that a significant proportion of the USD 100 billion raised would be spent on infrastructure". (Ibid., 24).

118 IFAD 2018a, para 11. As shown by Kamau and Colaicomo, while the grant element of the trust fund allowed IFAD to onlend the resources of the trust fund on concessional terms, these did not become part of IFAD's regular resources and could not, for that reason, be allocated through IFAD's performance-based allocation system (Ibid. para. 102).

119 Ibid, para. 103: "The first sovereign borrowing after the Spanish Trust Fund was designed to help bridge the difference between the IFAD9 target PoLG and the financing level achieved from the replenishment. A sovereign loan of keep with number 400 million was obtained from KfW with the agreement of the Executive Board in September 2014".

120 IFAD 2015. The sovereign borrowing from "KfW and the Spanish Trust Fund has allowed IFAD to finance a larger PoLG [programme of loans and grants] than would have been possible by relying only on replenishment contributions, loan reflows and Treasury income. Sovereign lending was IFAD's first step in introducing debt to leverage the equity in its balance sheet." (IFAD 2018, para 11).

121 IFAD 2018a, 97. It concluded that "four decades after its establishment, IFAD's financial architecture require[d] important reforms. These reforms concern[ed] the mobilization of financial resources, the system for allocating financial resources, the financial products

Under the eleventh Replenishment of IFAD (IFAD11), while Members' replenishment contributions remained at the time "the foundation of the Fund's capital and commitment capacity" (with a replenishment contribution target of USD 1.2 billion), borrowing from Member States and their institutions "was then fully integrated into the financial framework of the Fund for the first time".[122]

Since then, IFAD has taken a similar course as IDA by obtaining a credit rating. IFAD was the first UN Fund to do so. In October, Fitch gave an AA+ rating to IFAD.[123] While recognizing that "IFAD is inherently loss-making, owing to its business model", Fitch considered that this "is offset by the paid-in contributions it receives from its member states".[124] S&P harmonized its rating with that of Fitch by giving IFAD an AA+ rating as well.[125]

These ratings enhance IFAD's ability to mobilize resources[126] and are seen as a prelude to private placements.[127] While IFAD does not appear to plan issuing bonds anytime soon, such course of action might be considered at a later stage.[128]

---

available to respond to the need and demand of borrowing Member States, the financial sustainability of the Fund as well as internal and external financial governance features". (Ibid. 98) The said evaluation further recommended inter alia that. IFAD conduct "preparatory work for potential access to capital markets", stating. "Learning from the IDA case, it may not be strictly necessary for IFAD to be profitable to tap markets. However, a high credit rating is a condicio sine qua non and would in all likelihood require a restructuring of IFAD's financial architecture, by addressing those factors that create uncertainty." (Ibid., 99).

122 IFAD 2018b, para 4.

123 Fitch considered "IFAD's 'excellent' capitalisation as a key rating strength", primarily driven by [their] view that "IFAD's equity/assets ratio will continue to far exceed the 25% 'excellent' threshold over the medium term" and "supported by the fund's usable capital/risk-weighted assets (FRA) ratio, which also far exceeds the 35% 'excellent' threshold (end-2019: 75%)" (As of end-2019 this ratio was around 85%.). While recognizing that "IFAD is inherently loss-making, owing to its business model", Fitch considered that this "is offset by the paid-in contributions it receives from its member states". (FitchRatings 2020b).

124 FitchRatings 2020b. See also and McLellan 2020.

125 IFAD 2020.

126 As highlighted by IFAD's President: "With two positive ratings, we can mobilize more funds from various potential investors at a favourable cost. And this means we can do more to increase the incomes and food supply of the poor rural people who desperately need it. This is a prerequisite for building global stability and resilience". IFAD. 2020.

127 McLellan 2020.

128 Under IFAD's business model and financial framework for the years 2022–2024, IFAD will combine it Integrated Borrowing Framework with "the adoption of key principles" to support IFAD's financial sustainability as part of the revision of the existing procedures and definitions, and in addition, the Framework for Accelerated Repayments and Voluntary

6.2 *OPEC Fund*

The inherent problems of the revolving fund model have also manifested themselves in the case of the OPEC Fund. The fact that it was unable to have access to capital markets constrained its effectiveness. Hence, the OPEC Fund opted for a similar approach as IDA and IFAD, albeit with the difference that the OPEC Fund provides to a substantial extent financing on market-based terms. The high level of capitalization of the OPEC Fund enabled it to obtain a credit rating even though it cannot rely on callable capital to mobilize resources on capital markets.

In 2020, the Ministerial Council

> approved the Enhanced Management of OPEC Fund's Capital Resources, which entails (I) the establishment of the Special Capital Resources (SCR) fund through an initial transfer of loan and treasury assets from the existing capital resources of the OPEC Fund; and (II) the OPEC's Fund's existing capital resources being called Ordinary Capital Resources.[129]

Fitch rated the OPEC Fund on 29 July 2021 as "AA+ Outlook Stable" "based on the Standalone Credit Profile (SCP) of the institution" and, in particular, the "OPEC Fund's 'excellent' capitalisation as a key rating strength" and their expectation that the fund's equity/assets ratio, which was end-of 2000 around 91%, "will continue to far exceed the 25% 'excellent' threshold over the medium term".[130] A similar rating was given to the OPEC Fund also by S&P, which assigned the OPEC Fund an AA/A-1+ rating with a positive outlook.[131]

Hence, the capital structure of the OPEC Fund will resemble in the future that of ADB before the implementation of the project Galaxy when ADB leveraged resources on capital markets for its ordinary capital resources but the ADF was structured as a revolving fund to finance ADF loans and grants. As in line with Article 8 of the Agreement Establishing the OPEC Fund, the resources of the SCR must be held and managed entirely separately at all times from the OCR, any arrears or defaults on concessional loans do not affect the OCR balance sheet of the OPEC Fund or its credit rating.

Prepayments which constitutes a new instrument to boost IFAD's commitment capacity (IFAD. 2020, para. 17). IFAD will seek to increase its leverage "gradually and prudently" (IFAD. 2020, para. 140).

129 OPEC Fund 2021, 16.

130 FitchRatings. 2021c.

131 OPEC Fund Press Release 2021.

7 Market-Based (Hard) Windows

7.1 *Conceptual Architecture of Market-Based Windows*

The basic features of MDB capital structures are well known and do need to be explained for that reason in detail.

Mistry has well described the architecture of a hard window "which comprises the core 'development bank' in each institution" and has a "capital structure in two parts: *cash* capital and *callable* capital".[132] The "figment of confidence underlying the capital structure of MDBs is embedded in the notion of callable capital" which ensures "that each dollar lent is fully backed by a dollar of shareholder's equity, given the 1:1 limitation on the loan assets to capital ratio", even though "only a small fraction of the equity dollar in MDBs is paid-up front in cash".[133]

MDBs effectively can only perform their intermediation function if they can offer financing on favorable market-based terms.[134] Their ability "to leverage through their borrowings in international capital markets is significantly enhanced by their high credit standing", which is influenced notably by their "strong equity capitalization", i.e., equity to asset ratios that are higher than observed by commercial banks, as well as their "'shareholder support through 'callable capital' and their 'Preferred Creditor Status'".[135] As regards shareholder support, "[r]ating agencies tend to allow some proportion of this additional callable capital to count as actual capital, but it is less than 100 percent. Previously, S&P only recognized the callable capital of sovereigns with the same credit rating as that of the multilateral lending institution (MLI) concerned. Thus, for MLIs aiming for an AAA rating, S&P only [made] allowance for callable capital promised by shareholders that have AAA S&P ratings".[136] However, in 2018, S&P broadened their "definition of eligible callable capital to include sovereigns rated at least equal to the MLI's stand-alone credit profile (SACP)", which is a composite rating combining the assessments on capital adequacy

132 Mistry, 17.

133 Ibid., 22.

134 As stated by Humphrey: "The unique financial model of MDBs makes them extremely attractive for shareholders as it minimizes budgetary costs, but it means that the MDB has to be run in a way that ensure access to capital markets. Thus, MDBs have two sets of 'principals': the overt political and financial owners of the MDB (government shareholders) and the less obvious suppliers of liquidity essential for MDB operations (bond buyers)." Humphrey 2015b, 2.

135 Perraudin, Powell and Yang 2016, 8.

136 Ibid.

and funding and liquidity.[137] Fitch, on the other hand, applies a "usable capital to risk-weighted assets ratio" under which "[u]sable capital includes shareholders' equity plus a portion (10%) of callable capital subscribed by 'AAA'/'AA' rated shareholders".[138] Under the criteria used by both S&P and Fitch, there is an intrinsic relationship between membership composition and credit rating of MDB members and the rating of the MDBs.[139]

As the intermediation model is predicated on the ability of the financial intermediary to offer financing at preferential rates, the very sustainability of the financing offered by the intermediary is linked to their credit rating and may be seriously affected by any downgrade, in particular to Moody's BA category, or other comparable categories, where "obligations are judged to have speculative elements and are subject to substantial credit risk", or an even lower category.[140]

While the credit ratings of the members of financial intermediaries are of great importance for their own credit rating, it is possible that a financial intermediary may have a higher credit rating than the average credit rating of its members, in particular, if the capitalization of the intermediary is increased to well exceed a risk-adjusted capital ratio of 23.[141] This is confirmed, in particular, by the AAA-credit rating of IsDB which is higher than the average credit rating of its members. IsDB was able to obtain this rating as it has a stable capital structure and is one "of the strongest-capitalized MDBs with an equity-to-assets ratio of 39.6%".[142] Similar considerations also explain why the A+ credit

137 S&P Global 2018b, 2. On the SACP, see ibid., 5–7.

138 FitchRatings 2020a, 6.

139 Particular problems arise for borrower-dominated IFI, such as some of the sub-regional development banks which do not have, or only very few, AAA-rated members, and otherwise only members which lower credit ratings. The importance of these ratings can be illustrated by a comparison of the East African Development Bank (EADB) and the West African Development Bank (BOAD). The East African Development Bank (EADB) was upgraded in 2015 by Moody's from Ba1 to Baa3 (see EADB 2015). Still this rating is 9 notches lower on the Moody's rating scale that their Aaa rating of MDBs (the previous Ba1 rating was 10 notches lower). At this rating, EADB so far has been constrained to issuing local currency bonds, which tend to be rated higher by rating agencies than bonds issued in international capital markets. (See Capital Intelligence: Foreign Currency and Local Currency Ratings). The West African Development Bank, on the other hand, has a Baa1 rating which is 2 notches higher than that of EADB, partially because it benefitted from a World Bank project of capital market development (World Bank: Report No: ICR2565). (2013). It is able to issue bonds on international capital markets (See BOAD: BOAD issues the first African sustainability bond 2021).

140 Moody's Rating Scale and Definitions.

141 Under S&P's initial capital adequacy assessment, the risk-adjusted capital ratio is assessed as extremely strong if it is at 23% and above. See S&P Global Ratings 2018b, 16 (Table 10).

142 IsDB Investor Presentation 2019b, 14.

rating of the Corporación Andina de Fomento (CAF) by Fitch is higher than the average credit rating of CAF members.[143]

So far, none of the MDBs or IFIs that follow the intermediation model have ever made a call and, in essence, that model is predicated on the assumption that it will never be necessary to make such a call. As has been recognized with regard to the World Bank, if "the callable capital were ever called in, it would effectively be a nuclear option – so devastating as to effectively destroy the Bank itself".[144] Therefore, "as a buffer for very serious stress periods" callable capital remains untested as S&P highlighted in 2017.[145] Callable capital is "inferior to paid-in capital"[146] as for some member governments their ability to pay in distress scenarios is limited and for others payment requires legislative action, which makes the timeliness of payment an issue. "Finally, the directors who vote to make the call are appointed by the governments to which the call is made, which makes it difficult to assess with certainty under what degree of stress a board would make a capital call and what effect the nonpayment of a capital call by one member government would have on other members". For these reasons, and as indicated above, S&P does not view callable capital as a "substitute for paid-in capital".[147]

As prudence dictates that MDB borrowing and lending should be more appropriately "gauged against limits of *readily useable capital*; with capital increases being negotiated and concluded before borrowing or outstanding

143 Fitch stated in their 2019 Report that "CAF's intrinsic credit quality" drove their AA-rating of CAF. FitchRatings, Corporacion Andina de Fomento (CAF). Full Rating report 2019. Moreover, they highlight in the said report: "Excellent Capitalisation: CAF's equity/adjusted assets ratio averaged 30.4% from 2015 to end-December 2018, as sustained capital contributions and steady internal capital generation kept pace with growth. Its prudential framework requires a minimum total capital/weighted risks ratio (Basel II since 2007) of 30%. In practice, the reported ratio has been well above this minimum, reaching 41.1% in 2018." (Ibid.). In 2021, the rating of CAF was revised to A+ (See FitchRatings 2021). It was indicated in this context by Fitch: "The solvency assessment balances the bank's 'excellent' capitalisation with a 'moderate' risk profile. CAF's equity/adjusted assets ratio was 28.6% as of end-September 2020, above the threshold for an 'excellent' assessment (25%). The average for this metric was 30% over 2015–2019. Fitch's usable capital to risk-weighted assets (FRA) ratio, was 45% as of end-September 2020, also above the threshold for an 'excellent' assessment (35%)". See FitchRatings 2021.

144 Kapur and Raychaudhuri 2014, 3.

145 S&P Global. Supranationals: Special Edition 2017, 11.

146 Ibid., 12.

147 Ibid.

loans approach the limits of usable capital"[148] that notion is used in actual terms for determining when capital increases are required.

The ratings of MDBs do not only depend on their financial strength but also on their shareholders support which is affected, inter alia, if members deviate in raising capital from their historical share of paid-in to callable capital".[149] Hence, there is a limit regarding the extent to which MDBs and other IFIs can erode their paid-in capital ratios without effect on their credit rating.

Under their market-based windows, MDBs have to lend on market-related *hard terms* (hence the term *hard-window*); i.e., their interest charges must cover its own *borrowing cost* plus a spread or interest margin to cover its internal administrative and operating costs. Generally, MDBs provide loans with long maturities up to 20 years funded by borrowings with average life of about 5 years either with a fixed or variable spread (i.e., an interest mark-up over their own cost of borrowing).[150] While in the case of a variable spread the volatility of exchange rates is a risk of the borrower, the situation is different for loans with a fixed spread. In that case, the refinancing risk arising from this maturity mismatch is mitigated by the AAA-rating of MDBs which ensures a relatively stable funding cost. Any changes in funding cost will be passed on to the borrower through variable lending spread.[151]

In essence, the ability of MLIs to provide market-based financing is only constrained by the adequacy of their capital to sustain market-based borrowings. Thus, there is an intrinsic relationship between the unimpaired subscribed

---

148 Mistry 1995, 22. For the IBRD useable equity, see Word Bank Annual Report 2018 (Fiscal 2018), Table 27.

149 "This shareholder support is manifested in several ways. For shareholder governments that borrow from MDFIs, they show their support by servicing their loans from MDFIs in a timely manner, even in the event they do not service their commercial debt. For all shareholders, agreeing to cash capital subscriptions when needed and paying the capital subscriptions when due are tangible demonstrations of shareholder support. *Conversely, deviating from the institution's historical share of paid-in to callable capital by raising the share of callable capital (or, in particular, introducing callable capital into an MDFI's capital structure at a time when the global economy is only slowly recovering) could indicate a weakening of shareholder support, perhaps motivated by fiscal constraints that the shareholder governments themselves face*". (emphasis added) See S&P Rating Services 2009, 4.

150 See in detail Chris Humphrey 2014.

151 Memorandum from the World Bank President of 24 October 2019 on "IBRD Lending Rates and Spreads Applicable on or after October 1, 2019, 2" regarding the variable spread of the IBRD Flexible Loan product: "The pricing principle of IFL Variable Spread is to pass through changes in IBRD' s funding cost to Borrowers". The said Memorandum defines on pp. 2 and 3 the various components of the IFL variable spread.

capital of MLIs (as valued by each organization)[152] and the operational limit of the financing (headroom) which can be provided by them. As and to the extent that an organization is approaching its headroom, an increase in capital is required, which can take the form of a general capital increase or special (selective) capital increase. While in the case of general capital increases all members are given the opportunity to subscribe to a proportionate amount of the capital stock, special (selective) capital increases change the equilibrium of power between the members of the organization. This is the main reason why they often face obstacles.

7.2 *Capital Increases*

It is not possible to provide here a comprehensive review of the various capital increases of MDBs. Rather, only some significant features, issues and developments relating to the general and special (selective) capital increases of MDBs will be highlighted.

7.2.1 World Bank Group

7.2.1.1 *International Bank for Reconstruction and Development*

In the IBRD, general and selective capital increases are closely related. Therefore, it is useful to see the history of IBRD's general capital increases in conjunction with its selective capital increases. In this context, three periods can be distinguished.

During the period prior to 1984, nine increases in authorized capital stock were approved which increased the initial 100,000 shares allocated by the Articles of Agreement to 716,000 shares.[153] The first such increase in the amount of USD 10,000,000,000, is interesting as it involved an increase of callable capital only; it was approved in 1959 by the IBRD Board of Governors to support the growth in IBRD operations.[154] Prior to 1984, IBRD members were regularly eligible, to the extent that their IMF quotas increased as the result of a general quota review, for a selective capital increase in IBRD which aligned their IBRD shareholdings with their IMF quotas. In 1980, a first attempt was made to address the dilution of members' basic voting rights in the context of IBRD capital increases through the allocation of membership votes.[155]

152 While the constituent agreements of MDBs define the operational limit in similar terms, their interpretation has varied. For details see Sureda 2005, 229–232 Moreover, matters are further complicated due to open issues on the determination of standard of value and maintenance-of-value obligations. For details see Mistry, 38–45 and Sureda, 220–229.

153 IBRD Technical Note: Past IBRD Capital Increases 1987.

154 IBRD 1959, Board of Governors resolution No. 128.

155 IRBD Technical Note: Past IBRD Capital Increases 1987, 21.

As regards the period from 1984 until 2000, the 1988 General Capital Increase of IBRD, which increased the authorized capital of IBRD by USD 74,8 billion, and an Additional Capital Increase fell into this period.[156] During the above period, the parallelism between IMF general quota reviews and IBRD selective capital increases was increasingly decoupled. Rather, the focus moved to the question as and to what extent IBRD members' shareholdings can be aligned with their IDA contributions.

In 1984, the IBRD had a large selective capital increase which raised Japan, based on a 10% increase in its IMF quotas resulting from the Eights General Review of the IMF quotas, "to the position of second-largest shareholder of the IBRD".[157] While in the past, IBRD had followed the principle that "members' shareholding in the IBRD should be parallel to their relative quotas in the IMF", the 1984 SCI for Japan marked the beginning of the decoupling of the IBRD selective capital increases with IMF quotas".[158] As some countries hinted that their continued high IDA replenishment contributions might be subject to adjustments in their IBRD shareholdings, the focus moved instead on a possible linkage between IDA contributions and IBRD shareholdings. In 1987, while "rejecting any explicit and direct link between IDA contributions and IBRD shareholdings, a majority of Directors was prepared to support special share allocations for certain members in conjunction with the IDA8 negotiations reflecting more broadly these members' support to the World Bank Group [...]".[159]

The issue on whether there should be a linkage between IBRD members' contributions to IDA and their IBRD shareholdings surfaced again during the

156 IBRD 1988, Board of Governors resolutions Nos. 425 and 426.

157 Kapur, Lewis and Webb, 294.

158 In 1976, the IBRD had taken a first action to address the request of Japan first made during the IDA 5 replenishment negotiations (1975–77) that its IBRD shareholding should be harmonized with its cumulative contributions to IDA which were proportionately about twice as high as its IBRD shareholdings (Kapur, Lewis and Webb, 294). In case of Board of Governors Resolution No. 395 adopted on 30 August 1984, the principle that IBRD shareholding should be aligned with IMF quotas was partially dispensed with as the Executive Directors of the IBRD believed "that in calculating the special increases to be allocated only quota increases under the Fund Resolution in excess of 22.0833 percent of present quotas should regarded as special increases and that members be authorized to subscribe 50 percent of the shares as so calculated". (See the preamble of IBRD Board of Governors Resolution No. 395). (See Technical Note. Past IBRD Capital Increases. 1987, para. 31) Hence, under Resolution mentioned above which increased the capital stock of the IBRD by USD 7 billion, IBRD members were only allowed to subscribe to 50 percent of the shares which they would have been entitled to receive in parallel with IMF quota increase.

159 Memorandum from the World Bank President B. B. Conable to the Executive Directors 1987, 1.

IDA 11 Deputies' meetings, held in South Africa in June 1995 and in Washington D.C. in October 1995 when "several Deputies referred to the need to strengthen the linkage between IDA contributions and Bank shares".[160] At the 1996 Annual Meeting, the IBRD Executive Directors, noting the desire of Japan "to increase its subscription to the capital stock of the Bank by 33,230 shares", recommended this to the Board of Governors authorizing such a subscription which "would increase Japan's subscription from 93,770 shares or 6.15% of the authorized capital to 127,000 shares or 8.15% of the authorized capital".[161] Approval to that effect was given by the Board of Governors by Resolution No. 503 adopted on 14 June 1996.[162]

Starting in 2000, discussions on IBRD selective capital increases were linked to IBRD governance reform. Following the Monterrey Consensus, discussion in the World Bank focused on voice reform. A variety of options were considered in the context of the voice-reform process, which was implemented in two phases.[163] If anything, the voice-reform discussions underline the difficulties

---

160 "In their view, Bank shares, which reflect several historical factors, and IDA contributions, which tend to reflect more recent economic standing, have diverged sharply for some donors, and called for greater harmonization of the two. This would strengthen the Bank Group by recognizing more fully the changing relative economic positions of members and by encouraging donors to maximize their contribution to IDA". See IBRD, Note to Executive Directors on Possible Increase of IBRD Shareholdings of Certain Members 1995, 1.

161 IBRD Executive Directors Report 1 May 1996.

162 IBRD Board of Governors Resolution No. 503, 1996.

163 See Development Committee 2008 and Development Committee 2010. In this context, in particular, the following four issues were considered in the first phase. (I) First, a substantial problem arose from the fact that the 250 basic votes allocated to all IBRD members on an equal basis are defined in numeric terms (250 votes are allocated by Article V, Section 3 (a) of the IBRD Articles of Agreement) rather than based on a formula and were therefore diluted in the context of IBRD capital increases. (II) Second, the shareholdings of IBRD members, in particular, those of certain transitional economies, were no longer consistent with their important role in the world economy. (III) Third, certain areas, such as sub-Saharan Africa, were not adequately represented in the World Bank. (IV) Fourth, in the context of the voice reform process the need was stressed of improving the Board effectiveness and responsiveness to the views of developing and transitional countries. As part of the second phase, a shareholding review was to be conducted. See Development Committee 2010, paras. 34 to 36. As regards (I) above, it did not prove possible to reinstate the percentage of basic votes at the time when the IBRD Articles of Agreement took effect, i.e. 10,78% of total votes. Rather, in accordance with Resolution No. 596 (IBRD Board of Governors Resolution No. 596, 2009), in 2008 Art. V, Section 3 (a) of the IBRD Articles of Agreement was amended to read that "the basic votes of each member shall be the number of votes that results from the equal distribution among all members of 5.55 percent of the aggregate sum of the voting power of all the members". The proposal toward the "concept of parity between developed and DTC [developing countries and countries with

attached to any institutional reform. The changes which were eventually implemented came too late and achieved too little to address the concern of the transitional economies mentioned above.

A general capital increase and selective capital increase could only be implemented in 2018 after some of the U.S. concerns had been addressed, in particular those regarding IBRD loan pricing measures. Resolution No. 663[164] provided that the "authorized capital stock of the Bank shall be increased by 230,500 shares of capital stock", such shares being available for subscription by all members of IBRD as specified in the table of the Resolution and on such terms as specified in para. 3 of the Resolution.

Further, Resolution No. 664[165] provided that the IBRD capital stock should be increased by additional 245,773 shares. As under Resolution No. 663, all IBRD members were entitled to subscribe the number of shares specified in Resolution No. 664, but in a different proportion than under Resolution No. 663.

7.2.1.2 *International Finance Corporation*

The initial capitalization of IFC was relatively higher than that of the IBRD,[166] due to the fact that IFC provides financing without a sovereign guarantee. Hence, unlike the case of IBRD, where the paid-in portion of subscription payments initially was 20%, in the case of IFC payment for subscription had to be made in full by the original members and members admitted subsequently. While in the case of the IBRD, shareholdings were initially aligned with the IMF quotas, in the IFC, the shareholdings of the original members were in line with their IBRD shareholdings. This alignment was maintained in the early general

economies in transition] members into Bank governance" was not accepted as it would have represented "a paradigm shift requiring extensive dialogue among Shareholders". (See Development Committee 2008, para. 48) Hence, the realignments of shares provided for by para. 2 of Resolution turned out to be extremely modest, as reflected initially by Resolution No. 596 only 7,117 of the available unallocated shares were made available for subscription by 16 countries (IBRD Board of Governors Resolution No. 596, 2009). As regards the additional seat on the Executive Boards of the IBRD and IDA, this matter was eventually resolved after extensive discussion in 2010 (The World Bank (Board of Directors). https://www.worldbank.org/en/about/leadership/directors, accessed 21 April 2022). In 2016, a dynamic formula with two variables, a measure for economic weight and a measure for IDA contributions was proposed to the Development Committee. See Development Committee 2016, 3–6. Also on this matter Development Committee 2020b.

164 IBRD Board of Governors, Resolution No. 663.

165 IBRD Board of Governors, Resolution No. 664.

166 The initial subscription of original members was payable in full in gold or U.S. dollars. See Art. II, Section 3 (c) of the IFC Articles of Agreement.

capital increases,[167] but was later applied flexibly. In connection with a proposal to increase the IFC authorized capital by 150,000 shares for the former Soviet Republics,[168] an amendment to the IFC Articles was approved allowing the U.S. to exercise also in the future its *de facto* veto rights over IFC affairs.[169]

IFC was only included in the voice reform discussion at a late stage. Also, in the case of IFC, the core problem that the shareholdings of various IFC members (e.g., China and India) are no longer consistent with their role in the world economy, was not resolved. As for IBRD, it was also proposed for the IFC to improve Board representation for the then "47 countries of Sub-Saharan Africa (SSA) on all four Bank Group Boards, so that three Executive Directors would represent the SSA countries, rather than two".

Notwithstanding the recognition of the crucial role of the private sector in financing the post-2015 development agenda,[170] substantial problems arose in ensuring adequate provision of resources to IFC. One problem was that there was limited support for an increase of IFC's authorized capital stock, in particular, in the U.S. which has a *de facto* veto right over decisions approving an increase in authorized IFC capital stock, irrespective of whether the U.S. participates in such increase.

Eventually, the IFC members, including the U.S., agreed in 2018 to a general capital increase and selective capital increases subject to reforms designed, in part, to address a longstanding concern for many U.S. policymakers: high levels of World Bank lending to uppermiddle income countries, especially China.[171]

---

167 World Bank 1977. IFC Board of Governors resolution No. 100; World Bank. 1985. IFC Board of Governors resolution No. 149; World Bank Group 1992. IFC Board of Governors resolution No. 179.

168 IFC Board of Governors Resolution No. 196.

169 IFC Board of Governors Resolution No. 197.

170 Development Committee Discussion Note 2015, para 34.

171 In 2020, the IFC Board of Governors approved three important resolutions. The IFC Directors having determined "it would be desirable that each member be issued shares without any cash contribution", the IFC Board of Governors resolved by Resolution No. 270 to increase the IFC authorized capital stock by the creation of 16,999,998 additional shares to "implement the conversion of a portion of the retained earnings of the Corporation into paid-in capital" (IFC Board of Governors Resolution No. 270: "2018 Conversion of Retained Earnings and General Capital Increase" adopted on 16 April 2020). IFC Board of Governors Resolution No. 271 provided for an increase of IFC's authorized capital stock by 919,998 shares, each having a par value of one thousand United States dollars (D 1,000), and selective allocation of shares to members. Members included in the Table in para. 3 of Resolution No. 271 were authorized to subscribe up to the total number of shares indicated. (IFC Board of Governors Resolution No. 271 "2018 Selective Capital Increase" adopted on 16 April 2020, Para No. 5 (a), (c), (d) and (e)). Finally, a general capital increase, the first since 1992, was approved by the IFC Board of Governors by Resolution No. 272

A condition for these capital increases was a further amendment to the IFC Articles which allowed the U.S. to maintain its *de facto* veto right despite the fact that it did not subscribe to an increase of IFC's capital stock.[172] The terms of the general and the selective capital increases were very favorable to the U.S.[173] While similar issues also arose in other MDBs and IFIs, the IFI general and selective capital increases of 2020 show with particular clarity to which extent qualified majorities allow a single member (or a small group of member states) to shape the agenda of an organization.

7.2.1.3 *Multilateral Investment and Guarantee Agency*

The general capital increase of MIGA in 1988[174] is interesting as it was funded through a USD 150 million grant from IBRD, USD 150 million of paid-in capital and USD 700 million of callable capital. It has been so far the only general capital increase authorized by the MIGA Board of Governors and only involved very limited payment obligations for MIGA members. However, the MIGA Board of Governors increased by Resolutions Nos. 47[175] and 101,[176] consistent with Art. 22 of the MIGA Convention, the maximum aggregate amount of contingent liabilities that may be assumed by the Agency first from 150 percent to 350 percent, and subsequently to 500 percent of the amount of the Agency's unimpaired subscribed capital, reserves, and portion of its reinsurance cover determined by the Board of Governors.

---

which increased the IFC authorized capital stock by 4,579,995 shares, each having a par value of one thousand United States dollars (D 1,000). These were available for subscription by all members, however, the U.S., the largest IFC shareholder advised that that it would not exercise its rights under Article II, Section 2 (d) of the Articles to subscribe to its proportionate share of the general capital increase. 2018 General Capital Increase.

172 IFC Board of Governors Resolution No. 273: Amendment to the Articles of Agreement of the Corporation 2020, Art. II, Section 2 (c) para 1.

173 As indicated by Nancy Lee and Mark Plant: "By the numbers alone, this is a great deal for the American people. No new US taxpayer dollars will go to the IFC, but under the terms of the deal the US remains the largest shareholder and the only country with veto power over the most important voting decisions. As with any multilateral financial institution, the capital the US has contributed in the past has been multiplied many times over by other shareholders and translated into much larger financial flows to developing countries". Lee and Plant 2019, 42.

174 The capital increase was approved by MIGA Resolution of the Board of Governors No. 57.

175 World Bank 1994. MIGA Council of Governors resolution No. 47.

176 World Bank 2016. MIGA Council of Governors resolution No. 101.

7.2.2 Regional Development Banks and IFIs of Limited Membership

There have been shifts in the global financial architecture regarding the financing provided by international organizations. While until the "2008–09 global financial crisis, the World Bank was as large as the Inter-American, Asian and African banks combined, measured in terms of total capital to support ordinary lending", the "financial crisis increased the demand for lending from all the banks leading to capital increases ('recapitalizations') in 2011 at all the legacy banks except the EBRD. The increases were relatively larger at the three regional banks than at the World Bank, probably reflecting the greater interest of their regional borrowers in their banks" and the creation of the AIIB in 2015 added further to the share of the regional banks in total MDB (paid-in) capital; they now constitute more than 50 percent of total MDB capital.[177]

Hence, "the long-run trend appears to be relatively faster growth of the regional banks, where the middle-income countries have a relatively greater role and greater sense of 'ownership'".[178]

The IADB, AfDB and ADB epitomize that trend because they each dramatically increased their authorized capital. In the IADB and AfDB, where membership initially was limited to the members of the Organization of American States (OAS) and African countries, respectively, their opening to new members was instrumental to their increase of capital. The IADB Charter, which initially had been amended to admit Canada to membership, was subsequently further amended to allow members of the IMF and Switzerland to join in accordance with general rules to be established by the Board of Governors.[179] IADB initially amended the IADB Charter in 1976 to create an inter-regional capital stock[180] but deleted the provisions introduced to that effect already nine years later by providing for an automatic merger of inter-regional capital and ordinary capital stock.[181] In the context of nine increases in resources of the IADB, the IADB capital was increased to USD 170.9 billion.[182]

In the AfDB, the third general capital increase of AfDB or "GCI-3 (comprising the combined capital increases of 1979 and 1981) was very important as it entailed the admission of non-regional members into the shareholding of the AfDB, along with a substantial increase in the Bank's capital base to over USD

177 Birdsall 2018, 4.

178 Ibid.

179 IADB 1972, Board of Governors Resolution AG-4/72.

180 IADB 1976, Board of Governors Resolution AG-9/76.

181 IADB 1987, Board of Governors Resolution AG-8/87.

182 IADB Capital and Funds under Administration. Cordell, Bandura and Fernandez 2021 call for a new capital increase of IADB.

5 billion".[183] "The decision to open the Bank's capital to non-African participation proved very positive, in terms of membership and capital structure"[184] and set the path for the AfDB capital to multiply on several occasions. Thus, the Fourth General Capital Increase of the AfDB (GCI-4) increased the authorized capital stock of the AfDB by 200%. It took place in 1987 and was governed by a Resolution of the AfDB Board of Governors of 1987.[185] Under that Resolution, the authorized capital stock of the AfDB was increased from 5,400,000,000 U. A. to 16,200,000,000 U. A. by the creation of 1,080,000 new shares of a par value of 10,000 U. A. each share.[186] The new shares were allocated to regional and non-regional members in the proportion of 2:1.[187] As of the fifth General Increase in Resources, the preparation of general capital increases had become inextricably entwined with a review of the governance, financial, policy and operational agenda of AfDB. The review of GCI-V was completed in 1998 when it was approved by Resolution of the AfDB Board of Governors. Under that Resolution, the authorized capital stock was increased from 16,200,000,000 U.A. to 21,870,000,000 U.A. by the creation of 567,000 new shares.

The authorized capital of the AfDB further multiplied during the six and seventh general capital increase. GCI-VI was approved by the AfDB Board of Governors on 27 May 2010.[188] Under the Resolution adopted on that date, the authorized capital of AfDB was tripled through a 200% increase from U.A. 23,947,460,000 to U.A. 67,687,460,000 (then USD 100 billion) by the creation of 4,374,000 new shares, with a par value of ten thousand Units of Account (UA 10,000) for each share.[189] The seventh, and, so far, last general capital increase, took place in 2019. Discussion on GCI-VII started in 2018. Following a detailed review of AfDB, GCI-VII was the largest in the history of the AfDB and catapulted the AfDB to USD 208 billion, equivalent. Thus, currently, the AfDB has the highest approved capital of all regional development banks.[190]

As regards ADB, Erquiaga[191] has given in his financial history of ADB a detailed account of the five general capital increases of ADB. The last of these increases (GCI-V) increased the authorized capital of ADB in 2009 by

183 Mistry 1995, 28.
184 AfDB in Brief 2013, 10.
185 AfDB Board of Governors Resolution B/BG/87/11 (1987).
186 Ibid, para 1.
187 Ibid, para 2.1.
188 AfDB Board of Governors Resolution B/BG/2010/08 (2010).
189 Ibid.
190 AfBD 2019, 31.
191 Erquiaga 2016, 22.

200 percent to USD 165 billion. As in other organizations, ADB's general capital increases became the forum to review in general terms ADB financial policies.

Finally, EBRD has gradually increased its number of shareholders from 40 shareholders at origin to 66 (predominantly European countries and two supranational institutions, the European Union and the European Investment Bank). During the fourth capital resources review in May 2010, EBRD's shareholders decided to increase the bank's authorized capital to €30 billion from €20 billion. However, this capital increase did not raise shareholders' equity.[192]

There are substantial differences between IFIs in their capital ratios as shown by S&P Global.[193] Some IFIs, such as the AIIB, are listed by S&P Global as having exceptionally strong capital ratios, while these are substantially lower, even though still strong, in most of the traditional legacy MDBs, i.e., the World Bank, IADB, AfDB, ADB, and EBRD. As regards IBRD, IADB, ADB and AfDB, their paid-in capital ratios were substantially reduced over time in the context of their general capital increases.

From a conceptual point, it is not necessary at all for members to provide paid-in capital in the context of an increase in capital. As shown above, there have been various cases where the callable capital alone was increased without members being required to provide paid-in capital. Moreover, in the case of the AfDB, also temporary increases of callable capital were approved for certain members.[194] Also, as has been shown, increases in authorized capital can partially be funded by the grant of an organization, or conversion of retained income or from reserves. As and to the extent that paid-in capital was provided, the paid-in capital ratio generally was during more recent capital increases in the range between 2% and 6%. Neither the above reduction[195] in paid-in capital ratios nor the recent rapid expansion of IFI lending in the context of COVID19 has been of prejudice to the AAA rating of the MDBs mentioned above, as rating agencies tend to give a lot of weight to the strong stakeholder support of these institutions.

As regards the special or selective capital increases, it appears that these have been more effective instruments for rewarding donors for their contributions

192 "€1 billion was transferred from reserves to paid-in capital, and callable capital increased by €9 billion. Callable capital stood at €23.4 billion, and paid-in capital at €6.2 billion as of March 31, 2013. The increase in callable capital became effective in April 2011 upon receipt of more than 50% of the necessary subscriptions. As of Dec. 31, 2012, 2.2% of the callable capital shares (€0.2 billion) remain 'unsubscribed'". Standards & Poors Rating Services 2013.

193 S&P 2020b, 8–10.

194 AfDB Board of Governors Resolution 2019, para 1.

195 See on the "Diminution of Paid-Capital" Mistry, 35–37.

to soft windows through special (selective) capital increases in the market-based financing window than for aligning the shareholdings of countries with their role in the global economy. For the latter, the qualified majorities required for any amendment of constituent agreements of international organizations are formidable obstacles of reform as these give sometimes one country, or a small group of countries, a veto right. Moreover, in some organizations, members can also exercise preemptive rights in cases of proposed selective capital increases, which conceptually are inconsistent with the very purpose of the selective increase aimed at increasing the relative shareholdings of some members.

The core problem is that the richer countries find it difficult to increase their capital commitments but do not allow emerging economies to increase their share.[196] Against this background, the discussions on future capital increases have become a matter of substantial complexity as their main focus is on the measures to be taken by MDBs to maximize the availability of resources so as to avoid any major infusion of paid-in capital by their members.[197]

196 As highlighted by Kapur and Raychaudhuri: "The financial design of the IBRD required all member countries to contribute to the institution's capital, with the caveat that poor countries (the borrowers) had to contribute less, but then also had commensurately less power. The two principles – that power came with a price and there were no freeriders – ensured broad representation but strong creditor rights as well. Ironically, with the significant shifts in the balance of global power, the equity story of the IBRD faces a different 'free rider' problem today. In the past rich countries put brakes on IBRD capital increases because they did not want to the Bank to become so big as to crowd out private lenders and national agencies, whether private banks based in their countries or official Exim banks. Today, however, private banks are struggling. If the IBRD is to increase its lending substantively and in a manner that is financially prudent, it needs to increase its capital. Emerging economies are willing to put in capital to do so, but only if their ownership rights increase commensurately. However, the rich member countries have been disproportionately affected by the crisis and find it difficult to increase their capital commitments due to growing fiscal deficits. At the same time they are unwilling to let the emerging market member countries increase their share of capital that threatens the majority voting power of the rich countries". See by Kapur and Raychaudhuri, 3–4.

197 This is applicable for example to the discussion on a new general capital increase of IADB. In this context, IADB is requested inter alia to "enhance its financial reach, including 'sweating' its capital by optimizing its balance sheet", to be "instrumental in channeling private capital into development projects", "consider innovative ways to help catalyze additional investments through the domestic resources of developing countries", "establish local currency funds", and consider operational and institutional reforms". (See Runde, Cordell, Bandura and Fernandez, 4–5). Similar considerations also apply to a potential further capital increase of ADB.

8 Core Issues

In this overall context, some fundamental questions regarding the current market-based funding mechanisms of IFIs arise.

8.1 *Too Big to Fail?*

The increase in authorized capital of IFIs is best illustrated by the AfDB. In accordance with Art. 5, paragraph 1 of the Agreement establishing the African Development Bank, the initial authorized capital of AfDB was 250,000,000 units of account (U.A.), then defined as 0.88867088 gramme of fine gold.[198] As shown above, the capital of the AfDB has increased in the course of seven general capital increases to the equivalent of more than 200 billion USD. This increase can only be characterized as exponential. As shown above, also the IBRD and the IADB, AfDB and ADB have mirrored, even though to a somewhat lesser extent, the exponential increase of AfDB's authorized capital. The authorized capital of the IBRD, which was initially capitalized with USD 10 billion, has increased to USD 325 billion, and that of IADB and ADB, which were initially capitalized with USD 1 billion, has increased to, respectively USD 175 and 165 billion.

The borrowings of MDBs have sharply increased after the G20, at the 2015 November Antalya Summit, encouraged "Multilateral Development Banks (MDBs) to mobilize their resources, optimize their balance sheets, and catalyse private sector funding".[199] The "MDB Action Plan to Optimize Balance Sheets"[200] which was endorsed at the Antalya G20 Summit has been regularly updated, and in accordance with the recommendations contained in that plan MDBs enhanced their lending. Moreover, substantial pressure is being exercised by the G20, mostly indirectly, on rating agencies to relax their criteria.[201]

198 Mistry 1995, 289.

199 G20 Leaders Communiqué: Antalya Summit 2015, para 10.

200 G20, "Multilateral Development Banks: Action Plan to optimize Balance Sheets" (2015).

201 Humphrey, in his paper commissioned by the G24, criticized that "MDB operations do not come close to filling the gap between developmental needs and public and private sector financing" and that their rating methodologies have become "an increasing constraint on MDB operational capacity" as they are "weakening several key aspects of the MDB model, and hence restricting their potential to improve the lives of millions if not billions of the world's poor". (Humphrey 2015a, 1–2.) In addition, in 2016, Humphrey raised the question: "Could multilateral banks be lending an extra D 1 trillion?", suggesting the World Bank could collectively lend the amount mentioned above, which [then] represented "a 2% increase on their 2014 portfolios". (Humphrey 2016, 1.).

The MDBs, which already had increased their lending in previous years, have further expanded both their lending and borrowings. Thus, the World Bank Group announced in April 2019 that "given the unprecedented challenges that COVID-19 poses, the Bank Group expects to deploy up to USD 160 billion over the next 15 months to help countries protect the poor and vulnerable, support businesses, and bolster economic recovery".[202] Also, the other MDBs announced special measures to assist their members. Overall, as shown above, the various MDB assistance packages add up to more than 200 billion. As shown by S&P Global, the supranational debt totalled USD 1.43 trillion at the end of 2019, and it has further increased ever since.

The above shows how far the MDBs and other IFIs have come from their humble beginnings. It also shows, however, that the financial intermediation model espoused by the MDBs and other IFIs in a certain sense has become too big to fail. This finding has a variety of implications, inter alia, for the proposal that the IFIs should continue to draw on their alleged reserve capacity by further expanding their borrowing and lending programs without any further equity infusion.

It was warranted and appropriate that the MDBs assist their members in the COVID19 pandemic. Nevertheless, and even though according to the "Fitch Ratings 2020c Outlook: Supranationals", the "Rating Outlook for Supranationals is Stable",[203] there are some issues which are relevant to the discussion on whether MDBs and IFIs have a reserve capacity. Thus, Fitch also noted in their aforementioned outlook "the largest number of downgrades [of supranationals] in any given year", as well as a negative outlook for six institutions, due to concerns about their credit quality.

In this context, also the results of a stress test S&P conducted in 2020 are relevant. S&P then tested the capital bases of multilateral lending institutions (MLIs) to three hypothetical scenarios of stress.[204] The results of the stress tests suggested that "there won't be significant rating pressure under any of the three scenarios".[205] Nevertheless, for IBRD, S&P concluded that already the lowest impact scenario could bring IBRD's capitalization metric down to a level that could qualify for the same or a lower capital assessment, while

202 The World Bank. Feature Story: The World Bank Group Moves Quickly to Help Countries Respond to COVID-19. https://www.worldbank.org/en/news/feature/2020/04/02/the-world-bank-group-moves-quickly-to-help-countries-respond-to-covid-19, accessed 21 April 2022. See also World Bank 2021a.

203 FitchRatings 2020c.

204 S&P Global 2020a.

205 Ibid, 4.

considering this finding as mitigated as IBRD was likely to receive parts of its recently agreed general capital increase in 2021 and could rely on a significant buffer of callable capital.[206] It is also useful to reflect on the finding of S&P that "sovereign downgrade could erode the capital position" of multilateral lending institutions (MLIs), and "a very severe stress could put at risk the preferred creditor treatment (PCT) on which MLIs' business models rest, altering some institutions' credit profiles".[207]

While the above stress tests suggest that "MLIs have the capacity to weather the effects of the pandemic without significant erosion of their capital bases", it is doubtful that MDBs have "[h]alf a [t]rillion in [d]ry [p]owder",[208] as stated recently, or a spare capacity for further lending of USD 750 billion, as argued in 2020[209] about the same time when the above stress tests were made. It is a common trait of proposals as mentioned above and others like the one of Settimo,[210] who explores options for MDBs to operate at a lower than AAA-rating, that MDBs should accept higher levels of risk and expand their operations without any further substantial infusion of paid-in capital from their members. Calls to that effect have constantly been made by the G20 since 2015 on political grounds. The G20 not only supports a further far-reaching so-called "optimization of MDBs balance sheets" and revised (i.e., softer) criteria by rating agencies, but in addition it also has encouraged MDBs to engage in

206 Ibid. Moreover, as set out by S&P, "scenarios 2 and 3 depict substantially higher stress levels [....]." In addition to the increasing pressure on the entities already mentioned, African Development Bank, European Bank for Reconstruction and Development (EBRD), Council of Europe Development Bank (CEB), Islamic Development Bank (IsDB), Black Sea Trade and Development Bank (BSTDB), Islamic Corporation for the Development of the Private Sector (ICD), and the Caribbean Development Bank would approach or go below our capital thresholds. In all cases, except for the IsDB, ICD, and BSTDB, the entities have an ample buffer of eligible callable capital that could reinforce their financial risk profiles should capital levels deteriorate. (Ibid., 5).

207 Ibid, 1. Furthermore, also the asset quality of the non-sovereign operations of MDBs has deteriorated in the context of the COVID 19 – pandemic. As indicated by Fitch, almost all "MDBs focused on non-sovereign operations" and some "sovereign-focused MDBs" (including ADB, AfDB and IADB) have granted debt payment suspension to non-sovereign borrowers, mostly to those that "were current on their loan repayment but were facing short-term liquidity pressures". (FitchRatings 2021a, 2.). It is indicated in this context by Fitch: "Only a few MDBs have considered as impaired part of their exposures subject to debt suspension. [....] In Fitch's view, there is a risk that considering these exposures benefitting from temporary suspension of payments as 'performing' may mask the full negative impact of the crisis on MDBs' asset quality and only delay loan impairments". (Ibid.).

208 Landers and Aboneaaj.

209 See Humphrey 2020a, 1 and 2020b. See also Landers and Aboneaaj 2021.

210 See Settimo 2019.

advanced financial engineering (e.g., through an exchange of their sovereign exposures) and has urged them to participate in debt-stop initiatives. If MDBs should give in to the G20 pressure, they may risk losing their AAA-ratings and hence their ability to leverage resources on capital markets on the most favorable terms.

The fact that the G20 believes that it is entitled to direct the MDBs without any legal basis is of concern in itself.[211] However, it is questionable, in particular, inasmuch the G20 sees for itself a role in determining the capital adequacy of MDBs, because the very role of the G20 in this matter is highly problematic. The G20 is a political body which lacks the necessary independence and technical capacity for risk assessment and determining the capital adequacy of MDBs. It is also intrinsically conflicted in dealing with these matters as, even though never openly articulated, one of the main interests, if not the main interest of G20 members, is to minimize their own financial exposure and avoid the need for increases in authorized capital which may require an infusion of paid-in capital. Thus, the G20 should not be involved in the assessment of the capital adequacy of MDBs as a matter of principle.

Apart from the further erosion of paid-in capital ratios which is a corollary of proposals as mentioned above, they raise many other questions. These relate *inter alia* to the financial capacity of developing countries to serve such a rapid expansion of debt. Also, the question arises whether the crisis support by MDBs at times effectively aggravates rather than alleviates the debt problems of the poorest countries.

The President of the World Bank raised this question in 2019 at an IMF debt forum, where he stated: "We have a situation where other international financial institutions and to some extent development finance institutions as a whole, certainly the official export credit agencies, have a tendency to lend too quickly and to add to the debt problem of the countries". He said the Asian Development Bank was "pushing billions of dollars" into a fiscally challenging situation in Pakistan while the African Development Bank was doing the same in Nigeria and South Africa.[212]

Since the 2008 financial crisis, MDBs have increasingly been asked to provide crisis support to their members. However, while MDBs have a well-defined role in providing long-term capital for creating long-term productive assets, including economic infrastructure for human capital and education, and for matters such as climate change adaptation and mitigation and environmental

211 Droesse 2021.

212 Reuters 2020.

protection, they were not conceived as crisis management institutions. This is a function which should be entrusted to a new institution yet to be established. The purpose of development finance is not primarily to provide general budget support or fill 'financing gaps', but instead investing in the highest quality of development assistance operations that will deliver tangible and sustainable benefits. This matter does not appear to be given sufficient consideration in the deliberations of IFI assistance to developing countries. As and to the extent that MDBs provide longer-term loans (e.g., with maturities of 10–15 years) for general budget support or funding short-term needs of their members, they expose themselves and their members to three types of risk. First, in such a case, there often is a drastic mismatch between the maturities of the loan which has to be repaid over a longer term and the short-term nature of the support provided by IFIs. Second, the fact that MDB-financing is not used for generating assets but for funding current expenditures makes it more difficult for recipients to repay their loans. Third, such repayment is further aggravated by the fact that MDBs burden developing countries with the volatility of exchange rates as they provide emergency support generally in US dollar under loans which have to be repaid in US dollars, rather than in local currency. As a corollary of the above, there are risks that a further rapid "explosion" of MDB financing could lead to a need for far greater debt relief or even debt forgiveness in the future. The discussion on the optimization of MDBs balance sheets has been driven, so far, by the G20.

To be clear, MDBs and other IFIs should avail themselves of opportunities to enhance their impact and free headroom for operational activities. However, to avoid that the next global financial crisis may be one triggered by the IFIs, it would be best to entrust the determination on a future "optimization" of MDBs' balance sheets to an institution like the Basel Committee or to a committee with guaranteed independence and adequate technical capacity in dealing with these matters rather than entrusting it to the G20 which should not be involved in making determinations on the capital-adequacy of MDBs. Finally, to maintain their preferred creditor treatment, MDBs and other IFIs should resist any suggestions from the G20 or otherwise to participate with their own resources in debt stop or debt relief initiatives.

8.2 *Ownership of IFIs*

Traditionally, MDB and other IFI only admit states as members. Moreover, while so far private-sector entities, institutional investors and other stakeholders are consulted and involved in projects as recipients or in project implementation, their role does not need to remain limited to this role. Fact is that development finance institutions may be created by private-sector entities[213] and there is also no intrinsic reason as to why private-sector entities and other stakeholder should not be full members of IFIs.

It would serve no useful purpose to replicate the detailed discussion on this matter by this author.[214] As shown, it may have major positive effects if reputable private-sector entities which meet the highest standards of accountability and transparency become members or shareholders of IFIs.[215] The point which is stressed in this paper is that a paradigm shift is required which elevates participation of private-sector entities and other stakeholders to that of integral participants in the IFIs governance, funding and operational activities. As part of this paradigm shift, reputable export credit agencies (ECAs), reinsurance companies and similar entities should join forces with IFIs. Their full or partial membership in IFIs is an effective mechanism for enhancing the financial and risk-bearing capacity of IFIs and would allow them to expand their knowledge base and engage in new and advanced transactions.[216] It would be advisable for MDBs to consider amendments to their constituent agreements to fully exploit the positive aspects mentioned above. Pending, or as an alternative to such amendments, IFIs may enhance cooperation with reinsurances companies, export credit agencies and other stakeholders through secondary governance structures established under umbrella operational arrangements by the organization's governing bodies.[217]

Membership/shareholding of private-sector entities in IFIs may be of particular interest for borrower-owned development banks, such as some of the sub-regional development banks in Africa. These often have members with relatively lower credit ratings and therefore only credit ratings that are many notches below the AAA ratings of the MDBs. Opening membership of private-sector entities has the potential to increase substantially the equity of a borrower-dominated IFI. As the total adjusted capital is the "main capital measure for calculating RAC [risk adjusted capital] ratios",[218] an increase in equity may have a positive effect on the rating of an institution as indicted above. Effectively, such positive implications may not only apply in those cases where the institution does not pay a dividend but in certain circumstances also

213 This is epitomized recently by J.P. Morgan which uses IFC's Anticipated Impact Measurement & Monitoring (AIMM) framework, to perform an ex-ante assessment of J.P. Morgan's Corporate and Investment Banking (CIB) transactions. See J.P. Morgan. Development Finance Institution and J.P. Morgan. Methodology.

214 Droesse 2020.

215 Droesse 2020, 160–168.

216 Droesse 2020, 160–168.

217 Droesse 2020, 375; Droesse 2011c, 164–165 and Droesse 2011d, 297.

218 S&P Global Ratings (2018b), 4.

if a dividend is paid. Humphrey has shown in his analysis of the "Trade and Development Bank", which is a borrower-led African institution, that adding traditional equity investors in the ownership mix and offering them an actual financial return on their investment may be a "creative way of working to overcome the financial challenges posed by a borrower-led MDB in Africa".[219] Similar schemes might also be explored in other borrower-dominated development banks.

Unfortunately, the strong bias of rating agencies against membership of private-sector entities in IFIs entails serious constraints for involving non-state actors in the governance of IFIs. Such constraints are neither necessary nor are they justified. It appears that rating agencies are even more conservative than lawyers. While also lawyers used to focus exclusively on international and intergovernmental organizations established by a treaty, it is increasingly recognized in the legal community that new types of international organizations *sui generis* without a treaty foundation have emerged. It appears that among rating agencies such a recognition is still overdue and outstanding.

This is underlined by the focus of rating agencies on "supranational institutions" with a treaty basis[220] and their "Assessment of the Components of Policy Importance".[221] Furthermore, their conclusion that an MLI is expected not to be able to fulfil its public policy mandate if a large part of its activities is fulfilled by private entities, is intrinsically flawed.

It would be desirable for rating agencies to recognize that membership of private-sector entities in international financial institutions is not to be penalized *per se* but may strengthen not only the capital basis of the institution but also desired outcomes. Even in those cases where private-sector entities are admitted as members and most or all operational activities of an entity are

219 Humphrey (2019), 176 and 177.

220 Supranational institutions are defined "as those owned or established by governments of two or more countries. They are usually established by international treaties to pursue specified policy objectives and are generally not subject to commercial law. Multilateral lending institutions (MLIs) are a subset of this asset class. MLIs are usually established to promote economic development in their less-developed or regional member countries, facilitate regional integration, or expand cross-border trade". S&P, is of the opinion that, "the participation of private shareholders in an MLI's capital structure may also dilute its public policy role and affect its governance" because the goals of private and public shareholders may conflict, particularly in periods of stress. See: S&P Global, Supranationals: Special Edition 2020b, para 50.

221 Private-sector participation is classified in five categories from very strong to weak. In the latter category where a large part of the MLI's activity is fulfilled by private entities, the "MLI is expected not to be able in the future to fulfil its public policy mandate through the credit cycle." S&P Global 2020b, 51.

conducted by or through private-sector entities, a dilution of the public policy role of an IFI can be precluded through a variety of measures. This can be done *inter alia* by offering private-sector entities different categories of shares, by reserving decision-making in the plenary body of the organization to states only, by limiting private-sector representation in governing bodies of restricted membership, and by providing for qualified majorities, quorum requirements or voting rights which assure that all major decisions need to be approved by states. Where such measures are in place and the capitalization of the IFI is adequate, private-sector participation should not preclude a high credit rating, including a AAA-rating. In this context, it may give some hope that rating agencies have given CAF an A+ rating despite the fact that Series "B" shares of CAF can be subscribed inter alia by "private entities of Member Countries" and Series "C" shares may be subscribed "by legal entities or natural persons from outside the Member Countries".[222]

8.3 *Preferred Creditor Treatment*

Currently, MDBs and other IFIs benefit from a market practice known as Preferred Creditor Treatment (PCT). PCT "of the main IFIs is a longstanding puzzle in relation to sovereign lending".[223] It refers to the fact that sovereign borrowers typically continue to service their loans from MDBs even in the unlikely event that they default on other claims. This confers on the loans of MDBs a type of *de facto* seniority.

The justification for a continued preferred creditor status of MDBs, i.e., whether MDBs should legally be entitled to be given priority among individual creditors or classes of creditors in relation to the settlement of external debt, is currently being discussed. As shown by Martha, "general international law contains no compulsory standard of conduct requiring the preferential treatment of any external creditor".[224] Despite the lack of a strong backing for this principle in either general international law or constituent agreements of international organizations, great importance is attached to this principle by MDBs. While the principle of preferred creditor status goes back to the League of Nations, "the modern use of the term for MDBs, alternatively termed international financial institutions (IFIs) or multilateral lending institutions (MLIs), stems from the Paris Club renegotiations treatment of sovereign debt obligations to IFIs as exempt from rescheduling or default".[225]

222 See Art. I.
223 Cordella and Powel 2019a, 4.
224 Martha 1990, 825.
225 Kotecha 2019, 274.

The rationale for the preferred creditor treatment is often seen in the fact that the bylaws of IFIs:

> allow them to commit to (i) lend limited amounts at close to the risk-free rate under most circumstances, and (II) refrain from lending until any unpaid arrears are cleared. This avoids the possibility of debt dilution, sets IFI lending aside from private lenders, and explains why, in many instances, the presence of IFIs adds value.[226]

The PCT[227] has been called in question in some cases (e.g., when Greece fell into arrears with the IMF in July 2015)[228] and is strongly criticized in the literature by some authors.[229] Nevertheless, rating agencies have stressed the importance which this principle has for them and have clarified that an erosion of PCT could lead to lower rating of MLIs.[230]

All three rating agencies allow an uplift of the average borrower credit rating of MLIs based on their PCT for their sovereign operations. In the case of the IADB, "S&P reduces its estimate of the IDB's risk weighted assets (and hence of the capital it must hold to achieve a given standalone credit standing) for this purpose by 10 percent".[231] Hence, for the sovereign operations of MLIs, the PCT has important implications for their credit ratings and by implication for the terms on which they can borrow on capital markets[232] and which they charge

226 Cordella and Powell 2019a, 2.

227 Standards and Poor's Rating Services 2013, 1–8. As indicated by S&P.
"PCT status means that:
– MLIs have historically been exempt from participating in sovereign debt rescheduling coordinated by the Paris Club of bilateral creditors, while commercial lenders have generally not been exempt (under the principle of "comparability of treatment"); and
– When sovereigns do default to MLIs, these defaults are usually cured before commercial debt arrears because such clearance is usually a condition of resumed access to funding from the International Monetary Fund (IMF) and other MLIs". S&P Global Ratings 2018b, para 29.

228 Cordella 2019b, Paper 8941, 1.

229 Ibid.

230 Standards and Poor's Rating Services 2013.

231 Perraudin W, Powell A and Yang P 2016, 5.

232 S&P state in this context: "If sovereign borrowers' greater willingness to service their MLI debt were to lessen in the future, that potential change in the priority of payment could affect MLI ratings through different channels. [....] In distress, even if the MLI debt is current, our assessment of sovereign risk would be higher, implying, all else being equal, lower RAC ratios because the risk weightings charged to the MLI assets increase as the ratings decline. [....] These steps would reduce earnings and, with them, the MLI's capacity to generate capital internally, also potentially influencing our assessment of MLI capital adequacy". Standard and Poor's Rating Services 2013, 4.

to their borrowers. These are important reasons why PCT should be applied in the case of sovereign lending of IFIs.

A related but different question is whether MDBs and other IFIs should also be able to assert preferred creditor status in relation to their private sector operations with regard to access to foreign currency.

IFC managed to avail itself of that limited PCT regarding access to currencies,[233] consistent with Art. VI, Section 6 of the IFC Articles of Agreement which provides for the freedom of IFC assets from restrictions. Similar provisions are contained in the constituent agreements of other MDBs.

Nevertheless, from a policy-point of view it is questionable whether the limited PCT mentioned above is still justified. First, the need for such limited PCT may be questioned, as Moody's has concluded that both deposit freezes and private-sector external debt moratoriums which remain "the two quintessential forms of transfer and convertibility risk", both remain less frequent than sovereign defaults.[234] Second, unlike for sovereign operations, the more limited PCT for access to currencies which MDBs and other IFIs enjoy in relation to their private-sector operations is generally not taken into consideration for their credit rating.[235] Third, the question arises whether it is justified to give MDBs a general preference as regards access to currencies over other senior lenders. MDBs effectively have dispensed with that limited PCT in certain cases at their own volition, as it made collaboration with other senior lenders impossible or very difficult. As they have concluded deals with lenders like the US Exim which give these *pari passu* treatments,[236] it may be questioned whether it is still justified that MDBs claim in their private-sector operations preference as regards access to currencies over other lenders.

Furthermore, as will be discussed in further detail below, MDBs exchanged their foreign exchange exposures to avoid the penalty applied by MDBs for

233 In this regard, IFC states on its website: "As a multilateral development institution, IFC enjoys a de facto Preferred Creditor Status. This means that member governments grant IFC loans preferential access to foreign currency in the event of a country foreign exchange crisis. The Preferred Creditor Status therefore mitigates transfer and convertibility risk for IFC and its B Loan participants.

As is the case for the World Bank and other multilateral development institutions, Preferred Creditor Status is not a legal status, but is embodied in practice, and is granted by the shareholders of IFC (over 180 member governments). The Preferred Creditor Status of IFC has received consistent universal recognition from entities such as bank regulators, the Bank of International Settlement, rating agencies, and private PRI providers". See IFC Preferred Creditor Status".

234 Moody's 2020b, 1.

235 S&P state in relation to IFC.

236 Cohen 2020, 1–6.

portfolio concentration.[237] While by engaging in advanced financial engineering, they managed to increase the headroom for their operational activities, MDBs have opened in doing so a range of other issues relating, in particular, to the applicability of PCT to the exchanged exposures. In the absence of a firm legal basis, the ability of MDBs and other IFIs to assert PCT and ensure repayment of their loans is largely based on their relationship with their members. As will be further discussed below, there is a risk that in their attempt to avoid the penalty for credit concentration, MDBs may have overstretched their position and have weakened the acceptance of the PCT system.

IFIs "should be wary about the amounts they lend" as large "packages funded from IFI balance sheets lent to countries that do not have the incentives to repay may well end in failure".[238] Cordella and Powell discuss whether there are limits to the amounts for which MDBs can claim preferred creditor status relating to the total amounts lent to a country.[239] However, the question should better be addressed in the overall context of the share of a country's foreign debt which an MDB or other IFI holds. If an MDB would hold most of a country's foreign debt, it is difficult to argue that the MDB should enjoy PCT in respect of that debt. How can MDBs claim PCT if the most part of a country's foreign debt is senior?

As shown above, PCT does not have a firm legal basis and is, in essence, guaranteed as a market practice. Hence, it would be advisable for MDBs to exercise constraint in claiming PCT, particularly, in "expanding preferred creditor treatment beyond [their] own resources".[240] There is a risk that by overreaching their position (e.g., through the exchange of their foreign exposures), MDBs may potentially undermine the PCT system, with potentially far-reaching implications.

8.4 *Debt Relief or Debt Suspension Initiatives*

Finally, the question whether MDBs and other IFIs should participate in debt-relief initiatives has been discussed for a long time and has been raised in the context of the Heavily Indebted Poor Countries (HIPC) Initiative[241] and the Multilateral Debt Relief Initiative (MDRI).[242] These generally did not involve

237 S&P Global Ratings 2019, 3.
238 Cordella and Powell 2019a.
239 Ibid. See also Cordella and Powell 2019b.
240 Cordella and Powell 2019a.
241 IMF 2021, 1.
242 IMF 2017.

debt-relief granted by MDBs and other IFIs.[243] As the HIPIC Initiative and MDRI are extensively documented in the literature, in the context of this study only reference is made to the recent G20's Debt Service Suspension Initiative (DSSI) proposed in 2020 and the "G20 Common Framework for Debt Treatments beyond the DSSI" adopted in 2021.

While debt levels were high before the crisis, the COVID 19 pandemic "is pushing debt levels to new heights […] as countries seek to mitigate the health and economic effects of the crisis, while revenues are falling due to lower growth and trade, together raising debt burdens".[244]

The DSSI was launched in the context of the COVID 19 pandemic which resulted in a global economic collapse. It meant that bilateral official creditors were, "during a limited period, suspending debt service payments from the poorest countries (73 low- and lower middle-income countries) that requested the suspension".[245] It temporarily eased the financing constraints for these countries and helped address immediate liquidity needs but did not mean that existing debt sustainability problems in some of these countries would be resolved.[246]

The G20 initially "urged" MDBs to participate in the DSSI which offers "a temporary suspension of 'official sector' or government-to-government debt payments to 73 countries".[247] However, this was not pursued due to the opposition of rating agencies.[248]

243 However, a different approach was adopted in the case of ADB as the cost of debt relief to Afghanistan was funded from ADF resources. An amendment to the ADF Loan Regulations was required for this purpose. "Written consent from every ADF donor [was] obtained for the amendment of the ADF Regulations to allow the use of ADF resources (except the set-aside resources) for debt relief". ADB 2008, 9 (para. 29).

244 IMF 2021, 1–29.

245 Ibid.

246 Ibid.

247 The Action Plan adopted at the virtual G20 Meeting of 15 April 2020 asked "multilateral development banks to further explore the options for the suspension of debt service payments over the suspension period, while maintaining their current rating and low cost of funding". It called on the MDBs for "a swift implementation of the emergency response packages adopted by the World Bank and Regional Development Banks" amounting to over USD 200 billion and for a discussion on "the role of MDBs after the pandemic crisis, as they will have a key role to play to facilitate the recovery from the crisis and restore strong, sustainable, balanced and inclusive growth for developing countries". As reported by Reuters, the President of the World Bank said that "the Bank, the IMF and other multilateral lenders were exploring options for suspending their debt service payments while maintaining high crediting ratings on their bonds". See G20 2015.

248 Fitch have made it clear what the consequences of such a course of action would be. As reported by Boomberg: "Fitch Ratings warned that multilateral development banks could see their credit ratings suffer if they let the poorest nations suspend sovereign debt

Hence, MDBs did not participate in the DSSI. Instead, they increased their financing, including concessional financing, to DSSI-eligible countries. As indicated by the World Bank, from "April 2020 through June 2021, the World Bank committed USD 36.3 billion in financing for countries participating in the G-20 Debt Service Suspension Initiative (DSSI) – of which USD 11.8 billion was in the form of grants" and "disbursed USD 20.9 billion – including USD 5.6 billion in grants – to these countries. The total disbursement amount is roughly seven times the USD 3 billion in debt-service repayments received from DSSI countries".[249] Those resources were made available to enable the poorest countries to meet their obligations, including the payments which were due to the MDBs.

The "Common Framework for Debt Treatments beyond the DSSI" jointly endorsed in November 2020 by the G20 and Paris Club is an "an agreement of the G20 and Paris Club countries to coordinate and cooperate on debt treatments for up to 73 low-income countries that are eligible for the Debt Service Suspension Initiative (DSSI)". A detailed analysis of the Common Framework has been provided by Fitch.[250] As for the DSSI, the IMF and other IFIs were exempted from participating in the common framework. However, the IMF and World Bank were given in October 2020 a mandate by the Development Committee to "review the debt challenges of low-income countries and propose actions to address their fiscal and debt stress on a case-by-case basis and were encouraged to explore customized solutions for middle-income countries as well".[251]

Overall, the debt situation of many developing countries has deteriorated during the COVID-19 pandemic, and it is quite doubtful whether they will be able to repay their MDB and IFI debt. Also, it cannot be a sustainable solution in the long run that MDBs expand their lending to allow countries in debt-distress to service their own loans. Thus, it appears quite likely that there will be a renewed demand for restructuring of MDB and IFI debt in the future, possibly using similar approaches as under the HIPC Initiative and MDRI. The big question in this regard relates to the extent to which states will be prepared to allocate new and additional funds for that purpose.

payments, a move that governments from the world's biggest economies have urged them to explore. A reprieve of more than six months would lead Fitch to classify a development bank's full exposure as impaired and undercut preferred creditor status" and "also would increase the banks' credit risk and hurt their cash flow and liquidity [....]". See Martin 2020.

249 World Bank 2021b.

250 FitchRatings 2021b, 3.

251 Development Committee Communiqué 2020, 1.

9 New Funding Mechanisms

9.1 *Constraints of Current Funding Mechanisms*

The current market-based funding structures of MDBs and other IFIs are intrinsically constrained in two respects.

First, the international community "is pushing MDBs to do more to achieve international goals – filling the yawning infrastructure gap, improving social services and addressing global problems such as climate change, migration and pandemic disease", but unfortunately "the generosity of MDB member countries has not matched these ambitious goals".[252] Against this background, and giving the financial constraints of states in providing a major infusion of paid-in capital to MDBs for substantially extending the scope of their operations, other options for increasing the headroom of IFIs are being considered.

Second, it is a significant constraint for the effectiveness of MDBs and other IFIs that they still rely predominantly or exclusively on funding from their member states. They often have not even made an effort to attract substantial funding from sources other than their members. One of the reasons for this is that for attracting funding from outside resources, IFIs and Funds often need to implement substantial changes to their rules, procedures and practices. As doing so may be a painful process, MDBs and other IFIs tend to remain within their comfort zone.

9.2 *New Mechanisms for Increasing Headroom*

To increase headroom and availability of resources, various new mechanisms have been created. These relate, inter alia, to (I) synthetic securitization[253] (II) exposure exchange agreements, and (III) subordinated, hybrid capital.

9.2.1 Synthetic Securitization

The Room2Run may be seen as an interesting example in this category. It was the "first-ever synthetic portfolio securitization between a multilateral development bank (MDB) and private sector investors, pioneering the use of securitization and credit risk transfer technology in a new segment of the financial markets".[254] The transaction, which received a PRI [Principles of Responsible

252 Humphrey 2018.

253 On the difference between synthetic and true-sale securitization, see Orçun 2017.

254 Africa50. Room2Run Synthetic Securitization.

Investments] Award for 2019 shifted the "mezzanine risk on a USD 1bn portfolio of pan-African loans to private investors".[255]

In essence, the "deal functions like an insurance policy provided by investors on a chunk of AfDB loans", freeing up "space for the AfDB to make USD 650 million more in loans, without requiring further capital from shareholders".[256] In this context, Humphrey discusses various mechanisms for scaling up similar mechanisms for use by MDBs.[257] The potential of further amplifying approaches as mentioned above needs to be explored.

9.2.2 Exchange of Foreign Exposures

In addition, MDBs have started engaging in advanced financial engineering by exchanging their sovereign exposures. As the other initiatives aimed at a so-called "optimization" of MDBs' balance sheets, also this initiative was triggered by the G20.[258]

This tool was presented in 2015 by the World Bank as an "innovative framework agreement for an exchange of sovereign exposures that will collectively optimize their balance sheets for greater development effectiveness".[259] The President of the World Bank stated that this "innovative agreement" improved

255 "By absorbing losses on the mezzanine tranche of the portfolio, the transaction [reduced] the risk weight on the bank-retained senior portion of the structure, and hence the risk capital that the bank must hold. AfDB is then able to recycle this released capital, enabling D 650 million of new development lending in Africa". See PRI Awards 2019 case study: Room2Run 2019, 7–32.

256 Humphrey 2018.

257 Humphrey stresses that this type of synthetic securitization "differs from the sorts of securitizations that helped cause the financial crisis in important ways. Most notably, the loans themselves stay on the books of the AfDB – hence the AfDB has every incentive to ensure they are good projects and to engage in strong oversight. By contrast, commercial banks prior to the global crisis could actually sell off loans (like mortgages) to an investor and get rid of them entirely – hence they had little incentive to ensure those loans were high quality". See Humphrey 2018.

258 G20 2015.

259 It was indicated in this context: "The sovereign exposure exchange agreement is a risk management tool collaboratively developed by the major Multilateral Development Banks (MDBs). This initiative was launched in October 2013 by the World Bank Group's International Bank for Reconstruction and Development (IBRD) and endorsed by the MDB heads following a meeting of the G8 Ministers of Finance. Unlike commercial financial institutions, which diversify their loan portfolio across thousands, and sometimes millions, of borrowers, the MDBs lend to their sovereign shareholders. The resulting asset concentration reflects the strength of the relationship between MDBs and their borrowers, but it also requires MDBs to hold additional capital". See World Bank, Press Release: Development Banks Working Together to Optimize Balance Sheets 2015, 1.

collective financial capacity and development effectiveness.[260] Furthermore, also ADB offered similar explanations when introducing in 2020 a framework for exposure exchanges by exchanging on a pilot basis four country exposures.[261] It stated that exposure exchange is "a powerful and cost-effective way to improve the capital adequacy and creditworthiness of regional MDBs, whose portfolio diversification options can be otherwise limited".[262]

As MDBs "may have to extend large amounts of financing to a country or a private entity in difficulty" and "therefore generally have high levels of single counterparty concentration, especially compared to commercial banks", to a certain extent, concentration risk is a corollary of the "public interest mission".[263] "Concentration risk arises from an uneven distribution of loans to countries (single-name concentration) or through an unbalanced allocation of loans by region (regional concentration)".[264] Both single-name concentration and regional concentration may entail substantial risks and are therefore considered by rating agencies, such as S&P, according to their "Risk-Adjusted Capital Framework Methodology".[265]

To avoid the penalties for concentration risk applied to MDBs,[266] various MDBs consider that "[e]xchanging exposures provides an opportunity when two or more MDBs face different country concentrations; MDBs can reduce concentration risk by swapping exposures among themselves and thus rebalancing their portfolios".[267]

260 Ibid.

261 ADB 2020.

262 Ibid.

263 FitchRatings, 2020a.

264 Belhaj 2016, 79.

265 S&P 2020b.

266 The penalties which are applied by MDBs on that account are set out by Moody's in their score cards and are illustrated as follows: "For example, we may assign a score of Baa to a supranational institution whose development asset portfolio primarily consists of exposure to sovereigns that have strong credit quality (i.e., low A equivalent, incorporating preferred creditor status and credit protections) but with concentration risk that is characteristic of the Ba scoring category". See Moody's 2020a, 9.

267 They further indicated in this context: "Reducing concentration risk releases capital that can either be used to improve capital adequacy or support additional lending. An MDB EEA can have a similar impact on lending headroom as a capital increase, although in the case of the MDB EEA additional lending headroom is created by freeing up existing capital through balance sheet optimization, rather than through an injection of fresh capital". See Belhaj 2016, 80. A series of simulations have been conducted to demonstrate their approach (Ibid, 80–82.).

The Exposure Exchange Agreements (EEAs) between MDBs seek to achieve "a synthetic exchange of a portfolio of credit exposures".[268] Under the EEA, the "portfolios of exposures exchanged in the EEA between any two MDBs are equal in notional dollar values and in risk-weighted amounts at the time of the initial exchange".[269] "When the loans of a borrowing country included in an EEA transaction are placed in non-accrual status, the Provider of Protection on that exposure is obligated to compensate the Originating MDB under the EEA".[270] "Following a non-accrual event, the Provider of Protection would pay compensation to the Originating MDB for lost interest based on the EEA interest rate, which for the first EEAs has been defined as the sum of six-month Libor plus 75 basis points".[271]

While schemes as mentioned above have the potential of adding additional headroom for lending, they raise a number of fundamental issues.

First, already now, MDBs have in some cases imprudent and unsustainable single-name and regional concentration levels. The move of MDBs to advanced financial engineering by exchanging their foreign exposures is likely to aggravate this situation.

Second, a number of MDBs have explicit provisions in their constituent agreements to the effect that all their resources need to be used for the development of the developing member countries in their region.[272] As the Buyer of Protection remains under the EEA the lender of record, regional MDBs such as ADB will probably argue[273] that an exchange of foreign exposures is legitimate

---

268 "Under the EEA, there is a synthetic exchange of a portfolio of credit exposures of equivalent credit risk and dollar amount: one MDB assumes the credit risk on a portfolio of borrowing countries from another MDB in exchange for passing on the credit risk on a different portfolio of borrowing countries to the other MDB. In the event of a non-accrual event of one of the exchanged exposures, the MDB that has agreed to provide protection under the EEA (the Protection Provider) would compensate the Originating MDB for non-payment. There is no transfer or removal of loans from the Buyer of Protection's balance sheet: the Buyer of Protection remains the lender of record, and there is no impact on the borrower/lender relationship". Belhaj, 82.

269 Ibid., 83.

270 Ibid.

271 "If a non-accrual event on an underlying sovereign exposure in the EEA transaction occurs and has not been resolved by the end of the agreed EEA period, the Provider of Protection remains responsible for the payment of the compensation amount agreed under the EEA for that country exposure until a resolution of the non-accrual event takes place. This continued coverage, however, is limited to the country in non-accrual and does not automatically extend to the entire EEA portfolio". Ibid., 84.

272 E.g., ADB Charter 2001, Art. II.

273 Both ADB and IADB decided not to make available for review Board documents regarding the exchanges of foreign exposures concluded by them on a pilot basis.

for this reason and for the benefit of regional developing countries as it frees up capital for their development. Nevertheless, the fact remains that regional MDBs potentially will assume liabilities, even though on the basis of synthetic transactions, for billions of US dollars of debt from nonregional countries without having any control over such debt.

The third major issue relates to the implications of the scheme on the preferred creditor treatment. In this regard, it may be argued, as in relation to the exchange of four exposures between ADB and IADB approved on a pilot basis,[274] that the exchange will be "synthetic" in that it does not entail the actual transfer or removal of loans from either MDB's balance sheet and consequently does not change the relationship between the original lender and the borrower. Hence, the original lender will still be the point of reference for the PCT. Nevertheless, conceptually, any swap of foreign exposures, has implications for the relationship of MDBs and other IFIs with their members, which is crucial to the PCT. As any exchange of foreign exposures requires approval of the governing bodies of the organizations involved, it will most likely become known to borrowers that the original lender bought protection regarding their loan and will be compensated in the case of non-accrual status of that loan. In cases where a country is unable to service all its MDB loans, will this not have an influence on the decision of countries regarding the loans they want to service? Hence, the question may be asked whether exchange-of-exposure-schemes as mentioned above may have the potential of undermining the PCT system, which, as such, does not have a firm legal basis.

Fourth, in connection with the above, the question arises regarding the implications of an exposure-exchange scheme in case of another major global financial crisis where potentially a number of countries may not be able to service their MDB loans. The last global financial crisis has shown the far-reaching implications which advanced financial engineering may have and such implications should also be carefully evaluated in relation to the foreign exposure exchange scheme.

9.2.3 Subordinated Hybrid Capital

It is a very important development that rating agencies have accepted subordinated (hybrid) capital instruments to be included in the calculation of total adjusted capital of IFIs. To qualify for such inclusion, "a hybrid instrument must be able to absorb losses, demonstrate an ability to do so over time, and provide additional protection to the MLI's senior creditors while the MLI

274 ADB 2020.

remains current on its obligations toward them".[275] Moody's has well explained its "general approach to assigning equity credit for hybrid instruments (including shareholder loans) issued by non-banks". Where hybrid instruments are material and Moody's considers them relevant, Moody's "assigns equity credit and makes related financial statement adjustments".[276] Its "methodology applies to convertible and non-convertible hybrids issued by insurance companies finance companies, securities industry market makers, securities industry service providers, asset managers and non-financial corporations globally".[277] In assessing the amount of equity credit, Moody's considers in particular "whether the hybrid will be available to absorb losses when needed, which relates to its maturity" and, in this context, "the timing of the hybrid's redemption, the replacement security's features, and the expected evolution of the issuer's capital position over time".[278] Up to 100% of the subordinated debt may be recognized as equity. "Examples of hybrid instruments that may qualify for equity credit include redeemable shares where the MDB retains significant control over the ability to redeem and over the timing of any redemption; and subordinated debt facilities that would qualify for equity credit under [Moody's] cross-sector methodology".[279]

The issuance of subordinated, hybrid debt may give MDBs new opportunities to increase their capital. The question may be asked whether the pricing of subordinated (hybrid) debt may be an inherent constraint to the implementation of such a scheme as hybrids generally "are high-yielding because they are subordinated debt instruments whose rating is on average 2–3 notches lower than the same issuers' senior debt".[280] While these additional costs may have to be passed on to the borrowers of MDBs, this funding cost potentially might be blended with that from other sources of funding of MDBs. Moreover, it is conceivable that there may be entities that are prepared to take a position in subordinated, hybrid debt even without the higher yield of such debt due to its subordination to other senior debt. Subordinated hybrids issued by MDBs may offer private-sector or even civil society investors a less risky means of "social" or "activist" investing in areas such as the environment/climate change, green technologies, development of micro/small and medium-size enterprises, health innovation, among others. The "markets" for development-related

275 S&P Global, Supranationals Special Edition 2020, 56 (para. 66).
276 Moody's 2018, 1.
277 Ibid. 3.
278 Ibid.
279 Moody's Investors Service 2020a, 7.
280 Trigo 2019. 10 Questions to Understand Corporate Hybrid Bonds. BNP Paribas.

investing are diversifying, reflecting a wider spectrum of combinations of public and private goods and services and an attendant diversity in relevant financial models/structures. Hence, potentially a new market might be emerging for subordinated, hybrid debt. In this context, uniform pricing of MDB subordinated, hybrid debt and MDB lending may be less meaningful. Thus, pricing would not necessarily preclude a scheme as indicated above.

The biggest advantage of issuing subordinated, hybrid debt relates to the diversification of the equity base of MDBs. This mechanism is fundamentally different from those applicable in the case of increases of authorized capital in three respects. First, it does not require MDBs and IFIs to go through the excruciatingly difficult and extended process of negotiation with their members regarding increases of authorized capital. Second, it does not require a capital infusion of member states. Third, it does not entail changes to relative shareholdings of members, which are a common feature not only in the case for special (selective) capital increases which are expressly designed to change members relative shareholdings and voting rights, but also in case of general capital increases (in the latter case, all members have the opportunity to subscribe to a proportionate part of the capital increase, but some may not be able to do so for financial or other reasons, which decreases their relative shareholdings and corresponding voting rights). This makes them attractive to members as smart mechanisms for mobilizing capital, but it also makes IFIs less dependent on the whims of their member states in providing capital increases. However, it is precisely for this reason that mechanisms as those mentioned above are likely to be viewed critically at least by some states[281] which view capital increases as golden opportunities to extract concessions and impose conditionalities on MLIs. As the increased independence, which this new funding mechanism entails, reduces the leverage of states in making the infusion of new capital conditional on substantial changes to policies of MDBs and other IFIs, it is likely to be opposed for that very reason.

281 The position of the Trump Administration may serve as an example. As indicated by Hay, J. Global Capital; London (Jan 10, 2019): “Hopes of a thriving new market for securitizations by multilateral development banks hit a hole in the road in December, when the US Treasury said it disapproved of them and would seek to stop them”. It was stated that the US would seek, as part of its reform agenda for the MDBs, to “reverse the trend toward complex and expensive derivatives, the securitization of assets, and exposure swaps that circumvent governance”.

9.3 *Institutional and Financial Transformation of IFIs*

There are three ways how IFIs may be transformed into multi-stakeholder institutions. The first one is to allow non-state actors to become members or shareholders of IFIs. In that case, representation of non-state actors in the governing bodies of the IFI is a corollary of their membership, respectively, their shareholdings. Second, in those cases where membership is limited to states (and, possibly, international organizations), it is possible to define representation arrangements which give a voice to non-state actors. Third, it is possible to introduce multi-stakeholder features for international organizations by putting in place secondary governance structures. As has been shown above, in either case it is possible to ensure that membership of non-state actors does not dilute the policy mandate of the institution.

While transforming international organizations, including IFIs, into multi-stakeholder institutions may involve substantial benefits, such course of action is indispensable, in particular, for institutions or funds seeking to facilitate the transition of countries to a green economy. In that case, required resources are so high that they can never be financed through traditional public-sector funding mechanisms.[282] Indeed, in the case of the transition of countries to a green economy, innovative ideas are more important than money and active involvement with a wide range of stakeholders is of crucial importance. Hence, to be effective, any institution or fund seeking to facilitate the transition of countries to a green economy needs to be structured as a multi-stakeholder institution. Given the reduction of the cost of renewables, it is overall possible to mobilize resources for that purpose by offering bankable projects to the private-sector, institutional investors and other stakeholders for investments in the green economy.

The situation is similar for institutions seeking to facilitate investments in the Fourth Industrial Revolution and scaling 4IR technologies (artificial intelligence, robotics, the Internet of Things, autonomous vehicles, 3-D printing, nanotechnology, biotechnology, materials science, energy storage, and quantum computing).[283]

---

282 At the 2021 World Economic Forum, the green transition was discussed as an "D 50-trillion investment opportunity." (DW 2021) IRENA has shown that until 2050 for energy transition alone an investment worth D 131 trillion (D 4.4 trillion a year) in is required, notably for substantially increasing the share of renewables in the global energy mix. However, it was indicated in this context that the "sources of funds are not the problem per se, given that ESG (environmental, social and corporate governance) is the fastest-growing asset class and that several pandemic stimulus packages have a strong green focus". See Arab News 2021.

283 Schwab 2016, 1.

Moreover, new approaches are also required for filling the huge financing gap in basic infrastructure in emerging and developing countries (EMDCs) "of the order of USD 1 trillion per year between now and 2030".[284] This is another area where required investments are so large that they can never be met by public funds.

MDBs and IFIs can mobilize additional resources by maximizing the availability of internal resources. This might involve a review of IFIs policy-based lending and the question to what extent MDBs should effectively provide general budget support to their member countries even though they were not designed to provide such support. It may involve a review of the maturities of MDB loans and may imply that MDBs shift their activities to a greater extent to trade financing and other transactional profiles with shorter maturities. However, the core issue is that for the transition to a green economy, facilitating 4IR, filling the huge infrastructure gap and other related matters, main resources need to come from the private sector and institutional investors. This has implications for institutional frameworks for MDBs facilitating such pursuits as they need to give the private sector and institutional investors a voice in decision-making. Moreover, it will entail dramatic changes for the role and the operational modalities of MDBs and IFIs. Rather than loans with up to 20 years of maturity, short-term-bridge financing and seed-financing, as well as venture capital and innovation hubs will be of prime importance. Moreover, rather than from MDBs and other IFIs, the main funding for pursuits as mentioned above will come from the private-sector and institutional investors.

While trillions of USD are required for these purposes, the money *per se* is not the problem as IRENA has recognized when it showed for energy transition alone an investment worth USD 131 trillion is required until 2050. The situation is similar as regards filling the infrastructure gap. "Private investors – notably the roughly USD 100 trillion in institutional investor resources– would be able to help fill this gap, as infrastructure assets offer the kind of opportunities these investors seek".[285] The very magnitude of the required investments requires for MDBs new funding mechanisms,[286] including mechanisms as described below that are not linked to the capital base of MDBs.

---

284 Humphrey 2018, 7.

285 Ibid.,7.

286 Humphrey discusses for filling the infrastructure financing gap arrangements relating to projects bonds, securitization of infrastructure debt, MDB syndication arrangements and other related arrangements. Ibid. 14–29.

9.4 *Sponsoring Mechanisms Not Linked to Capital*

Given the fact that the paid-in capital ratios of MDBs are unlikely to increase substantially, it is necessary to explore new funding mechanisms not linked to the subscribed paid-in and callable capital of MDB members and the headroom for their operational activities.

MIGA is interesting in this context as it is funded through a combination of subscribed capital and sponsorship. While it was initially envisaged to fund MIGA entirely through sponsorship arrangements, such arrangements play now only an important supplementary role. As indicated by Shihata, "even if the applicable limit of MIGA's guarantee capacity is reached, the Agency will still be able to underwrite investments sponsored by member countries under the additional 'Sponsorship Trust Fund' facility".[287]

Similar sponsoring schemes could also be implemented by other MDBs. While in MIGA the sponsoring schemes are mostly used for high-risk activities to avoid that these become a burden for the balance sheet of MIGA, similar schemes might be given a wider application.

The Report of the G20 Eminent Expert Group on Global Financial Governance proposed multiplying "private capital by adopting system-wide approaches to risk insurance and securitization"[288] and to develop "system-wide political risk insurance and expand the use of private reinsurance markets".[289]

The Group also suggested that the "MDBs should, as a system, leverage on MIGA as a global risk insurer in development finance" and build on "MIGA's existing risk insurance capabilities to take on risk from the MDB system as a whole, and achieve the benefits of scale and a globally diversified portfolio".[290]

While the substantive proposals of the Eminent Expert Group deserve full support, it may be questioned whether it would be advisable to create a monopoly for risk related matters in MIGA. As an alternative, it might be considered to

287 Shihata 1988, 149. As stated in the Commentary to the MIGA Convention: The mechanics of sponsorship are as follows: A member proposing to the Agency the guarantee of an investment will incur a loss-sharing contingent obligation in the amount of the guarantee sponsored by it. Premiums and other revenues attributable to sponsored guarantees will be accumulated in a separate trust fund called the Sponsorship Trust Fund. The administrative expenses and payments on claims related to sponsored investments would be paid out of this Fund. After depletion of the Fund, any loss incurred on a sponsored guarantee would be shared by all sponsoring members" in proportion to the sponsored amount. See MIGA Commentary on the Convention: Establishing the Multilateral Investment Guarantee Agency 2010, 22–23.

288 Global Financial Governance: Report of the G20 Eminent Persons Group on Global Financial Governance 2018, 17.

289 Ibid, 39.g.

290 Ibid.

mainstream reinsurance and other risk-related activities in all MDBs through institutionalized cooperation (involving full or partial membership) with reinsurance companies and other stakeholders as proposed above. In the view of this author, this would be a much better option.

9.5 *Other Mechanisms*

In the case of MIGA's sponsoring arrangements, MIGA acts as the administrator of the sponsored funds. However, it is not necessary for MDBs and IFIs to assume such a role. There are a number of other innovative mechanisms which they can adopt which are not linked to their capital base.

Girishankar states that "four types of innovative mechanisms (private and solidarity mechanisms, public-private partnerships and catalytic mechanisms) make up the international landscape".[291] As shown by him, there are a flurry of proposals and ideas for each of these mechanisms, but his proposal requires elaboration regarding the question on how to create synergies between different mechanisms (in particular, between private mechanisms and the other three mechanisms that rely on public funding). Moreover, funding is not the only issue. There are a range of other matters where the availability of resources is not the problem as such and where ideas are more important than money. As shown, this relates, in particular, to the transition to a green economy and support to 4IR.

In this context, in the literature a range of "development-oriented instruments" is being discussed and interesting examples are given where such instruments have been implemented[292] and for a range of "commercially-oriented public instruments".[293] MDBs should explore options regarding such mechanisms to supplement their regular financial instruments, including mechanisms which are not dependent on their capitalization and the paid-in capital of their members. In doing so, they can charge fees for their services (e.g., on similar terms as MIGA in the context of sponsoring arrangements) and they can use such new mechanisms in connection with their regular

---

291 "Private mechanisms involve private-to-private flows in the market and in civil society. Solidarity mechanisms support sovereign-to-sovereign transfers and form the backbone of multilateral and bilateral ODA and other official flows (OOF). Public-private partnership (PPP) mechanisms leverage or mobilize private finance in support of public service delivery and other public functions, such as sovereign risk management. Catalytic mechanisms involve public support for creating and developing private markets (inter alia by reducing risks of private entry)". Girishankar, (I).

292 Große Puppendahl, Byiers and Bilal, 14–31.

293 Ibid.

market-based and concessional modalities of financing to upscale or supplement their regular modalities of financing and their activities.

While it is not possible to analyze the aforementioned instruments in any detail, specific reference to matchmaking mechanisms needs to be made as there are many instances where such mechanisms can be used.[294] MLIs should explore the full potential of such mechanisms which are particularly important because (i) major resources can be mobilized through such mechanisms (e.g., for undertakings such as the transition of countries to a green economy), and (II) the operational expenditures of such mechanisms can entirely be funded by the private sector and institutional investors.

Given the reduction of the price of renewables, investments in the green economy are viable on purely economic grounds. As financial resources are available, it may generally suffice if MDBs and other IFI facilitate investments in the green economy by matching the needs of states and public and private entities for funding with the interest of the private sector and institutional investors to invest in bankable projects regarding the transition to a green economy. Clearly, in some countries it will not be possible, however, to offer bankable project. In such cases, it may be possible to make projects bankable by including a first loss tranche or waterfall mechanism.[295]

The World Green Economy Organization in Dubai[296] has pioneered such a concept by organizing matchmaking meetings to which a great variety of stakeholders are invited. As the transition to a green economy involves a great variety of stakeholders, WGEO is organized as a fully-fledged multi-stakeholder institution. The activities of WGEO are implemented through entities participating in the seven platforms of WGEO.[297] While WGEO targets smaller projects in the range between 20 and 50 million USD and is still in the initial phase of its activities, the approach adopted by WGEO is conceptually sound and innovative. There is no reason why similar concepts should not work at a larger scale.

294 Ibid.

295 See Droesse 2011d, 248–249.

296 World Green Economy Organization (WGEO), https://worldgreeneconomy.org/, accessed 21 April 2022.

297 WGEO Platforms, https://worldgreeneconomy.org/platform-members/, accessed 21 April 2022.

10 Conclusion

As has been shown in this study, the organizational structures, institutional frameworks, and funding structures of IFIs and funds are intrinsically related. Whether different types of operations and financing are provided through institutions belonging to a group that are endowed with international legal personality and legal capacity under national law or under one legal personality by an organization administering different types of resources and providing different types of financing, has many legal implications for their governance structures, voting rights, and their funding mechanisms and operational modalities. As shown, special problems arise in the case of organizations which were not designed to leverage resources on capital markets against paid-in and callable capital. However, irrespective of their legal structures, IFIs need to respond to the same challenges. They need to find ways to maximize their impact by leveraging new resources and they need to find new ways to increase synergies between their various financing windows or the organizations forming an organizational group. To meet these objectives, they need to open themselves for participation by a wide range of stakeholders.

IFIs and export credit agencies, reinsurance companies and other stakeholders should join forces through coordination of their activities. An institutionalized participation of such and other stakeholders through full or partial membership would offer a very effective solution to achieve the above purpose. It would not only enhance the financial and risk-bearing capacity of IFIs but also their knowledge base and ability to engage in advanced transactions, in particular if it is accompanied through staff secondment and consultations at all levels.

The environment in which MDBs and other IFIs are operating is changing quickly and dramatically. The traditional financial intermediary model is intrinsically linked to the credit ratings of MDBs and other IFIs and their ability to leverage their capital base to mobilize resources on capital markets. However, states find it increasingly difficult to substantially increase their paid-in capital. The recognition of subordinated, hybrid debt offers in this context important new opportunities for MDBs and IFIs to expand and diversify their equity base. Also, securitization may offer opportunities for MDBs to free up resources. However, caution is required for MDBs to engage in advanced financial engineering or to further erode their paid-in capital ratios because in doing so they might lose their AAA-credit rating and undermine the financial strength in the long run.

The transition to a green economy and 4IR will fundamentally change the manner how MLIs conduct their business. One the one hand, such transition offers many opportunities to maximize the availability of internal resources. On the other hand, it involves financial demands of such magnitude that these can never be met through public-sector funding alone. This as such is not a problem *per se* as investments in the green economy and 4IR are viable on purely economic grounds. However, it requires that MDBs and other IFIs substantially change their strategic outlook and *modus operandi*. Hence, it is necessary to look for new financial paradigms that are not linked to the capital base of IFIs.

The sponsoring scheme of MIGA can be one example as it is not linked to the capital base of MIGA. However, while MIGA acts in this scheme as the administrator of the funds under that scheme, this is not intrinsically necessary and there are other ways for MDBs to enhance their impact. Any organization seeking to facilitate the transition to a green economy, to be effective, needs to be structured as a multi-actor and multi-stakeholder institution. Thus, changes in governance structures are a necessary corollary of the required changes in funding structures.

In addition to sponsoring mechanisms, MLIs should explore the potential of "development-oriented instruments" and "commercially-oriented public instruments". Particular attention should be given in this context to matchmaking mechanisms because these have the potential of mobilizing major resources for the transition to a green economy, and operational funding for such activities can come entirely from the private sector and institutional investors.

Hence, it is necessary for IFIs to explore new financing mechanisms and open themselves to the participation of other stakeholders. Moreover, irrespective of their legal structures, all funding windows need to embrace innovation and seek new ways to enhance their impact.

References

Africa50, "Room2Run Synthetic Securitization" <https://www.africa50.com/investing-for-growth/projects-investments/room2run-synthetic-securitization/> accessed 21 April 2022.

African Development Bank (AfDB), "AfDB in Brief" (2013) <https://www.AfDB.org/fileadmin/uploads/AfDB/Documents/Publications/AfDB_in_Brief.pdf> accessed 21 April 2022.

African Development Bank (AfDB), "Board of Governors Resolution B/BG/87/11: Concerning the general increase in the capital stock of the African Development Bank" (adopted 11 June 1987).

African Development Bank (AfDB), "Board of Governors Resolution B/BG/2010/08: Authorizing the Sixth General Capital Increase" (adopted 27 May 2010).

African Development Bank (AfDB), "Board of Governors Resolution B/BG/2019/09: Authorizing an Increase in the Authorized Capital Stock without Voting Power and the Subscription thereto by the Government of Canada" (adopted 12 June 2019).

African Development Bank (AfDB), "Board of Governors Resolution B/BG/87/11 concerning the general increase in the capital stock of the African Development Bank" (1987).

AfDB Board of Governors Resolution B/BG/2010/08 "Authorizing the Sixth General Capital Increase" adopted 27 May 2010, in: 2010 [AfDB] Annual Meetings Official Records <https://www.AfDB.org/en/documents/document/2010-annual-meetings-official-records-23777> accessed 21 April 2022.

African Development Bank (AfDB), "Annual Report 2019: Enhancing the Bank Group Capacity to deliver" <https://www.AfDB.org/en/annual-report/financial-report/enhancing-bank-groups-capacity-deliver> accessed 21 April 2022.

African Development Bank (AfDB), "Financing the Strategy" <https://www.AfDB.org/en/about/mission-strategy/financing-strategy> accessed 21 April 2022.

African Development Bank (AfDB), "AfDB's Strategy for 2013–2022" (2013) < https://www.afdb.org/sites/default/files/documents/publications/afdb_strategy_for_2013-2022_-_at_the_center_of_africas_transformation.pdf> accessed 21 April 2022.

African Development Bank (AfDB), "Group's Policy on Non-sovereign Operations" (AfDB 2015) <https://www.AfDB.org/fileadmin/uploads/AfDB/Documents/Policy-Documents/NSO_POLICY-En.pdf> accessed 21 April 2022.

African Development Bank (AfDB), "Investing in Africa's Future: The ADB in the 21st Century. Report of the High Level Panel" (2007) <www.AfDB.org/fileadmin/uploads/AfDB/Documents/Publications/27842402-EN-HLP-REPORT-INVESTING-IN-AFRICAS-FUTURE.PDF?bcsi_scan_7823DFCE46415F3E=0&bcsi_scan_filename=27842402-EN-HLP-REPORT-INVESTING-IN-AFRICASFUTURE.PDF> accessed 21 April 2022.

African Development Bank (AfDB), "Today is a day of joy for Africa: African Development Bank celebrates historic capital increase" (2019) <https://www.AfDB.org/en/news-and-events/today-day-joy-africa-african-development-bank-celebrates-historic-capital-increase-32349> accessed 21 April 2022.

African Development Bank (AfDB), "Reinvigorating African Concessional Finance". Report of the High-Level Panel on Transforming Trust in the AfDB Group into Influence (2017) <https://frmb.AfDB.org/documents/78/Reinvigorating%20African%20Concessional%20Finance%20-%20Report%20of%20the%20High%20Level%20Panel%20on%20Transforming%20Trust%20in%20the%20AfDB%20Group%20into%20Influence.pdf> accessed 21 April 2022.

African Development Bank (AfDB) Group, ADF-15 replenishment: Donors commit $7.6 billion, a 32% boost from last replenishment, in support of Africa's low-income, fragile, countries (2019) <https://www.AfDB.org/en/news-and-events/press-releases/adf-15-replenishment-donors-commit-76-billion-32-boost-last-replenishment-support-africas-low-income-fragile-countries-33074> accessed 21 April 2022.

Arab News. "$131 trillion needed to finance global energy transition, says IRENA" (2021) <https://www.arabnews.com/node/1826576> accessed 21 April 2022.

Asian Development Bank (ADB), "News Release: ADB Approves Policy Framework for Exposure Exchanges with Multilateral Development Banks" (2020) <https://www.adb.org/news/adb-approves-policy-framework-exposure-exchanges-multilateral-development-banks#:~:text=ADB%20Approves%20Policy%20Framework%20for%20Exposure%20Exchanges%20with%20Multilateral%20Development%20Banks,-News%20Release%20%7C%2010&text=ADB%20also%20approved%20a%20pilot,American%20Development%20Bank%20(IADB)> accessed 21 April 2022.

Asian Development Bank (ADB), "Policy for Providing Heavily Indebted Poor Countries Relief from Asian Development Fund Debt and Proposed Debt Relief to Afghanistan", 1–24 (2008) <https://www.adb.org/sites/default/files/institutional-document/33817/files/policy-providing-heavily-indebted-poor-countries-relief-adf-debt.pdf> accessed 21 April 2022.

Asian Development Bank (ADB), "Proposed Credit Guarantee and Investment Facility: Establishment of Trust Fund and Capital Contribution" (2010) <https://www.adb.org/projects/documents/proposed-credit-guarantee-and-investment-facility-rrp> accessed 21 April 2022.

Akin-Olugbade Adesegun and Augustin Flory. The Concessional Financing Windows of the African Development Bank Group: Organization, Decision Making, and Modalities, in Droesse 2011a, 401.

Belhaj Riadh, Merli Baroudi, Norbert Fiess, Jonas Campino de Olivera, Frank Sperling and Tim Turner, "Exposure exchange agreements among multilateral development banks for sovereign exposures: An innovative risk management tool" (2016) 10 Journal of Risk Management in Financial Institutions.

Birdsall Nancy, "The Dilemma of the African Development Bank: Does Governance Matter for the Long-Run Financing of the MDBs?" (Working Paper 498, 2018) Centre for Global Development <https://www.cgdev.org/sites/default/files/dilemma-AfDB-does-governance-matter-long-run-financing-mdbs.pdf> accessed 21 April 2022.

Blokker Neil M, "Proliferation of International Organizations: an Exploratory Introduction", in N. M. Blokker and H. G. Schermers (eds) "*Proliferation of International Organizations: Legal Issues*" (2001) (Kluwer Law International, The Hague/London/Boston 2001) <https://brill.com/view/title/10788> accessed 21 April 2022.

Bradlow, Daniel David, "International Law and the Operations of the International Financial Institutions" in D. Bradlow and D. Hunter (eds) "*International Financial Institutions And International Law*", (American University, WCL Research Paper No. 2011–14, Kluwer Press, 2010) <https://ssrn.com/abstract=1851849> accessed 21 April 2022.

Capital Intelligence, "Foreign Currency and Local Currency Ratings" <http://www.ciratings.com/page/rating-definitions/foreign-local-currency-ratings> accessed 21 April 2022.

Cohen Roger, "Berne Union: Capacity Sharing Market Place: BR3 Preferred Creditor Status" (2020) <https://uploads-ssl.webflow.com/5ef6f253d727ea76803f574a/60c1d5611cc311477c928305_BR3%20Preferred%20Creditor%20Status%0-%20Report%20Back.pdf> accessed 21 April 2022.

Corporación Andina de Fomento (CAF), "Agreement establishing CAF" (2015) <https://www.caf.com/media/29934/caf-agreement-establishing-10032015.pdf> accessed 21 April 2022.

Cordella Tito and Powell Andrew, "The preferred creditor puzzle in sovereign debt markets" (2019a) <https://voxeu.org/article/preferred-creditor-puzzle-sovereign-debt-markets> accessed 21 April 2022.

Cordella Tito and Powell Andrew, "Preferred and Non-Preferred Creditors: World Bank Group" (2019b) Policy Research Working Paper 8941 <http://documents1.worldbank.org/curated/en/578451563797490303/pdf/Preferred-and-Non-Preferred-Creditors.pdf> accessed 21 April 2022.

Credit Guarantee and Investment Facility (CGIF), "About Us" <https://www.cgif-abmi.org/about-us/> accessed 21 April 2022.

DDCAP Group, "ICD Returns to Market after Absence of Four Years with a Benchmark US$600m Sukuk to Help Member Countries' Private Sector Recover from COVID-19 Impact" (2020) <https://www.ddcap.com/icd-returns-to-market-after-absence-of-four-years-with-a-benchmark-us600m-sukuk-to-help-member-countries-private-sector-recover-from-covid-19-impact/> accessed 21 April 2022.

Development Committee Communiqué, "16 October 2020" <https://www.devcommittee.org/sites/dc/files/download/Communiques/2020-10/Final%20Communique%28E%29%2010.16.pdf> accessed 21 April 2022.

Development Committee. "2020 Shareholding Review: Report to Governors at the Annual Meetings" (DC2020-0009, 2020). 2020b <https://www.devcommittee.org/sites/dc/files/download/Documents/2020-09/Final%20DC2020-0009%20Shareholding.pdf> accessed 21 April 2022.

Development Committee Discussion Note, "From Billions to Trillions: Transforming Development Finance Post-2015" (2015) <https://www.devcommittee.org/sites/dc/files/download/Documentation/DC2015-0002%28E%29FinancingforDevelopment.pdf> accessed 21 April 2022.

Development Committee, "Enhancing Voice and Participation of Developing and Transition Countries in the World Bank Group: Options For Reform". (DC2008-0013) (2008) <https://www.devcommittee.org/sites/dc/files/download/Documentation/DC2008-0013%28E%29VoiceandParticipation.pdf> accessed 21 April 2022.

Development Committee. World Bank Group Voice Reform: Enhancing Voice and Participation of Developing and Transition Countries in 2010 and Beyond. DC2010-0006/1 (2010) <https://www.devcommittee.org/sites/dc/files/download/Documentation/DC2010-0006-1%28E%29Voice.pdf> accessed 21 April 2022.

Development Committee. Dynamic Formula Report to the Governors Annual Meetings 2016 (DC2016-0010, 2016) <https://www.devcommittee.org/sites/dc/files/download/Documentation/DC2016-0010.pdf> accessed 21 April 2022.

DW [Deutsche Welle]. "Davos: Green transition is '$50-trillion investment opportunity'" (2021) <https://www.dw.com/en/davos-green-transition-is-50-trillion-investment-opportunity/a-56375018> accessed 21 April 2022.

Development Finance Institutions (DFI) "DFI Working Group on Blended Concessional Finance for Private Sector Projects" (2020) <https://www.adb.org/sites/default/files/institutional-document/664336/joint-dfi-report-2020.pdf> accessed 21 April 2022.

Droesse Gerd, "Membership in International Organizations: Paradigms of Membership Structures, Legal Implications of Membership and the Concept of International Organization" (TMC Asser Press, The Hague 2020) <https://www.asser.n.l/upload/documents/20191220T151830-Frontmatter%20incl%20ToC.pdf> accessed 21 April 2022.

Droesse Gerd The replenishments of the Asian Development Fund: institutional development in the Asian Development Bank and the role of the legal counsel in resource mobilization. In: Quereshi AH, Gao X (eds) International Economic Organizations and Law. The perspective and role of the legal counsel. Wolters Kluwer, Alphen aan den Rijn (2012), pp 265–314.

Droesse Gerd, *Funds for Development: Multilateral Channels of Concessional Financing* (Manila: Asian Development Bank 2011a).

Droesse Gerd, "Introductory Remarks and Overview of Publication: Proliferation, Fragmentation and Earmarking of Concessional Financing" in Droesse Gerd (ed) *Funds for Development: Multilateral Channels of Concessional Financing* (Manila: Asian Development Bank 2011b).

Droesse Gerd, "Organizational Structures, Institutional Frameworks and Decision-Making Procedures of Multilateral Concessional Financing" in Droesse Gerd (ed) *Funds for Development. Multilateral Channels of Concessional Financing* (Manila: Asian Development Bank 2011c).

Droesse Gerd, "Modalities of Multilateral Concessional Financing" in Droesse Gerd (ed), *Funds for Development: Multilateral Channels of Concessional Financing* (Manila: Asian Development Bank 2011d).

Droesse Gerd, "Concessional Financing of the Asian Development Bank: The Asian Development Fund and Other Channels of ADB Concessional Financing" in Droesse Gerd (ed), *Funds for Development: Multilateral Channels of Concessional Financing* (Manila: Asian Development Bank 2011e).

Droesse Gerd, "Governance Changes in International Organizations: New trends and developments" in C. de Cooker (ed.) "Governance: International Organizations Adapting to a Changing Environment", International Institute for Administrative Services (IIAS), forthcoming in 2021.

East African Development Bank (EADB), "Moody's Upgrades East African Development Bank to BAA3 with a Stable Outlook" (2015) <https://www.eadb.org/news-events/moodys-upgrades-east-african-development-bank-to-baa3-with-a-stable-outlook> accessed 21 April 2022.

Edwards Sophie, "World Bank hits IDA replenishment target despite smaller US pledge" (2019) <https://www.devex.com/news/world-bank-hits-ida-replenishment-target-despite-smaller-us-pledge-96226> accessed 21 April 2022.

Standards & Poor's, European Bank for Reconstruction and Development (EBRD)(2013) <https://www.ebrd.com/downloads/capital/sp.pdf> accessed 21 April 2022.

European Investment Fund (EIF), "Governance of the European Investment Fund" <https://www.eif.org/news_centre/publications/eif_governance_en.pdf> accessed 21 April 2022.

European Investment Fund (EIF), "Who we are. Supporting entrepreneurship and innovation in Europe," <https://www.eif.org/who_we_are/>.

FitchRatings, "Corporacion Andina de Fomento (CAF): Full Rating report" (2019) <https://www.caf.com/media/2031962/fitch-report_corporacion-andina-de-fomento-caf-2019-05-31.pdf> accessed 21 April 2022.

FitchRatings, "Fitch Revises CAF's Outlook to Stable; Affirms at 'A+'" (2021) <https://www.fitchratings.com/research/sovereigns/fitch-revises-caf-outlook-to-stable-affirms-at-a-18-01-2021#:~:text=Fitch%20assesses%20CAF's%20liquidity%20as,debt%20at%20end%2DSeptember%202020.&text=Consistent%20with%20Fitch's%20Supranationals%20Rating,factor%20in%20the%20overall%20rating> accessed 21 April 2022.

FitchRatings, "Debt Suspensions May Mask Pandemic-Driven Deterioration in MDB Asset Quality" (2021a).

FitchRatings, "G20 Common Framework and Private-Sector Debt Restructuring" (2021b).

FitchRatings, "Fitch Affirms IBRD at 'AAA'; Stable Outlook" (2021c) <https://www.fitchratings.com/research/sovereigns/fitch-affirms-ibrd-at-aaa-stable-outlook-28-01-2021> accessed 21 April 2022.

FitchRatings, "Rating Action Commentary: Fitch Downgrades Islamic Corporation for the Development of the Private Sector to AA" (2018) <https://www.fitchratings.com/research/sovereigns/fitch-downgrades-islamic-corporation-for-development-of-private-sector-to-aa-05-10-2018> accessed 21 April 2022.

FitchRatings, "Supranationals Rating Criteria: Master Criteria" (2020a).

FitchRatings, "Fitch Rates International Fund for Agricultural Development 'AA+'; Outlook Stable" (2020b) <https://www.fitchratings.com/research/sovereigns/fitch-rates-international-fund-for-agricultural-development-aa-outlook-stable-02-10-2020> accessed 21 April 2022.

FitchRatings, "Fitch Ratings 2021 Outlook: Supranationals (2020c)

G20 Leaders Communiqué, "G20 Leaders Communiqué: Antalya Summit, 15-16 November 2015a" (2015) <https://www.mofa.go.jp/files/000111117.pdf> accessed 21 April 2022.

G20, "Multilateral Development Banks: Action Plan to optimize Balance Sheets" (2015) <http://g20.org.tr/wp-content/uploads/2015/11/Multilateral-Development-Banks-Action-Plan-to-Optimize-Balance-Sheets.pdf> accessed 21 April 2022.

Global Financial Governance, "Report of the G20 Eminent Persons Group on Global Financial Governance" (2018) <https://www.globalfinancialgovernance.org/assets/pdf/G20EPG-Full%20Report.pdf> accessed 21 April 2022.

Henry Glazer J. "A Functional Approach to the International Finance Corporation" (1957) 57 Columbia Law Review, 1089–1112 <https://www.jstor.org/stable/1119440> accessed 21 April 2022.

Haralz J H, "Nordic Development Fund: Ten Years of History" (1999) Helsinki NDF.

Humphrey Chris: "African Development Bank's landmark deal opens door to scaling up multilateral lending" (2018) <https://odi.org/en/insights/african-development-banks-landmark-deal-opens-door-to-scaling-up-multilateral-lending/> accessed 21 April 2022.

Humphrey Chris, "Are Credit Rating Agencies Limiting the Operational Capacity of Multilateral Development Banks?" (2015a) <https://www.academia.edu/19605819/Are_Credit_Rating_Agencies_Limiting_the_Operational_Capacity_of_Multilateral_Development_Banks> accessed 21 April 2022.

Humphrey Chris, "The Invisible Hand: Financial Pressure and Organisational Convergence in Multilateral Development Banks", The Journal of Development Studies, 2015b, 1-21 DOI: 10.1080/00220388.2015.1075978 (2015b).

Humphrey Chris, "Could multilateral banks be lending an extra $1 trillion?" (2016) <https://odi.org/en/insights/could-multilateral-banks-be-lending-an-extra-1-trillion/> accessed 21 April 2022.

Humphrey Chris, "Channelling private investment to infrastructure: what can multilateral development banks realistically do?" ODI Working Paper (2018) <https://cdn.odi.org/media/documents/12176.pdf> accessed 21 April 2022.

Humphrey Chris, “Minilateral Development Banks: What the Rise of Africa’s Trade and Development Bank says about Multilateral Governance” Vol.50 Development and Change 2019, 164-190 <DOI: 10.1111/dech.12467> accessed 21 April 2022.

Humphrey Chris, “Opinion: Multilateral banks have $750B in reserve financial capacity: Now is the time to use it” (2020a) Devex News <https://www.devex.com/news/opinion-multilateral-banks-have-750b-in-reserve-financial-capacity-now-is-the-time-to-use-it-97031> accessed 21 April 2022.

Humphrey Chris, “All hands on deck. How to scale up multilateral financing to face the Covid-19 crisis” (2020b) <https://odi.org/en/publications/all-hands-on-deck-how-to-scale-up-multilateral-financing-to-face-the-covid-19-crisis/> accessed 21 April 2022.

Humphrey Chris, “Six proposals to strengthen the finances of multilateral development banks” (ODI Working Paper 509, 2017) <https://www.odi.org/sites/odi.org.uk/files/resource-documents/11451.pdf> accessed 21 April 2022.

Humphrey Chris, “The politics of loan pricing in multilateral development banks” (2014) 21 Review of International Political Economy, 611–639.

Inter-American Development Bank (IADB) “Annual Report 2010” (2011a) <https://publications.iadb.org/publications/english/document/Inter-American-Development-Bank-Annual-Report-2010-The-Year-in-Review.pdf> accessed 21 April 2022.

Inter-American Development Bank (IADB) “Evaluation of the Bank’s Direct Private Sector Lending Program1995-2003 (Office of Evaluation and Oversight), 2004. <https://publications.iadb.org/publications/english/document/Evaluation-of-the-Bank-Direct-Private-Sector-Lending-Program-1995-2003.pdf> accessed 21 April 2022.

Inter-American Development Bank (IADB), “Capital and Funds under Administration” <https://www.iadb.org/en/idb-finance/capital-and-funds-under-administration> accessed 21 April 2022.

Inter-American Development Bank (IADB), “Concessional Resources” <https://www.iadb.org/en/about-us/concessional-resources> accessed 21 April 2022.

Inter-American Development Bank (IADB), “Approach Paper. Evaluation of the IDB Lab”, 2020 <https://publications.iadb.org/publications/english/document/Approach-Paper-Evaluation-of-IDB-Lab.pdf> accessed 21 April 2022.

Inter-American Development Bank (IADB), “Approach Paper. Evaluation of the Implementation of the Private Sector Merge-out” (IADB 2017) <https://publications.iadb.org/publications/english/document/Approach-Paper-Evaluation-of-the-Implementation-of-the-Private-Sector-Merge-out.pdf> accessed 21 April 2022.

Inter-American Development Bank (IADB), “IADB Board of Governors Resolution AG-4/72: Amendment of the Provisions of the Agreement establishing the Bank with respect to Membership and to related Matters” (Adopted on 23 March 1972)

<http://idbdocs.iadb.org/wsdocs/getdocument.aspx?docnum=EZSHARE-1983553961-15706> accessed 21 April 2022.

Inter-American Development Bank (IADB), "IADB Board of Governors Resolution AG-9/76: Amendments to the Agreement establishing the Bank with respect to the Creation of the Inter-Regional Capital Stock of the Bank and related Matters" (Adopted on 1 June 1976) <http://idbdocs.iadb.org/wsdocs/getdocument.aspx?docnum=EZSHARE-1983553961-13175> accessed 21 April 2022.

Inter-American Development Bank (IADB), "IADB Board of Governors Resolution AG-8/87: Merger of Inter-Regional and Ordinary Capital Resources" (Adopted on 24 December 1987).

Inter-American Development Bank (IADB), "Mid-term Evaluation of IDB-9 Commitments. Assessment of IDB-9's Private Sector Development Framework" (Background Paper 2013) <https://publications.iadb.org/publications/english/document/IDB-9-Assessment-of-IDB-9-Private-Sector-Development-Framework.pdf> accessed 21 April 2022.

Inter-American Development Bank (IADB), "Private Sector Development Strategy: Fostering Development through the Private Sector" (2011b) <https://issuu.com/idb_publications/docs/_en_70238> accessed 21 April 2022.

Inter-American Development Bank (IADB), "Report on the Ninth General Increase in the Resources of the Inter-American Development Bank" (AB-2764, 21 May 2010) <https://fundar.org.mx/mexico/pdf/gc19.pdf> accessed 21 April 2022.

Inter-American Development Bank (IADB), "Resolution AG-9/15 and CII/AG-2/15, Delivering the Renewed Vision: Organizational and Capitalization Proposal for the IDB Group Private Sector Merge-out" (2013) <https://idbdocs.iadb.org/wsdocs/getdocument.aspx?docnum=EZSHARE-1983553961-1378> accessed 21 April 2022.

Inter-American Development Bank (IADB), Board of Governors Resolution AG-09/01 "Lending to the Private Sector" (2001) <https://idbdocs.iadb.org/wsdocs/getdocument.aspx?docnum=EZSHARE-1983553961-14850> accessed 21 April 2022.

Inter-American Development Bank (IADB). "40 Years: More than a Bank" (2001) <https://publications.iadb.org/publications/english/document/40-Years-More-Than-a-Bank.pdf> accessed 21 April 2022.

Inter-American Development Bank (IADB) Invest, "Annual Report 2017" (2017) <https://idbinvest.org/en/publications/annual-report-2017> accessed 21 April 2022.

Inter-American Development Bank (IADB) Invest, "Annual Report 2018" (2018) <https://idbinvest.org/en/publications/annual-report-2018> accessed 21 April 2022.

Inter-American Development Bank (IDB) LAB, "About Us" <https://bidlab.org/en/about> accessed 21 April 2022.

International Development Association (IDA), "A landmark bond issue for IDA" (2018) <https://group.bnpparibas/en/news/landmark-bond-issue-ida> accessed 21 April 2022.

International Development Association (IDA), "IDA-IFC-MIGA Private Sector Window" <https://ida.worldbank.org/financing/ida-private-sector-window> accessed 21 April 2022.

International Development Association (IDA), "Increase in Authorized Capital and Subscription by Japan", Report of the Executive Directors of 8 July 1996, in The World Bank Group. 1996 Annual Meetings of the Boards of Governors. Summary Proceedings, 270–271.

International Development Association (IDA), "Press Release: Building out its Benchmark Curve IDA Prices 2 Billion 10-Year USD Bond" (2020a) <https://treasury.worldbank.org/en/about/unit/treasury/ida/ida-press-releases-fx#:~:text=The%20 10%2Dyear%20benchmark%20pays,%2Dannual%20yield%20of%201.065%25> accessed 21 April 2022.

International Development Association (IDA), "Report from the Executive Directors of the International Development Association to the Board of Governors – Additions to IDA Resources: Eighteenth Replenishment" (2017) <http://documents1.worldbank.org/curated/en/348661486654455091/pdf/112728-correct-file-PUBLIC-Rpt-from-EDs-Additions-to-IDA-Resources-2-9-17-For-Disclosure.pdf> accessed 21 April 2022.

International Development Association (IDA), "Report from the Executive Directors of the International Development Association to the Board of Governors – Additions to IDA Resources: Nineteenth Replenishment, Ten Years to 2030" (2020b) <http://documents1.worldbank.org/curated/en/459531582153485508/pdf/Additions-to-IDA-Resources-Nineteenth-Replenishment-Ten-Years-to-2030-Growth-People-Resilience.pdf> accessed 21 April 2022.

International Finance Corporation (IFC), "IFC Board of Governors resolution No. 21: Amendment of articles of agreement (English)" (1961) Washington D.C. World Bank Group. <http://documents.worldbank.org/curated/en/859621468180867492/International-Finance-Corporation-IFC-Board-of-Governors-resolution-no-21> accessed 21 April 2022.

International Finance Corporation (IFC), "BOG Resolution No. 273: Amendment to the Article II, Section 2 (c) of the Articles of Agreement of the Corporation" (Adopted on 16 April 2020) <https://documents1.worldbank.org/curated/en/314101587371306366/pdf/International-Finance-Corporation-IFC-Board-of-Governors-Resolution-no-273-Amendment-to-the-Articles-of-Agreement-of-the-Corporation.pdf> accessed 21 April 2022.

International Finance Corporation (IFC), "Board of Governors Resolution No. 272: 2018 General Capital Increase" (2020) <http://documents.worldbank.org/curated/en/952841587370588266/International-Finance-Corporation-IFC-Board-of-Governors-Resolution-no-272-2018-General-Capital-Increase> accessed 21 April 2022.

International Finance Corporation (IFC), "IFC Board of Governors resolution No. 271: 2018 Selective Capital Increase" (2018) Washington D.C. World Bank Group <https://documents1.worldbank.org/curated/en/756581587369597285/pdf/International-Finance-Corporation-IFC-Board-of-Governors-Resolution-no-271-2018-Selective-Capital-Increase.pdf> accessed 21 April 2022.

International Finance Corporation (IFC), "IFC Board of Governors resolution No. 270: 2018 Conversion of Retained Earnings and General Capital Increase" (2020) <http://documents.worldbank.org/curated/en/775571587368717297/International-Finance-Corporation-IFC-Board-of-Governors-Resolution-no-270-2018-Conversion-of-Retained-Earnings-and-General-Capital-Increase> accessed 21 April 2022.

International Finance Corporation (IFC), "IFC Board of Governors Resolution No.196: 1992 special capital increase". (1992) <http://documents.worldbank.org/curated/en/611201468330313949/International-Finance-Corporation-IFC-Board-of-Governors-resolution-no-196-1992-special-capital-increase> accessed 21 April 2022.

International Finance Corporation (IFC), "IFC Board of Governors Resolution No.197: Amendments to the articles of agreement of the corporation". (1992) <http://documents.worldbank.org/curated/en/723511468318550899/International-Finance-Corporation-IFC-Board-of-Governors-resolution-no-197-amendments-to-the-articles-of-agreement-of-the-corporation> accessed 21 April 2022.

International Finance Corporation (IFC), "Preferred Creditor Status" <https://www.ifc.org/wps/wcm/connect/corp_ext_content/ifc_external_corporate_site/solutions/products+and+services/syndications/preferred-creditor-status#:~:text=As%20a%20multilateral%20development%20institution,a%20country%20foreign%20exchange%20crisis> accessed 21 April 2022.

International Fund for Agricultural Development (IFAD), "Corporate-Level Evaluation on IFAD's Financial Architecture" (2018) < https://www.ifad.org/documents/38714182/40787225/cle_financial_architecture_full.pdf/3c2ecfae-85ea-42ad-90a9-3d81847bd712?t=1542890665000 > accessed 21 April 2022.

International Fund for Agricultural Development (IFAD), "Extending the IFAD programme through borrowing: Sovereign borrowing" (2018a) <https://www.ifad.org/documents/38714182/40787225/cle_financial_architecture_full.pdf/3c2ecfae-85ea-42ad-90a9-3d81847bd712?t=1542890665000architecture> accessed 21 April 2022.

International Fund for Agricultural Development (IFAD), "Spanish Food Security Cofinancing Facility Trust Fund agreements" (2012) (EB 2011/102/INF.13/Rev.1). <https://webapps.ifad.org/members/eb/102/docs/EB-2011-102-INF-13-Rev-1.pdf> accessed 21 April 2022.

International Fund for Agricultural Development (IFAD), "Sovereign Borrowing Framework: Borrowing from Sovereign States and State-Supported Institutions" (EB 2015/114/R.17/Rev.1, 23 April 2015) <https://webapps.ifad.org/members/eb/114/docs/EB-2015-114-R-17-Rev-1.pdf> accessed 21 April 2022.

International Fund for Agricultural Development (IFAD), "Report of the Consultation on the Eleventh Replenishment of IFAD's Resources. Leaving no one behind: IFAD's role in the 2030 Agenda (2018b) <https://webapps.ifad.org/members/gc/41/docs/GC-41-L-3-Rev-1.pdf> accessed 21 April 2022.

International Fund for Agricultural Development (IFAD), "IFAD12: Business Model and Financial Framework 2022-2024". IFAD12/2(R)/R.2. (2020) <https://webapps.ifad.org/members/repl/12/2/R/docs/IFAD12-2-R-R-2.pdf> accessed 21 April 2022.

International Fund for Agricultural Development (IFAD), "AA+ credit rating from Standard & Poor's will help IFAD increase investments to fight poverty and hunger" (2020) <https://www.ifad.org/en/web/latest/-/news/second-ifad-credit-rating-will-help-increase-investments-to-fight-poverty-and-hunger> accessed 21 April 2022.

International Islamic Trade Finance Corporation (ITFC) "What is ITFC" (2018) <https://www.itfc-idb.org/en/content/what-itfc> 21 April 2022.

International Monetary Fund (IMF), "Questions and Answers on Sovereign Debt Issues" (2021) <https://www.imf.org/en/About/FAQ/sovereign-debt> accessed 21 April 2022.

International Monetary Fund (IMF), "Multilateral Debt Relief Initiative – Questions and Answers" (2017) <https://www.imf.org/external/np/exr/mdri/eng/index.htm> accessed 21 April 2022.

Islamic Development Bank (ISDB), "42 Years in the Service of Development" (2016) <https://www.IsDB.org/sites/default/files/media/documents/2018-12/42%20Years%20in%20the%20Service%20of%20Development-1437H.pdf> accessed 21 April 2022.

Islamic Development Bank (ISDB), "2019 Financial Statements" (2020) <https://www.IsDB.org/sites/default/files/media/documents/2020-06/1%20Financial%20Statement%20English%202019%20Cleared%20%281%29_0.pdf> accessed 21 April 2022.

Islamic Development Bank (ISDB), "International Islamic Trade Finance Corporation to launch operations in January 2008" (2007) <https://www.IsDB.org/news/international-islamic-trade-finance-corporation-to-launch-operations-in-january-2008> accessed 21 April 2022.

Islamic Development Bank (IsDB), "Investor Presentation" (2019b) <https://www.IsDB.org/sites/%20Presentation%20(November%202019).pdftec> accessed 21 April 2022.default/files/media/documents/2019-11/IsDB%20Sustainable%20Investor

Islamic Development Bank (IsDB), "IsDB and ICD Sign Agency Agreement to Implement R2 COVID Support Line of Finance" (2021) <https://www.IsDB.org/news/IsDB-and-icd-sign-agency-agreement-to-implement-r2-covid-support-line-of-financehttps://www.IsDB.org/news/IsDB-and-icd-sign-agency-agreement-to-implement-r2-covid-support-line-of-finance> accessed 21 April 2022.

Islamic Development Bank (IsDB), "IsDB Group Entities Collaborate and Showcase Synergy to Support the OIC Member Countries" (2019c) <https://iciec.IsDB.org/node/919> accessed 21 April 2022.

Islamic Research and Training Institute (IRTI), "What we do" (2019) <https://irti.org/what-we-do/> accessed 21 April 2022.

Kaja Orçun, Synthetic securitization. Making a silent comeback (2017) <https://www.dbresearch.com/PROD/RPS_EN-PROD/PROD0000000000441788/Synthetic_securitisation%3A_Making_a_silent_comeback.pdf?undefined&realload=ujwh6RCGJn5x5UyOdr/RqHX9Qc~yuLQKu3ESSudr0xRk/kF6kMFNK~OXM0EAdw3B> accessed 21 April 2022.

Kamau Faith and Marieclaire Colaiacomo, "Financing for Development: Examining the Concept of Resource Mobilization for International Organizations, a case study of the International Fund for Agricultural Development (IFAD)" (2012) 9 International Organizations Law Review.

Kapur Devesh and Arjun Raychaudhuri, "Rethinking the Financial Design of the World Bank" (Working Paper 352, 2014) *Center for Global Development* <https://www.cgdev.org/publication/rethinking-financial-design-world-bank-working-paper-352> accessed 21 April 2022.

Kapur Devesh, John P. Lewis and Richard C. Webb, "*The World Bank: its first half century*" (Brookings Institution Press 2001).

Kotecha Mahesh K, "Rising Role of Preferred Creditor Status in Ratings of Multilateral Development Banks" (2019) <https://www.4scic.com/pdf/2%20Kotecha_Revitalizing%20the%20Spirit%20of%20Bretton%20Woods.pdf> accessed 21 April 2022.

Landers Clemence and Aboneaaj Rakan, "Half a Trillion in Dry Powder? The Time for MDB Financial Reform Is Now", Center for Global Development (2021) <https://www.cgdev.org/blog/half-trillion-dry-powder-time-mdb-financial-reform-now> accessed 21 April 2022.

Lee Nancy and Plant Mark, "Why Congress Should Authorize the IFC Capital Increase" (2019) Center for Global Development <https://www.cgdev.org/sites/default/files/Lee-Plant-Authorize-IFC-Capital-Increase.pdf> accessed 21 April 2022.

Martha Rutsel Silvestre J, "Preferred creditor status under international law: The case of the International Monetary Fund" (1990) International and Comparative Law Quarterly <https://wiki.duke.edu/download/attachments/75172973/Martha%2C%20Preferred%20Creditor%20Status%20under%20International%20Law%20The%20Case%20of%20the%20IMF.pdf?api=v2> accessed 21 April 2022.

Martin Eric, "Fitch Warns of Credit Risks If Development Banks Pause Repayment" (Bloomberg:2020) <https://www.bloomberg.com/news/articles/2020-04-23/fitch-warns-of-credit-risks-if-development-banks-pause-repayment> accessed 21 April 2022.

Mason Edward S, and Asher Robert E, "*The World Bank since Bretton Woods*" (Brookings Institution Press 2010).

McLellan Lewis, "IFAD gets credit rating in preparation for private placement issuance" (2020) <https://www.globalcapital.com/article/b1nmpkqcp9fs5p/ifad-gets-credit-rating-in-preparation-for-private-placement-issuance> accessed 21 April 2022.

Meenai Saeed Ahmed, "The Islamic Development Bank: a case study of Islamic co-operation" (1989) Routledge.

Memorandum (94490) from the World Bank President B. B. Conable to the Executive Directors, "Increases in Subscriptions of Certain Members to Capital Stock" (12 January 1987).

Memorandum from the World Bank President, "IBRD Lending Rates and Spreads Applicable on or after October 1, 2019" (October 24, 2019) <https://documents1.worldbank.org/curated/en/288111572632089775/pdf/IBRD-Lending-Rates-and-Spreads-Applicable-on-or-after-October-1-2019.pdf> accessed 21 April 2022.

Mendoza B Naki, "How the Inter-American Development Bank is restructuring its private sector financing" (*Devex Impact*, 03 May 2016) <https://www.devex.com/news/how-the-inter-american-development-bank-is-restructuring-its-private-sector-financing-88105> accessed 21 April 2022.

Mistry Percy S, "Multilateral Development Banks: an assessment of their financial structures, policies and practices" (1995) FONDAD, The Hague.

Moody's Investors Service, "Multilateral Development Banks and Other Supranational Entities Methodology" (2020a).

Moody's, "Hybrid Equity Credit" (2018).

Moody's, "Rating Scale and Definitions" <https://www.moodys.com/sites/products/productattachments/ap075378_1_1408_ki.pdf> accessed 21 April 2022.

Moody's, "Sovereign defaults, deposit freezes and private-sector external debt moratoriums" (2020b).

Moody's "International Development Association – Aaa stable" (2020c). <https://thedocs.worldbank.org/en/doc/103461606852699128-0340022020/original/MoodysIDACADec2020.pdf> accessed 21 April 2022.

Morgan. J. P. Development Finance Institution. Financing opportunities with anticipated development impact in emerging economies <https://www.jpmorgan.com/solutions/cib/investment-banking/development-finance-institution> accessed 21 April 2022.

Morgan. J. P. Development Finance Institution. Methodology <https://www.jpmorgan.com/content/dam/jpm/cib/complex/content/news/2020-dfi-announcement/pdf-1.pdf> accessed 21 April 2022.

Multilateral Investment Guarantee Agency (MIGA), "Commentary on the Convention: Establishing the Multilateral Investment Guarantee Agency" (1985). <https://www.miga.org/sites/default/files/archive/Documents/commentary_convention_november_2010.pdf> accessed 21 April 2022.

Multilateral Investment Guarantee Agency (MIGA), Board of Governors Resolution No. 57: 1998 general capital increase (1999) <http://documents.worldbank.org/curated/en/850471468332051811/Multilateral-Investment-Guarantee-Agency-MIGA-Council-of-Governors-resolution-no-57-1998-general-capital-increase> accessed 21 April 2022.

Multilateral Investment Guarantee Agency (MIGA), "MIGA Convention: Establishing The Multilateral Investment Guarantee Agency" (2010) 01 <https://www.piga.org/sites/default/files/archive/Documents/MIGA%20Convention%20February%202016.pdf> accessed 21 April 2022.

Nigeria Trust Fund (NTF), "About Us: Corporate Information" (1976) <https://www.afdb.org/en/about-us/corporate-information/nigeria-trust-fund-ntf> accessed 21 April 2022.

Nordic Development Fund (NDF), "Governing bodies and capital" <https://www.ndf.int/who-we-are/about-us/governing-bodies-and-capital.html> accessed 21 April 2022.

Nordic Finance Group, "Power Point Presentation" (2010) <https://www.nefco.int/wp-content/uploads/2019/10/Nordic-Finance-Group.pdf> accessed 21 April 2022.

Nordic Investment Bank (NIB), "Member countries, governing bodies and capital" <https://www.nib.int/who_we_are/about/member_countries_governing_bodies_and_capital> accessed 21 April 2022.

Nordic Investment Bank (NIB), "Statutes for the Cooperation Council of NIB, NDF and NEFCO" (as amended on 2006) <http://uniset.ca/microstates2/is_68-Statutes_CooperationCouncil.pdf> accessed 21 April 2022.

Nordic Investment Bank (NIB), Rules for the Cooperation Council (2009) <https://www.nib.int/files/106f0056c5b59c43d1ae3ff533e359c6e548f146/9188-rules-for-the-cooperation-council.pdf> accessed 21 April 2022.

Perraudin William, Powell Andrew and Yang Peng, "Multilateral Development Bank Ratings and Preferred Creditor Status" (IDB working paper series Nº IDB-WP-697 2016) <https://publications.iadb.org/publications/english/document/Multilateral-Development-Bank-Ratings-and-Preferred-Creditor-Status.pdf> accessed 21 April 2022.

Philip Erquiaga, "A History of Financial Management at the Asian Development Bank: Engineering Financial Innovation and Impact on an Emerging Asia" (2016) <https://www.adb.org/sites/default/files/publication/216736/history-financial-mgt-adb.pdf> accessed 21 April 2022.

Principles for Responsive Investment (PRI), "PRI Awards 2019 case study: Room2Run" (2019) <https://www.unpri.org/showcasing-leadership/pri-awards-2019-case-study-room2run/4848.article> accessed 21 April 2022.

Runde D. F, Cordell K. Bandura R. and Fernandez C., "The Right Time for a Capital Increase for the InterAmerican Development Bank (IDB)?" Center for Strategic and

International Studies (2021) <https://csis-website-prod.s3.amazonaws.com/s3fs-public/publication/210216_Runde_Capital_Increase.pdf?MCBtIQjAIXtTJ7xuT4MMePLCXCyrp.RM> accessed 21 April 2022.

Reuters "World Bank chief: some development banks worsening poor country debt burdens" (2020) <https://jp.reuters.+com/article/us-worldbank-debt-idUSKBN2050HT> accessed 21 April 2022.

S&P Global Ratings, "International Development Association 'AAA/A-1+' Ratings Affirmed: Outlook Remains Stable" (2018a) <http://pubdocs.worldbank.org/en/369221542732735867/ida-ratings-report-update-sp-20181113.pdf> accessed 21 April 2022.

S&P Global Ratings, "Multilateral Lending Institutions and other Supranational Institutions Ratings Methodology" (2018b).

S&P Global, "Can Multilateral Lenders' Capital Bases Hold Up Against COVID-19?" (2020a).

S&P Global, "International Finance Corporation, Ratings Affirmed At 'AAA/A-1+' On Criteria Revision: Outlook Remains Stable" (2019).

S&P Global, "Supranationals: Special Edition" (2020b) <https://www.spglobal.com/_assets/documents/ratings/research/100046890.pdf> accessed 21 April 2022.

S&P Global, "Supranationals: Special Edition" (2017) <https://www.spratings.com/documents/20184/908545/US_SR_Event_Webcast_MultilateralNov17_Article2.pdf/fc892865-5302-4dd6-93ca-8469c8752818> accessed 21 April 2022.

S&P Global Ratings, "Corporacion Andina de Fomento Outlook Revised to Stable from Negative; 'A+/A-1' Ratings Affirmed" (2020) <https://www.standardandpoors.com/en_US/web/guest/article/-/view/type/HTML/id/2462747> accessed 21 April 2022.

S&P Rating Services, "Rating Services. 2009". For Development Banks, Callable Capital Is No Substitute For Paid-In Capital (2009).

Settimo Riccardo, "Higher multilateral development bank lending, unchanged capital resources and triple-a rating. A possible trinity after all?" Banca d'Italia. Questioni di Economia e Finanza (Occasional Papers) No. 488 (2019) <https://www.bancaditalia.it/pubblicazioni/qef/2019-0488/index.html?com.dotmarketing.htmlpage.language=1> accessed 21 April 2022.

Schwab Klaus, "The Fourth Industrial Revolution: What it means, how to respond" (2016) <https://www.weforum.org/agenda/2016/01/the-fourth-industrial-revolution-what-it-means-and-how-to-respond/> accessed 21 April 2022.

Shihata Ibrahim F I, "The multilateral investment guarantee agency" (1986) 20 The International Lawyer, 485–497 <https://www.jstor.org/stable/40705744> accessed 21 April 2022.

Shihata Ibrahim F I, "MIGA and Foreign Investment: Martinus Nijhoff, Dordrecht Boston Lancaster" (1988).

Shihata Ibrahim F I, "Techniques to Avoid Proliferation of International Organizations – The Experience of the World Bank" in Blokker N. M. and Schermers

H. G. (ed) *Proliferation of International Organizations: Legal Issues* (The Hague, London, Boston: Kluwer Law International 2001).

Shihata Ibrahim F I, "The Multilateral Investment Guarantee Agency (MIGA) and the Legal Treatment of Foreign Investment" in *Collected Courses of the Hague Academy of International Law* (1987) <http://dx.doi.org/10.1163/1875-8096_pplrdc_A9789024737260_02> accessed 21 April 2022.

Shihata Ibrahim F I, "*The OPEC Fund for International Development: The Formative Years*" (1983) Routledge <https://books.google.de/books?id=H1B3a2JCeEsC&printsec=frontcover&source=gbs_atb&redir_esc=y#v=onepage&q=revision%20of%20the%20Agreement&f=false>

Shihata Ibrahim F I, "Organization of the Petroleum Exporting Countries: Agreement Establishing the OPEC Fund For International Development" (1980) 19 International Legal Materials <https://www.jstor.org/stable/20692184> accessed 21 April 2022.

Shihata Ibrahim F I. "The other Face of OPEC: Financial Assistance to the Third World" (1982) <https://agris.fao.org/agris-search/search.do?recordID=XF2015022200> accessed 21 April 2022.

Shihata Ibrahim F.I. "Organization of The Petroleum Exporting Countries: Agreement Establishing the OPEC Fund for International Development. (1980), Vol. 19, International Legal Materials, 879–885.

Standard and Poor's Rating Services, "How an Erosion of Preferred Creditor Treatment Could Lead to Lower Ratings on Multilateral Lending Institutions" (2013).

Standard and Poor's Global, "Credit Guarantee and Investment Facility 'AA/A-1+' Ratings Affirmed; Outlook Stable" (2017) <http://cgiftest.org/wp-content/uploads/2017/07/SP-Global-Ratings-2016_20170623.pdf> accessed 21 April 2022.

Sureda Andres Rigo, "The Law Applicable to the Activities of International Development Banks" in *Collected Courses of the Hague Academy of International Law* (Leiden: Martinus Nijhof 2005).

The International Bank for Reconstruction and Development (IBRD), "Technical Note: Past IBRD Capital Increases" (1987) Washington, D.C. <http://documents.worldbank.org/curated/en/645291468332351353/Past-International-Bank-for-Reconstruction-and-Development-IBRD-capital-increases-technical-note> accessed 21 April 2022.

The International Bank for Reconstruction and Development (IBRD), "Board of Governors resolution No. 128: Increase of $10,000,000,000 in Authorized Capital Stock and Subscriptions Thereto." (1959) Washington, D.C. <http://documents.worldbank.org/curated/en/819051468155112252/International-Bank-for-Reconstruction-and-Development-IBRD-Board-of-Governors-resolution-no-128-increase-of-10-000-000-000-in-authorized-capital-stock-and-subscriptions-thereto> accessed 21 April 2022.

The International Bank for Reconstruction and Development (IBRD), "Board of Governors Resolution No. 395: Increase of $7 Billion in Authorized Capital Stock and Special Increases in Subscriptions to Capital Stock" (adopted on 30 August 1984).

The International Bank for Reconstruction and Development (IBRD), "Note to Executive Directors on Possible Increase of IBRD Shareholdings of Certain Members" (10 November 1995) <http://documents.worldbank.org/curated/en/634061468162846618/pdf/767010BR0SecM100A2Ioreqest00PUBLIC0.pdf> accessed 21 April 2022.

The International Bank for Reconstruction and Development (IBRD), "IBRD Board of Governors Resolution No. 425: 1988 General Capital Increase" (Adopted on 27 April 1988) <http://documents.worldbank.org/curated/en/893681468337910240/International-Bank-for-Reconstruction-and-Development-IBRD-Board-of-Governors-resolution-no-425-1988-General-capital-increase> accessed 21 April 2022.

The International Bank for Reconstruction and Development (IBRD), "IBRD Board of Governors Resolution No. 426: 1988 Additional increase in authorized capital". (Adopted on 27 April 1988) <http://documents.worldbank.org/curated/en/815981468323360104/International-Bank-for-Reconstruction-and-Development-IBRD-Board-of-Governors-resolution-no-426-1988-Additional-increase-in-authorized-capital> accessed 21 April 2022.

The International Bank for Reconstruction and Development (IBRD), "IBRD Board of Governors Resolution No. 503 "Increase in Authorized Capital and Subscription by Japan" (Adopted on 14 June 1996) <http://documents.worldbank.org/curated/en/435381468038959245/pdf/854240IBRD50300PUBLIC00Box0382159B.pdf> accessed 21 April 2022.

The International Bank for Reconstruction and Development (IBRD), "IBRD Board of Governors Resolution No. 596: Enhancing Voice and Participation of Developing and Transition Countries" (Adopted on 30 January 2009).

The International Bank for Reconstruction and Development (IBRD), "IBRD Board of Governors Resolution No. 663: General Capital Increase" (2018a) <http://documents.worldbank.org/curated/en/668831538549114339/pdf/130434-BR-PUBLIC-resolution-ADD-SERIES-IBRD663-2018GeneralCapitalIncrease.pdf> accessed 21 April 2022.

The International Bank for Reconstruction and Development (IBRD), "IBRD Resolution No. 664: Selective Capital Increase (2018b) <http://documents.worldbank.org/curated/en/370231538549507417/pdf/130436-BR-PUBLIC-resolution-ADD-SERIES-IBRD664-2018SelectiveCapitalIncrease.pdf> accessed 21 April 2022.

The Islamic Corporation for the Development of the Private Sector (ICD), "Articles of Agreement: Establishing the Islamic Corporation for the Development of the Private Sector" (2012) <https://icd-ps.org/uploads/files/ICD%20Articles%20of%20Agreement%20(English)%20-%201603201315640351 57_2938.pdf> accessed 21 April 2022.

The Islamic Corporation for the Development of the Private Sector (ICD), "Power Point Presentation" (2018) <https://icd-ps.org/uploads/files/ICD%20Corporate%20Presentation%20-%20ENG%2018022018153576925_4104.pdf> accessed 21 April 2022.

The Islamic Corporation for the Insurance of Investment and Export Credit (ICIEC), "Who we are"< https://iciec.IsDB.org/about#> accessed 21 April 2022.

The Islamic Corporation for the Insurance of Investment and Export Credit (ICIEC), "2019 Annual Report" (2020) <https://iciec.IsDB.org/wp-content/uploads/2020/12/ICIEC-AR-2019-ENGLISH-FINAL-v3.pdf> accessed 21 April 2022.

The Islamic Corporation for the Insurance of Investment and Export Credit (ICIEC), "2019 Financial Statements" (Annual Report Vol. 02) <https://iciec.IsDB.org/wp-content/uploads/2020/12/English-AR-vol-2.pdf> accessed 21 April 2022.

The Islamic Corporation for the Insurance of Investment and Export Credit (ICIEC), "ICIEC Articles of Agreement, (2016) <https://iciec.IsDB.org/sites/default/files/ICIEC%20ARTICLE%20OF%20AGREEMENT%20%28ENG%29%20FAW.pdf> accessed 21 April 2022.

OPEC Fund for International Development, More Impact where it matters most. Annual Report 2019 (2020) <https://content.yudu.com/web/435ju/0A430b9/AnnualReport2019-EN/html/index.html?origin=reader> accessed 21 April 2022.

The OPEC Fund for International Development, "Financial Statements and Report of the Independent Auditors for the Years ended December 31, 2016 and 2015" (2017) <https://opecfund.org/var/site/storage/original/application/e8abf8730c6d335b7d2a429d1aa22d6c.pdf> accessed 21 April 2022.

The OPEC Fund for International Development, "What we Offer" <https://opecfund.org/what-we-offer/overview> accessed 21 April 2022.

The OPEC Fund for International Development, Report on the Audit of the Financial Statements of the Ordinary Capital Resources (OCR) for the year ended 31 December 2020 (2021) <https://opecfund.org/var/site/storage/original/application/e58c1837d5dcaecc0972b7c7075cb33f.pdf> accessed 21 April 2022.

The OPEC Fund for International Development, Press Release: "S&P assigns OPEC Fund AA/A-1+, Positive Outlook" (2021) <https://opecfund.org/media-center/press-releases/2021/s-p-assigns-opec-fund-aa-a-1-positive-outlook> accessed 21 April 2022.

The West African Development Bank (BOAD), "BOAD issues the first African sustainability bond" (2021) <https://www.boad.org/en/the-west-african-development-bank-boad-issues-the-first-african-sustainability-bond/f> accessed 21 April 2022.

The World Bank, "World Bank Annual Report, The International Bank for Reconstruction and Development (IBRD) and the International Development Association (IDA): Management's Discussion and Analysis and Financial Statements" (2018) <http://pubdocs.worldbank.org/en/474791538065340369/211296v2.pdf> accessed 21 April 2022.

World Bank Group, "Least Developed Countries Fund (LDCF)" (2016).

Trigo Thierry, "10 Questions To Understand Corporate Hybrid Bonds: BNP Paribas" (2019) <https://wealthmanagement.bnpparibas/en/expert-voices/10-questions-to-understand-corporate-hybrid-bonds.html> accessed 21 April 2022.

United Nations Treaties Series, "Agreement establishing the OPEC Special Fund" (28 January 1976, UN Treaty Series Vol. 2228, 125–134. <https://treaties.un.org/doc/Publication/UNTS/Volume%202228/v2228.pdf> <https://treaties.un.org/doc/Publication/UNTS/Volume%202228/v2228.pdf> accessed 21 April 2022.

Weill-Hallé Vera P., Cynthia Licul, and Itziar García Villanueva. Multilateral Concessional Financing of the International Fund for Agricultural Development in Droesse Gerd (ed), Funds for Development: Multilateral Channels of Concessional Financing (2011) (Manila: Asian Development Bank).

West-African Development Bank (BOAD), "BOAD Shareholders" <https://www.boad.org/en/who-we-are/> accessed 21 April 2022.

World Bank Group, "World Bank Group Guarantee Products Guidance Note" (2016). (2016) <https://ppp.worldbank.org/public-privatepartnership/sites/ppp.worldbank.org/files/documents/PPPCCSA_WBGGuarantees_Final%20_%20English%20_Printed%20Oct%202016.pdf> accessed 21 April 2022.

World Bank, "Report No: ICR2565. Implementation Completion and Results Report on a Credit in the Amount of SDR67 Million (US$96.39 Million Equivalent) to Banque Ouest Africaine de Developpement (BOAD) for a West Africa Economic And Monetary Union (WAEMU) Capital Market Development Project (2013) <http://documents1.worldbank.org/curated/en/302641468202198758/text/ICR25650P074520losed0March028020130.txt> accessed 21 April 2022.

World Bank Group, "International Finance Corporation (IFC) Board of Governors resolution No. 100: Increase of capital" (1977) Washington, D.C. <http://documents.worldbank.org/curated/en/891011468326694725/International-Finance-Corporation-IFC-Board-of-Governors-resolution-no-100-Increase-of-capital> accessed 21 April 2022.

World Bank, "International Finance Corporation (IFC) Board of Governors resolution No. 149: Increase of capital" (1985) Washington, D.C. <http://documents.worldbank.org/curated/en/957531468155723227/International-Finance-Corporation-IFC-Board-of-Governors-resolution-no-149-Increase-of-capital> accessed 21 April 2022.

World Bank Group, International Finance Corporation (IFC). "Board of Governors resolution No. 179: 1991 general capital increase" (1992) Washington, D.C. <http://documents.worldbank.org/curated/en/564931468158370897/International-Finance-Corporation-IFC-Board-of-Governors-resolution-no-179-1991-general-capital-increase> accessed 21 April 2022.

World Bank Group,. International Finance Corporation (IFC): "IFC Board of Governors resolution no. 196: 1992 special capital increase (English). (1992) Washington,

DC: World Bank Group <http://documents.worldbank.org/curated/en/61120146833 0313949/International-Finance-Corporation-IFC-Board-of-Governors-resolution -no-196-1992-special-capital-increase> accessed 21 April 2022.

World Bank Group. International Finance Corporation (IFC). "IFC Board of Governors Resolution; no. 196: 1992 special capital increase" (1992). Washington, D.C.: World Bank Group <http://documents.worldbank.org/curated/en/611201468330313949/ International-Finance-Corporation-IFC-Board-of-Governors-resolution-no-196 -1992-special-capital-increase> accessed 21 April 2022.

World Bank Group, "Multilateral Investment Guarantee Agency (MIGA) Council of Governors resolution No. 47: Increase in overall limit of guarantee capacity" (1994) Washington D.C. <http://documents.worldbank.org/curated/en/186611468153855 347/Multilateral-Investment-Guarantee-Agency-MIGA-Council-of-Governors -resolution-no-47-increase-in-overall-limit-of-guarantee-capacity> accessed 21 April 2022.

World Bank Group, "Multilateral Investment Guarantee Agency (MIGA) Council of Governors resolution No. 101: Increase in Overall Limit on Guarantee Capacity" (2016) Washington D.C. <http://documents.worldbank.org/curated/en/6751614 79292137152/Multilateral-Investment-Guarantee-Agency-MIGA-Council-of-Govern ors-resolution-no-101-Increase-in-Overall-Limit-on-Guarantee-Capacity> accessed 21 April 2022.

World Bank, "World Bank Annual Report 2021" (2021a) <https://www.worldbank .org/en/about/annual-report/covid-response#:~:text=paying%20their%20work ers.-,The%20Bank%20Group%20expects%20to%20deploy%20up%20to%20 %24160%20billion,private%20sector%20solutions%20that%20promote> accessed 21 April 2022.

World Bank, "Press Release: Development Banks Working Together to Optimize Balance Sheets" (22 December 2015) <https://www.worldbank.org/en/news/press -release/2015/12/22/development-banks-optimize-balance-sheets> accessed 21 April 2022.

World Bank Group, "World Bank Group Guarantee Products: Guidance Note" (2016a) <https://ppp.worldbank.org/public-private-partnership/sites/ppp.worldbank.org/ files/documents/PPPCCSA_WBGGuarantees_Final%20_%20English%20_Prin ted%20Oct%202016.pdf> accessed 21 April 2022.

World Bank, "The World Bank Group Moves Quickly to Help Countries Respond to COVID-19" (2020) <https://www.worldbank.org/en/news/feature/2020/04/02/ the-world-bank-group-moves-quickly-to-help-countries-respond-to-covid-19> accessed 21 April 2022.

World Bank, Debt Service Suspension and COVID-19 (2021b). <https://www.worldbank .org/en/news/factsheet/2020/05/11/debt-relief-and-covid-19-coronavir> accessed 21 April 2022.

World Food Conference, "Report of The World Food Conference, Resolution XIII: International Fund for Agricultural Development" (5–16 November 1974) Rome <https://digitallibrary.un.org/record/701143?ln=en> accessed 21 April 2022.

CHAPTER 9

The Green Climate Fund

A Unique Financing Vehicle among International Organizations

Douglas Leys and Rosanna Anderson***

Abstract

Global efforts to prevent catastrophic climate change have given rise to international collaboration, including between developed and developing countries. However, contentious issues around accountability for and financing of climate action remain. Within this context, this chapter explores how the Green Climate Fund (GCF) has navigated these issues to build collaboration and to effectively fulfill its mandate to accelerate low-emission and climate-resilient development in developing countries. The first section of this chapter outlines where GCF fits within the international climate change regime, including underlying principles. Section 1.2 then reviews key provisions of GCF's Governing Instrument, including the composition of its Board and its financing sources. Section 2 of this chapter analyses the development of GCF's capital raising processes, from the initial resource mobilization to the transition to a formal replenishment process. This section also examines how the organization has sought to balance diverse needs, including the need for oversight with accessibility of funding. The third section examines GCF's resource mobilization policies in detail, to provide insight into how its unique mandate, governing structure and fundraising modalities are functionally supported and made operational. The fourth and final section concludes the analysis of GCF's financing modalities and provides an indication of potential future directions for GCF.

* General Counsel of the Green Climate Fund, dleys@gcfund.org.

** Department of Public Law and Governance of Tilburg Law School, the Netherlands, r.j.anderson@tilburguniversity.edu.

DOI:10.1163/9789004460010_010

1 Introduction***

The Green Climate Fund (GCF) is the world's largest dedicated climate change fund and its work is inherently connected to the intricate international politics in this field, as well as broader efforts to combat the effects of climate change. The impacts of climate change vary across regions, countries and populations, with many developing countries bearing the worst consequences with limited capacity to adapt.[1] Additionally, oversight of funds for climate change mitigation and adaptation is necessary to ensure effective results are achieved with integrity, transparency and accountability. Accordingly, GCF inhabits a space of compromise and collaboration, where these different needs must be recognised and balanced. This chapter will explore how GCF has sought to develop suitable policies to respond to this challenge and, in particular, how its representative governance has impacted this process. The first section focuses on the international climate change regime and how this has shaped GCF, particularly in relation to its governing structure. The second section explores the process and politics of GCF's first resource mobilisation and the transition to a formal replenishment. To highlight its unique legal framework, final sections of the chapter review GCF's resource mobilisation and relevant operational policies in detail.

1.1 *International Climate Change Regime and the Green Climate Fund*

GCF is established under the United Nations Framework Convention on Climate Change[2] (UNFCCC or the Convention). The Convention was adopted in 1992, entered into force in 1994 and now has almost universal membership with 197 country Parties. Its ultimate objective is the "stabilization of greenhouse gas concentrations in the atmosphere at a level that would prevent dangerous anthropogenic interference with the climate system". In the 2015 Paris Agreement, which was adopted in Paris at the 21st session of the Conference of the Parties (COP 21) to the UNFCCC on 12 December 2015 and entered into force on 4 November 2016, this goal was further refined to, amongst others, keeping the "increase in the global average temperature to well below 2°C above pre-industrial levels and pursuing efforts to limit the temperature

*** Early drafts of this paper benefitted from inputs by Raj Bavishi, Senior Counsel at the Green Climate Fund Office of the General Counsel.

1 Intergovernmental Panel on Climate Change 2018, 9 para B.5.1.

2 United Nations Framework Convention on Climate Change (adopted 9 May 1992, entered into force 21 March 1994) 1771 U.N.T.S. 107 (the Convention).

increase to 1.5°C".[3] Achieving this goal and addressing the impacts of climate change requires a significant investment of resources. Assigning responsibility for financing climate action, and determining how to distribute those funds, is an ongoing issue in global climate change negotiations. In light of GCF's role as a climate change fund, these matters are central to its governance, operations and other modalities.

The Convention provides guidance on apportioning responsibilities related to climate change action and finance. Article 3.1 of the Convention establishes that the principle of Common but Differentiated Responsibilities and Respective Capabilities (CBDRRC) should apply and that developed country Parties should be taking the lead on climate change action. Consistent with this principle, Article 4.3 of the Convention states that developed country Parties shall transfer financial resources to meet the costs incurred by developing country Parties in complying with their obligations under the Convention. This obligation is reiterated in Article 9.1 of the Paris Agreement, with Article 9.2 encouraging other Parties to provide voluntary support. Article 11 of the Convention also provides that there shall be a financial mechanism for the provision of financial resources on a grant or concessional basis. As GCF was entrusted as one of the operating entities of the financial mechanisms, Article 11 lays down the foundations of GCF's accountability and governance structure.

1.2 *Governing Instrument of the Green Climate Fund*

The Conference of the Parties (COP), the highest decision-making body under the Convention, established GCF in 2010 at its 16th Session.[4] A year later at COP 17, GCF's Governing Instrument (GI) was approved, further defining the objectives and structure of the Fund.[5] Pursuant to the GI, GCF's purpose is to make a significant and ambitious contribution towards attaining the goals set by the international community to combat climate change, particularly the Paris Agreement goals. Further, within the UNFCCC framework, GCF is to promote the paradigm shift towards low emission and climate-resilient development pathways by providing support to developing countries to limit or reduce their greenhouse gas emissions and to adapt to the impacts of climate change. Another crucial element from the GI are the principles which guide

3 Conference of the Parties (adopted 12 December 2015, entered into force 4 November 2016) U.N. Doc. FCCC/CP/2015/L.9/Rev/1 (the Paris Agreement).

4 Conference of the Parties, 'Decision 1/CP.16' FCCC/CP/2010/7/Add.1 (2011).

5 Conference of the Parties, 'Decision 3/CP.17' FCCC/CP/2011/9/Add.1 (2012), 55–66 (the Governing Instrument).

GCF's work: GCF is to provide additional, adequate, and predictable financing to catalyse climate investment in both the public and private sphere, with balanced impacts in both adaptation and mitigation. In achieving these aims, GCF must be transparent, accountable, country-driven, while also promoting environmental, social, economic and development co-benefits and taking a gender-sensitive approach. To ensure GCF has the necessary tools to transform these important objectives into reality, the GI prescribes that GCF shall have juridical personality, legal capacity as necessary for its functions and privileges and immunities necessary for the fulfilment of its purposes.

The foundations for the governance structure and decision-making authority for GCF are set out in decision 1/CP. 16[6] and the GI.[7] Specifically, decision 1/CP. 16 requires that GCF be governed by a Board of 24 members, composed of an equal number of representatives from developing and developed country Parties, including representatives from Small Island Developing States (SIDS) and Least Developed Countries (LDCs).[8] The GI also provides the Board with full responsibility over the funding decisions of GCF.[9] The Board is supported by an independent GCF Secretariat which manages day to day operations and whose Executive Director (ED) enjoys only limited authority which has been delegated by the Board or as otherwise set out in the GI.[10] This Board structure is extremely unusual amongst international financial institutions which generally, though not exclusively, leave a majority of Board seats for donors or funders. As a result, decision-making in GCF requires a balancing act between the different regional, financial and ideological interests on the Board. In particular, the collaboration and compromise between developed and developing party representatives has influenced many of GCF's core policies for receiving and distributing funds.

Another central aspect of GCF shaped by the GI is GCF's financing sources. As previously noted, GCF operates within the UNFCCC framework which requires developed countries to take the lead and transfer financial and technological resources to developing countries.[11] This is codified in the distinction between paragraphs 29 and 30 of the GI: Paragraph 29 mandates that the Fund will receive financial inputs from developed country Parties to the Convention, while paragraph 30 makes it optional for GCF to receive financial inputs from a

6 See note 4, [103].
7 See note 5, [II.C.1.9].
8 See note 4, [103].
9 See note 5, [II.A.5].
10 See note 4, [108]; See note 5.
11 The Convention 2015, Article 3.1.

variety of other sources, both public and private. Within these provisions, the GCF Board has authority to further define the parameters of raising capital. In this context, the representative governance on the Board reinforces the focus on ensuring developed countries fulfil their financing responsibilities under the international climate change regime while also striving for stringent financial oversight.

GCF is not the only operating entity under the UNFCCC's financial mechanism provision. The Global Environment Fund (GEF) is the other functioning operating entity and uses similar contribution-based financing, although it splits the funds between its five conventions.[12] The five conventions are respectively: The Convention on Biological Diversity (CBD), the Minamata Convention on Mercury, the Stockholm Convention on Persistent Organic Pollutants (PoP), the United Nations Convention to Combat Desertification (UNCCD), and the UNFCCC. UN agencies similarly rely on contributions. However, they receive a combination of assessed contributions and voluntary contributions. Multilateral Development Banks (MDBs) also fund projects similar to those in GCF's portfolio. In contrast to GCF, GEF and UN agencies, MBDs predominately provide finance through loans and raise funds in more varied ways, including leveraging their share capital and engaging with capital markets. As demonstrated, GCF is thus unique in its reliance on voluntary contributions for a single purpose.

2 How the Green Climate Fund Raises Capital

2.1 *Launching the Initial Resource Mobilization*

This section discusses the rationale surrounding the timing and nature of the first resource mobilisation effort by GCF. The Board decision for GCF to launch an ad hoc Initial Resource Mobilization (IRM) and transition later to a formal replenishment process was made at the Fifth Board Meeting, held in October 2013.[13] By decision B.07/09 in May 2014, the Board confirmed that certain requirements relating to the Fund's capacity to receive, manage, programme and disburse financial resources had been met and that the IRM process should commence.[14] The Board requested that pledges be received by November 2014,

12 Global Environment Facility 2019, 9–10.

13 Green Climate Fund, 'Decisions of the Board – Fifth Meeting of the Board' GCF/B.05/23 (2013), 12.

14 Green Climate Fund, 'Decisions of the Board – Seventh Meeting of the Board' GCF/B.07/11 (2014), 11.

with the acknowledgment that the process may extend beyond this date. To begin the IRM process, the Board also endorsed arrangements proposed by the Secretariat for the collective engagement of interested contributors.[15] These arrangements included a series of meetings to assess the overall performance, as well as virtual communication between meetings as necessary; two technical sessions and a high-level pledging conference.[16]

2.2 *Themes and Priorities*

At the first and second meetings of interested contributors to the Initial Resource Mobilization Process, held respectively in June/July and September 2014, differing views emerged regarding GCF's financial policies as well as governance matters.[17] These debates then carried over to the eighth Meeting of the Board and subsequent board meetings. The discussion on the policies for contributions at the eighth Board Meeting highlights some of the key contentious issues, including potential earmarking or targeting of financial contributions, proposed linkage between contributions and decision-making in order to incentivise more fundraising and the division of roles between the Board and Secretariat.[18] Procedures for decision-making in the absence of consensus, a matter the Board was mandated by the GI to resolve, also remained a controversial issue for many years. Despite these tense negotiations, the policies for contributions for the IRM were eventually endorsed at the eighth Board Meeting,[19] which paved the way for contributors to make pledges to the Fund.

Of note, the IRM Contributions Policy reaffirms that GCF would accept only the following types of contributions: (a) grants from public and private sources (noting that private sources would require the development of a separate policy); (b) contributions from public sources; and (c) concessional loans from public sources.[20] It was held that grants must "significantly exceed" loan amounts[21] and limitations were set on the uses of loans, for example, they

15 Ibid.

16 Green Climate Fund, 'Arrangements for the first formal replenishment of the Green Climate Fund' GCF/B.21/30/Rev.01, (2018), 4.

17 Green Climate Fund, 'Outcome of the First and Second Meetings of Interested Contributors to the Initial Resource Mobilization Process of the Green Climate Fund' (2014) GCF/B.08/15.

18 Green Climate Fund, 'Report of the Eighth Meeting of The Board' GCF/B.08/46 (2014), [287]-[341].

19 Green Climate Fund, 'Decisions of the Board – Eighth Meeting of the Board' GCF/B.08/45 (2014), [22].

20 Ibid, Annexes XIX–XXIII.

21 Ibid, Annex XIX [III.10].

were not available for non-reimbursable uses such as to finance the administrative budgets of the Fund. It was also agreed that contributions in the form of loans or capital would be accompanied by a minimum grant contribution to the Fund to cover administrative costs[22] and that loan contributions would also be accompanied by a grant contribution to cushion any non-performing loans.[23] Many of these core provisions have carried through to GCF's first replenishment.

2.3 *Pledges as Part of the Initial Resource Mobilization*

After finalizing the policies and other arrangements for contributions, the High-Level Pledging Conference was planned for 20 November 2014 in Berlin, Germany. Even before the Conference, however, almost USD 3 billion had already been pledged.[24] Twenty-one more countries, including four developing countries, pledged at the High-Level Pledging Conference, resulting in a total of the equivalent of approximately USD 9.3 billion.[25] Between the Pledging Conference and COP 20, there were additional pledges announced from Spain, bringing its total pledge to EUR 120 million, and Canada (CAD 300 million).[26] Further pledges were announced at COP 20, with some original contributors increasing contributions and other contributors pledging for the first time. Ultimately, the pledges amounted to the equivalent of approximately USD 10.2 billion and were received from 32 countries, including eight developing countries.[27] The final hurdle for GCF before allocating resources towards projects and programmes, was to reach effective commitment authority. This required 50 % of contributions pledged by November 2014 to be confirmed by fully executed contribution agreements/arrangements by the Secretariat no later than 30 April 2015.[28] In May 2015, GCF was confirmed to have reached the necessary threshold for commitment authority to become effective.[29] Resulting from the contributions from both developing and developed countries, this milestone highlights the collaborative approach of GCF.

---

22 Ibid, Annex XIX [IV.13(c)].

23 Ibid, Annex XIX [VI.25(f)(II)].

24 Green Climate Fund, 'Outcome of the First GCF Pledging Conference and Pledges as of December 31, 2014' (2015) GCF/BM-2015/Inf.01/Rev. 01, [I.2].

25 Ibid, [II.10].

26 Ibid, [III.13].

27 Ibid, [III.14].

28 Ibid, [IV.15].

29 Green Climate Fund, 'Fourth Report of the Green Climate Fund to the Conference of the Parties to the United Nations Framework Convention on Climate Change' GCF/B.10/08 (2015), [V.5.4.3.25].

2.4 *The Green Climate Fund's First Formal Replenishment ("GCF-1")*

One of the major factors influencing the move towards a formal replenishment cycle model was the predictability of funding – an underlying principle required by GCF's GI. During the years following the completion of the IRM, the COP was also active in urging the Board to "agree on the arrangements for the first formal replenishment process of the GCF as soon as feasible"[30] at COP 21 and to launch the replenishment process at COP 23.[31] The COP also noted the importance of the mandate of GCF, particularly in the context of the Paris Agreement and the commitment of developed countries to mobilise USD 100 million per year for climate action.[32] Linkages between the Paris Agreement and UN Sustainable Development Goals and Agenda 2030 have also been highlighted to emphasise the crucial nature of GCF's work.

Turning to the arrangements for the first replenishment process, the Board discussions returned to old debates concerning the balance between oversight and accessibility of GCF funds. Board discussions also considered the desired ambition of the replenishment, with developing countries especially looking for increased scale and potential targets to match the goals outlined under the UNFCCC. While targets did not ultimately form part of the replenishment arrangements, these discussions underlined the urgency and importance of GCF for sustainable development in many countries.

2.5 *Decision to Trigger the Replenishment*

In undertaking the replenishment process, one matter which remained consistent over the years was the proposed trigger for the replenishment. In the first meetings with Interested Contributors for the IRM process and Policies for Contributions to the IRM, held in 2014, there was agreement that the formal replenishment process should be triggered "once the Fund's cumulative funding approvals exceed 60 % of the total contributions"[33] and this number was reaffirmed in subsequent policies. At the twenty-first Meeting of the Board, practical issues with the trigger arose, as there were different potential methods for calculating the Fund's total contributions. Of particular note was the question whether or not to count the USD 2 billion of the pledged USD 3 billion which had not been confirmed by a fully executed contribution agreement. As a result, the decision at the Twenty-first Meeting of the Board[34]

30 Conference of the Parties, 'Decision 7/CP.21' FCCC/CP/2015/10/Add.2 (2015), [10].
31 Conference of the Parties, 'Decision 9/CP.23' FCCC/CP/2017/11/Add.1 (2017), [17].
32 See note 31, [53].
33 See note 22, Annex XIX [1.1(d)].
34 Green Climate Fund, 'Decisions of the Board – Twenty-first meeting of the Board' GCF/B.21/34 (2018), [58].

to commence the formal replenishment did not reference the 60 % trigger, but instead noted the importance of replenishment in accordance with GCF's mandate and its increased capabilities to support low-emission and climate-resilient development.[35]

Echoing the IRM, the first replenishment process was structured around two consultation meetings in April and August of 2019.[36] The actual Pledging Conference for the first replenishment was then held in Paris, France on 24–25 October 2019 and secured financing for a four-year period from 1 January 2020 to 31 December 2023. A total of 30 countries and one region (Wallonia of Belgium) pledged to GCF, including two representing developing countries (Indonesia and Republic of Korea).[37] Total pledges, including pledges made since the high level pledging conference, amounted to over USD 10 billion.[38] The legal arrangements which made this process possible are discussed in the sections below.

3 Legal Aspects of the Green Climate Fund's Fundraising

3.1 *Legal Authority and the Green Climate Fund's Fundraising*

The legal basis for GCF's authority to raise funds can be found in Articles 4.3, 4.4 and 11 of the Convention, Articles 9.1, 9.2 and 9.8 of the Paris Agreement and are operationalised in the context of GCF by paragraphs 29 and 30 of the GI. GCF's Board, with its representative governance, retains much of the authority over decisions which shape GCF's legal framework. Through a decision-making process originally based on consensus, now supplemented by a novel voting procedure adopted in July 2019,[39] the Board determines the basis on which GCF receives contributions. The Executive Director and Secretariat have limited authority to engage in this process, and their roles are predominately restricted to negotiating, accepting and signing agreements on contributions within policy parameters. In certain cases, despite the delegation of authority to the ED, the Board has approved certain contribution agreements which

35 Ibid.

36 Green Climate Fund, 'GCF First Replenishment (GCF-1): Replenishment Summary Report' GCF/B.24/11 (2019), [10].

37 Green Climate Fund, 'Status of Pledges and Contributions' (First Replenishment: GCF-1) (2019).

38 Green Climate Fund, 'Green Climate Fund exceeds USD 10 billion replenishment mark' (2020).

39 Green Climate Fund, 'Decisions of the Board – Twenty-third meeting of the Board' GCF/B.23/23 (2019), [16].

contained conditions which could be regarded as outside the policy on contributions. For example, the first contribution agreements to the GCF came in the form of loans from Canada and France and this established a precedent by which contributions could take form of loans to the GCF on concessionary terms and conditions.[40] Another case was the Board's approval of the contribution from Spain at the Twelfth Board Meeting. Spain requested that as condition of its contribution there should be a provision in the contribution agreement requiring that the Board must approve no less than four projects in any given calendar year in which the payment schedule fell, in order for the Spanish contribution to become valid.[41] After some discussion, the contribution agreement was endorsed by the Board, and the ED stated that the Secretariat would continue to bring contributions containing special and novel provisions to the attention of the Board.[42] However, the Board in general is reluctant to approve contributions which contain conditions. This runs contrary to the spirit of the UNFCCC and the Paris Agreement which require developed country Parties to make contributions to developing country Parties to promote a paradigm shift towards low emission and climate resilient pathways.

3.2 *From Whom Does the Green Climate Fund Receive Contributions and Why?*

This section explores how the underlying objectives and governance elements of GCF played a fundamental role in shaping its contribution policies. Due to the legal structure of GCF, GCF has no share capital, nor does it receive assessed contributions. At present, the GCF does not raise funds from the capital markets. Assessed contributions in the UN system, for example, are mandatory contributions made by Member States[43] in accordance with Article 17(2) of the Charter of the United Nations. Calculated based largely on per capita income, they are required from even the least developed countries. However, the unique mandate of GCF to facilitate the transfer of financial resources from developing to developed countries is at odds with requiring mandatory contributions from all country Parties and could undermine its critical objective. This distinctive objective means that GCF's main source of contributions is developed countries, as outlined in paragraph 29 of the GI.

40 Green Climate Fund, 'Decisions of the Board – Twelfth Meeting of the Board' GCF/B.12/32 (2016), [35].

41 Green Climate Fund, 'Report of the Twelfth meeting of the Board' GCF/B.12/33 (2016), [199]-[205].

42 Ibid, [203].

43 United Nations, 'Charter of the United Nations', (1945), 4(1).

However, the GCF resource mobilisation processes have attracted contributions from developing countries, indicating the collaboration and urgency at the heart of its work.

Theoretically, as per the Paris Agreement and paragraph 30 of GCF's GI, GCF may also receive financial inputs from alternative sources. The Policy for Contributions to GCF for the first replenishment therefore provides that, in addition to developed country Parties, GCF may receive financial inputs from:

(a) Non-Parties to the Convention;
(b) Public and private entities; and
(c) Philanthropic foundations, among others.[44]

In practice, obtaining Board approval and developing policies in relation to contributions received from alternative sources has been a drawn-out process. In July 2018, at the Twentieth Meeting of the Board, a document outlining policies and procedures for contributions from philanthropic foundations and other non-public and alternative sources was tabled in the agenda.[45] While some Board members indicated they felt the policy was already overdue, Board members from developing country Parties indicated a preference to keep the focus on ensuring developed country Parties fulfil their financial obligations under the Convention and the Paris Agreement. In light of the lack of consensus, the policy was not discussed during the Board meeting and will be considered by the Board at a later date.[46]

Additional sources of funds for GCF may also include investment income earned on the balance of the Green Climate Fund Trust Fund and reflows from outgoing loans and other financial products, including interest and principal repayments, net of repayments to loan contributors, as well as returns on equity investments.[47] The Green Climate Fund Trust Fund was established at the 16th session of the COP to the UNFCCC, inviting the International Bank for Reconstruction and Development (IBRD), also referred to as the World Bank, to serve as the interim trustee of GCF.[48]

44 Green Climate Fund, 'Decisions of the Board – Twenty-fourth meeting of the Board' GCF/B.24/17 (2019), Annex I section II.4.

45 Green Climate Fund, 'Policies for contributions from philanthropic foundations and other alternative sources' GCF/B.20/08/Rev.01 (2018).

46 Green Climate Fund, 'Report of the Twentieth Meeting of the Board' GCF/B.20/26 (2018), [59]-[122].

47 See note 50, Annex I [II.4].

48 Green Climate Fund, 'Agreement on the Terms and Conditions for the Administration of the Green Climate Fund Trust Fund', (2013).

3.3 *Legal Agreements/Arrangements for Contributions*

A pledge to GCF is a political commitment signifying a willingness to contribute funds. This statement must undergo an important conversion process in order to become funds which are accessible to GCF. GCF's funds are held in trust in accordance with the Amended and Restated Agreement on the Terms and Conditions for the Administration of the Green Climate Fund Trust Fund (Amended and Restated Terms and Conditions).[49] These provide that the World Bank (the Trustee) must establish and administer a Trust Fund to receive contributions from contributors in accordance with the terms of the contribution agreements entered into with the Contributors. The Standard Provisions Applicable to the Green Climate Fund Trust Fund (Standard Provisions)[50] also form part of the governing documentation for the trust arrangements, by outlining key definitions and detailing other aspects of how the Trustee may use the funds. In accordance with these terms and provisions, the Trustee may only administer the funds and assets which make up the Trust Fund in accordance with the relevant decisions of the Board of GCF or other designated person(s). This includes, for example, the policies governing the process by which the Trustee may receive and credit any return or reflow of funds to the Trust Fund.

A key legal requirement outlined in the Amended and Restated Terms and Conditions is that each contribution be formalised in a contribution agreement, executed by the Fund, the Trustee and the Contributor. The Contributor is authorized to make contributions to the resources of the GCF within the parameters set out in the GI. The Fund will not only receive financial inputs from country Parties to the Convention but also may receive financial outputs from a "variety of other sources, public and private, including alternative sources".[51] The Standard Provisions provide that contribution agreements include all contribution agreements and arrangements, including loan agreements. Contributors may negotiate regarding the terms and form of their contributions. One illustration of this, particularly common for large contributions to GCF, is when a Contributor requests to formalize their pledge through the use of a non-legally binding contribution arrangement instead of a legally binding agreement. This requires the clauses and language used in the agreement to be tailored accordingly. The arbitration clause, for example, may be

---

49 Green Climate Fund, 'Decisions of the Board – Nineteenth meeting of the Board' GCF/B.19/43 (2018), [16].

50 Green Climate Fund, 'Decisions of the Board – Second Meeting of the Board' GCF/B.02-12/12 (2012), [9].

51 Conference of the Parties, 'Decision 3/CP.17' FCCC/CP/2011/9/Add.1 (2012), 55–66 (the Governing Instrument), [29]-[30].

modified and a disclaimer added to indicate that the document is an 'administrative arrangement' rather than a contractual agreement.

In fulfilling its role executing contribution agreements and managing GCF's day-to-day functions, the GCF Secretariat is held to high policy and fiduciary standards.[52] The policies, as decided by the Board, require having appropriate measures in place to prevent corrupt, fraudulent, and otherwise illegal practices, including the prevention of the use of Fund resources to finance terrorist activity. Similarly, the Secretariat is required to adopt best practice fiduciary principles and standards relating to anticorruption, countering of financing of terrorism, fraud, financial sanctions, embargoes and anti-money laundering, as well as such other fiduciary principles as may be identified by the Board as best practices.[53] These fiduciary principles and standards, including anti-money laundering and counterterrorism financing, are also imposed on entities accredited by the Fund via accreditation master agreements and/or arrangements with accredited entities.[54] Any allegations of violation of the relevant fiduciary principles and standards is to be reported to, and investigated by, GCF's Independent Integrity Unit.[55]

3.4 *Types of Contributions and Policy Conditions*

The terms and conditions under which these financial resources may be provided to the Fund are approved by the Board. The policies therefore reflect the priorities and compromises of the diverse governing caucus, as well as GCF's operational needs. For example, there are a number of risks which GCF is exposed to as a result of its unique funding modality. Most notably, GCF's contributions policies must account for risks such as unfulfilled pledges, underperforming loans and loss as a result of fluctuating exchange rates. In its most recent iteration, the Policy for Contributions to GCF for the first replenishment thus authorises and outlines the conditions for making contributions to the Fund while imposing protective measures. In accordance with the Policy for Contributions, contributions to GCF may take the form of grants, loans or capital payments and are authorised via contribution agreements/arrangements signed by the contributors, GCF and the Trustee.[56] While the Board has final

---

52 See note 18, Annex II.

53 Green Climate Fund, 'Decisions of the Board – Eighteenth Meeting of the Board' GCF/B.18/23 (2017), [8].

54 Green Climate Fund, 'Template AMA: GCF Accreditation Master Agreement' (2020).

55 Green Climate Fund, 'Decisions of the Board – Twenty-Second Meeting of the Board' GCF/B.22/24 (2019), Annex XIV.

56 See note 50, Annex I [IV.12].

authority over such matters, the ED has been delegated the authority to enter into contribution agreements which are consistent with applicable Board policies.

Reflecting their low level of risk and other respective benefits, contributions in the form of grants enjoy the greatest flexibility and may be used for any financial instrument (e.g., grants, concessional loans, equity, guarantees), administrative budgets, and the accredited entity fees. As a result of limitations on other forms of contributions, grant contributions must significantly exceed amounts contributed in the form of loans and capital.[57]

Capital contributions may be used for financial instruments which are meant to generate reflows. Capital contributions may not be used to finance grants or administrative budget, unless the specific terms of such capital contribution allow for such use. Consequently, capital contributors are required to make a grant contribution to cover administrative budgets and AE fees, amounting to at least 10 % of the amount of the pledged capital contribution. Overall, it is recommended that aggregate capital contributions do not exceed 20 % of the total aggregated amount of pledges for the replenishment period, a threshold which may be reviewed in the future.[58] Both grants and capital contributions may be paid in the form of cash or promissory notes. The encashment of promissory notes will be based on an encashment schedule agreed between the contributor and GCF to ensure a predictable and reliable cash flow.

In relation to loan contributions, GCF prohibits cross-subsidization between providers of grants and providers of loans to ensure the financial sustainability of GCF. The use of loan contributions is also limited to the financing of loans on terms less concessional than the loan contributions and is unavailable for non-reimbursable uses, such as to provide grants or to finance the administrative budgets and AE fees. Similar to capital contributions, loan contributors are therefore required to provide a grant contribution to cover these non-reimbursable costs, in the amount of at least 10 % of the amount of the pledged loan contribution. Loan contributions from an individual contributor are also limited to 40 % of their total contribution, unless the grant contribution from that individual contributor exceeds the grant contribution provided in the previous resource mobilization period.

GCF's Policy for Contributions for the first replenishment provides protective provisions for non-performing loans which requires that losses from non-performing loans will be borne on a pro-rata basis by contributors whose contributions were allocated to loans. Fulfilling this condition requires GCF to

57 Ibid, Annex I, Section V.

58 Ibid.

model and monitor cash-flows. In addition, in accordance with the prudential debt limit considerations and principle of no cross-subsidization, a portion of the total grant contributions provided by loan contributors are held as a cushion for non-performing loans. The cushion for the first replenishment was set at 20 % of the total loan amount for the loan contributor.

3.5 *Other Potential Conditions on Contributions*

On numerous occasions the GCF Board has rejected proposals, primarily from developed, contributor country Parties, to attach additional conditions onto contributions and the use of GCF's financial resources. Since early Board meetings, proposals were made to link contributions and decision-making to encourage contributions and to allow the targeting or earmarking of contributions. At the Eighth Meeting of the Board, for example, an attempt to allow up to 20 % of total confirmed contributions to be targeted was removed prior to the Board's adoption of the Policies for Contributions for the IRM.[59] Decisions on policies perceived to be imposing new conditions on access to and use of GCF's financial resources have generally been unable to gain the consensus needed for adoption. However, there remain avenues through which country Parties condition, at least informally, the making of their contribution on certain policies being adopted. Noteworthy examples include the adoption of the decision-making procedures in the absence of consensus at the Twenty-third Meeting of the Board and the adoption of the Updated Gender Policy and Action Plan 2020–2023 at the Twenty-fourth Meeting of the Board, which are examined below.

The Board is mandated by paragraph 14 of the GI to develop decision-making procedures in the absence of consensus. For some Board members, obtaining agreement on these decision-making procedures had been a priority for years. As a result of this, during the IRM, attempts were made to make the approval of decision-making procedures in the absence of consensus a required condition for contributions. However, this position was strongly rejected on the basis that contributions should be strictly unconditional. Nevertheless, concerns around the perceived governance gap persisted and re-emerged as a significant issue in the lead up to the first replenishment. In July 2019, significant progress was made at the Twenty-third Board Meeting when the procedure on decision-making in the event that all efforts at reaching consensus have been exhausted was adopted.[60] Consultations on the first replenishment were then

59 See note 21, [296]-[324].

60 See note 44, [16].

held in August of the same year, during which another ongoing policy matter, the importance of which had been emphasized by contributors, was raised; namely, the need to update GCF's gender policy. A successful pledging conference for GCF's first replenishment was held in October 2019, demonstrating strong and continued confidence in the Fund's ability to fulfil its mandate.[61] The following month, at the Twenty-fourth Meeting of the Board, the Board ultimately adopted both the Policy for Contributions to the Green Climate Fund for the first replenishment[62] and the Updated Gender Policy and Action Plan 2020–2023.[63] Considering prior difficulties to gain consensus on both the decision-making policies and gender policy, the timing of their adoption, and the proximity to the first replenishment pledges, is noteworthy.

Another method through which contributors seek to exert soft influence over the use of GCF's financial resources is through accompanying letters, setting out priorities regarding the use of contributions. Recent examples include the letter of 3 July 2020 from the Government of Japan, regarding Japan's pledge of up to USD 1.5 bn.[64] In the letter it outlines four key expectations of Japan, namely, that GCF will promote infrastructure-related projects, further promote adaptation financing, enhance application of wide-ranged knowledge and expertise of climate change in GCF projects and realise balanced geographical representation in the composition of GCF Secretariat staff. By way of another example, in a letter dated 9 October 2020, the United Kingdom confirmed its additional contribution of GBP 1.44 billion and emphasised its keen interest in GCF taking all reasonable and adequate steps to tackle sexual exploitation, sexual abuse and sexual harassment.[65] It must be noted that these letters do not carry legal weight and the Board retains authority with regard to the financial decisions of GCF. However, as an entity relying on voluntary contributions, there is an incentive for the Board to consider the views of contributors.

3.6 *The Green Climate Fund's Commitment Authority*

GCF's commitment authority is calculated by reference to the total amount of available resources in the form of cash and promissory notes in the Trust Fund, which are yet to be committed by GCF. As a result, the commitment authority of GCF varies based on receipt of funds and promissory notes and

61 Green Climate Fund 'Pledging Conference for GCF's First Replenishment' (2019).
62 See note 50, [19].
63 Ibid, [39].
64 Green Climate Fund 'Contribution Arrangement with Japan (GCF-1)' (2020), 7–8.
65 Green Climate Fund 'Contribution Arrangement with the United Kingdom (GCF-1)' (2020), 6–9.

commitments. Based on the tracking by GCF, as part of risk management, it is expected that there will always be sufficient commitment authority available in the Trust Fund to meet GCF's obligations and support funding decisions. In the unlikely event that GCF has insufficient commitment authority, there is a policy to prioritize how the funds will be committed and transferred.[66]

3.7 *The Green Climate Fund's Risk Management*

The inevitable financial risks faced by GCF as a result of its funding structure are acknowledged in its policies dealing with the different types of contributions GCF receives. Managing these risks has always been a priority for GCF, as evidenced by the fact that the financial risk management and investment frameworks were one of the eight essential requirements for the IRM to proceed.[67] Risk policies have continued to be updated since this time, to provide appropriate buffers and protect GCF's interests and resources.

The first specific risk managed by GCF worth noting is liquidity risk, which refers to the possibility of having insufficient available cash in the Trust Fund to meet payment obligations of GCF. Liquidity concerns would arise, if GCF's cash position was lower than its scheduled or unscheduled payment obligations at any point in time. The mechanisms implemented to manage this risk require GCF to commit only available cash and promissory note deposits, not amounts based on pledges. In addition, GCF closely monitors the risk of non-payment and set aside a financial reserve from the funding available for the minimum liquidity requirements as determined by GCF's risk management framework. The Fund's liquidity risk appetite in the Risk Appetite Statement requires GCF's liquidity reserve (on any day) to be sufficient to sustain GCF's net funding requirements for at least one year.[68] The Risk Appetite Statement aims to provide guidance on: overall level of risk that GCF is willing to take on, types of risk to be monitored, and qualitative appetite statements and quantitative metrics in the day-to-day operations of specific business units.[69]

The related risk of non-payment of contributions, which similarly could affect the ability of GCF to finance programs and projects, arises when pledges fail to be converted or when pledge agreements/arrangements are otherwise not honoured. This risk is particularly acute in the case of contribution arrangements which are non-legally binding documents and thus more susceptible to

66 See note 50, Annex I, Section VII.

67 See note 17, Annex XXII.

68 Green Climate Fund, 'Decisions of the Board – Seventeenth Meeting of the Board' GCF/B.17/21 (2017), Annex VI.

69 Green Climate Fund, 'Risk appetite statement (Component II)', (2017), [4].

political changes. In order to minimise this risk, the Secretariat must monitor contributions and report on them to the Board, convert pledges or encash promissory notes in a timely and scheduled manner, regularly and actively engage with relevant contributors and diversify contributors.

GCF must also grapple with the potential risk of incurring losses in the value of contributions due to Foreign Exchange (FX) rate fluctuations, referred to as the FX risk. Due to constantly changing nature of FX rates, the USD equivalent value of contributions denominated in non-USD currencies varies over time, resulting in increases or decreases in the USD equivalent value, to which the Fund is exposed.[70] The prevailing approach has been natural hedging and, where possible, matching currencies of loan contributions to the currencies of GCF's commitments to AEs. For instance, if the main currency is USD in the country in which an AE is incorporated, then any potential exchange risk is mitigated by ensuring that the loan to that country is disbursed in USD accordingly. For various reasons, these approaches have proven an insufficient buffer. Accordingly, GCF is currently in the process of examining alternative options for mitigating the FX risk. Additional options outlined in a recent report to be considered by the Board include the establishment of an FX reserve to act as an FX commitment risk buffer, the limited use of hedging in the FX Market and the adoption of the EUR as the accounting base currency.[71]

3.8 *Trigger for the Green Climate Fund's Replenishment*

In contrast to the 60 % trigger initially adopted for the first replenishment, there has since been a movement towards launching GCF's next replenishment a fixed 30 months after the beginning of the first replenishment programming period, i.e. July 2022.[72] There was strong support from several contributors to have a fixed four-year period as this enhances the predictability of contributions and sound financial management.[73] The changing of the trigger for the next replenishment reflects ongoing efforts by GCF to pursue best practice in fulfilling its mandate, specifically in relation to the need to provide predicable financial resources to developing countries.

---

70 Green Climate Fund 'Initial analysis of options to minimize the effects of currency fluctuations on the commitment authority of the GCF' GCF/B.27/18 (2020), [3].

71 Ibid, [14]-[33].

72 Green Climate Fund 'Summation by the Global Facilitator – First Replenishment of the Green Climate Fund First Consultation Meeting' (2019), [20].

73 Ibid.

4 Conclusion

At its core, GCF is a mechanism for the crucial transfer of financial resources from developed countries to developing countries to accelerate climate action and achieve the goals set out in the Paris Agreement and the Convention. GCF's success as the leading climate finance institution depends to a great extent on the sustainability of its model and its ability to garner widespread international support. Broad and representative participation in the governance of GCF is therefore key to ensuring its actions and policies respond to the diverse needs of the global community. For example, the composition of GCF's Board is, in essence, the operationalisation of genuine North-South cooperation in action. It is unique to the GCF that the Board is composed of an equal number of members from the developing (South) and developed (North) country Parties. The board consists of 24 members in total and a two-thirds majority of the members must be present at decision making procedures to constitute a quorum. Decisions are made by consensus and in the event consensus cannot be achieved and the voting procedures are triggered, any such decision must have a four fifths majority before the decision can be valid and effective. Furthermore, the voluntary deployment of resources to GCF and its vast network of accredited and direct access entities is a model to be emulated in not only addressing climate change but wider issues such as poverty alleviation and sustainable development. It is from this perspective that GCF is unique in its quest to advance the frontiers of North-South cooperation in a tangible way. To retain its central position in the field of climate finance and continue to accelerate the green transition, GCF must maintain its participatory governance and decision-making procedures, monitor its policies for effectiveness, and continue to evolve based on lessons learnt.

References

Conference of the Parties to the UNFCCC

Report of the Conference of the Parties on its sixteenth session, held in Cancun from 29 November to 10 December 2010 Addendum Part Two: Action taken by the Conference of the Parties at its sixteenth session FCCC/CP/2010/7/Add.1 (2011).

Report of the Conference of the Parties on its seventeenth session, held in Durban from 28 November to 11 December 2011. Addendum. Part two: Action taken by the Conference of the Parties at its seventeenth session FCCC/CP/2011/9/Add.1 (2012).

Report of the Conference of the Parties on its twenty-first session, held in Paris from 30 November to 13 December 2015 Addendum Part two: Action taken by the Conference of the Parties at its twenty-first session FCCC/CP/2015/10/Add.2 (2015).
Report of the Conference of the Parties on its twenty-third session, held in Bonn from 6 to 18 November 2017 Addendum Part two: Action taken by the Conference of the Parties at its twenty-third session FCCC/CP/2017/11/Add.1 (2017).

Green Climate Fund

Decisions of the Board – Second Meeting of the Board GCF/B.02-12/12 (2012).
Decisions of the Board – Fifth Meeting of the Board GCF/B.05/23 (2013).
Decisions of the Board – Seventh Meeting of the Board GCF/B.07/11 (2014).
Outcome of the First and Second Meetings of Interested Contributors to the Initial Resource Mobilization Process of the Green Climate Fund (2014) GCF/B.08/15.
Decisions of the Board – Eighth Meeting of the Board GCF/B.08/45 (2014).
Report of the Eighth Meeting of The Board GCF/B.08/46 (2014).
Outcome of the First GCF Pledging Conference and Pledges as of December 31, 2014 (2015) GCF/BM-2015/Inf.01/Rev. 01.
Fourth Report of the Green Climate Fund to the Conference of the Parties to the United Nations Framework Convention on Climate Change GCF/B.10/08 (2015).
Decisions of the Board – Twelfth Meeting of the Board GCF/B.12/32 (2016).
Report of the Twelfth meeting of the Board GCF/B.12/33 (2016).
Decisions of the Board – Seventeenth Meeting of the Board GCF/B.17/21 (2017).
Decisions of the Board – Eighteenth Meeting of the Board GCF/B.18/23 (2017).
Decisions of the Board – Nineteenth meeting of the Board GCF/B.19/43 (2018).
Policies for contributions from philanthropic foundations and other alternative sources GCF/B.20/08/Rev.01 (2018).
Report of the Twentieth Meeting of the Board GCF/B.20/26 (2018).
Decisions of the Board – Twenty-first meeting of the Board GCF/B.21/34 (2018).
Decisions of the Board – Twenty-Second Meeting of the Board GCF/B.22/24 (2019).
Summation by the Global Facilitator – First Replenishment of the Green Climate Fund First Consultation Meeting (2019).
Pledging Conference for GCF's First Replenishment (2019).
Status of Pledges and Contributions (First Replenishment: GCF-1) (2019).
Decisions of the Board – Twenty-third meeting of the Board GCF/B.23/23 (2019).
GCF First Replenishment (GCF-1): Replenishment Summary Report GCF/B.24/11 (2019).
Decisions of the Board – Twenty-fourth meeting of the Board GCF/B.24/17 (2019).
Template AMA: GCF Accreditation Master Agreement (2020).
Contribution Arrangement with Japan (GCF-1)' (2020).
Contribution Arrangement with the United Kingdom (GCF-1) (2020).

Initial analysis of options to minimize the effects of currency fluctuations on the commitment authority of the GCF GCF/B.27/18 (2020).

Green Climate Fund exceeds USD 10 billion replenishment mark (2020) <https://www.greenclimate.fund/news/green-climate-fund-exceeds-usd-10-billion-replenishment-mark> accessed 12 November 2020.

Template AMA: GCF Accreditation Master Agreement (2020) <https://www.greenclimate.fund/sites/default/files/document/accreditation-master-agreement-template.pdf> accessed 19 January 2021.

Global Environment Facility, Instrument for the Establishment of the Restructured GEF (2019).

Intergovernmental Panel on Climate Change, 'Summary for Policymakers' in Global warming of 1.5°C: An IPCC Special Report on the impacts of global warming of 1.5°C above pre-industrial levels and related global greenhouse gas emission pathways, in the context of strengthening the global response to the threat of climate change, sustainable development, and efforts to eradicate poverty (2018).

Paris Agreement Under the United Nations Framework Convention on Climate Change (adopted 12 December 2015, entered into force 4 November 2016) U.N. Doc. FCCC/CP/2015/L.9/Rev/1.

The White House: Office of the Press Secretary 'Statement by President Trump on the Paris Climate Accord' (2017) <https://it.usembassy.gov/statement-president-trump-paris-climate-accord/> accessed 25 November 2020.

United Nations Framework Convention on Climate Change (adopted 9 May 1992, entered into force 21 March 1994) 1771 U.N.T.S. 107.

CHAPTER 10

Developments in the Labelled Bond Concept

More than just Green

*Heikki Cantell**

Abstract

Multilateral development banks (MDBs) are typically established by a treaty among sovereign states which are the shareholders of these organizations and subscribe to their capital. Beyond shareholding, Member countries do not finance these entities' activities directly. Instead, MDBs fund themselves on the capital markets by issuing bonds. These bonds, however, have not traditionally been linked to specific types of projects financed by such MDBs to fulfil their mandates. In a major departure from established practice, from 2007 onwards, two of the largest MDBs started issuing bonds dedicated to environmental projects. These bonds came to be known as "green bonds". After close to a decade and a half of mainly green bonds, the markets have seen an acceleration in the growth and diversification of bonds relating to defined project types or themes, known as labelled bonds. This chapter is written in light of these rapid developments, which deserve to be better explored and understood in the literature. Furthermore, in the broader society and even among some practitioners in the field, there is a need for further awareness of and discussion about the various types of bonds, their taxonomy and their related legal and policy considerations. To achieve these aims, this chapter begins by describing the origins of the labelled bond concept, starting with green bonds to then turn to the current array of social, sustainability and sustainability-linked bonds. To illustrate the legal aspects associated with this evolving labelled bond concept, this article uses COVID-19 Response Bonds as a case study. Following this, the discussion turns to the latest developments in, and future prospects of, the labelled bond concept, including in the context of major initiatives in the European Union and increasing market demand. The chapter concludes by arguing that labelled bonds have a critical and possibly under-appreciated role to play in financing a sustainable response to, and recovery from, the pandemic, as well as a transition to a lower-carbon future. MDBs have a key role to play in this regard.

* General Counsel and Head of Legal, Nordic Investment Bank, heikki.cantell@nib.int.

 | DOI:10.1163/9789004460010_011

1 Introduction

MDBs are supranational institutions typically established and owned by states.[1] Some MDBs have entities other than states as members; the European Bank for Reconstruction and Development (EBRD), for instance, comprises the European Investment Bank (EIB) as a shareholder.[2] While they differ in terms of membership, purpose and geographical scope, MDBs are united in their function of lending money to sovereign or non-sovereign borrowers to promote social and economic goals and achieve a variety of development goals based on the particular MDB's mandate and mission.[3]

The states that establish an MDB, along with states who become members of the MDB after its formation, also own the MDB as shareholders. At the time of establishment, typically there is an injection of initial capital in proportion to the organization's ownership structure. This capital injection allows the organization to begin its operations, such as acquiring a headquarters and hiring initial staff. After this point, the member states' financial contributions stop and the usual way an MDB funds its ongoing operations is through the issuance of bonds on the international debt capital markets, where MDBs raise the large quantities of funds needed to finance their loans. In this way, as this article underscores, MDBs play an important role not only through their financings, but also via their engagement in the international debt capital markets.

Until recently, such bonds issued by MDBs were not linked to specific types of projects that the MDB was financing under its mandate and mission. The proceeds of a bond issue would typically be included in an MDB's ordinary resources and be used to finance such MDB lending activities in general. Beyond this, however, MDBs' bond frameworks did not provide for bond proceeds to apply differently based on any eligibility criteria related to the type or theme of a project.

However, in a major departure from established practice, starting in 2007 two of the largest MDBs – the EIB and the International Bank for Reconstruction

1 In this article, "multilateral development bank" is given a broad meaning and includes international financial institutions (IFIs), such as the Nordic Investment Bank, and other related multilateral entities engaged in cross-border project financing. Some MDBs, such as the European Investment Bank, can arguably be considered to be both an investment bank and a global development bank.

2 European Bank for Reconstruction and Development *'EBRD Shareholders and Board of Governors'*, <https://www.ebrd.com/shareholders-and-board-of-governors.html>, accessed 21 October 2021.

3 For an overview of the main global, regional, and sub-regional MDBs, see Delikanli, Dimitrov and Agolli 2018.

and Development (World Bank) – started issuing bonds dedicated to environmental projects. Now known as green bonds, these are fixed income debt instruments whose proceeds are dedicated to projects, activities and assets that are meant to benefit the environment.[4] Following the emergence of green bonds, there has in the latter part of the last decade been a steady acceleration in the growth and diversification of bonds relating to defined project types or themes. These are known as themed or labelled bonds.[5] While the most well-known type of labelled bond remains the green bond, this article argues that the significance, impacts and prospects of the expansion of the labelled bond concept allows for a much wider range of subject matters than just the environment.

This chapter is written in light of these rapid developments in the labelled bond concept, which deserve to be better explored and understood in the literature.[6] Furthermore, in the broader society and even among some practitioners in the field, there is a need for further awareness of and discussion about the various types of labelled bonds, their taxonomy and their related legal and policy considerations. Similarly, greater attention should be given to the role labelled bonds can play in responding to – and recovering from – the COVID-19 pandemic, as well as to mitigate climate change risks in the longer term.

Against this backdrop, this chapter will provide a brief history of the development of green bonds. Following this, the focus will turn to the rapid evolution and expansion of the labelled bond concept, including, most recently, sustainability-linked bonds. As a case study, COVID-19 Response Bonds provide a timely and relevant illustration of the emerging types of thematic bonds and their attendant legal issues. The chapter will then look at the latest developments related to, and the future of, the labelled bond concept. Finally, a call for further innovation and growth in themed bonds, and the critical role of MDBs in this connection, will accompany other concluding thoughts.

---

4 Park 2018, 1.

5 The terms “themed”, “thematic” and “labelled” are synonymous. For the purposes of simplicity and consistency, in this article, “labelled” bonds will be used.

6 As Maltais and Nykvist note: “Despite significant growth there has to date been very little academic research on green bonds”: Maltais and Nykvist 2020, 2.

2 Tracing the Emergence of Green Bonds

This section provides a summary of the background to the emergence of green bonds in the context of MDBs, starting with traditional bond issuance, key developments, and ongoing diversification of the green bond issuer base.

MDBs have a long experience in financing their lending activities by borrowing money from international debt capital markets by issuing bonds. Distilling these to their essence, bonds are commoditized debt instruments representing, in substance, a promise from the issuer to repay the principal of the bond to the holder at maturity in addition to, if applicable, a periodic coupon over the life of the bond. The World Bank, for instance, has issued bonds since 1947 to finance its development projects.[7] These bonds issued by MDBs were historically not linked to specific or thematic project types.

However, in 2007 and 2008, two watershed events occurred that paved a new way for MDBs to raise money on the debt capital markets. In 2007, EIB issued a "Climate Awareness Bond". The issue of this bond marked a turning point as proceeds were for the first time "ring-fenced" in a specific portfolio.[8] Shortly thereafter, in 2008, the World Bank issued its first green bond in response to market demand and involving a diverse range of stakeholders. The proceeds of this particular bond would be applied exclusively to eligible environmental projects and impact reporting was included as a key element of the process. An interdisciplinary research body, the Centre for International Climate and Environmental Research (CICERO), was closely involved in the green bond's development and provided the first research-based evaluation of the green bond investment framework to evaluate its environmental robustness (known as a second opinion).[9] Setting aside their tailored use of proceeds wording and any corresponding additional disclosure, green bonds otherwise closely follow the issuance process used for classic unlabelled bonds (including in respect of

7 World Bank, '*10 Years of Green Bonds: Creating the Blueprint for Sustainability Across Capital Markets*', <https://www.worldbank.org/en/news/immersive-story/2019/03/18/10-years-of-green-bonds-creating-the-blueprint-for-sustainability-across-capital-markets>, accessed 21 October 2021.

8 European Investment Bank. '*Climate Awareness Bonds*', <https://www.eib.org/en/investor_relations/cab/index.htm>, accessed 21 October 2021.

9 World Bank, '*10 Years of Green Bonds: Creating the Blueprint for Sustainability Across Capital Markets*', <https://www.worldbank.org/en/news/immersive-story/2019/03/18/10-years-of-green-bonds-creating-the-blueprint-for-sustainability-across-capital-markets>, accessed 21 October 2021.

the applicable documentation, financial disclosure requirements and placement process).[10]

Initially, only MDBs issued green bonds, and the volumes were small. Volumes have since increased remarkably, as shown in Graph 10.1 below. Growth in volume has gone hand in hand with a diversification of the issuer type.[11] Presently, in addition to MDBs, green bonds are also issued by commercial banks, corporates, sovereigns and a number of government agencies. A notable agency example is Fannie Mae, which in 2020 was the largest issuer of green bonds by volume with total a total issuance of USD 13 billion.[12]

Despite this growth in volume and diversification, the overall green bond market represented less than 1% of the total bond market in 2019 and was

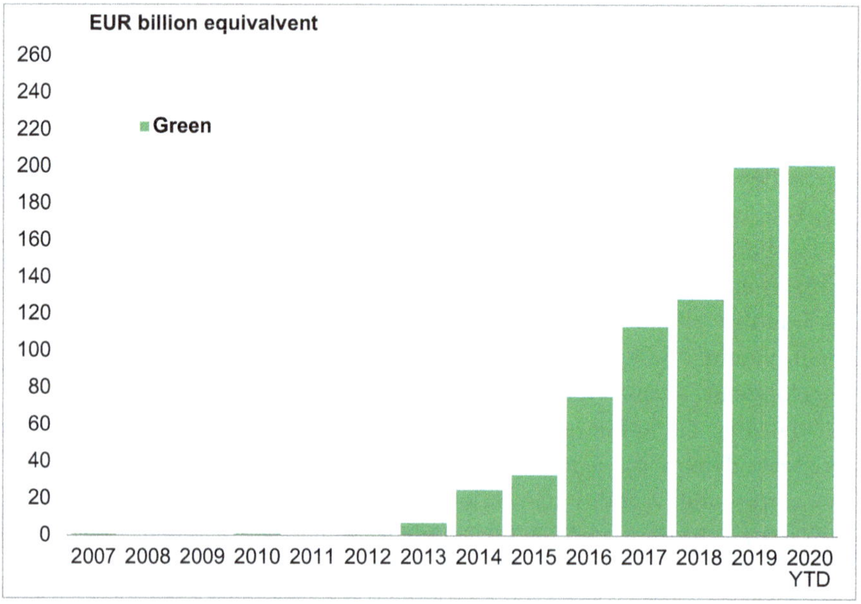

GRAPH 10.1 Growth in issuance of green bonds 2007 – Nov. 2020
SOURCE: CRÉDIT AGRICOLE CIB SUSTAINABLE BANKING (AS OF 20 NOVEMBER 2020)

10 Ketterer et al. 2019, 3.

11 *Ibid*, pp. 2–3.

12 Climate Bonds Initiative, *'Record $269.5bn green issuance for 2020: Late surge sees pandemic year pip 2019 total by $3bn'*, <https://www.climatebonds.net/2021/01/record-2695bn-green-issuance-2020-late-surge-sees-pandemic-year-pip-2019-total-3bn>, accessed 21 October 2021.

concentrated in a handful of countries and regions, namely Europe, the United States and China.[13]

3 Beyond Green: Evolution and Expansion of the Bond Concept

Following the initial green bond issuances in the late 2000s, green bond design underwent a rapid evolution to cover even more targeted themes than "just" green. An illustrative example is the Nordic Investment Bank's (NIB) inaugural Nordic–Baltic "Blue Bond" for water management and protection. This Nordic–Baltic "Blue Bond" was issued in February 2019 and was the first blue bond listed on Nasdaq's Nordic Sustainable Debt Market. For context, NIB has been issuing green bonds since 2011, for a total of almost EUR 5 billion, financing over 90 projects. Given NIB has an explicit environmental mandate and that it had been assessing the environmental impact of projects for a long time prior, issuing green (and other themed) bonds was a logical (and easy) step for NIB. The same can be said, *mutatis mutandis*, for a number of MDBs.

The Nordic–Baltic "Blue Bond" was issued under NIB's Environmental Bond (NEB) Framework. This Framework has a "Dark Green" second opinion from CICERO, which is the highest possible grade.[14] The NEB framework allows NEB bonds to finance projects from several of NIB's seven eligible project categories, or to just focus on one type, which was the case for the Nordic–Baltic "Blue Bond". The proceeds of the Nordic–Baltic "Blue Bond" were designated for eligible projects in the fields of wastewater treatment and water pollution prevention. More specifically, eligible projects under the Nordic–Baltic "Blue Bond" included those with the aim of (I) reducing discharges into water (mainly phosphorus, nitrogen, organic matter, heavy metals, plastics and pharmaceuticals); (II) supporting pollution prevention and the development of climate change resilient infrastructure; and (III) minimizing groundwater extraction and contamination, and improving the replenishment of aquifers, extending protected areas, and strengthening the protection and restoration of water and marine ecosystems, and biodiversity (such as wetlands, rivers and lakes, coastal areas and open sea zones).[15]

---

13 Ketterer et al. 2019, 1.

14 CICERO's 'Shades of Green' methodology provides information on how well a green bond aligns with a low-carbon resilient future. The two other lower grades are Light Green and Medium Green. For more, see CICERO. *'Shades of Green: Green Bonds'*, <https://cicero.green/green-bonds>, accessed 21 October 2021.

15 Nordic Investment Bank 2020, *'NIB SEK 1.5 billion 5-Year Nordic-Baltic Blue Bond'*, <https://www.nib.int/files/03c2a48e4c0d142117199687ccf1fee4cca6d8f5/10464-2020-joint-press-release-nib-nordic-baltic-blue-bond-6-october-2020.pdf>, accessed 21 October 2021.

The Nordic–Baltic "Blue Bond" saw high demand from investors based in the region (from Sweden in particular). Investors expressed strong interest in the development of such a product, thereby showing that market demand is driving not just bond volumes but also thematic focus. The novelty of the Nordic–Baltic "Blue Bond" lead to a Bond Award for innovation in 2020, with the judges noting the specialized water management product design which was "unique" to NIB.[16] A second Nordic-Baltic "Blue Bond" was issued in October 2020, again meeting high investor demand.

The first Nordic–Baltic "Blue Bond" issued by NIB is one among an increasing number of bonds whose proceeds are ring-fenced to fund specified categories of eligible projects. Presently, four main categories of labelled bonds can be observed in the market. First, Green Bonds, the proceeds of which, as described above, are used to finance eligible environmental projects. Second, Social Bonds are loans used to finance, as the name implies, eligible social projects. An example is the African Development Bank's Social Bond, the proceeds of which are used to finance projects including rural electrification, last mile connectivity for rural communities, sustainable water supply and sanitation delivery, as well as other categories of projects with positive social impact and outcomes.[17] The third type of labelled bonds are "Sustainability Bonds", the proceeds of which are used to finance a combination of eligible green and social projects. An example is "Sustainable Development Bonds" issued by the World Bank, investing in which supports the World Bank Group's twin goals of ending extreme poverty and promoting shared prosperity, as well as supporting the Sustainable Development Goals and positive social and environmental outcomes in countries.[18] And fourth, Sustainability-linked Bonds, the financial and/or structural characteristics of which vary depending on whether the issuer achieves predefined sustainability or other environmental, social or governance (ESG) objectives. This type of labelled bond is still in the nascent phase of development, with the first issue taking place in late 2019 by the

16 Environmental Finance 2020, *'Award for innovation – use of proceeds (green bond) – Nordic Investment Bank'*, <https://www.environmental-finance.com/content/awards/green-social-and-sustainability-bond-awards-2020/winners/award-for-innovation-use-of-proceeds-(green-bond)-nordic-investment-bank.html>, accessed 21 October 2021.

17 African Development Bank 2017, *'Social Bond Framework'*, <https://www.afdb.org/fileadmin/uploads/afdb/Documents/Generic-Documents/AfDB_Social_Bond_Framework.pdf>, accessed 21 October 2021.

18 World Bank, *'IBRD Funding* Program', <https://treasury.worldbank.org/en/about/unit/treasury/ibrd>, accessed 21 October 2021.

Dutch-registered finance company Enel Finance International. In June 2021, Enel subsequently launched another such bond linked to the achievement of Enel's sustainable objective related to the reduction of direct greenhouse gas emissions, contributing to UN Sustainable Development Goal 13 (climate action), and in accordance with the group's Sustainability-Linked Financing Framework.[19]

Labelled bonds are regulated like any other fixed-income securities. Additionally, a number of industry bodies have designed frameworks governing best practices regarding labelled bonds, namely the International Capital Market Association (ICMA's) Green Bond Principles, Social Bond Principles, Sustainability Bond Guidelines and Sustainability-Linked Bond Principles (SLBP). ICMA is a highly regarded non-governmental entity in the capital markets that sets industry best practices and could be regarded as exercising a quasi-regulatory function. These ICMA Principles are voluntary guidelines developed in collaboration with market players (issuers, investors, arranging banks, etc.) and, while they carry weight, are not formally binding legal standards.

As with green bonds, other new types of labelled bonds have experienced rapid expansion in terms of volumes and diversity of issuers. As the graph below (Graph 10.2) illustrates, the labelled bond market has grown from EUR 7 billion in 2013 to a projected EUR 352 billion in 2020. Green bonds still constitute the bulk of outstanding labelled bonds; however, social and to a lesser extent, sustainability bond volumes have increased rapidly, particularly over the last couple of years.

As a proportion of total bonds issued, as of late 2020, green, social, sustainability, and sustainability-linked bonds – issued by MDBs and other market players – represented almost 14% of bonds issued in EUR. By way of contrast, in 2013, the same amount stood at just 0.4%.[20]

---

19 World Business Council for Sustainable Development 2021, *'Enel successfully places a triple-tranche 3.25 billion euro sustainability-linked bond in the eurobond market, the largest sustainability-linked transaction ever* priced', <https://www.wbcsd.org/Overview/News-Insights/Member-spotlight/Enel-successfully-places-a-triple-tranche-3.25-billion-euro-sustainability-linked-bond-in-the-eurobond-market-the-largest-sustainability-linked-transaction-ever-priced>, accessed 21 October 2021.

20 Crédit Agricole CIB Sustainable Banking (As of 20 November 2020); excludes Sustainable Development Bonds which are not ICMA compliant; percentages in graph refer to bonds in EUR (ex-gov).

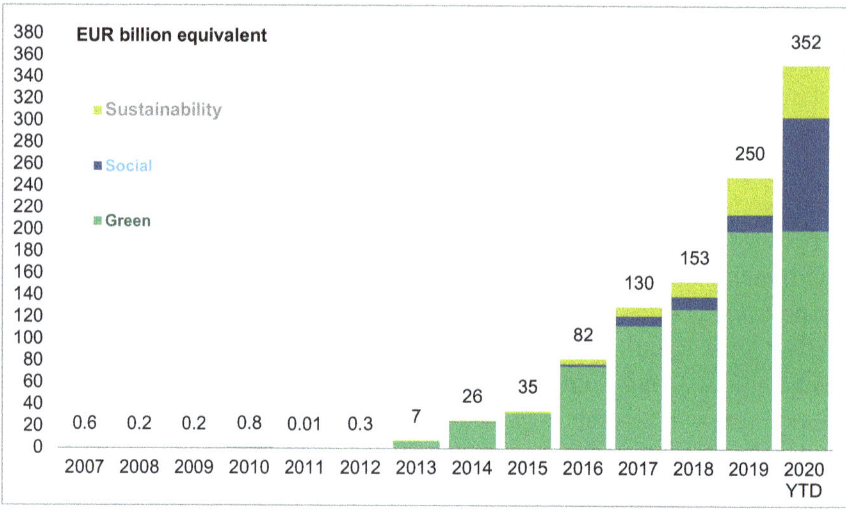

GRAPH 10.2 Volume and type of labelled bonds issued 2007 – Nov. 2020
Note: Excluding sustainability-linked bonds.
SOURCE: CRÉDIT AGRICOLE CIB SUSTAINABLE BANKING (AS OF 20 NOVEMBER 2020); EXCLUDES SUSTAINABLE DEVELOPMENT BONDS WHICH ARE NOT ICMA COMPLIANT; PERCENTAGES IN GRAPH REFER TO BONDS IN EUR (EX-GOV)

4 Case Study: COVID-19 Response Bond Frameworks

To illustrate the rise of labelled bonds beyond the most well-known green bond type (in addition to the above-mentioned blue bond), the global tragedy of the coronavirus pandemic – still ongoing at the time this chapter was written – provides a timely, if not sobering, opportunity for a case study in the form of COVID-19 Response Bonds.

COVID-19 first emerged in early 2020 and subsequently spread around the world resulting in 116 million confirmed cases and 2.5 million deaths as of early March 2021.[21] The effects of the COVID-19 pandemic go beyond its impact on global health, with profound social and economic consequences and suffering businesses, leading to, among others, increased unemployment and underemployment. In this particular context, regular bond issuers – including states and government agencies, and international and supranational organizations, as well as corporates – needed additional resources to effectively react to the

21 BBC, *Covid map: Coronavirus cases, deaths, vaccinations by country*, <https://www.bbc.com/news/world-51235105>, accessed 21 October 2021.

negative consequences of the pandemic. While the amounts raised, maturity dates and spreads differ, a common feature of these COVID-19 Response Bonds is that they are all specifically targeted at mobilizing additional financing that, in turn, will be made available to eligible borrowers to mitigate the effects of the COVID-19 pandemic.

MDBS were at the forefront of issuing this new type of bond. In particular, some MDBS used their existing social bond frameworks to issue bonds in relation to COVID-19. For example, the Council of Europe Development Bank (CEB) responded to the COVID-19 crisis by quickly leveraging off its existing Social Inclusion Bond framework in order to support its member countries, whilst being in line with existing initiatives, to launch a EUR 1 billion seven-year COVID-19 Social Inclusion Bond on 2 April 2020. Later the same year, a USD 500 million three-year Global COVID-19 Response Social Inclusion Bond followed.[22]

In contrast, other MDBS created new bond frameworks in response to the pandemic. For example, NIB issued its first Response Bond in March 2020 (for EUR 1 billion) in response to a call from its Governors to take decisive action in response to the COVID-19 pandemic. This Response Bond financed eligible projects that aimed at alleviating the social and economic consequences caused by the COVID-19 pandemic in NIB's member countries in the Nordic-Baltic region. NIB has no explicit "social mandate", but social aspects are captured under its "productivity" mandate which are reflected in the purpose of the Bank and its constituent documents. In addition, NIB's defined purpose implies that it can also play a stabilizing role during economic crises.

To issue these bonds, NIB created a brand new "Response Bond Framework" under which two transactions (as at 15 October 2021) have been taken. This Response Bond Framework includes a description of, among other matters, the eligible project selection process, the use and management of proceeds from the sale of such bonds, and the corresponding reporting.[23] The bonds issued under NIB's Response Bond Framework are intended to fund eligible response loans extended by the Bank, with such bonds otherwise following all financial, risk and liquidity policies and guidance under which NIB normally issues debt.[24] Market demand was strong: the EUR 1 billion issue, for example,

22 CEB 2020, *'CEB issues second COVID-19 Social Inclusion Bond'*, <https://coebank.org/en/news-and-publications/news/ceb-issues-second-covid-19-social-inclusion-bond/>, accessed 21 October 2021.

23 NIB 2020, *'NIB Response Bond Framework'*, <https://www.nib.int/files/adb67bf11f99d9cc9d191bb28cbd22ee2c200c3c/10456-nib-response-bond-framework-.pdf>, accessed 21 October 2021.

24 *Ibid*, at p.3.

was several times oversubscribed with more than 80 investors in a few hours. The transaction priced tighter than initial guidance, representing the largest-ever orderbook for a EUR benchmark from NIB.

An early question that arose when COVID-19 Response Bonds began to be issued to finance the response to the COVID-19 pandemic was the categorization of these bonds. In this respect, COVID-19 Response Bonds are best apprehended of as a new type altogether of social bond. As alluded to earlier, social bonds finance projects aimed at either a specified social issue or which seek to achieve a desired social outcome. A cursory review of COVID-19 Response Bonds, including those issued by NIB, shows that COVID-19 Response Bonds are typically designed to address the health, social or economic consequences of the coronavirus.

From the perspective of ICMA, debt capital market issuers can indeed issue a Social Bond related to COVID-19 even if they have not previously issued a Social Bond. But when doing so, the body has underscored the importance of addressing the four key components of ICMA's Social Bond Principles.[25] Those four components relate to the use of proceeds, project evaluation and selection, proceeds management and reporting. Proceeds must go exclusively towards addressing or mitigating social issues wholly or partially emanating from the coronavirus outbreak.[26] There is, however, no list published by ICMA regarding these social issues. Having said that, in the early stages of the pandemic, the International Finance Corporation noted for illustrative and guidance purposes some industry-specific case studies of use of proceeds. For example, in the MDB sphere, use of proceeds could finance loans to small businesses affected by the adverse economic effects of the pandemic. Another example, for corporate issuers in the pharmaceutical industry this time, would be use of proceeds covering financing COVID-19 testing, vaccine or medication research and development. In the manufacturing industry, use of proceeds could target the manufacturing or modification of machines to produce safety equipment and hygiene supplies.[27]

25 ICMA, *'Q&A for Social Bonds related to Covid-19'*, <https://www.icmagroup.org/assets/documents/Regulatory/Green-Bonds/Social-Bonds-Covid-QA310320.pdf>, accessed 21 October 2021.

26 *Ibid.*

27 IFC 2020, *Social bonds: Illustrative use-of-proceeds case studies: Coronavirus*, <https://www.ifc.org/wps/wcm/connect/3d1ccd21-ad12-4468-b03d-251cd6421bc5/SB-COVID-Case-Study-Final-30Mar2020-310320.pdf?MOD=AJPERES&CVID=n4RsBEk>, accessed 21 October 2021.

A range of other industry bodies and consulting firms have published similar guidance.[28]

While COVID-19-related bonds issued by MDBs as Social Bonds should follow the Social Bond Principles, a departure from those principles may be justified by the nature of the circumstances. When doing so, the reasons for, and the fact of, non-adherence to the Social Bond Principles must be articulated clearly. For example, NIB specifically mentions in its Response Bond Framework that: "[T]he framework has not obtained a Second Party Opinion. Despite playing an important role in societies' response to the crisis, the framework should not be considered compliant with the Social Bond Principles".[29]

This was a conscious choice given the urgency and severity of the situation, and because NIB was not fully certain that it could adhere in total to the Social Bond Principles. Therefore, it was a more short-term solution rather than NIB's normal long-term view and proper assessment of projects upfront before financing.

NIB's experience in using COVID-19 Response Bonds illustrates the tensions associated with balancing a "need for speed" with adequate commitment regarding the use of proceeds, project evaluation and selection, proceed management and reporting elements of social bonds. "Green washing" has been cited as a common problem in respect of green bond issues. This refers to the phenomenon where bonds labelled as "green" have in fact little positive environmental impact and may actually harm the environment instead.[30] Similarly, there is a risk that social bonds issued in response to the pandemic may involve "social washing". It goes without saying that this is to be avoided at all costs when MDBs issue response bonds, and that transparency and accountability is vital for the credibility and viability of social bonds and labelled bonds in general.

To conclude, the usual considerations concerning transparency relating to management of proceeds, monitoring requirements, mechanisms to track funds, impact measurement, third-party assessments, and other reporting elements should be respected in the context of COVID-19 Response Bonds, the issuance of which follows the Social Bond Principles. For those Response

28 See e.g. Sustainalytics 2020, *'Responding to COVID-19 through Social Bonds'*, <https://www.sustainalytics.com/esg-research/resource/corporate-esg-blog/responding-to-covid-19-through-social-bonds>, accessed 21 October 2021.

29 NIB 2020, *'NIB Response Bond Framework'*, <https://www.nib.int/files/adb67bf11f99d9cc9d191bb28cbd22ee2c200c3c/10456-nib-response-bond-framework-.pdf>, accessed 21 October 2021.

30 Rajwanshi 2019.

Bonds that do not adhere to the Social Bond Principles, the fact of and justification for non-adherence must be articulated clearly in the documentation and relevant public-facing information. Research has underscored that strong governance is important to not only ensure a well-priced bond issue, but also more broadly to support the development of the labelled bond market and meaningfully contribute to sustainable development.[31]

Therefore, in the absence of strong governance, there are increased risks for not only the integrity of individual COVID-19 bond issues but also the broader market when departing from the Social Bond Principles in the interests of speed. This emphasizes the more fundamental need for MDBS to operate with sound banking principles and the highest standards of good governance.

5 Latest Development and Future Prospects for Labelled Bonds

This section discusses some of the emerging trends and developments in the sphere of labelled bonds, as well as some possible future trajectories.

First, as demonstrated by the rapid growth in green bond volumes and diversification in the issuer and investor bases, it is likely that labelled bonds will play an increasingly important role in mobilizing financing needs. This is not only in response to the COVID-19 pandemic, but also in the longer-term, in response to the impact of climate change.

Much has been written about human-induced global warming and how this affects the climate system.[32] This has been increasingly recognized in the financial sector. A watershed moment in this respect was the speech given by the then Governor of the Bank of England and Chairman of the Financial Stability Board, Mark Carney, in 2015. In his speech, titled "Tragedy on the Horizon", Carney observed that: "With better information as a foundation, we can build a virtuous circle of better understanding of tomorrow's risks, better pricing for investors, better decisions by policymakers, and a smoother transition to a lower-carbon economy. By managing what gets measured, we can break the Tragedy of the Horizon".[33]

For many reasons, including increasing government, public and investor awareness of climate change, green bonds are likely to continue to be issued in increasing volumes by an increasingly diversified issuer base. This is a

31 See e.g. Berensmann et al. 2018.

32 See e.g International Panel on Climate Change (IPCC), Chapter 3, <https://www.ipcc.ch/sr15/>, accessed 21 October 2021.

33 Carney 2015.

positive development given that green bonds help raise awareness of the risks and impacts caused by and associated with climate change. In addition, green bonds represent an avenue for investors – particularly larger, institutional investors – to direct financial flows towards investments that help mitigate the risks and impacts of climate change.

In addition, a second meaningful development to look out for relates to the rise of ESG considerations and the important role played by investor activism in that regard. As the World Bank's first green bond showed, investor demand has from early on driven the development of labelled bonds. Strong investor demand is appealing to market newcomers who take full advantage of it. For instance, in October 2020, the European Commission's first social bond (EUR 17 billion issued) was 13 times oversubscribed.[34] This insatiable investor demand reflects the increased efforts of the global community towards addressing the impacts of climate change and the increased appeal of financings for investments providing ESG benefits. Hence it is not only states, supranational organizations and MDBs, but also institutional investors – including large asset managers – that are increasingly incorporating ESG-related considerations into their investment decisions and channelling growth in sustainable financing.

ESG has emerged as a core concept in defining sustainability, and there are now a wide range of industry-supported sustainability initiatives that link ESG with financing. These include the Global Impact Investing Network,[35] the Equator Principles[36] and the Principles of Responsible Investment.[37] In relation to bonds specifically, ICMA has noted that Sustainability-Linked Bonds aim at furthering the key role that debt markets can play in funding and encouraging issuers that contribute to sustainability from an ESG perspective.[38] Hopefully, the enhanced focus on ESG considerations will further drive investor preference toward sustainable financing and impact investing, including labelled

---

34 European Commission 2020, *'EUR 17 billion EU SURE social bond listed on LuxSE'*, <https://ec.europa.eu/commission/presscorner/detail/en/IP_20_1981>, accessed 21 October 2021.

35 The Global Impact Investing Network, *'COMPASS: The Methodology for Comparing and Assessing Impact'*, <https://thegiin.org/research/publication/compass-the-methodology-for-comparing-and-assessing-impact>, accessed 21 October 2021.

36 The Equator Principles 2020, <https://equator-principles.com/wp-content/uploads/2021/02/The-Equator-Principles-July-2020.pdf>, accessed 21 October 2021.

37 The Principles of Responsible Investment, *'About the PRI'*, <https://www.unpri.org/pri/about-the-pri>, accessed 21 October 2020.

38 International Capital Markets Association 2020, *'Sustainability-Linked Bond Principles'*, <https://www.icmagroup.org/assets/documents/Regulatory/Green-Bonds/June-2020/Sustainability-Linked-Bond-Principles-June-2020-171120.pdf>, accessed 21 October 2021.

bonds. This will likely go hand in hand with increased expectations regarding the measurement of the impact of such labelled bonds.

A third major trend that is expected to continue is the role taken by MDBS in the development of the labelled bond concept and the stimulation of the labelled bond market. In this respect, it is important to note that MDBS are not only issuers, but also investors, including in labelled bonds. For example, NIB has allocated EUR 500 million in liquid assets for investments in green bonds, social bonds, sustainability bonds and sustainability-linked bonds issued by companies or municipalities in NIB's member countries. These investments are used to finance environmentally sustainable projects that can contribute to mitigating climate change and achieve positive social outcomes in the Nordic-Baltic region. This, in turn, contributes to NIB fulfilling its mandate.[39]

In addition, researchers have argued that MDBS can be seen as "norm entrepreneurs" in light of their role as a – perhaps the – key catalyst in the development of sustainable banking norms and practices.[40] This "entrepreneurial spirit" can be observed clearly in the role that MDBS have played in the development of the labelled bond concept. Indeed, the Addis Ababa Action Agenda encouraged MDBS to play their role by developing financial instruments – including green bonds, and by extension labelled bonds more generally – to direct the resources of long-term investors towards sustainable development.[41] The various ways in which MDBS are in fact achieving this goal has been explained above.

Furthermore, the measuring, tracking and reporting on the impact of bonds is now established market practice even where there is no legal obligation to do so. One striking example of thought leadership in this respect is the World Bank Sustainable Development Bonds and Green Bonds Impact Report (earlier the "Green Bond Impact Report") which includes dedicated chapters for sustainable development bonds and green bonds and presents results highlights, issuance, commitment and allocation figures.[42] The Report is widely respected by the industry – as well as other MDBS – as a useful reference point and benchmark for impact reporting standards. This shows that MDBS are

39 Nordic Investment Bank, *'Investments in labelled bonds'*, <https://www.nib.int/what_we_offer/investments_in_labelled_bonds>, accessed 21 October 2021.

40 Mendez and Houghton 2020, 12; 972.

41 United Nations Inter-agency Task Force on Financing for Development, *'Multilateral development banks'*, <https://developmentfinance.un.org/multilateral-development-banks>, accessed 21 October 2021.

42 World Bank, *'World Bank Impact Report: Sustainable Development Bonds and Green Bonds'*, <https://treasury.worldbank.org/en/about/unit/treasury/impact/impact-report>, accessed 21 October 2021.

shaping not only the narrative but also the normative framework applicable to the reporting, tracking and dissemination of impact investments.

The fourth development we wish to highlight regarding the future of labelled bonds is the emergence of Sustainability-Linked Bonds. A key development in this regard is the publication by ICMA of its Sustainability-Linked Bond Principles. In a nutshell, the idea behind this type of labelled bonds is that their financial performance should be a function of whether the issuer succeeds in achieving predefined sustainability/ESG objectives.[43] This type of bond is "forward looking", and is a performance-based instrument where an issuer commits explicitly to future improvements in sustainability outcome(s) within a set timeline. Sustainability-linked bonds represent a fascinating development from a legal perspective, perhaps foreshadowing a shift in focus away from use of proceeds to an analysis of the performance and/or impact of a business or other relevant entity.

One key legal question concerns the consequences of an issuer not achieving the predefined goals in terms of bond performance and default. If an issuer does not achieve its targets, the bond will specify the consequences. As the Sustainability-Linked Bond Principles provide: "The cornerstone of a SLB is that the bond's financial and/or structural characteristics can vary depending on whether the selected KPI(s) reach (or not) the predefined SPT(s), i.e. the SLB will need to include a financial and/or structural impact involving trigger event(s)".[44]

The usual main consequence is a higher interest rate and hence higher coupon yield. In situations where the bond's targets cannot be satisfactorily observed, the Sustainability-Linked Bond Principles note that fallback mechanisms should be included.[45] Potential exceptional or extreme events – such as drastic changes in the regulatory environment that could substantially impact the calculation of the KPI – should also be explained in the bond documentation.[46] Otherwise, generally speaking, there are no other adverse contractual consequences – for example, breach of covenant – for the issuer not achieving the bond's goals. This similarly holds for event of default; to the author's best knowledge, no MDB issue has ever used the concept of "ESG default".

---

43 As defined in ICMA in the *Sustainability-Linked Bond Principles: Voluntary Process Guidelines* 2020, <https://www.icmagroup.org/assets/documents/Regulatory/Green-Bonds/June-2020/Sustainability-Linked-Bond-Principles-June-2020-171120.pdf>, accessed 8 March 2021.

44 International Capital Markets Association 2020, 5.

45 *Ibid.*

46 *Ibid.*

For the viability and credibility of sustainability-linked bonds in the long term it seems, however, crucial that consequences for not achieving the set goals shall be pre-defined. It appears inevitable that, at some point, a wider question of a themed bond not in fact financing what had been promised and agreed will become an issue leading to disputes. This will also require an analysis of which entities will be best suited and have the right skills to help evaluating in substance if the engagements given by the issuer of a themed bond have indeed been fulfilled.

Sustainability-linked bond issuance remains novel and niche but is likely to grow. In late 2020, the European Central Bank (ECB) decided that sustainability-linked bonds would be eligible as collateral for Eurosystem credit operations, and also for Eurosystem outright purchases for monetary policy purposes.[47] In making this decision, sustainability-linked bonds were given legitimacy as a discrete form of instrument and, more broadly, signaled clearly to the market the EU's strong and growing support for sustainable finance. MDBs, given their mandates and expertise, are uniquely placed to finance environmentally sustainable projects funded by sustainability-linked bonds. In this respect, the role of MDBs in moving forward innovation and regulation remains central and should be encouraged. For example, from 2021 onwards, NIB is one of the coordinators of the Working Group on Sustainability-Linked Bonds.

A fifth future prospect relates to the significance of major European Union regulatory initiatives. The EU's "Green Deal" of December 2019 underlined the need for long-term signals to direct financial flows to green investments. The Taxonomy Regulation, which entered into force on 12 July 2020, represented a significant development as it establishes a common set of criteria for determining whether an economic activity qualifies as environmentally sustainable.[48] The Taxonomy Regulation establishes six environmental objectives, including climate change mitigation and climate change adaptation.[49]

---

47 European Central Bank 2020, *'ECB to accept sustainability-linked bonds as collateral'*, <https://www.ecb.europa.eu/press/pr/date/2020/html/ecb.pr200922~482e4a5a90.en.html>, accessed 21 October 2021.

48 Regulation (EU) 2020/852 of the European Parliament and of the Council of 18 June 2020 on the establishment of a framework to facilitate sustainable investment, and amending Regulation (EU) 2019/2088.

49 The four other objectives are: Sustainable use and protection of water and marine resources; the transition to a circular economy; pollution prevention and control; and the protection and restoration of biodiversity and ecosystems: European Commission, *'EU taxonomy for sustainable activities'*, <https://ec.europa.eu/info/business-economy-euro/banking-and-finance/sustainable-finance/eu-taxonomy-sustainable-activities_en>, accessed 21 October 2021.

To remain relevant and up to date, the Taxonomy relies on a Platform on Sustainable Finance composed of 57 members which assists the European Commission in further developing the Taxonomy and sustainable finance policies more generally.[50] In addition, the Commission established a Technical Expert Group (TEG) on Sustainable Finance that issued a final report on EU taxonomy on 9 March 2020. This report included recommendations on the overall design of the Taxonomy and guidance on how disclosures can be made using the Taxonomy. This initiative will help provide credibility and reliability to Taxonomy users when implementing it in their activities.

The Taxonomy is still in its infancy and its legal consequences for labelled bond issuance continue to evolve quickly. Taking green bonds as an example, the EU Commission has announced the establishment of a voluntary EU Green Bond Standard open to all issuers of green bonds, including to MDBs. A core requirement of the proposed framework will be Taxonomy-alignment—that is, funds raised by the bond should be allocated fully to projects that are aligned with the EU Taxonomy. The other key elements are transparency on how the bond proceeds are allocated, external review to ensure compliance with the Taxonomy Regulation, Taxonomy-alignment of the funded projects and supervision by the European Securities Markets Authority of reviewers.[51]

In light of the Taxonomy and related laws, it can be expected that MDBs issuing green bonds (and other relevant bonds) in the EU will address Taxonomy-alignment in their bond issuances. The EIB's initiatives in this respect provide an illustrative case study. In late 2020, the EIB's Board of Directors approved the Climate Bank Roadmap 2021–2025 outlining the EIB's goals for climate finance that support the European Green Deal.[52] The Climate Bank Roadmap provides that the EIB aims to align its tracking methodology for green finance with the EU Taxonomy and reflect the alignment to capital markets through an extension of the eligibility criteria for Climate Awareness Bonds and Sustainability Awareness Bonds.[53] The Roadmap also aims to align those bonds over time with the proposed EU Green Bond Standard, and the

---

50 See European Commission, *'Platform on sustainable finance'*, <https://ec.europa.eu/info/business-economy-euro/banking-and-finance/sustainable-finance/overview-sustainable-finance/platform-sustainable-finance_en>, accessed 21 October 2021.

51 European Commission, *'European green bond standard'*, <https://ec.europa.eu/info/business-economy-euro/banking-and-finance/sustainable-finance/european-green-bond-standard_en>, accessed 21 October 2021.

52 EIB, *'The EIB Group Climate Bank Roadmap 2021–2025'*, <https://www.eib.org/en/publications/the-eib-group-climate-bank-roadmap.htm>, accessed 21 October 2021.

53 EIB, *'Climate Awareness Bonds'*, <https://www.eib.org/en/investor-relations/cab/index.htm>, accessed 21 October 2021.

EIB has already amended its bond documentation in light of the evolving EU Taxonomy legal framework.[54]

6 Conclusion

There are a variety of labelled bonds that have quickly emerged on the debt capital markets. Labelled bonds have a critical and possibly under-appreciated role to play in financing a sustainable response to, and recovery from, the pandemic, as well as a transition to a lower-carbon future. MDBs have and will play a central role in driving the innovation, growth and diversification of labelled bonds. Green and other labelled bonds are important tools to finance responses to climate change risks, which remain the greatest risks in the longer run. When the pandemic ends, the international community must be prepared to re-build and MDBs have a key role to play in financing the recovery, and further on the horizon, in financing long-term responses – including major infrastructure projects – to climate change. MDBs have and will continue to play a key role in international debt capital markets by contributing to guiding regulatory developments and in setting high standards for other (labelled) bond issuers.

References

African Development Bank, *Social Bond Framework*, (September 2017), <https://www.afdb.org/fileadmin/uploads/afdb/Documents/Generic-Documents/AfDB_Social_Bond_Framework.pdf>, accessed 21 October 2021.

BBC, *Covid map: Coronavirus cases, deaths, vaccinations by country*, (21 October 2021), <https://www.bbc.com/news/world-51235105>, accessed 21 October 2021.

Berensmann K, Dafe F and Lindenberg N, *Demystifying green bonds*, in: Boubaker S, Cumming D and Nguyen D K (ed), *Research Handbook of Investing in the Triple Bottom Line*, (Edward Elgar Publishing 2018).

Carney M, *Breaking the tragedy of the horizon – climate change and financial stability*, Speech at Lloyd's of London (London, 29 September 2015), <https://www.bis.org/review/r151009a.pdf>, accessed 21 October 2021.

54 *Ibid.*

Council of Europe Development Bank, *CEB issues second COVID-19 Social Inclusion Bond*, (3 June 2020), <https://coebank.org/en/news-and-publications/news/ceb-issues-second-covid-19-social-inclusion-bond/>, accessed 21 October 2021.

Center for International Climate Research (CICERO), *Shades of Green: Green Bonds*, (n.d.), <https://cicero.green/green-bonds>, accessed 21 October 2021.

Delikanli I U, Dimitrov T and Agolli R, *Multilateral Development Banks: Governance and Finance*, (Springer 2018).

Environmental Finance 2020, *'Award for innovation – use of proceeds (green bond) – Nordic Investment Bank'*, <https://www.environmental-finance.com/content/awards/green-social-and-sustainability-bond-awards-2020/winners/award-for-innovation-use-of-proceeds-(green-bond)-nordic-investment-bank.html>, accessed 21 October 2021.

European Central Bank, *ECB to accept sustainability-linked bonds as collateral*, (22 September 2020), <https://www.ecb.europa.eu/press/pr/date/2020/html/ecb.pr200922~482e4a5a90.en.html>, accessed 21 October 2021.

European Commission, *EUR 17 billion EU SURE social bond listed on LuxSE*, Press Release (27 October 2020) <https://ec.europa.eu/commission/presscorner/detail/en/IP_20_1981>, accessed 21 October 2021.

European Commission, *Platform on sustainable finance*, (n.d.), < https://ec.europa.eu/info/business-economy-euro/banking-and-finance/sustainable-finance/overview-sustainable-finance/platform-sustainable-finance_en>, accessed 21 October 2021.

European Commission *European green bond standard*, (n.d.), <https://ec.europa.eu/info/business-economy-euro/banking-and-finance/sustainable-finance/european-green-bond-standard_en>, accessed 21 October 2021.

European Commission, *EU taxonomy for sustainable activities*, (n.d.), <https://ec.europa.eu/info/business-economy-euro/banking-and-finance/sustainable-finance/eu-taxonomy-sustainable-activities_en>, accessed 21 October 2021.

European Investment Bank, *Climate Awareness Bonds*, (n.d.), <https://www.eib.org/en/investor_relations/cab/index.htm>, accessed 21 October 2021.

European Investment Bank, *The EIB Group Climate Bank Roadmap 2021–2025*, <https://www.eib.org/en/publications/the-eib-group-climate-bank-roadmap.htm>, accessed 21 October 2021.

European Investment Bank, *Climate Awareness Bonds*, (n.d.), <https://www.eib.org/en/investor-relations/cab/index.htm>, accessed 21 October 2021.

The Equator Principles, (July 2020), <https://equator-principles.com/wp-content/uploads/2021/02/The-Equator-Principles-July-2020.pdf>, accessed 21 October 2021.

The Global Impact Investing Network, *COMPASS: The Methodology for Comparing and Assessing Impact*, (n.d.), <https://thegiin.org/research/publication/compass-the-methodology-for-comparing-and-assessing-impact>, accessed 21 October 2021.

International Capital Markets Association, *Q&A for Social Bonds related to Covid-19*, (n.d.), <https://www.icmagroup.org/assets/documents/Regulatory/Green-Bonds/Social-Bonds-Covid-QA310320.pdf>, accessed 21 October 2021.

International Capital Markets Association, *Sustainability-Linked Bond Principles*, (June 2020), <https://www.icmagroup.org/assets/documents/Regulatory/Green-Bonds/June-2020/Sustainability-Linked-Bond-Principles-June-2020-171120.pdf>, accessed 21 October 2021.

International Finance Corporation (IFC), *Social bonds: Illustrative use-of-proceeds case studies: Coronavirus*, (March 2020), <https://www.ifc.org/wps/wcm/connect/3d1ccd21-ad12-4468-b03d-251cd6421bc5/SB-COVID-Case-Study-Final-30Mar2020-310320.pdf?MOD=AJPERES&CVID=n4RsBEk>, accessed 21 October 2021.

International Panel on Climate Change (IPCC), *chapter 3*, <https://www.ipcc.ch/sr15/ > accessed 21 October 2021.

Ketterer J A, Andrade G, Netto M, and Haro M I, *Transforming the Green Bond Market. Inter-American Development Bank*, (2019), <https://publications.iadb.org/publications/english/document/Transforming_Green_Bond_Markets_Using_Financial_Innovation_and_Technology_to_Expand_Green_Bond_Issuance_in_Latin_America_and_the_Caribbean_en.pdf>, accessed 21 October 2021.

Maltaisand A and Nykvist B, *Understanding the role of green bonds in advancing sustainability*, (2020), Journal of Sustainable Finance & Investment, <https://www.tandfonline.com/doi/pdf/10.1080/20430795.2020.1724864?needAccess=true>, accessed 21 October 2021.

Mendez A and Houghton D P, *Sustainable Banking: The Role of Multilateral Development Banks as Norm Entrepreneurs*, (2020), Sustainability, <doi:10.3390/su12030972>.

Nordic Investment Bank, *NIB Response Bond Framework*, (version 2, 2 April 2020), <https://www.nib.int/files/adb67bf11f99d9cc9d191bb28cbd22ee2c200c3c/10456-nib-response-bond-framework-.pdf>, accessed 21 October 2021.

Nordic Investment Bank, *Investments in labelled bonds*, <https://www.nib.int/what_we_offer/investments_in_labelled_bonds>, accessed 21 October 2021.

Nordic Investment Bank, *NIB SEK 1.5 billion 5-Year Nordic-Baltic Blue Bond*, (6 October 2020), <https://www.nib.int/files/03c2a48e4c0d142117199687ccf1fee4cca6d8f5/10464-2020-joint-press-release-nib-nordic-baltic-blue-bond-6-october-2020.pdf>, accessed 21 October 2021.

Park S, *Investors as Regulators: Green Bonds and the Governance Challenges of the Sustainable Finance Revolution*, (2018), Stanford Journal of International Law, Vol. 54, No. 1, 2018, University of Connecticut School of Business Research Paper No. 18–12, https://ssrn.com/abstract=3142887.

The Principles of Responsible Investment, *About the PRI*, <https://www.unpri.org/pri/about-the-pri>, accessed 21 October 2020.

Rajwanshi Y, *Are Green Bonds as Good as They Sound?*, (26 November 2019), Berkeley Economic Review Vol. 10, <https://econreview.berkeley.edu/are-green-bonds-as-good-as-they-sound/>, accessed 21 October 2021.

Sustainalytics, *Responding to COVID-19 through Social Bonds*, (7 April 2020), <https://www.sustainalytics.com/esg-research/resource/corporate-esg-blog/responding-to-covid-19-through-social-bonds>, accessed 21 October 2021.

United Nations Inter-agency Task Force on Financing for Development, *Multilateral development banks*, <https://developmentfinance.un.org/multilateral-development-banks>, accessed 21 October 2021.

World Bank, *10 Years of Green Bonds: Creating the Blueprint for Sustainability Across Capital Markets*, <https://www.worldbank.org/en/news/immersive-story/2019/03/18/10-years-of-green-bonds-creating-the-blueprint-for-sustainability-across-capital-markets>, accessed 21 October 2021.

World Bank, *IBRD Funding Program*, (n.d.), <https://treasury.worldbank.org/en/about/unit/treasury/ibrd>, accessed 21 October 2021.

World Bank, *World Bank Impact Report: Sustainable Development Bonds and Green Bonds*, <https://treasury.worldbank.org/en/about/unit/treasury/impact/impact-report>, accessed 21 October 2021.

CHAPTER 11

Smart Infrastructure

The New Sustainable Development Paradigm

*Arthur M. Mitchell**

Abstract

International Financial Institutions (IFI) play a critical role in promoting the development and financing of infrastructure projects in the world today and will continue to do so in the future. Many of these institutions have gained valuable experience over a number of years, but the inclusion of new "smart" technologies into infrastructure projects is proceeding at an exponential pace and fundamentally shifting the approach to the design of infrastructure development projects. In order to provide added value to project sponsors and the affected people, these institutions must ensure that their policies and procedures contribute to enhancing the positive aspects while mitigating any negative outcomes of technological development. As it is likely that most, if not all, infrastructure will include some elements of these new technologies in the future, a keen awareness of how to encourage smart and sustainable projects is necessary. IFIs may need to review or create new policies and procedures to address these issues, particularly with respect to governance, privacy, cyber security, data protection, the regulation of artificial intelligence and anti-corruption techniques.

1 Introduction

While IFIs have focused on improving social and economic outcomes in their mandated areas of operations,[1] in line with global momentum, these

---

* Arthur M. Mitchell is Senior Advisor in the Tokyo office of White & Case LLP, amitchell@whitecase.com. He was formerly General Counsel of the Asian Development Bank (2003–2007). The views expressed in this chapter are strictly those of the author and should not in any way be attributed to White & Case LLP or members of the firm. The content hereof is not intended to be legal advice. The valuable assistance of Sean Curran of White & Case LLP Singapore in the preparation of this chapter is acknowledged with gratitude.

1 The original IFIs – the Bretton Woods Institutions – which include the World Bank and the IMF, originally focused on rebuilding countries devastated by World War II and providing a mechanism for international cooperation in managing the global financial system. In time,

DOI:10.1163/9789004460010_012

institutions are increasingly concerned with sustainability themes in connection with their operations.[2] Smart infrastructure presents many opportunities for development financiers to maximize the development impact of their funding operations in a manner that is aligned with sustainability-linked thematic priorities. However, smart infrastructure also presents certain risks as well as novel challenges and concerns. IFIs will need to consider these issues from a policy perspective if smart infrastructure is to be harnessed by these institutions towards the achievement of their institutional objectives, in a manner which is consistent with their respective risk tolerances and their publicly accountable status.

While not intended to provide a comprehensive treatment of the issues related to smart infrastructure, this chapter will first explain the concept of smart infrastructure and its link with sustainability and then consider a few use cases involving smart supply chains, smart construction, smart cities and smart grids. Finally, it will review some of the most relevant risk factors and regulation and policy concerns relating to smart infrastructure. Because changes in law and technology are happening on a daily basis, definitive answers for all of the issues that are likely to arise cannot be comprehensively addressed here, but it is hoped that shedding light on some recent developments and issues that may arise will be a good start to the discussion.

the mandates of these institutions shifted towards a focus on development, poverty reduction and economic stability. See <https://www.worldbank.org/en/about/history>, accessed 8 February 2021, <https://www.worldbank.org/en/about/history/the-world-bank-group-and-the-imf>, accessed 8 February 2021, and <https://www.imf.org/external/about/history.htm>, accessed 8 February 2021 for a summary of the history of the Bretton Woods Institutions, accessed 8 February 2021.

2 The Asian Infrastructure Investment Bank (AIIB) mission statement – Infrastructure for Tomorrow (i4t) – establishes AIIB's commitment to sustainability in its operations: <https://www.aiib.org/en/about-aiib/who-we-are/infrastructure-for-tomorrow/overview/index.html>, accessed 8 February 2021; the Asian Development Bank's (ADB) corporate strategy – Strategy 2030 – highlights sustainability as one of its key strategy concerns: <https://www.adb.org/documents/strategy-2030-prosperous-inclusive-resilient-sustainable-asia-pacific>, accessed 8 February 2021; since 2005, the European Bank for Reconstruction and Development (EBRD) has issued an annual Sustainability Report in which it details its support for sustainable development in its countries of operations in the relevant year: <https://www.ebrd.com/sustainability-reporting.html>, accessed 8 February 2021.

2 Smart Infrastructure

2.1 *Characteristics of Smart Infrastructure*

Broadly speaking, smart infrastructure is understood as being the result of combining traditional physical (or "hard") infrastructure with technology-based digital infrastructure. Digital infrastructure is characterized by the interconnection of technological solutions, such as sensors, cameras and drones and related software, designed to collect and analyze data. The addition of "digital" solutions to physical infrastructure yields improved information relating to the status and operation of physical infrastructure assets, with the aim of enabling more efficient and precise decision making with respect to the design and ongoing operations and maintenance of such assets, essentially rendering physical infrastructure "smart" by providing it the ability to communicate and synthesize information relating to its status and/or operation.

Smart infrastructure will typically rely on the internet as a communication channel. The concept of the Internet of Things (IoT) has emerged as a term to describe the modern phenomenon relating to the interconnectedness of physical devices, which are embedded with smart technologies, through the internet. The IoT includes consumer devices, such as connected vehicles and home appliances, with remote monitoring capabilities, as well as industrial devices, such as the digital infrastructure components, which are incorporated in transportation networks and smart cities.

Connecting smart devices to the internet enables them to communicate with each other in real-time, without involving a human being. These communications can, in turn, be analyzed and processed by systems which deploy artificial intelligence (AI) technologies and, depending on their application, systems may then make operating decisions based on the information that they have received. The aim of this automated process of information communication, analysis, processing and actioning is to deliver efficient and precise operations which maximize the resources used to deliver the relevant outcome.

2.2 *Delivering Sustainable Outcomes*

The benefits of the addition of appropriately designed and implemented digital infrastructure to physical infrastructure include: (I) more intelligent operation of mature networks, (II) longer life and more efficient operation of new infrastructure, and (III) in relation to any infrastructure asset, whether new or old, better whole-life value of the infrastructure asset. Whether considered from an environmental or financial perspective, the sustainability benefits of smart infrastructure are clear: a more efficient use of resources.

Companies and project developers are coming to recognize the importance of "sustainability governance" as a top management issue. When employed correctly, all critical functions, such as the office of the CEO, sales and marketing, IT, finance and procurement, human relations, R&D, manufacturing and the sustainability office, share data links which direct their attention to the environmental social and governance (ESG) goals of the enterprise and track how results are being delivered on a real-time basis. In addition to providing a new management tool, sustainability governance will make it easier for the enterprise to report and disclose its progress in its journey, and for its financiers to monitor compliance with the terms and conditions of their financing documents.

3 Use Cases

3.1 *Introduction*

Our modern world has become increasingly characterized by the prevalence of technology and interconnectedness, and it would be difficult to isolate an industry or sector which has not been affected by smart technologies in some way.[3] From a development perspective, there are certain key use cases which highlight the focus on sustainability, including: smart supply chains, smart construction, smart cities and smart grids. These use cases are discussed in further detail below.

3.2 *Smart Supply Chains*

The digital and physical infrastructures of the world are converging and this is visible in smart supply chains. Increasingly supply chains have been digitized to become instrumented, interconnected and intelligent.[4] Instrumented means that information that was previously created by people is being generated by

3 Many commentators argue that we are in the midst of a "Fourth Industrial Revolution" which is driven by the way that technologies like artificial intelligence, autonomous vehicles and the IoT are radically affecting our daily lives. The concept of the Fourth Industrial Revolution was introduced to a global audience in 2016 through the World Economic Forum. For further discussion of the "Fourth Industrial Revolution" in the context of infrastructure development see the Community Paper released by the World Economic Forum in November 2019 which is available here: <https://www3.weforum.org/docs/WEF_Technology_in_Infrastructure.pdf>, accessed 8 February 2021.

4 Carroll 2010. But see the discussion at section 4.1 below for a more up-to-date definition of "smart" characteristics.

sensors, RFID tags,[5] meters, actuators, GPS and other devices. Interconnected means that customers, suppliers and IT systems will interact with each other in real time. Intelligent means that users will be able to assess a myriad of constraints and alternative courses of action by simulating various and diverse options for any given scenario.

One relevant use case is a platform pioneered by Minehub Technologies Inc. The MineHub platform is designed to improve efficiency in trading operations, with an eye toward evaluating ESG[6] issues in mining and metals supply chains. By using blockchain open-source code technology, MineHub allows parties involved in selling, buying, delivering and paying for a cargo of minerals to collaborate securely in real-time rather than couriering or emailing paper documents that are subject to interception and fraud. The platform helps to standardize, structure and digitize marketing and trading administration, including in relation to contracts, trade confirmations, assays, and letters of credit. Importantly, the MineHub platform can be used by a wide variety of companies, of various types and sizes, including SMEs and large corporate miners, trading houses, financial institutions, alternative financiers, logistics companies and assayers.

In keeping with the direction of modern regulation and commercial requirements, MineHub has recognized the value of incorporating information relating to the specific ESG characteristics of the minerals and metals that are traded on its platform. MineHub will allow functionality that enables users to attach, certify and verify evidence related to the ESG specifications and emissions footprint of their materials and shipments in upstream and downstream supply chains. This will be a step towards making ESG characteristics one of the defining attributes of the raw materials which are traded on its platform. In time, it is expected that, through the assimilation of information from both upstream and downstream sources, MineHub will be able to provide a mechanism which industry participants will be able to use to evidence their compliance with ESG targets.

3.3 *Smart Construction*

It is fair to say that all major companies are considering how to make their operations more efficient, in part by focusing on digital transformation, to

5 Radio Frequency Identification (RFID) is the wireless non-contact use of radio frequency waves to transfer data. Marking items with RFID tags allows users to automatically and uniquely identify and track inventory and other assets.

6 Investors are increasingly applying environmental, social and governance (ESG) parameters as part of their analysis to identify material risks and growth opportunities in projects.

maintain a competitive edge. Realizing that technology can be used to perform diagnostic operations on equipment, in order to anticipate maintenance requirements and replacement part needs, many manufacturers have been attaching sensors to their products. By taking advantage of the vast amount of data that can be collected in this manner, they are finding new ways to provide valuable services to their customers. For example, with almost a hundred years of experience, Komatsu Ltd, an old-line manufacturing (monozukuri) company, is pioneering smart construction in order to make the entire job site visible to contractors and analyze relevant data in real time. Komatsu's equipment is fitted with sensors which upload site data to drones, GPS systems and the cloud.[7] The data produced is made available to the contractors through smart phones and computer tablets. It allows them to see the entire project from start to finish in a 3D format, which includes financial and scheduling information. Thus, Komatsu is not only a traditional manufacturer but also a tech-enabled solution provider to its customers. The new visibility that project owners will gain about their construction site will allow them to better monitor compliance with their own ESG requirements.

3.4 *Smart Cities*

With respect to smart cities, to start with, we must recognize that not all smart cities are the same. Each of Tokyo, New York, Toronto, Paris, London, Berlin, Copenhagen, Barcelona, Vienna and Hong Kong is often mentioned as being typical of a smart city. However, even these cities have not taken a holistic approach towards smart infrastructure. Recently, Toyota's Woven City project and Neom in Saudi Arabia have been promoted as planned mega-cities which will incorporate the latest smart city technologies in a comprehensive manner, although most smart city initiatives to date have taken a more modest approach, by focusing on discrete projects that can be scaled up over time.

In the past the concept of a "smart city" has been used to describe many different types of cities, based on attributes such as environmental sustainability, efficient and well-functioning infrastructure, entrepreneurial economies, and/or flourishing technology industries.[8] Until recently, there was no particular focus on any single end-goal included in the concept of a smart city but, rather, the term was used as a descriptor for cities which focused on some of the attributes mentioned.

---

7 The "cloud" refers to software and services that run on the internet, as opposed to locally on a user's computer. The term is often used to refer to online storage systems.

8 McKinsey Global Institute 2018.

In more recent times, the concept has been refined to specifically capture cities where public and/or private actors make use of digital infrastructure to "improve the quality of life".[9] Public agencies can use data produced by digital technology, such as sensors, cameras and drones, to collect information, with a view to making more precise decisions which, in turn, leads to efficiencies in the running of the city. Companies and individuals can use data produced by smart city technologies to make decisions that reduce their overall use of resources, with yields benefits including lower operating/living costs and a more sustainable use of resources by the city.

With urbanization and population increases, climate change challenges and public health concerns, among other issues, cities around the world are facing daunting infrastructure challenges. Smart technologies provide tools that allow cities to get more out of their existing infrastructure, and to design future infrastructure in a more informed way to address the challenges they face. Use of smart technologies can lead to improvements, such as cleaner air for citizens to breathe, safer communities, less traffic congestion, and a more efficient use of water and energy resources. These improvements deliver a higher quality of life for citizens of smart cities.

Notwithstanding the fact that there is no one mold for a smart city project, there are certain areas of focus which are common amongst smart city projects, and environmental sustainability is often at the top of the list. Industry analysts have estimated that deployment of a range of smart city applications, to the most reasonable extent, could, in the context of any specific city: reduce greenhouse gas emissions by 10% to 15%, lower water consumption by 20–30 percent and reduce the volume of solid waste per capita by 10–20 percent.[10] Greenhouse gas emissions could be reduced, through the use of building automation systems,[11] in commercial buildings and homes. Strategic use of air quality sensors could help identify patterns and sources of emissions. Deploying sensors and analytics in water systems could help identify leakages

---

9 The International Telecommunications Union (ITU), the United Nations specialized agency for information communication technologies, has proposed the following definition: "A smart sustainable city is an innovative city that uses information and communication technologies and other means to improve quality of life, efficiency of urban operation and services, and competitiveness, while ensuring that it meets the needs of present and future generations with respect to economic, social, and environmental aspects." See Smart sustainable cities: An analysis of definitions, ITU-T Focus Group on Smart Sustainable Cities, 2014.

10 McKinsey Global Institute 2018.

11 Building automation systems are automated centralized control systems, designed to automatically control elements of building functionality, such as heating/cooling, lighting, electrical and security systems, among others.

to help reduce losses. Unrecycled solid waste could be reduced by incentivizing users to recycle through digital waste tracking technologies and payment for disposal. Ultimately, strategic use of digital technologies, to address the challenges that modern cities face, can deliver a cleaner and more sustainable environment.

The United Nations (UN) recognized the importance of making cities sustainable when adopting the UN Sustainable Development Goals (SDGs) in 2015.[12] The UN SDGs are a set of interlinked goals which are aimed at mobilizing efforts to end poverty, fight inequalities and tackle climate change. The UN SDGs were universally adopted by all UN member states as a call to action to deliver a series of global socio-economic and environmental ambitions by 2030. UN SDG 11 establishes the goal to make cities and human settlements inclusive, resilient and sustainable.[13] Rapid urbanization, carbon emissions and resource usage are highlighted by the UN as some of the key issues to address in the challenge to make cities more sustainable. Smart solutions are seen as one of the key tools to enable cities to make progress towards meeting the UN SDGs.[14]

3.5 *Smart Grids*

We now know that further development of electricity grids, to incorporate renewables in a distributed fashion, is a requirement to achieve a carbonless future. For example, Japan has embarked on a major project to install smart meters in every home. The Tokyo Electric Power Company (TEPCO) and Chubu Electric Power Co., Inc. (Chubu Electric) together have rolled out close to 36 million such devices. Both of these companies have teamed up with private suppliers and will finance the relevant equipment costs through user fees. One of the challenges will be to make sure that the technology solutions supplied by numerous vendors will be interoperable. For example, power line communications, cellular networks and wireless radio frequencies must work together to connect the utilities, homes and consumer devices in a seamless way. Because systems are often installed and controlled by the consumer, distributed energy resources can put the power grid as a whole at risk. In order to make these systems properly work together, new industry standards may be required.

12 For more information on the UN Sustainable Development Goals see <https://www.un.org/sustainabledevelopment/>, accessed 8 February 2021.

13 See: <https://www.un.org/sustainabledevelopment/cities/>, accessed 8 February 2021.

14 See generally: McKinsey Global Institute 2018.

4 Involvement of International Financial Institutions in Smart Infrastructure

IFIs have become interested in promoting and financing smart infrastructure and it is likely that this activity will only increase across a broad spectrum of projects. Some recent examples of IFI involvement in smart infrastructure projects are set out below in this section.

4.1 *The European Bank for Reconstruction and Development* (EBRD)

As part of its flagship "Green Cities" urban sustainability initiative, which launched in 2016, EBRD has been working with partner cities located in its countries of operations to reduce energy use and greenhouse gas emissions.[15] EBRD works with each of its Green Cities to design a tailor-made program of planned improvements called a Green City Action Plan (GCAP). It aims to support the implementation of each GCAP through municipal investments. EBRD and other development-focused organizations have noted that cities worldwide are the source of at least 70% of greenhouse gas emissions.[16] Therefore, in recognition of the urgent need to address the causes of climate change, EBRD recently announced that it is doubling its funding to support its Green Cities initiative.[17]

According to EBRD, while the concept of a smart city is not necessarily synonymous with a green city, the digital technologies used in the design of smart cities can be used to improve cities' environmental performance. Therefore, smart city tools can be employed as a means to support green cities.[18] In recognition of the impact that smart technologies can have towards achieving cities' sustainability targets, the EBRD methodology for its GCAPs has recently been updated to specifically incorporate a "smart" assessment component from the start of its GCAP design process.[19] Recently launched Green Cities partnerships with Kyiv, Ukraine and Novi Sad, Serbia will be the first partnerships to deploy the new smart assessments as part of their respective GCAPs. However, cities

15 Further details relating to the EBRD's Green Cities initiative are available here: <https://ebrdgreencities.com/>, accessed 8 February 2021.

16 United Nations Sustainable Development Goals, Goal 11 Make cities inclusive, safe, resilient and sustainable, https://www.un.org/sustainabledevelopment/cities/, accessed 22 August 2022.

17 European Bank for Reconstruction and Development 2020.

18 European Bank for Reconstruction and Development 2016, 14.

19 European Bank for Reconstruction and Development 2020.

which are already in the program will have smart components retrofitted into their planning.[20]

4.2 *The Asian Development Bank (ADB)*

The ADB has been active across a broad spectrum of smart infrastructure projects, including intelligent transport systems, mobility as a service, clean energy and renewables, financial markets and smart cities.[21] The ADB recently co-financed an intelligent transport system project in Shaanxi Province in the People's Republic of China, aimed at reducing greenhouse gas emissions produced by the local transport and logistic sector, by improving operations efficiency and building green facilities.[22] The project involved developing low-carbon and intelligent logistics and transport systems, along with an integrated information and communications technology system aimed at enhancing the local government's ability to manage real-time transport and logics issues and to disseminate information to industry partners.

4.3 *The Asian Infrastructure Investment Bank (AIIB)*

Under its Infrastructure for Tomorrow corporate strategy, one of AIIB's key thematic priorities is to empower its clients through digital infrastructure and broader technology-enabled infrastructure.[23] AIIB has pursued this priority through several innovative means, including, notably, its participation in the Lightsmith Climate Resilience Partners private equity fund, a specialist growth fund focusing on climate resilience technology solutions. This fund makes growth equity investments in technology companies that build resilience to the physical damage and disruption, risk and volatility and resource scarcity resulting from climate change.[24] The fund represents the first known instance

20 *Ibid.*

21 Details relating to ADB projects can be found on the ADB website: <https://www.adb.org/projects>, accessed 8 February 2021.

22 Details relating to ADB's Shaanxi Green Intelligent Transport and Logistics Management Demonstration Project are available on the ADB website: <https://www.adb.org/projects/51401-002/main>, accessed 8 February 2021.

23 Further details on AIIB's Infrastructure for Tomorrow corporate strategy can be found on the AIIB website: <https://www.aiib.org/en/about-aiib/who-we-are/infrastructure-for-tomorrow/overview/index.html>, accessed 8 February 2021.

24 The details relating to AIIB's investment in the Lightsmith Climate Resilience Partners fund are available on the AIIB website: <https://www.aiib.org/en/projects/details/2020/approved/Multicountry-Lightsmith-Climate-Resilience-Partners.html>, accessed 8 February 2021.

of a private equity fund with an investment strategy focused on climate resilience and adaptation solutions.

As can be seen from the EBRD, ADB and AIIB examples noted above, IFIs have recognized the potential for smart technologies to provide solutions to some of the most challenging development and sustainability issues faced by our global society. IFI strategies and initiatives are increasingly placing emphasis on innovation and smart technology solutions as essential components to development projects. Given that the developing countries in which IFIs focus their efforts often suffer from decades of underinvestment in infrastructure, one of the great opportunities to be realized from investments in smart technology solutions is to provide these countries with the opportunity to "leapfrog" from their current out-of-date status to a "smart", sustainable future.

5 Project Risks and Regulation

5.1 *Introduction*

The promise of smart infrastructure, which employs sensors, connectivity and data analytics, is one of better, more convenient and cheaper outcomes for users. However, even those with the most extreme "techno-centric" views cannot ignore the potential risks associated with AI and big data, that are integral to it. As these technologies are spreading rapidly into all aspects of our lives, it is important for IFIs to ensure that the smart infrastructure projects they finance adequately address issues such as privacy and information security, fairness, inclusion and corruption.

The establishment of applicable laws, regulations and institutional/organizational policies, relating to the use of smart technologies and the concerns which they raise, has, in general, been slow to develop. For example, several of the world's major economies have only recently put in place comprehensive laws and regulations relating to privacy, information confidentiality and security and processing, a lead that developing economies have followed.[25] Within the community of IFIs too there exists a policy lacuna with respect

25 The European Union's General Data Protection Regulation (GDPR), which came into effect on May 25, 2018 has many implications in the context of smart infrastructure in the EU and is internationally recognized as the reference standard for data protection laws; India is in the process of introducing an overhaul to its data protection legislation, in the form of the Personal Data Protection Bill (PDP), which incorporates many elements of the GDPR; China has recently enacted its Personal Information Protection Law (PIPL) which is its first dedicated law on personal data protection; UNCTAD has conducted a comprehensive review of the status of data protection and privacy legislation worldwide,

to specific issues which arise in the context of smart infrastructure projects, such as concerns relating to the use of artificial intelligence and information privacy and security matters. If IFIs are to fully participate in the realization of the smart infrastructure development opportunities, appropriate risk assessments on the use of smart technology in infrastructure projects will need to be undertaken, and identified risks will need to be adequately addressed though institutional policies.

Smart infrastructure projects raise many of the same legal, economic, commercial and/or political risks as traditional hard infrastructure projects. But they also present some unique risks relating to governance, privacy, cybersecurity, data protection and the use of AI. A few of the most important considerations relating to risks that arise in the context of smart infrastructure projects are mentioned below.

5.2 *Governance*

A key determinant of the success of a smart infrastructure project will be the governance model[26] that is applicable to the project. In many cases, the administrative capacity and regulatory framework is not suited to the adoption of new technologies, particularly when the project crosses jurisdictional lines between local and national authorities.[27] In order to achieve successful project implementation, effective partnerships and collaboration among various stakeholders is imperative.

In the context of smart city projects, The Social Smart City Framework[28] outlines an inclusive governance model for smart cities, which promotes e-enabling, e-engaging and e-empowering of key stakeholders in decision-making, thereby ensuring appropriate buy-in and support from them.

5.3 *Privacy*

The interconnected nature of the digital platforms previously discussed, using ubiquitous sensors and cameras, can lead to many societal benefits such as reduction of a city's carbon footprint, better traffic management and crime detection and prevention. However, when combined with such technologies as facial recognition and other AI technologies, the risks to individual privacy

available here: <https://unctad.org/page/data-protection-and-privacy-legislation-worldwide>, 8 February 2021.

26 In this context, "governance model" refers to the structures and processes by which the local government operates.

27 European Commission 2020.

28 Effing and Groot 2016.

become obvious. For example, what is the right balance between surveillance and privacy when people are in public spaces? Projects which fail to adequately address "privacy by design" will likely face public opposition. Governments and project sponsors need, at a minimum, to be transparent with respect to the rules on the collection and processing of data, indicate how the relevant data will be shared with third parties and explain what the data will be used for and how long it will be retained.[29]

5.4 *Cybersecurity and Data Protection*

Governments, companies and individuals suffer cyberattacks on a daily basis and the methodologies of bad actors are constantly evolving. One of the principal advantages of smart infrastructure is connectivity through the IoT, but this is also the source of one of its greatest vulnerabilities. This is related to the convergence of the cyber and physical worlds, the interoperability of legacy and new systems and the integration of city services and enabling infrastructure.[30] For example, in relation to the smart cities use cases cited above, one can easily imagine a city where the streetlights, public parking spaces and electricity grid are all connected, in order to manage traffic, reduce pollution and save budgetary resources. But the lack of consistent cybersecurity standards and procurement of technology from disparate suppliers can lead to vulnerabilities in the related cyber landscape.

5.5 *Regulation of Artificial Intelligence*

The advantages of data analytics cannot be fully achieved without artificial intelligence. The challenge is that there is no single system of regulation that covers AI at this stage. Various laws are applicable (or potentially applicable) to the development and implementation of AI technologies. These laws include those related to intellectual property, data protection, consumer protection and privacy, products liability, computer misuse and human rights. The EU is taking the lead in developing new legal standards[31] with the European Commission publishing a comprehensive draft regulation on the use of AI, in April 2021. It is widely expected that this draft AI regulation will be adopted, in some form, and become legally enforceable in the EU in a few years. When coupled with GDPR, it will likely form the global baseline for the regulation of

29 Appleton 2020.

30 Deloitte Insights 2019.

31 News European Parliament, <https://www.europarl.europa.eu/news/en/press-room/20201016IPR89544/parliament-leads-the-way-on-first-set-of-eu-rules-for-artificial-intelligence>, accessed 9 February 2021.

AI and privacy. This framework will have significant implications for certain social considerations, such as the rights of affected communities, in projects financed by IFIs.

5.6 *Anti-corruption*

IFIs have comprehensive policies against corruption, a concern that is particularly relevant to parties that participate in development of physical infrastructure projects.[32] Their integrity departments should be able to use AI-enhanced tools to detect (and possibly predict) indicators of corruption (i.e., red flags) in construction projects by accessing data from e-procurement systems and building information modeling/management (BIM) software that is commonly used by EPC contractors globally.[33] If this data is coupled with the sensors and other IoT services, the investigators will be able to monitor projects in real time and enhance their ability to dramatically reduce corruption. This will in turn lead to better economic performance and productivity, lower prices and poverty reduction.

6 Conclusion

Smart infrastructure poses some challenging questions for governments, project sponsors and financiers, some of which have been outlined above. In the Asian context, these challenges have not stopped the governments and the private sector in Japan, China and South Korea from aggressively promoting the development of smart cities and smart infrastructure, both domestically and generally in South East Asia.[34] IFIs such as AIIB, ADB and EBRD have an important role to play because these types of technologies will become embedded in the infrastructure projects they finance. Through negotiations with counterparties and the implementation of their policies, IFIs operate as standard setters in the context of international development projects. Accordingly, there is an important opportunity for them to assume the same role in relation to the financing of smart infrastructure projects. The good news is that effective policy and smart regulation can achieve the right balance between the positive and negative aspects inherent in these projects. This will be the new paradigm for sustainable infrastructure development.

---

32 Note the widespread corruption in the construction industry; Craig 2017.

33 Autodesk, Building Information Modeling, <https://www.autodesk.com/solutions/bim>, accessed 8 February 2021.

34 Nikkei Asian Review 2020.

References

Appleton J, *Citizen's perspectives on data privacy in smart cities*, (2 November 2020), <https://hub.beesmart.city/en/strategy/citizens-perspective-on-data-privacy-in-smart-cities>, accessed on 9 February, 2021.

Asian Development Bank's (ADB), Strategy 2030, (July 2018) <https://www.adb.org/documents/strategy-2030-prosperous-inclusive-resilient-sustainable-asia-pacific>, accessed 1 November 2021.

Asian Infrastructure Investment Bank (AIIB), Infrastructure for Tomorrow (i4t), <https://www.aiib.org/en/about-aiib/who-we-are/infrastructure-for-tomorrow/overview/index.html>, accessed 1 November 2021.

Carroll T, The Smarter Supply Chain of the Future (October, 2010), <https://www.ibm/legal/copytrade.shtml>, accessed 8 February 2021.

Craig D, *Construction Corruption Bleeds the Industry's Productivity*, Jobsite (1 May 2017), <https://www.procore.com/jobsite/construction-corruption-bleeds-the-industry-s-productivity/>, accessed 8 February 2021.

Deloitte Insights, *Making smart cities cybersecure*, (2019), <https://www2.deloitte.com/content/dam/Deloitte/de/Documents/risk/Report_making_smart_cities_cyber_secure.pdf>, accessed 9 February 2021.

Effing R and Groot B P *Social Smart City: Introducing Digital and Social Strategies for Participatory Governance in Smart Cities* (2016). In: Scholl H. et.al (eds) *Electronic Government. EGOV 2016*, Lecture Notes in Computer Science, vol 9820. Springer, Cham, <https://doi.org/10.1007/978-3-319-44421-5_19>.

European Bank for Reconstruction and Development (EBRD), Sustainability Reporting, <https://www.ebrd.com/sustainability-reporting.html>, accessed 1 November 2021.

European Bank for Reconstruction and Development (EBRD), EBRD's Green Cities initiative, <https://ebrdgreencities.com/>, accessed 1 November 2021.

European Bank for Reconstruction and Development (EBRD), Green Cities Programme Methodology, (2016), <https://www.ebrdgreencities.com/assets/Uploads/PDF/6f71292055/Green-City-Action-Plan-Methodology.pdf>, accessed 1 November 2021.

European Commission, *The making of a smart city: policy recommendations*, (2020), <www.smartcities-infosystem.eu>, accessed 8 February 2021.

McKinsey Global Institute, Smart Cities: Digital Solutions for a livable future (June 2018), <https://www.mckinsey.com/business-functions/operations/our-insights/smart-cities-digital-solutions-for-a-more-livable-future>, accessed 8 February 2021.

Nikkei Asian Review, $2.4bn Japan fund to help decarbonization in 26 ASEAN cities, (17 December 2020), <https://asia.nikkei.com/Spotlight/Environment/2.4bn-Japan-fund-to-help-decarbonization-in-26-ASEAN-cities>, accessed 8 February 2021.

United Nations (UN), Sustainable Development Goals, <https://www.un.org/sustainabledevelopment/>, accessed 8 February 2021.

United Nations Conference on Trade and Development (UNCTAD) *Data Protection and Privacy Legislation Worldwide*, (14 December 2021), <https://unctad.org/page/data-protection-and-privacy-legislation-worldwide>, accessed 8 February 2021.

United Nations Development Programme (UNDP), *Catalyzing Private Sector Investment in Climate Smart Cities*, (11 August 2020), <https://www.undp.org/publications/catalyzing-private-sector-investment-climate-smart-cities>, accessed 8 February 2021.

United Nations Sustainable Development Goals, *Goal 11 Make cities inclusive, safe, resilient and sustainable*, https://www.un.org/sustainabledevelopment/cities/, accessed 22 August 2022.

World Economic Forum (WEF), Community Paper (November 2019), <https://www3.weforum.org/docs/WEF_Technology_in_Infrastructure.pdf>, accessed 1 November 2021.

PART 4

Innovations in Structure and Development

CHAPTER 12

The Flood of the Private Sector Funding in Development and USAID's Maneuvers to Ride the Wave

*Gayle Girod**

Abstract

While USAID's goals have shifted, from the early days of implementing the Marshall Plan, which focused on reducing the risk of communism and increasing market opportunities for the U.S. by decreasing poverty and increasing production in developing countries, to the Biden Administration's USAID intention to focus on programming that "advances U.S. national security and economic prosperity, demonstrates American generosity, and promotes a path to recipient self-reliance and resilience", the underlying motivations are similar – understanding that the United States' success is contingent on the World's success. However, USAID's methods of operating to reach those goals have shifted, to match the shifting landscapes in the countries in which it works, recognizing the invaluable role that private sector business and investments can play in reaching its development objectives. With creative use of its authorities, USAID is advancing new approaches to development.

* Gayle Girod is Chief Innovation Counsel and the Assistant General Counsel for the Bureau for Development, Democracy, and Innovation (DDI) at USAID, ggirod@usaid.gov. Gayle joined the USAID Office of General Counsel in May 2011 after working for three years at World Vision as Associate General Counsel, advising on compliance, policy, and operational issues, primarily related to U.S. Government grant matters. Prior to World Vision, Gayle practiced government contracts law in Washington, D.C. (Reed Smith – 2003 to 2008, Morgan, Lewis and Bockius – 1996–2003, and Howrey & Simon – 1995–1996), advising clients on contract and grant compliance matters, and representing companies in contract negotiations and litigation, including claims and bid protests. Gayle clerked for the Honorable Kenneth R. Harkins, Court of Federal Claims (1994–1995). Originally from Michigan, Gayle is a graduate of Michigan State University and the University of Toledo College of Law. The opinions and views expressed are those of the author and not those of USAID.

 | DOI:10.1163/9789004460010_013

1 Introduction

USAID celebrated its 60th anniversary in 2021, one of the first, and still the premier, international development agency, currently providing more than USD 20 billion a year in development assistance worldwide. However, the development landscape has shifted since its founding in 1961. In its early years, U.S. development aid dwarfed other means of financial assistance to developing countries and the U.S. was one of the few players in this field. In the intervening decades, the needs of target countries have changed and there is now a greater flow of money to developing countries from international development agencies, accompanied by an exponential increase in private sector investment in development. In response, USAID programs are evolving to most efficiently meet the needs of the world's poor by tapping into these additional funding streams, by partnering with other donors and, increasingly, the private sector.

2 A Brief History

Following the end of World War II in 1945, the U.S. recognized the benefits of rebuilding war-torn Europe, including the bolstering of the U.S. economy. Rebuilding Europe's industrial and agricultural production capability, and supporting its financial stability, would reduce poverty and unemployment, facilitate international trade and stem the spread of communism in Europe. George C. Marshall, Secretary of State from 1947 to 1949, proposed the first large scale iteration of international development assistance under the European Recovery Program,[1] better known as the Marshall Plan, a massive U.S. sponsored program to provide financial and technical assistance to Europe, to stabilize it by rebuilding its infrastructure and economy.

Feeding on the fear of the spread of communism, following the collapse of European economies, as a result of the Second World War, the U.S. Congress passed the Economic Cooperation Act[2] (ECCA) in April 1948, to implement the Marshall Plan. Providing financial and technical support to other nations, as envisaged by the ECCA, was deemed to be in the interest of the United States.

1 According to the Council on Foreign Relations, the United States spent USD 13.2 billion on the Marshall Plan from 1948 to 1952. See <https://www.cfr.org/blog/it-takes-more-money-make-marshall-plan> accessed 16 June 2022.

2 The European Recovery Program (ERP), informally known as the Marshall Plan, was legislated as Title I under the Economic Cooperation Act.

Specifically, Section 102(a) of the ECCA provided as follows: "Recognizing the intimate economic and other relationships between the United States and the nations of Europe, and recognizing that disruption following in the wake of war is not contained by national frontiers, the Congress finds that the existing situation in Europe endangers the establishment of a lasting peace, the general welfare and national interest of the United States, and the attainment of the objectives of the United Nations".[3] The Economic Cooperation Administration (ECA) was set up as an independent government agency to implement the ECCA and administer the Marshall Plan.

In his inaugural speech on January 20, 1949, for his second term of office, President Truman embraced the early successes of the Marshall plan and articulated his vision of international assistance as the fourth point of his foreign policy objectives (referred to as the Point Four Plan) as follows:

> We must embark on a bold new program for making the benefits of our scientific advances and industrial progress available for the improvement and growth of underdeveloped areas. More than half the people of the world are living in conditions approaching misery. Their food is inadequate. They are victims of disease. Their economic life is primitive and stagnant. Their poverty is a handicap and a threat both to them and to more prosperous areas. For the first time in history, humanity possesses the knowledge and skill to relieve suffering of these people. The United States is pre-eminent among nations in the development of industrial and scientific techniques. The material resources which we can afford to use for assistance of other peoples are limited. But our imponderable resources in technical knowledge are constantly growing and are inexhaustible.[4]

The Point Four Program focused on two goals: (I) Creating markets for the United States by reducing poverty and increasing production in developing countries; and (II) diminishing the threat of communism by helping countries prosper under capitalism.

During its short operation from 1948 to 1951, the ECA provided USD13 billion in development aid, the vast majority in the form of direct grants. Such assistance helped strengthen industrial and agricultural production and improved financial stability in Europe. The countries receiving aid under the Marshall

---

3 Economic Cooperation Act of 1948, Section 102(a).

4 See Harry S. Truman Inaugural Address, January 20, 1949. See <https://www.bartleby.com/124/pres53.html> accessed 16 June 2022.

Plan increased their gross national product by 15–25%, based on the support received. It transformed the perception of foreign aid, making it a legitimate and effective part of U.S. policy on the world stage.

In 1953, George Marshall was awarded the Nobel Peace Prize for his contribution to the recovery of post-war Europe. He was the first general to win the Peace Prize, a controversial choice for that reason.

The ECA operated for only three years before being abolished. Its functions were first transferred to the newly created Mutual Security Agency (MSA) (1951–1953) and then to the Foreign Operations Administration (FOA) (1953–1955). The MSA and FOA both expanded their purpose, from solely economic support, as was the case with the ECA, to coordinating U.S. policy related to the "cooperative development of economic and military strength among the nations of the free world".[5] Thereafter, U.S. government international development activities had a six year home in the International Cooperation Administration (ICA) (1955–1961), established by the State Department to coordinate non-military security programs and administer/ implement economic assistance and technical cooperation programs.

In a March 1961 Special Message to the Congress on Foreign Aid, President John F. Kennedy stated that "[t]here is no escaping our obligations: our moral obligations as a wise leader and good neighbor in the interdependent community of free nations – our economic obligations as the wealthiest people in a world of largely poor people, as a nation no longer dependent upon the loans from abroad that once helped us develop our own economy and our political obligations as the single largest counter to the adversaries of freedom".[6]

On November 3, 1961, the United States Agency for International Aid (USAID) was born, with the passage of the Foreign Assistance Act of 1961 (FAA).[7] Recognizing the "interdependence of nations", the FAA declared that United States development cooperation policy should emphasize five principal goals:

(1) the alleviation of the worst physical manifestations of poverty among the world's poor majority;

5 See Letter to Secretary Dulles Regarding Transfer of the Affairs of the Foreign Operations Administration to the Department of State, April 17, 1955, <https://www.presidency.ucsb.edu/documents/letter-secretary-dulles-regarding-transfer-the-affairs-the-foreign-operations> accessed 16 June 2022.

6 President Kennedy Special Message to the Congress on Foreign Aid, March 22, 1961, <https://www.presidency.ucsb.edu/documents/special-message-the-congress-foreign-aid-1> accessed 16 June 2022.

7 The Foreign Assistance Act of 1961 (P.L. 87–195; 22 U.S.C. 2151 et seq.).

(2) the promotion of conditions enabling developing countries to achieve self-sustaining economic growth, with equitable distribution of benefits;
(3) the encouragement of development processes in which individual civil and economic rights are respected and enhanced;
(4) the integration of the developing countries into an open and equitable international economic system; and
(5) the promotion of good governance through combating corruption and improving transparency and accountability.[8]

Until the mid-1970s, U.S. development assistance was focused on large technical and capital assistance programs, primarily, infrastructure loans. With a revision to the FAA in 1973, USAID funding became more focused on smaller technical assistance awards, to address "basic human needs", such as: Food and nutrition, population planning, health, education and human resources development.[9]

In 1973, Congress passed a resolution directing USAID to focus its economic aid on the poorest populations in the poorest countries. Consequently, USAID increased the number of its missions in the 1970s from 38 to 62, with 20 new missions in Africa. Over the next two decades, USAID reaffirmed its commitment to broad-based economic growth, emphasizing employment and income opportunities through a revitalization of agriculture and expansion of domestic markets.

In the 1990s, USAID programs became more holistic, with integrated country programs intended to be more sustainable and to bolster the host country's ability to care for its people. The 2000s saw a large increase in U.S. aid, primarily to Afghanistan and Iraq. Consequently, USAID programmed large infrastructure and other projects that were closely aligned with U.S national security policy in the region. It also greatly expanded its stable of implementing partners, to include the private sector, foundations and other donor agencies, thereby increasing the impact of its foreign assistance funding.

Now, 60 years since its founding, USAID is the largest U.S. development agency, accounting for more than half of the total foreign assistance provided by the U.S.[10] Currently, USAID provides contracts, grants, and other types of

8 The Foreign Assistance Act, section 101 (22 U.S.C. 2151).

9 PUBLIC LAW 93-189-DEC. 17, 1973, Section 2(2)(B), Amending the FAA.

10 "With a budget of over USD 27 billion, USAID is one of the largest official aid agencies in the world and accounts for more than half of all U.S. foreign assistance – the highest in the world in absolute dollar terms". <https://en.wikipedia.org/wiki/United_States_Agency_for_International_Development> accessed 16 June 2022.

funding to advance U.S. development and other policy goals. Additionally, USAID's staff includes technical experts who guide activity design and provide technical direction to a network of thousands of USAID implementing partners, through whom USAID currently disburses more than USD 20 billion for development and humanitarian assistance, in more than 100 countries, supporting the provision of cash transfers, procurement of equipment and commodities, building and maintenance of reliable infrastructure, improvement of educational systems, and the provision of training and technical assistance.[11]

USAID's goals have always been two-fold: humanitarian relief to people around the world who are suffering, as well as to advance U.S. national security interests by creating a stable socio-economic and political global environment. From the objective in the initial days of implementing the Marshall Plan to stem the growth of communism, to today's efforts to providing people with the means to fight poverty and hunger, and resist a myriad of corrupt and disruptive influences, USAID has advanced U.S. policy objectives through overseas development assistance.

USAID's programs run the gamut, from traditional agreements,[12] supporting an implementing partner's program, to more innovative programs[13] to support and encourage investments abroad. While all of these programming methods have a place in a comprehensive development system, there is a long-standing recognition that USAID needs to consider the private sector as a valuable development partner. To do this ever more effectively, USAID will need to meet the private sector where they are, which will require a creative use of USAID resources to fit the square peg of the private sector's needs, e.g. profit, workforce development etc., into the round hole of USAID's policies and objectives, as well as its regulatory and statutory framework.

3 USAID's Legal Framework

Like other U.S. government entities, USAID operates within prescribed regulations. For each project in which it is involved, USAID must have specific authority. While private sector organizations are generally free to do anything

11 See USAID Fiscal Year 2020 Agency Financial Report <https://www.usaid.gov/sites/default/files/documents/USAID_FY2020_AFR-508.pdf> accessed 16 June 2022.

12 USAID has traditionally used cost reimbursement grants and cooperative agreements to support implementing partners in executing their programs.

13 As described below, USAID is using its authority, including grants and cooperative agreements, in new and creative ways, e.g. milestone based awards, to achieve greater impact.

that is not prohibited by applicable laws and regulations, USAID, like other U.S. government agencies, operates within the confines of authorities provided by Congress, through authorizing legislation, annual appropriations, and other laws and regulations.

The FAA is USAID's primary statutory authority, providing it with the authority to "take the lead in concert with other nations to mobilize [resources from wealthy] public and private sources".[14] Its development assistance is to be carried out within its policy parameters to "promote private sector activity in open and competitive markets in developing countries, recognizing such activity to be a productive and efficient means of achieving equitable and long-term economic growth".[15] Further legislation over the years have provided USAID with additional authority. This includes:

- The Support for East European Democracy (SEED) Act of 1989 and the FREEDOM Support Act (FSA) of 1992 (providing support to Central and Eastern European countries following the fall of the Berlin Wall);
- The U.S. Leadership Against HIV/AIDS, Tuberculosis, and Malaria Act of 2003 (the primary legislation behind the President's Emergency Plan for AIDS Relief (PEPFAR), for HIV/AIDS treatment, prevention, and research); and
- Most recently, the Better Utilization of Investments Leading to Development Act of 2018 (the BUILD Act) (providing USAID authority to access the tools of the new U.S. International Development Finance Corporation (DFC), such as loan guarantees, loans, political-risk insurance and equity).

Under Section 635(b) of the FAA, USAID is authorized to "make loans, advances, and grants to, make and perform agreements and contracts with, or enter into other transactions with, any individual, corporation, or other body of persons, friendly government or government agency, whether within or without the United States and international organizations in furtherance of the purposes and within the limitations of this Act". This provision of the FAA is the basis of USAID's ability to implement foreign assistance through implementing partners.

In addition to affirmative authorities for it to operate, USAID's statutory framework provides numerous prohibitions that must be considered in each program and activity, including a prohibition on aid to certain countries, such

14 The Foreign Assistance Act, section 102(a) (22 U.S.C. 2151 et seq.).

15 The Foreign Assistance Act, section (b)(14) (22 U.S.C. 2151 et seq.), added by section 301 of the International Security and Development Cooperation Act of 1985 (Public Law 99–83; 99 Stat. 190).

as North Korea and Iran, a prohibition on the U.S. government holding equity, and prohibitions on certain types of programs, including those that support abortion as a method of family planning or provide assistance to the police or military in a recipient country.

USAID contracts and assistance awards (grants and cooperative agreements) require many standard terms and conditions, which are mandated by statute, regulation, or policy. All USAID contracts are subject to the Federal Acquisition Regulations (FAR), which provide a regulatory framework for awarding and managing U.S. government contracts. It contains 51 parts addressing issues relating to contract award and management, as well as Part 52, containing over 600 potential contract clauses, and Part 53, providing dozens of government forms. There is also a supplement to the FAR, which contains additional USAID specific clauses. USAID assistance awards are managed by USAID personnel under the USAID Automated Directive System (ADS) 303, which includes sets of standard provisions, to be used depending on the assistance recipient and type of award. Like the FAR for contracts, this regulatory framework also provides structured clauses to address cost principles, audit rights, reporting, etc., as well as "power of the purse string" clauses that require contractors to maintain a drug-free workplace and reach certain U.S. small business subcontracting goals.

In addition to compliance with the myriad of required terms and conditions, the U.S. government budget process can make it difficult for agencies like USAID to have the right funding available at the right time, to facilitate private sector partnerships, including navigating congressional appropriations, adhering to the timing, purpose and amount of the appropriated funds, which are frequently out of step with private sector needs. USAID's annual appropriations, which include additional authorities, specify the amount of funding to be allocated to specific types of programming or towards various Congressional priorities. The timing of the U.S. government's budget cycle can be challenging when funding is requested years in advance of when it is received and made available by USAID for disbursement.

4 Structural Impediments

In addition to the legal hurdles, there are also a few "self-made" obstacles to engaging the private sector that are attributable to the way in which USAID operates. For example, only very recently has it begun to capture indicators that measure the success of private sector partnerships, which is needed to incentivize staff to take the extra time that a private-sector partnership may take to identify, negotiate, and execute.

Additionally, USAID is very decentralized, with missions in more than 80 countries. This can make it difficult to imbed the cultural shift that is required to include the private sector in a majority of USAID's programs. USAID also has a lot of staff turnover, with Foreign Service postings lasting one to four years, in addition to political appointments, which change when the administration in Washington changes. Usually, new leadership comes with new or different priorities. Additionally, USAID decisions can be driven by the desire to have an "announcable" for a public event, which is not ideal. There has also been an overall low risk tolerance within USAID, which can impede progress and innovation.

5 Expanding the Impact of USAID Funding

USAID's traditional methods for expending funds operate easily within the parameters of its statutory and regulatory authorities, restrictions, procedural framework, and appropriations cycle. Usually, USAID issues a solicitation for an identified activity, accepts proposals/applications in respect thereof, and ultimately awards a cost reimbursement contract or assistance award following a technical review. Such awards are generally for five years, but may be extended. The implementing partner is paid as funds are expended, and additional funds are allocated to the award each year, as USAID receives its annual budgetary appropriation.

In December 2018, USAID published a Private Sector Engagement Policy (PSE Policy), recognizing that the amount of government funding it receives cannot address the full range of issues that developing countries face. Increasingly, with the billions of dollars of private sector funding flowing into these countries, USAID's goal is to engage in market-based programs, to encourage private sector investment towards desirable development outcomes.

USAID is not new to working with the private sector. Even prior to 2018, it engaged in thousands of private sector partnerships, leveraging billions of private sector dollars, across many sectors, such as economic growth, agriculture, health, education, environment, democracy, water and sanitation, gender issues, and humanitarian assistance. However, USAID is looking to continue to progress across the spectrum of private sector activity, from accessing corporate philanthropy to private enterprise-driven development. Consequently, USAID's relationship with the private sector has expanded to aligning with its profit-making motivation where it intersects with USAID's development goals.

On the philanthropic end of the spectrum, USAID engages in public-private partnerships with corporations to steer their charitable contributions to USAID directly, using USAID's gift authority, or, more likely, to USAID implementing partners for use by them to supplement USAID funded activities. Such philanthropic partnerships include monetary contributions or volunteer work from a private sector partner in countries/communities where a company may operate or sell products. Over the years, such philanthropy has expanded to include the concept of "corporate social responsibility",[16] where USAID can help guide corporations to align social, environmental and developmental issues with their business strategy and operations.

The next phase on the spectrum of public-private partnerships, beyond charitable giving and corporate social responsibility, requires USAID to identify the shared values between its corporate partners and USAID's development goals, to co-create partnerships that address long-term strategic business interests, while also creating sustainable development impact. Such co-investment by the private sector and USAID can accommodate the private sector's expectations of a reasonable return on investment, as a core objective of the partnership, alongside sustainable development. Such mutually beneficial projects, tapping into commercial, market-based solutions, can mean more sustainable initiatives beyond USAID's traditional 5- to 10-year programs.

FIGURE 12.1 Intersection of business and development goals

16 According to Investopedia, "[c]orporate social responsibility (CSR) is a self-regulating business model that helps a company be socially accountable – to itself, its stakeholders, and the public. By practicing corporate social responsibility, also called corporate citizenship, companies can be conscious of the kind of impact they are having on all aspects of society, including economic, social, and environmental. To engage in CSR means that, in the ordinary course of business, a company is operating in ways that enhance society and the environment, instead of contributing negatively to them", <https://www.investopedia.com/terms/c/corp-social-responsibility.asp> accessed 16 June 2022.

As shown above, the private sector and USAID share common interests and collaboration provides the private sector with needed resources, including people and natural, while helping to advance development goals, economic growth and public welfare.

6 New Models of Development

Years ago, traditional international foreign aid (IFA), i.e. development funding from public entities, was the largest source of external funding going into developing countries. Now, in some countries, private investment dwarfs aid from public sources. According to the Global Philanthropy Tracker 2020, international private sector funding going into target countries was more than three times the amount of IFA received. Aid agencies want, and need to tap into these private sector funds to supplement and enhance funding from public sources.

It is important to view international private sector funding as an additional source of development funding, to augment the impact of IFA rather than supplant it. In some developing countries, international private sector funding is not effective, because there isn't a functioning legal or economic structure to support it, including laws addressing tax and intellectual property, a sufficiently trained work force or a viable value chain infrastructure. IFA can help fund programs to support the building blocks to a strong economy, so that international private sector funding can reach its full potential.

Even within the confines of the statutory and regulatory infrastructure that determines what it can and cannot do, USAID is able to employ a wide variety of methodologies to address market constraints, create incentives for private sector investment and otherwise leverage the private sector's unique expertise to solve development and humanitarian challenges more efficiently, and sustainably, than development agencies can do alone.

As detailed below, USAID employs unique models of development to tap into the billions of dollars of foreign investment in developing countries, using innovative blended-finance and investment-mobilization platforms to raise private capital at scale to accomplish ambitious development goals. Working alongside private sector actors, with a profit motivation, provides many benefits to USAID, and to development as a whole, beyond just the additional resources that the private sector can bring to bear. USAID can encourage and help the private sector to promote more inclusive and sustainable business practices. In return, the private sector can provide USAID with additional technical expertise and significantly expand the pool of stakeholders and resources available for investing in development. Such partnerships also harness the synergies between the private sector and development goals, such as improved value chains, better trained local workforces, and new potential solutions to other societal challenges.

7 What USAID Has to Offer the Private Sector

The work that USAID accomplishes and supports furthers a strong business environment. Health, education, and gender programs all help to provide a healthy and productive workforce. Democracy and economic growth programs help develop a strong and sustainable political and social framework that is integral to a productive private sector. Equally, energy and infrastructure programs provide valuable resources for business ventures.

USAID also partners with host governments and civil society organizations.[17] Private sector entities partnering with USAID can leverage these deep and long relationships to strengthen their in-country presence and aid in effective use of host government systems. Partnering with USAID can establish and grow strong brand recognition and goodwill for such entities.

USAID has many programs focused on reducing market barriers and risks to investment. USAID works not just at the systemic and governmental level, but also has programs designed to reduce investment risk in individual projects. USAID programs create new markets and customers for the private sector.

USAID is driven to finding new, innovative solutions to development concerns, as evidenced by the newly formed Bureau for Development, Democracy and Innovation (DDI), which includes the Innovation, Technology, and Research Hub (ITR), to lead "USAID's work to identify, research, explore, integrate and experiment with innovative technologies, processes, and practices that amplify the success of USAID's programming. DDI/ITR develops and maintains technical expertise and partnerships critical to supporting and accelerating modern and ever-evolving approaches and solutions, from concept to

17 While there are many ways to define civil society, the United Nations states, "[a] civil society organization (CSO) or non-governmental organization (NGO) is any non-profit, voluntary citizens' group which is organized on a local, national or international level. Task-oriented and driven by people with a common interest, civil society organizations (CSOs) perform a variety of services and humanitarian functions, bring citizens' concerns to Governments, monitor policies, and encourage political participation at the community level", <https://www.un.org/en/civil-society/page/about-us> accessed 16 June 2022.

common practice". The entire agency works to identify new, and enhance existing, technologies to further the impact of its development programs, designed to have a positive impact on the host country's business environment.

8 How USAID Is Overcoming Obstacles to Development

USAID's 2018 Private Sector Engagement (PSE) Policy has had a significant and positive impact on legal and structural impediments to development, by taking concrete steps to move the ball forward on private sector engagement. As provided in the PSE Policy, "[p]utting this policy into practice will take an [a]gency-wide effort through several complementary work streams. The policy prizes flexibility, creativity, and aggressiveness among USAID's leadership and staff to define the policy's implementation and tailor it to each [o]perating [u]nit's unique context and role". It is no coincidence that this policy follows on the heels of the agency's Risk Appetite Statement in June 2018, where USAID adopted a high tolerance for risk in programs that partner with the private sector, as follows:

> We will co-design and co-invest with private-sector entities that promise to leverage or mobilize additional resources or expertise to amplify the impact of our work, while recognizing that sometimes such partners will fail to mobilize promised capital, or deliver on commitments.[18]

9 How USAID Engages the Private Sector

USAID has various institutional means to engage with the private sector. The Global Development Alliance (GDA) is USAID's flagship private sector program, established in 2001. The GDA aligns the U.S. government and private sector interests, and crafts an activity that benefits both. Generally, this involves a private sector partner who provides resources in support of the relevant activity, and an implementing partner who implements the activity with the help of USAID funding. The activity in question is "co-created" by USAID, along with the resource and implementing partners, to achieve both business and

18 See U.S. Agency for International Development Risk Appetite Statement – June 2018, p. 8–9, <https://www.usaid.gov/sites/default/files/documents/1868/USAID_Risk-Appetite-Statement_Jun2018.pdf> accessed 16 June 2022.

development goals on a market-based approach. Public and private resources are provided, ideally at least at a 1:1 ratio. However, frequently government funding is leveraged at a much higher ratio. The end-result is more sustainable development than if USAID funded the activity alone.

USAID has greatly increased its use of co-creation, to collaborate with the private sector and other stakeholders, in order to "crowd-source" solutions to identified problems. While USAID has the necessary technical expertise, it recognizes that incorporating varied perspectives and motivations can yield better development results. Much of USAID's formal "co-creation" has occurred through Broad Agency Announcements (BAA). BAAS are solicitations for research and development, to address a stated problem or challenge. BAAS ask for short submissions providing potential solutions.[19]

Frequently, these submissions form the basis for USAID's decision regarding who is qualified to help craft a solution. Those with expertise to contribute are invited to participate in a facilitated "co-creation" event to discuss and brainstorm the issues. Ultimately, with a BAA, some of the participants may be asked to submit concept papers to be funded. The "co-creation" event also serves as a networking opportunity for future endeavors or to receive funding from USAID as part of a consortium. For instance, in 2015, USAID issued a BAA, looking to "collaborate in the research, development, piloting, testing, and scaling of innovative, practical and cost-effective interventions to catalyze private investment in developing countries". Over a dozen companies were represented at the resulting "co-creation" workshop, where USAID noted that this was not "business as usual", and that it was seeking creative solutions to support investments. The result was a contract that included opportunities for many of the workshop participants to receive USAID funding, and created a network of partners for USAID missions to tap into the right expertise to support future local investment opportunities and prepare the investments to receive private sector funding by reducing entry barriers and investment risk. Meanwhile, the prime contractor facilitates knowledge management, through which information is shared and best practices are identified, and provides proper monitoring and evaluation. Awards such as this tap into a broad range of stakeholder expertise and are structured to capture and respond to lessons learned from the experience of past projects.

USAID's Development Innovation Ventures (DIV) program funds solutions to development problems and helps scale-up those with strong evidence of positive impact and cost-effectiveness. DIV provides various levels of funding

19 See FAR Part 35.016.

for innovations at different stages of development: At stage 1 (proof of concept) up to USD 200,000 in funding; at stage 2 (testing and positioning for scale) up to USD 1,500,000 in funding; at stage 3 (scaling) up to USD 5,000,000 in funding and "Evidence Grants" of up to USD 1,500,000. The DIV program employs evidence-based technical analyses to identify innovations with strong indicators of positive impact, cost-effectiveness and a viable pathway to scale and sustainability. Michael Kremer, a co-founder of DIV, who recently won the Nobel Prize in Economics, noted as follows: "[DIV] is deliberately open across sectors and geographies, and to innovations intended to scale either commercially or through developing country governments or donors. We complement this openness with a tiered evidence-based approach to funding. DIV makes small investments to pilot and rigorously test promising ideas and larger ones to help innovations that are supported by rigorous empirical evidence to transition to scale". Since 2010, DIV has funded 200 innovations, in 45 countries, positively impacting 55 million lives. Following on the success of the DIV model, USAID supported the UK Department for International Development (DFID) in creating the Global Innovation Fund (GIF) in 2014, which follows the DIV model. To date, GIF has invested USD 101 million in 51 innovations, expected to positively impact 130 million lives. France recently launched its own program, *Fonds d'Innovation pour le Développement* (the Fund for Innovation for Development), modeled after the DIV.

For many years, USAID has also been funding loan guarantees using its Development Credit Authority (DCA), to reduce the risk of lending to underserved markets, to establish new relationships with financial institutions and to demonstrate the viability of lending to the development community. From 1999 to 2018, DCA made USD 5.5 billion worth of credit available in 80 countries. Loan guarantees, backed by the full faith and credit of the U.S. Treasury, are an effective development tool on their own or as a companion to other development financing. Additionally, the BUILD Act of 2018 created the DFC, which combined the Overseas Private Investment Corporation and USAID's DCA authority to consolidate certain finance solutions, including loan guaranties, direct loans, equity investments, and political risk insurance. USAID is able to access these products through the DFC.

As stated above, many of USAID's funding activities are usually on a reimbursement basis, where the implementing partner is reimbursed for all reasonable, allowable, and allocable costs incurred. While this is a viable option for some awards, using a fixed-priced, milestone-based funding approach can frequently lead to better results. In a milestone-based approach, USAID only pays as the milestones are met. However, the contractor is not paid anything if the milestones in question are not met. Additionally, while USAID does not have to pay for the contractor's costs in excess of the negotiated milestone payments, the contractor does not have to return any funding if its costs are less than the negotiated milestone payments. This means that accurately selecting, defining and pricing the milestones at the beginning of the award process are crucial to craft an activity that is equally beneficial to the government and the implementing partner. The payments agreed should adequately remunerate the partner, but must also reflect value to USAID. If structured effectively, administering activity in this manner can be much easier than in a traditional award. There are fewer administrative burdens on the partner, including fewer expenditures, such as travel, purchase or hire of vehicles, subcontractors, etc., that are subject to USAID approval, and the partner does not have to submit to a financial audit for the award. In addition, the implementing partner is provided greater leeway on how to accomplish the milestones, and can better calibrate performance based on lessons learned during the process.

USAID has creatively used this fixed-price model for a number of successful projects, including development impact bonds and prizes. "Development impact bonds" (DIBs), also known as "social impact bonds" (SIBs), are not "bonds" in the traditional sense, but a fixed-priced model where, in addition to the funding and implementing party/ies, there is an investor who is willing to provide the money up-front to the implementing party, with the promise of being repaid by the funding when the milestones are met. This basic model can get more complex as more parties are added, including potentially a third-party evaluator and intermediary. Like other models of development, DIBs/SIBs are but one tool in the toolbox, and are most effective when they are the right tool for the desired outcome.

The first "social impact bond" (SIB), the Peterborough Social Impact Bond, was developed in part by Social Finance,[20] in 2010, in the UK. The Peterborough SIB was a six-year project, whereby Social Finance would be paid based on its ability to reduce the rate of recidivism for certain prisoners, with a goal of reducing recidivism by 10%. Social Finance was free to determine what interventions it deemed would be effective. The investors paid for the services and would only be repaid if re-offending was reduced by at least 7.5%.[21] Social

20 Social Finance is a non-profit organization specializing in impact investing. See <https://socialfinance.org/> accessed 16 June 2022.

21 The project, split into two cohorts, achieved sufficient results to trigger an outcome payment, with an overall reduction in recidivism in the sample population of 9%. See <https://assets.publishing.service.gov.uk/government/uploads/system/uploads/attachment_data/file/486512/social-impact-bond-pilot-peterborough-report.pdf and

Finance indicates that "[t]here are now over 160 impact bonds across 28 countries, with more than 25 in the United States".[22]

The use of DIBs and SIBs is most appropriate when the entity that will benefit from the outcome, generally the host government in the development context, is actively involved in the DIB/SIB in question. Hence, in the UK example, it would make sense for the "outcome funder" to be the government entity that would accrue significant savings from a reduction in recidivism (i.e. they would not have to pay the high costs of incarceration for repeat offenders), than for a development agency to fund the relevant project in that role. This is because, in a DIB/SIB, there is also an investor involved who stands to make a return on its investment. Therefore, if the outcome funder agrees to pay USD 100 for each person who does not go back to prison, and the implementer ends up spending USD 90 on interventions for each person who does not go back to prison, then the investors earn a USD 10 profit. If the outcome funder is the government agency that pays USD 200 for each person who returns to prison, they are happy to pay USD 100 to keep them out of prison – that is a huge win. If the outcome funder is a development agency, then it may be that they could have simply reimbursed the costs to the implementer and paid only USD 90, instead of USD 100. However, there may be other reasons for the development agency to entertain a DIB/SIB; perhaps to encourage other investors to the table.

USAID has a significant role to play in private sector impact investment in developing countries, where the investment achieves a positive social and/or environmental impact, in addition to the financial upside for investors. USAID can contribute by advancing a healthy business environment, through an active civil society and stable government regulation, that mitigate risks to individual investments. USAID is able to support investment funds, which combine resources from many investors, to provide much needed capital to small and medium sized enterprises. A recent example is the Althelia Biodiversity Fund (ABF), a USD 100 million, 11-year impact investment fund for Brazil. Through a USAID implementing partner, the International Center for Tropical Agriculture (CIAT), USAID was able to have a seat at the table in a project to provide technical expertise and to ensure that the fund furthers biodiversity conservation and sustainable development goals in the Brazilian Amazon. Mirova Natural Capital eventually aims to raise USD 100 million from private sector impact investors to invest in sustainable activities that will

---

https://www.gsef-net.org/sites/default/files/publication/peterborough-social-impact-bond-cohort-2-results-report_1.pdf> accessed 16 June 2022.

22 See <https://socialfinance.org/social-impact-bonds/> accessed 16 June 2022.

protect, restore, or otherwise improve biodiversity and community livelihoods in the Amazon basin.[23] Recognized by Environment Finance as the 2020 fund of the year,[24] the ABF will invest to ensure the integrity and conservation of the Brazilian Amazon ecosystem over the next 20 years.

As another example of USAID creatively supporting the private sector with the creative use of its authorities, USAID determined that a major impediment to effectively addressing the Ebola crisis in Liberia was the lack of an internet infrastructure; It partnered with Google to replicate the success of previous Google efforts in Ghana and Uganda to make "commercially driven investments in broad-band enabled infrastructure".[25] USAID was able to provide milestone-based funding directly to Google to support its efforts in a way that would lead to positive development outcomes, including ensuring reliable internet connectivity to key government ministries and health facilities, as well as the University of Liberia.

Prizes and "challenges" are another way that USAID uses a fixed-priced structure to support the private sector to achieve positive development impact. At its most basic level, a prize is a thing of value provided for meeting a set goal or for winning a competition. There are two sides to the prize equation: The "ask", which is the action required by the offeror to be taken in order to be considered for the award, and the "prize", which is the thing of value provided to the winner. Selection of the winner may be random, based on meeting certain criteria, or a combination of the two.

The "ask" can be as simple as inviting submission of an entry to a competition, or it may require fulfilling certain criteria, for example, from merely submitting your entry to the Publishers Clearing House (and maybe ordering a magazine subscription or two) to being the first non-governmental organization to launch a manned spacecraft into space (as with the Ansari X prize). The "ask" might be something that the offeror is itself seeking, for instance a prize for an application or piece of equipment, but, just as often, it may confer an incidental benefit to the entity running the prize, for instance, building a valuable mailing list from the information obtained in the entry process. Or in the case of the Ansari X Prize, to encourage private investment in the space

23 Mirova is an impact investment manager. See <https://www.mirova.com/en> accessed 16 June 2022.

24 Environment Finance is an online news and analysis service reporting on sustainable investment, which provides annual awards in a number of categories, recognizing excellence in sustainable investments. See <https://www.environmental-finance.com/content/awards/sustainable-investment-awards-2020/winners/> accessed 16 June 2022.

25 See <https://www.csquared.com/about-us/> accessed 16 June 2022.

industry. A prize may be cash, some other form of value, public recognition or an opportunity to do or participate in an event or project, or a combination of one or more of these incentives. For example, Nobel prizes come with a cash prize also, although the value of the recognition may outweigh the cash prize for many.

When determining if a prize is the right method for USAID, USAID must, as with all programming, determine the desired outcome. A prize can be a useful means for generating enthusiasm or interest in a certain area of development, or it may provide USAID a solution that it is looking for to address a given development challenge. At its best, a prize would accomplish both ends, i.e., spur interest amongst a large number of potential solution providers as well as multiple solutions for the challenge(s) at hand. Of course, USAID must also determine the prize itself. As stewards of taxpayer resources, USAID must ensure that the value of the prize yields equivalent value to USAID. In some cases, there may be ample participants in response to offers of recognition or just the opportunity to participate in an event. However, where there is a significant investment required in order to participate, recognition alone may not be enough to incentive participation. A prize with monetary value may be required, in essence to pay for the participation. Such prize may be a lump sum or the promise of future funding, such as the award of a grant.

A good example of USAID promoting private sector innovation through a prize competition is the USAID Global Health Savings Lives at Birth (SLAB) challenge, started in 2011, that has been held each year since. SLAB uses a prize-like competition to provide funding for innovations that address health risks during childbirth and in the days immediately thereafter, a time when mothers and babies are at much greater risk of death. To date, SLAB has funded 120 innovative tools and approaches, which is a significant proportion of all early-stage innovations funded worldwide, that are estimated to be benefiting about two million women and children. USAID multiplied the power of its impact by partnering with other development funders, such as Grand Challenges Canada, the Bill and Melinda Gates Foundation, the U.K. Department for International Development and the Korea International Cooperation Agency. The unique features of SLAB are the specificity of the outcome sought and the breadth of innovation that could potentially deliver it. The goal is to reduce the risk of maternal-child death and disease at birth, but innovation run the gamut, from identification of information to dissemination to new device technologies. Each year, SLAB holds a multi-day conference, featuring its finalists as part of the competition. In addition to the potential for funding, the participants are provided a public venue at which to showcase their innovations. SLAB provides funding at three levels, early-stage seed, proof of concept, and transition to scale funding, allowing a broad range of solutions to be eligible, and seeks to tailor the prize purse to the solution. Following the success of SLAB, USAID has launched a number of other "grand challenges", to address an array of development needs, including improving literacy and government accountability, and fighting Ebola.

10 Conclusion

The above are but a few examples of USAID's role in partnering with the private sector. While many of these unique structures are accomplished by using USAID's traditional awards – cost reimbursement contracts and cooperative agreements – to achieve non-traditional results, USAID continues to explore its unique authorities to maximize the impact of both development and private sector funding to address the world's development needs. As USAID continues to better understand the private sector's needs, drivers, capabilities and hurdles, it expects to identify even more robust opportunities for collaboration and delivery for development.

References

Economic Cooperation Act of 1948, <https://www.marshallfoundation.org/wp-content/uploads/2014/06/California_The_Economic_Cooperation_Act_of_1948.pdf>, accessed 30 November 2021.

Eisenhower D D, Letter to Secretary Dulles Regarding Transfer of the Affairs of the Foreign Operations Administration to the Department of State, (17 April 1955), <https://www.presidency.ucsb.edu/documents/letter-secretary-dulles-regarding-transfer-the-affairs-the-foreign-operations>, accessed 30 November 2021.

Federal Acquisition Regulation, FAR Part 35.016., <https://www.govinfo.gov/content/pkg/CFR-2011-title48-vol1/pdf/CFR-2011-title48-vol1-sec35-016.pdf>, accessed 30 November 2021.

Kennedy J F, Special Message to the Congress on Foreign Aid, (22 March 1961), <https://www.presidency.ucsb.edu/documents/special-message-the-congress-foreign-aid-1>, accessed 30 November 2021.

The Foreign Assistance Act of 1961, <https://www.foreign.senate.gov/imo/media/doc/Foreign%20Assistance%20Act%20Of%201961.pdf>, accessed 30 November 2021.

Truman H S, Inaugural Address, (20 January 1949), <https://www.bartleby.com/124/pres53.html>, accessed 30 November 2021.

United States Agency for International Development (USAID), USAID Risk Appetite Statement – June 2018, (2018) <https://www.usaid.gov/sites/default/files/documents/1868/USAID_Risk-Appetite-Statement_Jun2018.pdf>, accessed 30 November 2021.

United States Agency for International Development (USAID), Fiscal Year 2020 Agency Financial Report, (2020), <https://www.usaid.gov/sites/default/files/documents/USAID_FY2020_AFR-508.pdf>, accessed 30 November 2021.

US Congress, Public Law 93-189 / Amendment Foreign Assistance Act of 1973, (17 December 1973), <https://www.govinfo.gov/content/pkg/STATUTE-87/pdf/STATUTE-87-Pg714.pdf#page=1>, accessed 30 November 2021.

US Congress, Public Law 99-83 / International Security and Development Cooperation Act of 1985, (8 August1985), <https://www.govinfo.gov/content/pkg/STATUTE-99/pdf/w-99-Pg190.pdf>, accessed 30 November 2021.

CHAPTER 13

Multilateral Development Banks as Agents of Private Contract

*Ilias Bantekas**

Abstract

This article shows how and in what manner international financial institutions (IFIs) and multilateral development banks (MDBs) have complemented their public international law character with the extensive use of private (contract) law for the purpose of attracting and disbursing funds. The following analysis contains selective examples of such innovative contractual practices by a number of IFIs, i.e., the legal framework of intergovernmental trust funds, the contractual relationships with private donors, donor commitments by public donors, and the extensive use of memoranda of understanding (MoU). Finally, the constitutional, democratic, and human rights implications of the use of MoUs in the case of the Greek sovereign debt crisis are highlighted. This brief case study sheds light on the possible normative implications of the use of private (contract) law as a substitute for more traditional treaties.

1 Introduction

A radical transformation has taken international law by surprise since the late 1990s, if not earlier. During the Cold War inter-state relations were not only formal, but quintessentially formalistic. This meant that because relatively few concrete international rules existed, states were very cautious about what they "said" or did, in order to avoid being bound to prior conduct, whether in the form of binding unilateral acts or conduct seen as entailing *opinio juris*, and thus leading to participation in the formation of custom. No wonder, then, that treaties involved a grand ceremonial dimension, with senior government officials attending signature events. Nowadays, with some exceptions, there is very little interest in such things. The regulation of state conduct is much

* Professor of Transnational Law, Hamad bin Khalifa University (Qatar Foundation) College of Law and Adjunct Professor, Georgetown University, Edmund A Walsh School of Foreign Service, ibantekas@hbku.edu.qa.

DOI:10.1163/9789004460010_014

more comprehensive, but not through solemn treaties and customary international law. It is sometimes forgotten that treaties and custom are not sources of international law as such.[1] Rather, obligations are sources of international law, whether for one or more states, and such obligations can be contained in treaties and custom. Hence, treaties and custom are the vehicles for the expression of mutual obligations, the governing law of which is general international law.[2] In this sense, states may just as well exchange these two obligation-bearing vehicles with new vehicles; and, indeed, they have. This author is not aware of any concrete studies with empirical evidence about the contractual practices of states, but anecdotal evidence suggests that save for matters of a constitutional/global nature, such as the prohibition of torture, most other matters are regulated through less grandiose and much less flexible legal forms.

As this article will demonstrate, MDBs, particularly the International Bank for Reconstruction and Development (IBRD), as well as IFIs, such as the International Monetary Fund (IMF), effectively engineered a variety of mechanisms by which they could invite, hold, invest, and finance funds provided to them without any real liability to states, markets, investors, and intended beneficiaries. Some of these took the form of trusts, lacking the contractual or trustee obligations typically associated with trusts; or by requiring borrowing states to borrow under private terms and wholly outside their constitutional frameworks. As a result, sovereign debt management, liquidity and guarantees to states by IFIs or MDBs[3] have been transformed from a transaction between two or more public actors predicated on public (international) law, to an agreement based on private law and subject to the jurisdiction of arbitral tribunals or the courts of a neutral state. The governing law of such agreements is seldom international law, but typically English law.[4] This author has elsewhere expressed the opinion that while reliance on private law has several positive effects, in the manner it is being employed by IFIs and investors almost always leads to the loss of economic and fiscal self-determination.[5] This article attempts to merely show how and in what manner international development

1 See e.g. Tomuschat 2018, 185–204.

2 This is in accordance with Art 2(1)(a) Vienna Convention on the Law of Treaties 1968 (VCLT).

3 IFIs and MDBs are not synonymous. Rather, MDBs are a subcategory of IFIs. The IMF is not a development bank and not part of the World Bank Group although it is frequently mentioned in this paper.

4 By way of illustration, the insertion of English law clauses in sovereign debt instruments (including bonds, borrowing agreements and others) is now common practice. In fact, the financing document is now modeled around boilerplate, standardized, instruments produced by the London Loan Market Association. See Schwarcz 2017.

5 See Bantekas, Vivien 2016.

banks have shed their public international law character in favor of private (contract) law.

To understand why the "public" has been eroded from "international law" it is important to have an overview of the broader context. Since at least the mid-1980s, although certainly from the early 1970s, a period known as "monetarism", financial markets became the key vehicle of growth for liberal democracies.[6] From 1940 to the late 1960s, the U.S. reversed its Great Depression with high volumes of manufacturing, which led to universal employment, which in turn culminated in high volumes of consumerism and so-called "growth". It was during this time that growth was measured in quantitative terms on the basis of gross domestic product (GDP). GDP was the measure of success and prosperity of nations in accordance with liberal economists at the time, who must have assumed that growth can be perpetual.[7] The global oil crisis of the early 1970s clearly showed that continuous growth was a fallacy, but instead of turning to a different model of development, manufacturing-based growth was replaced with financial markets-based growth. This latter model spectacularly crashed at least twice, once in the early 1990s and again around 2007–08, largely as a result of the absence of even rudimentary regulation of the financial sector and private markets.[8] GDP-based growth and scare mongering by the financial markets that there is no alternative model to growth-based economics is key to understanding many of the political decisions of modern times, such as climate change politics, as well as the privatization of services that are fundamental to the enjoyment of basic human rights.

It was only natural that in such an environment IFIs would be bound by the choices dictated by their creators. When states decided to de-regulate financial markets and transnational corporations (TNCs), they implicitly (but very much consciously) agreed to confer a significant part of state affairs to the financial sector; specifically, elements of economic and fiscal policy. Markets not only generate money, but more importantly generate much needed liquidity required for the sustenance and survival of states themselves. If a private financial institution is the sole supplier of liquidity to a state, it can very much dictate the terms for the provision of such liquidity, which in turn impacts on the borrowing state's fiscal and economic policies.[9] Moreover, if the lender can dictate a state's fiscal policy, by implication it can also impose its preferred

---

6 See Chrystal 1990.

7 Pilling 2018.

8 Varoufakis 2015, Bantekas 2012, *Wealth and Growth-based Policies have Augmented Global Poverty and Eroded Human Rights: A Return to Human-Centred Thinking.*

9 See Lienau 2008.

form of agreement. This will naturally be a contract or even an agreement lacking the qualities of contracts if it satisfies the interests of the lender. In fact, such contractual arrangements are not averse to national governments. A private contract, or a MoU, need not (always) go through various rounds of parliamentary scrutiny; can be subjected to confidentiality demands; bypass strict constitutional guarantees; hide elements of corruption or bribery and; in any event, governments can claim to their electorates that the form of agreement is not as important as the terms of the agreement themselves.

Given that liquidity was and is provided by financial markets, in conjunction with IFIs, it is only natural that IFIs could not dictate contractual forms that were antithetical to the interests of their founding states and private financial markets, which are at the heart of liberal democracies' growth-based policies. Although it may seem that the World Bank Group, particularly the IBRD, as well as the IFM, were promoting contractual forms that borrowing states were bound to follow, the reality is rather different. It is now well documented that entrepreneurial lawyers in top international law firms engineered many of the contractual terms and forms associated with sovereign lending,[10] as well as that the political protagonists of the Washington Consensus were responsible for the mass privatizations imposed or suggested by the IMF on developing states in exchange for liquidity and aid. Behind these political protagonists one naturally finds all those TNCs eager to take over for a mere pittance badly managed, but overly lucrative state monopolies, as well as negotiate zero tax policies in exchange for their "investment".[11]

10 At the behest of some of the biggest law firms, several courts have been convinced to construe the *pari passu* clause in bonds and loan agreements in a manner that allows holdout creditors to sue the sovereign debtor even if all other creditors have agreed on a restructure of the debt. *See NML Capital, Ltd. et al. v. The Republic of Argentina*, 699 F. 3d 246 (2d Cir. 2012). The U.S. Court of Appeals effectively held that because of Argentina's debt restructuring it was not technically bankrupt, in which case there would be a ranking of its debt. As a result, the *pari passu* clause in its sovereign bonds entailed that Argentina could not (even through an IMF-backed debt restructuring process) arbitrarily prioritize its super-majority creditors to the detriment of the unsecured creditors.

11 See Bantekas 2021, *The Linkages Between Business and Human Rights and their Underlying Causes*, 118; see also Bantekas 2021, *The Emerging UN Business and Human Rights Treaty and its Codification of International Norms*, 12.

2 A Brief Note on the Interface between Global Administrative Law and Transnational Law

This paper subscribes to the idea that in the absence of detailed regulation in founding treaties or other instruments, international organizations (IOs) have established their own processes and mechanisms by which to fulfil their mandates. Such processes and mechanisms are based on their implied powers and as a result it is now firmly accepted that a global administrative law (GAL) exists by which to apply and enforce international law.[12] The more complex an organization becomes, so too its web of internal and external processes will become and it will generate more and more detailed regulation, whether in the form of internal by-laws as well as instruments through which to contract with third entities.

Transnational law only slightly overlaps with GAL and particularly with the means and modalities of contracting with third entities. Transnational law should be viewed as a sphere of regulation that is distinct from the spheres of domestic law(s) and public international law and is broader than the set of universes that exist within it. Domestic law is a vertical system of regulation where rules are made by the state. International law, on the other hand, consists of a horizontal system of regulation that is based on state consent. Transnational law is different from its other two counterparts. It makes no hierarchical distinction between its various participants (i.e. between states and private entities) and all are conferred equal legal status and standing to create industry-wide rules through consent-based self-regulation. Of course, it is acknowledged that some participants are much more influential than others and such power may dictate the exercise, boundaries, and outcomes of self-regulation, but this is no different to the myth of sovereign equality of states under international law. An illustrative example may be offered by the various standards adopted by the transnational construction industry.[13] Self-regulation that produces rules internal to an industry may (although not necessarily) culminate in its replication in domestic law, as either an acknowledged – albeit unwritten – business custom or a fully-fledged written law. What is important is that the authority to self-regulate and the 'rules' emanating therefrom (*lex*

12 See the pioneering works of Cassese 2005, 37; Kingsbury, Krisch and Stewart 2005, 15.

13 The construction industry's FIDIC rules are distinguished threefold as follows: construction contracts per se (red book); plant and design-build (yellow book) and; EPC turnkey contracts (silver book). See Bantekas 2009, *The Private Dimension of the International Customary Nature of Commercial Arbitration*, 449.

mercatoria)[14] is part of a wider process that has become a new *sphere* comprising many disparate self-regulations and even more "rules".[15]

IOs and particularly IFIs transact with third entities on a frequent basis, but this does not mean that they do so exclusively in the sphere of transnational law. IFIs may well, in certain cases, want to attach all possible formalities to an agreement with a state and thus endow said agreement with the attributes of a traditional treaty. In other cases, many of which are described in this article, such formality may be viewed as inefficient and commercially harmful. Given that IFIs manage significant funds and operate (even to a limited degree) as commercial banks (e.g. when they agree to a commission in the management of funds), they must compete with other private and public actors for their "livelihoods". If their competitors operate in a sphere that is largely unregulated and where industry rules apply, then IFIs have little choice but to operate there too (for specific purposes at least).

In equal measure, IFIs are cautious about how they transact with third entities. Where the third entity in question is in a dire financial situation IFIs may impose any terms that are beneficial to themselves, in a manner that would resemble an adhesion contract under domestic law. GAL allows the IFI to make the pertinent choice and although the treaty form is used, it is hardly prevalent or consistent.[16]

---

14 The ultimate validation of *lex mercatoria* rests on the fact that not all legal orders are created by the nation state and accordingly that private orders of regulation can create law. Teubner 1997, *Global Bukowina: Legal Pluralism in the World Society*, in: Teubner (ed) 1997, *Global Law without a State*, 15.

15 See Bantekas 2021, *The Contractualization of Public International Law and its Impact on the Rule of Law*, 2.

16 By way of illustration, although loan facilities issued by the IMF may be described as treaties under certain circumstances, they are typically provided as stand-by-arrangements. These are regulated under Art XXX(b) of the IMF's Articles of Agreement, with the IMF having consistently described them as non-contractual in nature. In order to clarify that stand-by-agreements are not in fact contracts the IMF adopted two distinct decisions: Decision No 2603-(68/132) 20 Sep 1968 and Decision No 6056-(79/38) 2 March 1979. In particular, para 7 of the 1968 Decision stated that "in view of the character of stand-by-arrangements, language having a contractual flavour will be avoided in stand-by-documents". See generally: Gold 1980.

3 Multilateral Development Banks as Trustees of Member State Funds

One ingenious way of attracting financing by states is the intergovernmental trust model. The donor-trustee relationship is established through agreement, but this is a *sui generis* agreement that excludes, for example, the element of bargain or consideration and in which, typically, the trustee endeavors to assume as few obligations as possible.[17] Given the sovereign and public international law nature of most donors (states) and trustees (typically IOs),[18] one would expect the agreement setting out this relationship to be recorded in the form of a traditional treaty; this is, in fact, quite rare, although it will not be uncommon for MDBs to enter into treaties with states in respect of other matters. It is not uncommon for the trust agreement to take the form of an MoU[19] – which, in general terms, is intended as an agreement lacking consideration or an intention to create a legal relationship[20] – or other agreement, many times lacking the binding nature of contracts. A contract, as a matter of general principles, is a binding agreement that is the product of an offer, an acceptance, and an intention to be bound. Common law jurisdictions further require consideration (effectively a bargain or benefit for each party), whereas civil law jurisdictions typically require a good or legal cause (so-called *causa*).[21]

---

17 This is, of course, not surprising for the World Bank. See Krever 2011, 287, who traces the rule of law discourse in the Bank to show its narrow understanding of the rule of law and distancing from concrete human rights obligations.

18 See Bantekas 2020, *The Legal Personality of World Bank Funds under International Law*, 101–143.

19 MoU between the Swedish Ministry of Sustainable Development and UNEP (Feb 2005); see also UN-HABITAT MoU with Canada for Contributing to the Water and Sanitation Trust Fund.

20 This is not always the case, however. In Case C-258/14, *Eugenia Florescu and Others* v *Casa Jude¸teana˘ de Pensii Sibiu and Others*, Judgment of the Court (Grand Chamber) of 13 June 2017, EU:C:2017:448, para 36, the CJEU came to the conclusion that MoU concluded under EU financial assistance mechanisms and balance-of-payment processes qualified as EU acts under art 267(1)(b) TFEU, and hence susceptible to interpretation by the Court. Moreover, in Joined Cases C-8-10/15P, *Ledra Advertising Ltd and Others v. European Commission and European Central Bank*, EU:C:2016:701, where the CJEU held that where the EC Commission is involved in the signing of MoU within the framework of the European Stability Mechanism it is acting within the sphere of EU law. Therefore, it is bound to refrain from MoU that are inconsistent with EU law, including the EU Charter of Fundamental Rights.

21 See Art 2.1.1 UNIDROIT Principles of International Commercial Contracts (2010). See also Smits 2017, 41–63.

Apart from the initial act of appointment of a trustee, a future donor may wish to participate in the trust arrangement, whether by simply depositing an amount of money in the trust account, by concluding a bilateral agreement with the trustee for the same purpose, or by acceding to the original trust agreement. In all of these cases we find a convergence of consent, since even the mere deposit of funds in an account must meet the approval of the trustee, which is manifested by the maintenance of the funds in the trust account, or their subsequent withdrawal for disbursement purposes. The donors to a particular intergovernmental trust may turn out to be numerous and not all endowed with the same amount of international legal personality, thus involving, besides states, IOs, physical persons, multinational corporations, and legal persons with limited international legal personality. It is obvious that a traditional treaty would not constitute the appropriate arrangement for all these actors, thus necessitating a series of distinct legal transactions by the trustee with each individual entity. In such cases, some contractual arrangements will possess a private law character, without, however, detracting from the international legal nature of the trust.[22]

In accordance with its operational policies, the World Bank, when acting as a trustee, enters into framework agreements with its donors.[23] Under said policies, donors are required to enter into an additional Trust Fund Administration Agreement (TFAA) on the basis of which the Bank recovers its costs to manage and administer the trust fund.[24] The elaborate mechanism by which the above agreements are drafted, signed and implemented, as well as the absence of any "lighter" – non-binding – alternative, suggests that the intention of the World Bank is to conclude binding agreements with contributing states, private entities and IOs. In fact, the Bank, where possible, enters into standard binding agreements with all donors to a particular trust fund in order to harmonize results and reduce cost.[25] The Bank's Standard Provisions applicable to each

22 No doubt, in order to avoid a series of individually negotiated transactions, a single instrument may be used by the trustee, which may or may not have a binding character. Instruments of commitment (IOCs) are common to the work of conferences of states parties (COP) to multilateral treaties, as well as large inter-governmental funds such as GEF. See Churchill and Ulfstein 2000, 623.; equally: Weiss 2014, 83. See also: Bantekas 2009, *United Nations Employment Law and the Causes for the UN's Failed Female Senior Appointments Record*, 225.

23 IBRD Operational Policy (OP) 14.40 on Trust Funds, Art 1 and Bank Policy (BP) 14.40, "on Trust Funds" Art 1.

24 Ibid., Arts 7–8.

25 Agreement between the UK and IBRD/IDA for the ASEM-EU Asian Financial Crisis Response Fund (TF 020147) of 29 June 1998; Agreement between Denmark and IBRD/IDA for the ASEM-EU Asian Financial Crisis Response Fund (10 Nov 1998).

trust fund are expressly stated in each Letter of Agreement as forming an integral part thereof.[26] That the parties intend to create a binding legal relationship is manifested by the language employed in these instruments. For example, in the Agreement between the EC Commission and the World Bank for the ASEM Trust Fund of 23 December 1998, it is stated in the relevant part: "We are pleased to confirm the intention of the Commission to make available to the World Bank the sum of [...]". Equally, "the contribution shall be used for the purposes [...]" and "the Commission shall deposit [...]", whereas "the Bank shall make available to the competent bodies of the EC, upon request, all relevant information [...]".[27] Such agreements are of a binding but *sui generis* nature.

It is suggested that there is no indication in the text that they are meant to be treaties and none make reference to a governing law, although many do provide reference to modalities for dispute resolution.[28] For example, the TFAA between the Tunisian Ministry of Development and the IBRD to finance the Marseilles Center for Mediterranean Integration Multi-Donor Trust Fund[29] states in Annex 1, article 9, that in the event of dispute the Permanent Court of Arbitration (PCA) would assume jurisdiction. The fact that article 9.1 therefore refers to the PCA's Optional Rules for Arbitration Between International Organizations and States, however, does not alter the conclusion on the nature of the TFAA. The Optional Rules do not as a rule serve to define whether the underlying referral agreements are a treaty or otherwise. Even so, article 33(1) of the Optional Rules expressly states that:

> In resolving the dispute, the arbitral tribunal shall apply the rules of the organization concerned and the law applicable to any agreement or relationship between the parties, and, where appropriate, the general principles governing the law of international organizations and the rules of general international law.

The TFAA in question, as is the case with all TFAAs this author has seen, contains Standard Provisions that serve the purpose of a governing law and in any event, the World Bank's operational policies on trusts and other matters will fill any remaining gaps. What is clear is that the Bank and its TFAA donor states desire to retain their public international and sovereign nature, while at the

26 Ibid.

27 TF 020147, Project No ALA/ASI/98/0419, preamble.

28 See Bantekas 2021, *Effective Management of International Aid through Inter-governmental Trust Funds*

29 TF071415 (2013).

same time entering into a binding agreement that is not a traditional treaty. The TFAA contains all the elements of a contract, while not being grounded in the law of any jurisdiction.

It is also common practice, although by no means universal, for donors to conclude an MoU with the potential trustee and recipient states.[30] The purpose of these instruments is not to set up the trust fund or agree on the terms of the donation/contribution, but rather to "record the intention of the parties to enter into appropriate agreements in due course". This was expressly mentioned in the various identical MoUs between the Netherlands, on the one hand, and Indonesia and the World Bank, on the other, regarding the Establishment of a Multi-Donor Trust Fund following the catastrophic effects of the 2004 earthquake and tsunami.[31] Eventually, given that the World Bank was appointed trustee to the Multi Donor Fund (MDF) for Indonesia, contribution agreements were entered into with each one of the state donors in the form of treaties. Because the Bank's policy is to treat all donors equally, whereby as a result agreements must be "substantially the same", disagreement arose among the various departments in the Bank as to whether "substantially the same" means word-for-word identical, or whether a request by a donor state that did not alter the obligations of the agreement could in fact be accommodated.[32] Disagreement arose in connection with a formal cap on administrative costs, the designation of terrorism therein, and the conclusion of an expiration date for the agreement. In connection with the terrorism language, for example, one donor was content with the definition, but because it imposed a condition on the funds, the MDF was forced to amend its Standard Provisions. This, however, meant that a subsequent agreement had to be reached on this issue anew with all the donors.[33]

Finally, accession to Donor Agreements is possible through an appropriate provision in the General Agreement – where applicable – or each individual agreement. Article 3 of the Donor Agreement for the Establishment of an Anti-Corruption Activities Fund, concluded between Norway and the Inter-American Development Bank (IDB), states that the Fund shall accept contributions from any donor through the subscription of a Letter of Adherence to the Donor Agreement.[34] Arrangements may potentially become complicated

---

30 See Kellerman, 107.

31 Adopted on 25 April 2005.

32 *Review of Post-Crisis Multi-Donor Trust Funds* (February 2007) 51.

33 Ibid.

34 The Agreement is attached to IDB Doc CC-6146 (26 February 2007).

where new contributors include, besides states and IOs, also private entities.[35] In this case, since the Donor Agreement in question is a traditional treaty, it is not possible for the private entity to accede to this instrument. Therefore, it must be assumed that the trustee will enter into a new agreement with the private donor under the terms of a private agreement, whether in the form of a contract or other. In this case, it is assumed that since any entity can contribute funds, then agreements with private entities may be accomplished in the form of private contracts or agreements lacking the attributes of contracts.

4 Multilateral Development Banks as Agents of Private Donors

Private parties must, like states, contract with the trustee, rather than the trust fund, in respect of any of their transactions with trust funds or other mechanisms set up by MDBs. Such agreements, whether in the form of contracts, or agreements lacking the attributes of contracts,[36] will be governed by the law chosen by the parties.[37] Given that contracts must be "substantially the same" so as to ensure equality of treatment of the contracting entities, the governing law will be different in the trustee's agreements with the private donors; this is most likely to be the law of the seat of the trustee, but where the contract is to be performed in a third territory, the applicable law may well be the law of that country.[38] This is certainly a matter of choice between the parties and subject to the general principle of party autonomy. Generally, although state donors will face administrative costs in setting up the trust fund, this is not the case with private parties. Indeed, the contractual terms for the latter are far simpler since the constitutional formalities relating to treaty making for states are absent in the case of private parties. Nonetheless, any liability that may possibly accrue from such a relationship will burden the private entity on account of its lack of privileges and immunities,[39] in contrast to the World Bank or

35 Private entities typically enter the picture at the procurement phase and are subject to several layers of regulation. See Williams-Elegbe 2017, Chapter 3.

36 For example, agreements involving offer, acceptance and intention to be bound, but without the element of consideration, are considered contracts in civil law jurisdictions but not (generally speaking) under English law. This is a very complex issue in English law and there exist a long list of exceptions. See Peel 2007, 3–150; von Mehren 1959, 1009.

37 See Mann 1959, 34.; Morlino 2019, 261.

38 Delaume 1997.

39 It is usual for trustees to be mandated by the donors to enter into arrangements with the private entity in order to provide it with tax deductibility allowances in respect of its donation. See Art 27(a)(1)(2) of the Global Fund for AIDS Framework Document. Otherwise, the relevant financial or operational regulations clearly stipulate that no

the UN, for example, which is endowed with such protections. The privileges and immunities may be waived by contract and in any event are inapplicable where a state is acting as *fiscus* (i.e. in a commercial capacity).[40] The privileges and immunities of IOs are typically negotiated in advance and are embodied in the organization's founding charter, headquarters (HQ) agreement with the host state, the host state's law, as well as customary international law.[41]

Obviously, in its mutual relationship with the private party, the trustee will be an equal contractual partner. Private entities may, where applicable, be entitled to simply transfer or deposit money in a trust fund without the requirement of a written agreement. All that may be needed is a letter of notification to the trustee that the money has been deposited. In this case, since the private entity is not a state, its acts cannot be assimilated to a unilateral act – with or without legal obligation. The legal nature of these types of acts will be determined on the basis of the applicable banking and contract law governing a particular transaction.[42] Whether they entail, however, an intention to create a binding legal relationship is a matter of construction of the agreement in question.[43]

It is not unusual for private parties to wish to make a contribution without the formality of a binding agreement. The adoption of non-binding private instruments should not be excluded where the institutional rules of the trustee either allow, or omit reference to, such informal arrangements. The World Bank's policies generally exclude the possibility of such agreements,[44]

---

special advantages or benefits should accrue to private donors, such as Art 6 of the World Bank's OP 14.40. Equally, s 2.13 *et seq* of the World Bank Trust Fund Hand-Book, IBRD Doc 17304 (April 1997) warns the Bank, when acting as trustee, to avoid providing any benefits to private investors that would give rise to a conflict of interest or a distortion of its procurement rules.

40 See Art 17 of the UN Convention on Jurisdictional Immunities of States and their Property. O'Keefe and Tams 2013, 284.

41 Okeke 2018, 265–81.

42 This is a complex issue that is not susceptible to generalizations. The Court of First Instance (CFI) of the EU has long confirmed that the law of EU member states is not applicable to public contracts granted by entities set-up by the EU Council of the EU. Case T-411/06, *Sogelma – Societá generale lavori manutenzioni appalti Srl v European Agency for Reconstruction* (*AER*), ECLI:EU:T:2008:419, para 115. The CFI argued that such a principle was applicable, unless otherwise provided, to any international organization in the EU.

43 The requirement of an intention to be bound should not be conflated by the existence of an offer and acceptance. Either of these may simply be made in the form of an invitation to treat, or there might well be significant dissensus between what is offered and what is actually accepted. Dissensus does not allow the creation of a contract. See note 21, Smits 63–89.

44 In 2016 an updated standardized Administration Agreement template with sixteen of the World Bank's largest donors who provide 90 per cent of IBRD/IDA trust fund

whereas the other United Nations Specialized Agencies that administer trust funds have taken a varied approach to the legal modalities of private contributions.[45] The legal nature of the agreement will also depend on the type of contribution made. It is common for private contributors, particularly those in a specific industry, to donate in-kind, rather than cash. In 2003, the pharmaceutical corporation Novartis agreed to provide Tuberculosis medicine for the treatment of 500,000 sufferers over a period of five years. This undertaking was consummated through an MoU and not a formally binding contract. The medicines were delivered to the Global Drug Facility (GDF) of the Stop Tuberculosis Partnership for use in programs supported by the Global Fund against AIDS, Tuberculosis and Malaria.[46]

5 The Persistent Problem of Donor Commitments

Consistent state practice in the field of international donor conferences clearly demonstrates that a pledge should not be given the same meaning as that of a promise (in the form of a unilateral act) that otherwise may, but does not always, constitute a binding expression of will by the promising state.[47] Rather, the legal nature of a pledge is anything but a binding promise.[48] In fact, the

---

resources was adopted, including standard provisions on disclosure of information and communication on fiduciary issues. This was supplemented with a series of notes on governance arrangements in trust funds, preferencing arrangements, donor reporting, managing trust funds for results, and indicative budgets. See: Guidance Note on Governance Models: An Overview and Proposed Approaches, <http://bit.ly/GovernanceGuidance>, last accessed: 1 February 2022.

45 Art 18 of the UN Secretary-General's Guidelines on Cooperation between the UN and the Business Community (17 July 2000) envisages five types of partnership arrangements. Of interest in this connection is para (a) dealing with direct contributions, whereby it is advised that this be accommodated through a trust fund or special account agreement with the partner subject to the applicable Rules and Regulations of the UN.

46 IFPMA, Partnerships to Build Healthier Societies in the Developing World (September 2006), 37.

47 This distinction is not made by the ILC Rapporteur, V R Cedeno, in his Report on Unilateral Acts of States, UN Doc A/CN.4/486 (5 March 1998), para 91ff.

48 This is not very different from the treatment of promises in domestic contract law, where generally a binding offer is distinguished from a mere invitation to treat (which does not amount to a binding offer). Advertising-related cases, which involve an alleged unilateral act (by the seller) provide significant evidence to this effect. See the English leading case of *Carlill v Carbolic Smoke Ball Co* [1893] 1 QB 256 and *Fisher v Bell*, (1961) 1 QB 394. The position in the US is similar. *Lefkowitz v Great Minneapolis Surplus Store*, 86 NW 2d 689 (Minn 1957). Equally in the civil law tradition, albeit more cautious. See s 145 of the German Bürgerliches Gesetzbuch (BGB) [Civil Code] and the Federal Supreme Court

only binding act of the potential donor is the act of contribution itself, which materialises with the actual transfer of funds or goods to the recipient collecting entity. It is only at the moment of receipt or deposit that the donor is bound to honour the transaction. A pledge, on the other hand, is merely considered an expression of intent to provide a voluntary contribution of funds.[49] In international law, therefore, it constitutes solely a non-binding announcement of an intended contribution,[50] unless it is expressed, of course, under the form and content of a binding agreement.[51] There does exist an intermediate category between pledging and contribution though; it is that of commitment, which consists in the creation of a legal, contractual obligation between the donor and recipient entity, and which specifies the committed amount.

In order to avoid hosting donor conferences in which the outcome is the mere making of pledges that do not translate into concrete cash contributions, it became evident that the culmination of a conference must involve binding commitments. Paragraph 29 of the United Nations Secretary-General's Bulletin[52] aims exactly to remedy this lacuna by requiring a degree of formality concerning pledges. At this stage it is also worth noting that only a portion of the funds committed and collected as a result of donor conferences is earmarked for trust funds. Depending on the experience of the trustee in the administration of funds and his powers of influence, as well as on the basis of the mandate received by the creators of the trust fund, the trustee may well attempt to set up a particular legal mechanism by which to turn pledges into concrete commitments. To a large degree, the World Bank has managed to

---

(BGH) judgment in NJW (1980) 1388, which held that the display of goods in a window is not an offer but merely an invitation to make an offer.

49 The matter is not beyond contention in domestic law. In the US, for example, there is sharp disagreement between two distinct camps. The first asserts that pledges made to charitable organizations should not be treated any different to ordinary principles of contract formation, arguing that unless agreed otherwise such pledges are invitations to treat or unenforceable promises. *Maryland Nat'l Bank v. United Jewish Appeal Fed'n of Greater Washington, Inc.*, 407 A2d 1130, 1136 (Md 1979). The other camp argues that such pledges should be enforced on public policy grounds and the philanthropic purposes underlying charities. See *Jewish Fed'n of Cent. N.J. v. Barondess*, 560 A2d 1353, 1354 (NJ Super Ct Law Div 1989); see also *Salsbury v. Nw. Bell Tel. Co.*, 221 NW2d 609, 613 (Iowa 1974).

50 See Archibald 2004, 329. Archibald rightly comments that with regard to unpaid voluntary contributions, the UN does not invoke Art 19 of the UN Charter, at 325–26.

51 See also Silvestre and Martha 2014, 263. The issue has not received any particular treatment in general international law, nor in the expert work on unilateral acts of the UN International Law Commission (ILC). See Eckart 2012.

52 UN Secretary-General's Bulletin on the Establishment of Trust Funds, UN Doc ST/SGB/188 (1 March 1982).

standardize and streamline this process, but only in respect of particular trust funds. A typical example is the Global Environment Facility (GEF), whereby donors must sign an Instrument of Commitment, which constitutes a binding agreement subject to ratification by national parliaments. The trustee has established the same type of binding commitment in respect of the various replenishments required to keep the GEF alive.[53]

6 The Rise of Memoranda of Understanding

Given that both the United Nations and its Specialized Agencies do not generally require a treaty format for concluding trustee (administration) or donor agreements – in fact, the relevant Financial Regulations do not stipulate the two as separate contracts – it is not surprising that several MoUs have appeared in this respect. There is no single general definition of MoU,[54] but in general terms they constitute agreements lacking the binding nature of contracts, thus effectively missing the parties' intention to be bound by the terms of the agreement.[55] No doubt, just because the parties label an agreement an MoU does not necessarily entail that the agreement in question is not framed in binding terms. If this is in fact the case, the MoU will be deemed binding and therefore assume the qualities of a contract.[56]

Typical examples, albeit not as trust agreements, are the MoU between the conference of parties (COP) of the Convention to Combat Desertification and the International Fund for Agricultural Development (IFAD)[57] regarding the

53 The Instrument for the Revitalized Global Environmental Facility (GEF) of March 2008, Annex C.

54 Even so, an excellent definition is provided by the UN Treaty Handbook [in the Glossary section] as follows: "The term memorandum of understanding (M.O.U.) is often used to denote a less formal international instrument than a typical treaty or international agreement. It often sets out operational arrangements under a framework international agreement. It is also used for the regulation of technical or detailed matters. An M.O.U. typically consists of a single instrument and is entered into among States and/or international organizations".

55 Markakis 2018, Bailouts, the Legal Status of Memoranda of Understanding, and the Scope of Application of the EU Charter: Florescu, 643.

56 The ICJ pointed out in *Qatar v Bahrain* (Maritime Delimitation and Territorial Questions between Qatar and Bahrain), (2001) ICJ Rep 40, that the characterization of an MoU as a treaty will depend on its actual terms, the inclusion of actual commitments and the particular circumstances (eg Ministerial level signatures as opposed to directors).

57 The practice of most COP confirms that because they must interact with other actors they must be assumed to possess some, at least, legal personality. COP to environmental treaties regularly, for example, adopt decisions by which they appoint a third entity

Modalities and Administrative Operations between the Global Fund,[58] as well as the MoU between the COP to the Biological Diversity Convention and the GEF regarding the Institutional Structure Operating the Financial Mechanism of the Convention.[59] The GEF and IFAD serve as financing mechanisms for the purposes of these conventions and not as trustees. Their role is to finance part or all of the projects decided by the COP to these conventions, as long as these decisions are consistent with the respective constitutional instruments of IFAD[60] and the GEF.[61] In the case of the COP-GEF MoU, one may obviously argue that the choice of this instrument is necessarily dictated by the fact that neither of the two entities possesses sufficient legal personality[62] such that would enable them to conclude a treaty, or other binding agreement.[63] In any event, while the parties to such MoU are generally presumed to have intended to desist from assuming any binding obligations, the non-binding character of these instruments may, nonetheless, be questioned on several grounds.

---

as a trustee to a financing mechanism stipulated under their founding treaty followed thereafter by the conclusion of an MoU with the designated trustee. See UN Doc UNEP/CBD/COP/1, Decision1/2, para 2 and UN Doc UNEP/CBD/COP/2/19, Decision II/6, para 1. MoU between the COP to the Convention on Biological Diversity (CBD) and the Council of the Global Environmental Fund (GEF), UN Doc UNEP/CBD/COP/3/38, Decision III/8; see also the MoU between COP to the Convention to Combat Desertification (CCD) and the International Fund for Agricultural Development (IFAD) regarding the Modalities and Administrative Operations of the Global Mechanism, UN Doc ICCD/COP(3)/10 (30 August 1999), Annex I.

58 Art 2. The MoU is attached as Annex I in Doc UNEP/CBD/COP/3/10 (11 October 1996).

59 Art II(C). The Draft MoU is attached as Annex I to Doc ICCD/COP (3)/10 (30 August 1999).

60 According to Art 2 of the 1976 Agreement Establishing the IFAD, the objective of the Fund shall be to mobilize additional resources under concessional terms for agricultural development in developing member states. This involves projects designed to introduce, expand or improve food production systems and to strengthen related policies, taking into consideration the need to increase food production in the poorest food-deficit countries, the need to increase food production in other developing countries and the importance of improving the nutritional level of the poorest populations. IFAD has entered into an agreement with the UN under Art 57 of the UN Charter and is a specialized agency thereof. See IFAD Lending Policies and Criteria, adopted by IFAD Governing Council on 14 Dec 1978 (as recently amended by Res 106/XXI (12 Feb 1998)).

61 The Restructured GEF Instrument is reproduced in (1994) 33 ILM 1273, as subsequently amended in March 2008, para 2. Para 3 stipulates also "that the agreed incremental costs of other relevant activities under Agenda 21 that may be agreed by the Council shall also be eligible for funding insofar as they achieve global environmental benefits by protecting the global environment in the focal areas".

62 See Bantekas 2020, *The Legal Personality of World Bank Funds under International Law*, 101–143.

63 Matz 2005, 265; 285.

Firstly, and in respect to trust agreements established by MoU, the trustee is appointed as the account holder (where applicable) and administrator of the trust fund and its assets. This in itself entails a reciprocal obligation and moreover the trustee owes particular duties to the donors, which can hardly be assumed on a non-binding basis. As most of these duties stem from widespread practice in the field of international law trust funds, it is not out of the question to posit that they have become part of customary international law between States and trustees, and as such are binding and not merely voluntary. Moreover, the trustee owes some fiduciary duties to the beneficiaries once these have been designated.[64] It would thus be unreasonable for the trustee and the donors to appoint the trustee without either of these entities owing any obligations to the beneficiaries at any stage of the trust process.

In practice, the vast majority of commentators argues that despite the relevant MoU, the GEF is not legally bound by decisions of the COP.[65] Although the intention of the parties entering into such MoU should be respected, the very content of such instruments necessarily entails a plethora of binding obligations, whether implicitly by the very function of the trustee's role or as a result of customary international law. Perhaps, therefore, the best way of approaching the normative character of such agreements is article-by-article. Alternatively, it may be argued that the parties to an MoU establishing a trust relationship are aware of and accept the binding duties arising from such a relationship and thus the role of the MoU is to emphasize the non-binding character of all the other aspects of this relationship. It should be noted, of course, that the parties to the aforementioned MoU are not states in their vast majority but IOs. Moreover, it is true, as already explained, that the intergovernmental status of others, such as the GEF, may be in doubt. Nonetheless, it is undeniable that these institutions enjoy at least some international legal personality, and even if they are unable to enter into treaties as quasi-intergovernmental organizations, they are competent to conclude contracts under domestic law.[66] The MoU route, therefore, does not have to be the only option. Overall, the

64 See Bantekas 2011, 224; 231; equally Bantekas 2021, *The Contractual and Transnational Nature of Sovereign Donor-Trustee International Aid Contributions*, (forthcoming).

65 In fact, the COP to the CBD, in its first review of GEF effectiveness as the CBD's financial mechanism expressed discontent with the GEF's level of compliance. See note 63, Matz, 285–86.

66 The private law of the host state will dictate the terms of an entity's competence, typically through the civil code. Civil codes distinguish between physical persons and legal persons. See e.g. Bantekas and Al-Ahmed 2022, Qatari Law of Contracts, chp 4. In addition, the legal personality of trust entities, will be set out in their HQ agreements, although this will not depart from the relevant provisions of the civil code.

problematic nature of MoUs serving as administration agreements is limited to a small number of cases that do not generally involve state entities.

7 Memoranda of Understanding Adopted by International Financial Institutions in the Greek Sovereign Debt Crisis: Constitutional, Democratic and Human Rights Considerations

A particular type of MoU that has emerged in the post-2008 financial crisis era concerns the role of IFIs, such as the IMF, in the provision of liquidity to distressed sovereigns. Sovereign financing is typically achieved through syndicated and bonded loans. In syndicated loans, a number of banks pool financial resources in favor of a single borrowing state, not only in order to diversify the risk but also because a single bank may not have sufficient resources.[67] The lenders (or holders of the loan) may subsequently sell their portion of the loan to the secondary market, whether through novation or assignment. In novation, the initial financing contract is terminated and a new contract between the new novator and novatee state is established. Similar arrangements are made in the case of assignment. The exposure of banks involved in syndicated loans to severe non-performance necessitated a change in the financing of states. This came about through the process of bonded loans. There are two types of bond issuance, namely direct placement through an auction, and indirect placement by means of an international issuance. It is in respect of the latter that investment banks play a key role because the loan possesses an international character and banks possess the attributes of foreign investors protected under bilateral investment treaties (BITs).[68]

Debt relief under IMF initiatives has been supplied either by the Paris Club or through other forms of debt restructuring. Since the adoption of the Poverty Reduction and Growth Facility, the Paris Club has offered better debt restructuring to countries eligible under the Heavily Indebted Poor Countries (HIPC) Initiative than to non-HIPC countries. Participating creditor countries and the debtor country usually sign an Agreed Minute at the end of a negotiation session. This is not a legally binding document but merely a recommendation by the heads of delegations of participating creditor countries to their governments to sign a bilateral agreement implementing the debt treatment. When there are only a few creditors concerned, the Paris Club agreement is

67 See Mugasha 2007, 88–91.

68 See Megliani 2018, *Private Loans to Sovereign Borrowers*, in: Bantekas and Lumina (eds) 2018, *Sovereign Debt and Human Rights*, 74–76.

exchanged through mail between the Chair of the Paris Club and the government of the debtor country and is called "terms of reference". In some cases, the multilateral debt agreement is implemented (in addition) through an MoU. As regards non-Paris Club creditors, they typically enter into bilateral agreements with debtor states, either under the HIPC Initiative or independently of it. Numerous bilateral agreements have been concluded in this manner, whether as treaties or MoUs.[69]

As this section will go on to show, IFIs should be cautious about their use of MoUs in light of the manner these have been employed by the IMF and the European Central Bank (ECB), whereby the aim was to bypass constitutional procedures for transposing agreements into the domestic legal order.[70] This section intends to highlight the arbitrary and largely adhesive nature of such agreements and so emphasize the importance of prudence by IFIs. In the case of modern post-2010 Greece, since entering into its "bail out" agreements in 2010, a supervisory authority known as the "Troika" and composed of the EU (Commission), the ECB, the IMF, and later the European Stability Mechanism (ESM) was imposed by Greece's multilateral creditors.[71] Given that the bulk of the conditionalities were contained in MoUs, the aim of which was to render any issues arising therefrom inadmissible from local or international courts,[72] the authority of the "Troika" was exceptionally broad and in practice could sanction any policy or law, even if not directly related to the Greek debt-restructuring plan. In order to secure implementation of these conditionalities, it was necessary to bypass constitutional requirements. According to article

69 See IMF, HIPC Initiative: [Report on the] Status of Non-Paris Club Official Bilateral Credit Participation (10 Oct 2007) 7–11. The IMF and the Paris Club have identified several legal impediments to debt relief agreements. Among these one may note: a) impediments arising where central banks are the holders of the debt; b) those cases where some creditors have argued that the mandate of specialized agencies holding guaranteed claims does not allow them to provide debt relief at HIPC Initiative terms; c) sale of HIPC claims to private investors, which increases the likelihood of litigation. Id, IMF HIPC Report, 12–13.

70 See Bantekas 2021, *The Contractualisation of Fiscal and Parliamentary Sovereignty: Towards a Private International Finance Architecture?*, (forthcoming).

71 Bilateral creditors in the troika are represented and coordinated by the EC Commission – on the basis of an Inter-creditor agreement concluded among themselves on 8 May 2010 – whereas the IMF represents itself. The text of the Consolidated version of the Inter-creditor agreement is available at: <http://www.irishstatutebook.ie/eli/2010/act/7/schedule/1/enacted/en/html>, accessed: 17 August 2022.

72 It was only in Case C-258/14, *Eugenia Florescu and Others* v *Casa Jude¸teana˘ de Pensii Sibiu and Others*, Judgment of the Court (Grand Chamber) of 13 June 2017, EU:C:2017:448, para 36, that the CJEU came to the conclusion that MoU concluded under EU financial assistance mechanisms and balance-of-payment processes qualified as EU acts under art 267(1)(b) TFEU, and hence susceptible to interpretation by the Court.

36(2) of the Greek Constitution, international agreements must be ratified by an implementing law adopted by the plenary of Parliament. International agreements require a qualified majority of three fifths of the deputies in accordance with article 28(2) of the Constitution.[73] The Loan Agreement of 8 May 2010 (as amended by a subsequent agreement of 12 December 2012), however, was not even distributed to Parliament, nor was it publicly discussed, including the severe austerity measures contained therein. In fact, in a document entitled "Statement on the support to Greece by Euro area Members States" of 11 April 2010,[74] it was announced that the Euro Area Member States, together with the ECB and the IMF, were prepared to provide a loan to Greece and that the terms of the loan had "already been agreed". This demonstrates that none of the parties involved had any intention of respecting the procedures of the Greek Constitution or to comply with even elementary requirements of transparency.[75]

Moreover, article 1(4) of Law 3845/2010 granted the Finance Minister authority to negotiate and sign the texts of all pertinent loan and financing agreements (including treaties, contracts and MoUs). Although it was required under the Constitution that all such agreements be subject to parliamentary ratification, this never happened. Five days after its adoption, article 1(9) of Law 3847/2010 modified article 1(4) of Law 3845 by stipulating that the term "ratification" [by parliament] is replaced by "discussion and information". Moreover, all pertinent agreements (irrespective of their legal nature) were declared as producing legal effect upon their signature by the Finance Minister.[76] Hence, articles 28 and 36 of the Constitution were effectively abolished by a mere legislative amendment. What is more, Law 3845 included two of the three MoUs as mere annexes, relegating them to the status of "programme plan".[77]

73 See Judgment No 668/2012 (20 February 2012), para 29, decided by the Plenary of the Greek Conseil d'Etat (ΣτΕ), the majority of whose members agreed with such an interpretation of Art 28(2).

74 Law no 3845/2010, Annex II.

75 See principles 28–32 of the UN Guiding Principles on Foreign Debt and Human Rights, UN Doc A/HRC/20/23 (10 April 2011), which render transparency a cardinal principle.

76 Case C-258/14, *Eugenia Florescu and Others* v *Casa Jude¸teana˘ de Pensii Sibiu and Others*, Judgment of the Court (Grand Chamber) of 13 June 2017, EU:C:2017:448, para 41. See Markakis 2018, Bailouts, the Legal Status of Memoranda of Understanding, and the Scope of Application of the EU Charter: Florescu, 643.

77 Greek Parliament 2015, Debt Committee on the Truth of the Public Debt, 'Preliminary Report', 48–49. Available at: <http://cadtm.org/IMG/pdf/Report.pdf>, accessed: 17 August 2022.

In the context of the Greek sovereign debt crisis, the use of MoUs were clearly intended to produce binding legal consequences. It was evident to both parties that one party (the Greek state) was distressed and hence willing to bypass its constitutional arrangements under which a sovereign parliament could discuss and approve the loans and attendant austerity measures. That the measures in the MoUs gave rise to grossly disproportionate rights and obligations was beyond doubt and, unlike other agreements between sovereigns, access to a fair dispute resolution mechanism was effectively dispelled.[78] It is important that the deployment of informal agreements like MoUs by IFIs respects parliamentary sovereignty as in this manner such agreements will command legitimacy and respect.

8 Conclusion

IFIs play a significant role in the global financial architecture and the pursuit of development. In doing so, they must, by necessity, develop instruments by which to transact with their direct stakeholders. They must compete for scarce funding not only among their creators and member states, but also from third parties, private donors, and others. This process requires flexibility and a significant degree of entrepreneurship. MDBs in their role as trustees of assets have bypassed traditional channels of transacting. This is a fascinating development that while flexible and adaptable to the needs of other stakeholders, is not without its share of consequences. Agreements in the form of contracts may be governed by a foreign substantive law,[79] or disputes submitted to commercial arbitration. MDBs may agree to waive their jurisdictional immunities or otherwise agree to perilous promises by donors on the basis of informal instruments, such as MoU or other types of written commitments. By doing so, they become agents of contract and in the process, they must become effective contract managers in the same manner that law firms or in-house legal departments undertake the same role on behalf of their principals or clients. This is not necessarily a negative development. MDBs are now competing – and this will intensify in the future – with a number of non-governmental entities for the best possible developmental use of donor funding. In equal measure, despite Sustainable Development Goal (SDG) pledges, the public and private nature of the funding is not always clear, nor is the degree to which aid is

78 See Bantekas 2018, 52–80; equally, Bantekas 2020, *The Rise of International Commercial Courts: The Astana International Financial Center Court*, 1.

79 See Bantekas 2021, *The Globalisation of English Contract Law: Three Salient Illustrations*, 130.

currently tied. This means that MDBs must strive to prove that they constitute the best possible mechanisms for receiving, managing, and ultimately disbursing developmental funds to appropriate recipients. This can only be achieved by competing not only as better managers but as more creative and adaptable lawyers.

The mix of contractual practices analyzed in this article is hardly exhaustive. It serves as an illustration of what is out there and how this is different from the types of transactions typically associated with creatures of international law. Trust funds and MDBs have proven to be resourceful and adaptable to the changing market forces. Their continued success will be measured not only by how they employ and operate various forms of agreements (whether MoU, contracts, treaties, or others), but crucially also by the legitimacy of the contents and processes underlying these agreements. It is also important that, whatever the form of agreement, MDBs focus on the developmental goals as well as fundamental human rights underlying these agreements. This is important because the practice of BITs as well as that of IMF-led programs has sadly lost sight of both development and human rights.[80]

References

Archibald J E, *Pledges of Voluntary Contributions to the United Nations by Member States: Establishing and Enforcing Legal Obligations*, (2004) 36 Geo Wash Int'l LR 317, 317–18, 329.

Bantekas I, *The Private Dimension of the International Customary Nature of Commercial Arbitration*, (2009) 25 Journal of International Arbitration 449.

Bantekas I, *United Nations Employment Law and the Causes for the UN's Failed Female Senior Appointments Record*, (2009) 6 International Organizations Law Review 225.

Bantekas I, *The Emergence of the Intergovernmental Trust in International Law*, (2011) 81 British Yearbook of International Law 224, 231.

Bantekas I, *Wealth and Growth-based Policies have Augmented Global Poverty and Eroded Human Rights: A Return to Human-Centred Thinking*, (2012) 1 International Human Rights Law Review 30.

Bantekas I and Vivien R, *The Odiousness of the Greek Debt in Light of the Findings of the Greek Debt Truth Committee*, (2016) 22 European Law Journal 539.

80 See Bantekas 2020, *The Human Rights and Development Dimension of Foreign Investment Laws: From Investment Laws with Human Rights to Development-Oriented Investment Laws*, 339.

Bantekas I, *A Human Rights-Based Arbitral Tribunal for Sovereign Debt*, (2018) 29 American Review of International Arbitration 52–80.

Bantekas I, *The Rise of International Commercial Courts: The Astana International Financial Center Court*, (2020) 33 Pace International Law Review 1.

Bantekas I, *The Human Rights and Development Dimension of Foreign Investment Laws: From Investment Laws with Human Rights to Development-Oriented Investment Laws*, (2020) 31 Florida Journal of International Law 339.

Bantekas I, *The Legal Personality of World Bank Funds under International Law*, (2020) 56 Tulsa Law Review 101–143.

Bantekas I, *The Emerging UN Business and Human Rights Treaty and its Codification of International Norms*, (2021) 12 George Mason International Law Journal 1–43.

Bantekas I, *The Linkages Between Business and Human Rights and their Underlying Causes*, (2021) 43 Human Rights Quarterly 118.

Bantekas I, *The Globalisation of English Contract Law: Three Salient Illustrations*, (2021) 137 Law Quarterly Review 130.

Bantekas I, *The Contractualization of Public International Law and its Impact on the Rule of Law*, (2021) International Journal of Law in Context 1.

Bantekas I, *The Contractual and Transnational Nature of Sovereign Donor-Trustee International Aid Contributions*, (2021) 49 Syracuse Journal of International Law and Commerce (forthcoming).

Bantekas I, *Effective Management of International Aid through Inter-governmental Trust Funds*, (2021) 10 Loyola Chicago International Law Review 1.

Bantekas I, *The Contractualisation of Fiscal and Parliamentary Sovereignty: Towards a Private International Finance Architecture?*, (2021) 10 Global Constitutionalism 1.

Bantekas I and Al-Ahmed A, *Qatari Law of Contracts*, (Cambridge University Press 2022).

Carlill v Carbolic Smoke Ball Co [1893] 1 QB 256, (1961).

Cassese S, *Administrative Law without the State? The Challenge of Global Regulation*, (2005) 37 NYU J Int'l L & Pol 663.

Cedeno V R, *Unilateral Acts of States*, UN Doc A/CN.4/486, (5 March 1998).

Chrystal A, *Monetarism*, (Edward Elgar 1990).

Churchill R and Ulfstein G, *Autonomous Institutional Arrangements in Multilateral Environmental Agreements: A Little Noticed Phenomenon in International Law*, (2000) 94 AJIL 623.

Delaume G, *Proper Law of State Contracts Revisited*, (1997) 12 ICSID Review Foreign Investment Law Journal 1.

Eckart C, *Promises of States in International Law*, (Hart 2012).

Fisher v Bell, (1961).

Gold J, *The Legal Character of the Fund's Stand-by-Arrangements and Why it Matters*, (IMF Pamphlet Series No 35, 1980).

Greek Conseil d'Etat, *Judgment No 668/2012, para 29, decided by the Plenary of the Greek Conseil d'Etat (ΣτΕ)*, (20 February 2012).

International Bank for Reconstruction and Development (IBRD), *Bank Policy (BP) 14.40, on Trust Funds,* 1997 <https://documents.worldbank.org/en/publication/documents-reports/documentdetail/932661468162558092/op-bp-14-40-trust-funds-with-supporting-documents>, accessed 15 April 2021.

International Bank for Reconstruction and Development (IBRD), *Operational Policy (OP) 14,40 on Trust Fund,* 1997 <http://web.worldbank.org/archive/website01541/WEB/0__C-150.HTM>, accessed 15 April 2021.

International Fund for Agricultural Development (IFAD), *Lending Policies and Criteria, adopted by IFAD Governing Council on 14 Dec 1978* (as recently amended by Res 106/XXI), (12 Feb 1998).

International Monetary Fund (IMF), *Decision No 2603-(68/132)*, (20 Sep 1968).

International Monetary Fund (IMF), *Decision No 6056-(79/38)*, (2 March 1979).

International Institute for the Unification of Private Law (UNIDROIT), *Principles of International Commercial Contracts*, (2010).

Jewish Fed'n of Cent. N.J. v. Barondess, 560 A2d 1353, 1354 (NJ Super Ct Law Div 1989).

Kellerman M, *The Proliferation of Multilateral Development Banks*, (2019) 14 Review of International Organizations 107.

Kingsbury B, Krisch N and Stewart R B, *The Emergence of Global Administrative Law*, (2005) 68 Law and Contemporary Problems 15.

Krever T, *The Legal Turn in Later Development Theory: The Rule of Law and the World Bank's Development Model*, (2011) 52 Harvard International Law Journal 287.

Ledra Advertising Ltd and Others v. European Commission and European Central Bank, EU:C:2016:701, (2016).

Lefkowitz v. Great Minneapolis Surplus Store, 86 NW 2d 689 (Minn 1957).

Lienau O, *Who is the "Sovereign" in Sovereign Debt? Reinterpreting a Rule-of-Law Framework from the Early Twentieth Century*, (2008) 33 Yale J Int'l L 63.

Mann F A, *The Proper Law of Contracts Concluded by International Persons*, (1959) 35 British Yearbook of International Law 34.

Markakis M, *Bailouts, the Legal Status of Memoranda of Understanding, and the Scope of Application of the EU Charter: Florescu*, (2018) 55 Common Market Law Review 643.

Maryland Nat'l Bank v. United Jewish Appeal Fed'n of Greater Washington, Inc., 407 A2d 1130, 1136 (Md 1979).

Matz N, *Financial Institutions between Effectiveness and Legitimacy: A Legal Analysis of the World Bank, Global Environmental Facility and Prototype Carbon Fund*, (2005) 5 Int'l Environmental Agreements 265, 285.

Megliani M, *Private Loans to Sovereign Borrowers*. In: I Bantekas, C Lumina (eds), *Sovereign Debt and Human Rights*, (Oxford University Press 2018) 69, 74–76.

Mehren v. AT, *Civil law Analogues to Consideration: An Exercise in Comparative Analysis*, (1959) 72(4) Harvard Law Review 1009.
Morlino E, *Procurement by International Organizations: A Global Administrative Law Approach*, (Cambridge University Press 2019) 261.
Mugasha A, *The Law of Multi-Bank Financing*, (Oxford University Press 2007) 88–91.
NML Capital, Ltd. et al. v. The Republic of Argentina, 699 F. 3d 246 (2d Cir. 2012).
Norwegian Agency for Development Cooperation (NORAD), *Review of Post-Crisis Multi-Donor Trust Funds*, (February 2007) 51.
O'Keefe R, Tams CJ, *The United Nations Convention on Jurisdictional Immunities of States and their Property: A Commentary*, (Oxford University Press, 2013), 284.
Okeke E C, *Jurisdictional Immunities of States and International Organizations*, (Cambridge University Press, 2018) 265–81.
Peel E, *Treitel: The Law of Contract*, (Oxford University Press, 12th edn 2007) 3–150.
Pilling D, *The Growth Delusion: The Wealth and Well-Being of Nations*, (Bloomsbury 2018).
Qatar v. Bahrain (Maritime Delimitation and Territorial Questions between Qatar and Bahrain), (2001).
Salsbury v. Nw. Bell Tel. Co., 221 NW2d 609, 613 (Iowa 1974).
Schwarcz S, *Sovereign Debt Restructuring and English Governing Law*, (2017) 12 Brooklyn J Corp Fin Comm L 1.
Smits J, *Contract Law: A Comparative Introduction*, (2nd ed Edward Elgar 2017) 41–63.
Silvestre R and Martha R J S, *The Financial Obligation in International Law*, (OUP 2014) 263.
Teubner G, *Global Bukowina: Legal Pluralism in the World Society*, In: Teubner G (ed), *Global Law without a State*, (Dartmouth, 1997), 15.
Tomuschat C, *General International Law: A New Source of International Law?*, In: Pissillo Mazzeschi R, de Sena P (eds), *Global Justice, Human Rights and the Modernisation of International Law*, (Springer 2018) 185–204.
United Nations, *Secretary-General's Bulletin on the Establishment of Trust Funds* (UN Doc ST/SGB/188), (1 March 1982).
United Nations, *UN Doc UNEP/CBD/COP/1/8, Decision1/2, para 2*, (6 October 1994).
United Nations, *UN Doc UNEP/CBD/COP/2/19, Decision II/6, para 1*, (30 November 1995).
United Nations, *UN Doc UNEP/CBD/COP/3/10*, (11 October 1996).
United Nations, *UN Doc UNEP/CBD/COP/3/38, Decision III/8*, (11 February 1997).
United Nations, *UN Doc ICCD/COP(3)/10*, (30 August 1999).
United Nations, *UN Secretary-General's Guidelines on Cooperation between the UN and the Business Community*, (17 July 2000).
United Nations, *UN Convention on Jurisdictional Immunities of States and their Property*, (2 December 2004).
United Nations, *UN Guiding Principles on Foreign Debt and Human Rights, UN Doc A/HRC/20/23*, (10 April 2011).

Varoufakis Y, *The Global Minotaur: America, Europe and the Future of the Global Economy*, (2015).

Weiss E B, *Voluntary Commitments as Emerging Instruments in International Environmental Law*, (2014) 44 Environmental Law and Policy 83.

Williams-Elegbe S, *Public Procurement and Multilateral Development Banks* (Hart 2017).

Appendices

CHAPTER 14

2020 AIIB Law Lecture

The Judicial Role of the International Court of Justice in the Development of International Law

*H.E. Judge Xue Hanqin**

Abstract

At the heart of modern international law stands the principle of peaceful settlement of international disputes. Traditionally, States' right to resort to war for the resolution of international disputes was seldomly challenged. For centuries, use of force or threat of use of force was common in international relations. Not until the founding of the United Nations (UN) and the adoption of the Charter of the United Nations was non-use of force in international relations legally prohibited, and peaceful settlement of international disputes established as one of the fundamental principles in international law.[1] In this development, the International Court of Justice (ICJ) was and continues to be a key actor. As will become clear in the following, however, the role of the Court goes beyond settling disputes. It has entailed the significant task of developing, without legislating, international law through judicial law-making. The case law analysed in this chapter shows that this is particularly the case when the existing law is inadequate, unclear or uncertain, and when the law needs to be developed first through progressive interpretation. In this role, the Court faces a tension inherent in the nature of law as such, i.e., between stability on the one hand, and evolution in view of economic and social progress on the other hand. This raises the question whether and to what extent self-restraint by the Court might be necessary. The chapter concludes by emphasizing three core challenges the Court faces, and how they might impact its work in the future.

* Judge, International Court of Justice, h.xue@icj-cij.org. This article is based on the 2020 AIIB Law Lecture delivered by the author on 11 December 2020.

1 Charter of the United Nations, art 2(3) and (4). Although the 1928 Kellogg-Briand Pact (Renunciation of War as an Instrument of National Policy) was considered the first international treaty that prohibited Sates to use force for the "solution of international controversies, and … as an instrument of national policy in their relations with one another" (art 1), that was not accepted as part of general international law. See, for example, Miller 1928; Shotwell 1929; Brownlie 1963.

 | DOI:10.1163/9789004460010_015

1 Introduction and Historical Context

The world has gone a long way in searching for effective, reliable, and trustworthy mechanisms for dispute resolution with a view to maintaining peace and normal conduct of State relations. Apart from bilateral negotiations, third-party dispute settlement mechanisms, in particular those with binding effect, such as arbitration and judicial settlement, were long pursued but with very few successes. The first international court for the peaceful settlement of international disputes was not the ICJ, but the Permanent Court of Arbitration (PCA), which was established by the two Peace Conferences held in the Hague respectively in 1899 and 1907. However, the PCA is not a physically-standing court in the true sense of the term. It is a mechanism, with one permanent Bureau, a set of rules of arbitration and a roster of arbitrators appointed by States.[2] It serves primarily to standardize and facilitate international arbitrations for the peaceful settlement of international disputes.

The idea to set up a world court for judicial settlement of international disputes, a step further from arbitration, was raised during the Hague Conferences, but was rejected by the participating States. Apart from the reason that States would not wish to submit their national affairs to a few judges, they very much doubted that there could be any effective way to ensure that independent judges be chosen and able to act impartially and conscientiously.[3] The idea to establish a world court was finally materialized when the Permanent Court of International Justice (hereinafter "PCIJ") was founded in 1922 by the League of Nations. The Court was composed of fifteen judges, who were elected jointly by the Council and the Assembly of the League. Besides, the League would also ensure budget for the operation of the judicial organ.[4] This model, as well as its

2 See 1899 Convention for the Pacific Settlement of International Disputes, Chapter 2; 1907 Convention for the Pacific Settlement of International Disputes, Chapter 2.

3 At the second Hague Peace Conference, a recommendation for a Judicial Arbitration Court was adopted. Elihu Root, the then American Secretary of State, in his instructions to the American delegates to the 1907 Hague Peace Conference, as recorded, stated: "There can be no doubt that the principal objection to arbitration rests not upon the unwillingness of nations to submit their controversies to impartial arbitration, but upon an apprehension that the arbitrations to which they submit may not be impartial. It has been a very general practice for arbitrators to act, not as judges deciding questions of act and law upon record before them under a sense of judicial responsibility, but as negotiators effecting settlements of the questions brought before them in accordance with the traditions and usages and subject to all the considerations and influences which affect diplomatic agents [...]" (Hobér 2006).

4 Although institutionally the Permanent Court of International Justice (PCIJ) was not part of the League, the election of the judges and the budget of the Court were controlled by the League. Covenant of the League of Nations, art 14; Statute of the Permanent Court

Statute and Rules of Procedure, to a large extent, was adopted by the ICJ subsequently.[5] Thanks to this institutional link, the PCIJ and the ICJ are frequently referred to as "the World Court".[6]

After nearly a century of judicial practice, the World Court has, to a large extent, won the trust and confidence of States as an effective and reliable means for the settlement of international disputes and States in general attach importance to its settled jurisprudence.

2 Institutional Design and Jurisdiction

The ICJ is one of the six major organs and the principal judicial organ of the UN.[7] According to the UN Charter, its Statute forms an integral part of the Charter, to which all UN members are *ipso facto* parties.[8] The Court, composed of fifteen judges who are elected jointly by the General Assembly and the Security Council must, as a whole, represent the main forms of civilization and the principal legal systems of the world.[9]

The Court has general jurisdiction over disputes between States. It can deal with all cases that States submit to it and all matters specially provided for in the Charter or in treaties and conventions in force. Generally speaking, the Court is competent to deal with two kinds of cases: to adjudicate disputes

of International Justice, arts 3, 4, 32 and 33. Under the 1920 Statute, the PCIJ consisted of eleven judges and four deputy-judges, who would not sit on the bench unless any judges could not perform their functions. The 1929 revised Statutes expanded the number of judges from eleven to fifteen and added a new chapter addressing advisory opinions. In 1930, the Assembly decided to elect fifteen judges and four deputy-judges. The deputy-judges ceased to exercise their function when the revised Statute came into force in 1936. The PCIJ received 63 cases (36 contentious cases and 27 requests for advisory opinions) on its docket in the 18 years of its judicial function from 1922 to 1940. The Court ceased to function after 1940 because of the outbreak of the Second World War. For the history of the Permanent Court of International Justice, see further, for example, Hudson 1944; Spiermann 2005; Rosenne 2006.

5 Charter of the United Nations, art 92.

6 Another example for the institutional link between the PCIJ and the ICJ: in October 1945, the PCIJ met for the last time and decided to transfer its archives and effects to the ICJ. The election of the first members of the ICJ took place six days after the resignment of all the judges of the PCIJ at the First Session of the UN General Assembly and Security Council on 6 February 1946. Months later, Judge José Gustavo Guerrero (El Salvador), the last President of the PCIJ, was elected as the first President of the ICJ.

7 Charter of the United Nations, arts 7 and 92.

8 Charter of the United Nations, arts 92 and 93.

9 On the composition of the Court and the election of judges, see Statute of the International Court of Justice, arts 2–15.

between States (contentious cases) and to answer legal questions requested by the General Assembly, the Security Council or any other competent organ of the United Nations (advisory proceedings). In contentious cases, the judgment of the Court is binding on the parties in respect of the case concerned.[10] In the advisory proceedings, although the advisory opinion is not binding, it carries significant legal weight.

One essential feature of the Court is that the jurisdiction of the Court must be based on the consent of the States. In other words, both parties to a dispute must agree to submit their case to the Court for settlement.[11] There are several ways by which a State may accept the jurisdiction of the Court. They may do so by concluding a special agreement, or by accepting the dispute settlement clause (the compromissory clause) of a treaty, or by a declaration.[12] This voluntarism stands in sharp contrast with the compulsory nature of domestic jurisdictions. In respect of advisory proceedings, according to Article 96 of the Charter, the General Assembly or the Security Council may request an advisory opinion from the Court on any legal question of international law. Other UN organs and specialized agencies which are duly authorized by the General Assembly, may request advisory opinions from the Court on a legal question that arises from the scope of their activities.

---

10 Statute of the International Court of Justice, art 59.

11 The Court has consistently stressed: "a State is not obligated to allow its disputes to be submitted to judicial settlement without its consent." *Western Sahara, Advisory Opinion of 16 October 1975, I.C.J. Reports 1975*, p. 25, para. 33; *Applicability of Article VI, Section 22, of the Convention on the Privileges and Immunities of the United Nations, Advisory Opinion of 15 December 1989, I.C.J. Reports 1989*, p. 191, para. 37; *Legal Consequences of the Construction of a Wall in the Occupied Palestinian Territory, Advisory Opinion of 9 July 2004, I.C.J. Reports 2004*, p. 158, para. 47. Similar pronouncement was made in a series of contentious cases, for instance, *Monetary Gold Removed from Rome in 1943 (Italy* v. *France, United Kingdom of Great Britain and Northern Ireland and United States of America), Preliminary Question, Judgment of 15 June 1954, I.C.J. Reports 1954*, p. 32; *Continental Shelf (Libyan Arab Jamahiriya/Malta), Application to Intervene, Judgment of 21 March 1984, I.C.J. Reports 1984*, p. 24, para. 38; *Land, Island and Maritime Frontier Dispute (El Salvador/Honduras: Nicaragua intervening), Application to Intervene, Judgment of 13 September 1990, I.C.J. Report 1990*, p. 115, para. 54; *Certain Phosphate Lands in Nauru (Nauru* v. *Australia), Preliminary Objections, Judgment of 26 June 1992, I.C.J. Reports 1992*, p. 260, para. 53.

12 Among 193 States parties to the Statute, 74 States have made declarations accepting the compulsory jurisdiction of the Court. There are over 300 treaties which contain a clause providing that if a dispute relating to the interpretation and application of the treaty cannot be settled by negotiation or other means, at the request of one party, the dispute may be submitted to the Court for settlement. If a State party did not make a reservation to such a clause at the time it became a party to the treaty, it means it has accepted the jurisdiction of the Court.

The ICJ, in the course of its 75 years of judicial function, has dealt with a very broad range of subject-matters of public international law, from traditional subjects of territorial disputes and maritime delimitation to contemporary areas of international law, such as human rights, use of force, environmental law, sanctions, etc. Its rich jurisprudence has been an imperative source of legal studies for the development of international law. To date, there have been 150 contentious cases filed in the Court and 27 requests for advisory opinions. Over 100 States have appeared before the Court in contentious cases and more than 130 States have participated in the advisory proceedings.[13]

3 Judicial Function of the Court

In accordance with the Statute, the judgment of the Court is final and without appeal.[14] States parties undertake legal obligations under Article 94 of the Charter to comply with the decision of the Court if it is a party to the case. Moreover, if any party to a case fails to do so, the other party may request the Security Council to take measures so as to give effect to the judgment. Throughout the Court's history, the Security Council has rarely got involved in the implementation of the Court's judgments. For the most part, the Court's judgments have been respected and implemented; in some complicated cases, the process of implementation may extend over a long period of time.[15]

---

13 For States' participation in contentious cases, see "Contentious cases organized by State on the website of the ICJ", available at: <https://www.icj-cij.org/en/cases-by-country>. For States' participation in advisory proceedings, see "The International Court of Justice: Handbook", pp. 87–88, available at: <https://www.icj-cij.org/public/files/publications/handbook-of-the-court-en.pdf> The statistics in the Handbook were as of 31 December 2018.

14 Statute of the International Court of Justice, art 60.

15 For instance, in *Gabcikovo-Nagymaros Project (Hungary/Slovakia)*, one year after the Court rendered its Judgment of 25 September 1997, Slovakia filed in the Registry of the Court a request for an additional judgment in the case due to the alleged unwillingness of Hungary to implement the Judgment. After the filing by Hungary of a statement of its position on Slovakia's request, the Parties resumed negotiations and informed the Court on a regular basis of the progress. On 30 June 2017, Slovakia requested that the Court place on record the discontinuance of the proceedings for an additional judgment, to which Hungary did not oppose. However, both Parties reserved their respective right under Article 5, paragraph 3, of the Special Agreement to request the Court to render an additional judgment to determine the means of executing its Judgment of 25 September 1997, and the case remains pending on the Court's General List till the present day.

The progressively strengthened role of the Court in the peaceful settlement of disputes did not come easily. In the early days of the World Court, there was a severe insufficiency of codified international law; the Court was often alarmed to find that it had to settle disputes on the basis of vague principles and the rules to be interpreted and even created by itself. The idea of developing international law through the restatement of existing customary rules or through making new rules did not arise only in the time of the PCIJ. Serious attempts to develop international law were made since the late eighteenth century by prominent scholars, learned societies (e.g., Institut de Droit International and International Law Association),[16] and Governments, before and after the First World War,[17] notwithstanding their limited success and Euro-centric nature.

The situation was greatly improved after the Second World War, when the UN Charter laid down fundamental principles and norms of international law as the basis of the post-War world order. For that purpose, the General Assembly was entrusted with the responsibilities under Article 13 of the Charter to initiate studies and make recommendations for the purpose of encouraging "progressive development of international law and its codification". In 1947, it established the International Law Commission (ILC) to codify international law, preparing legal instruments for the adoption by States. The ILC is composed of eminent legal experts of international law; currently there are thirty-four members. They are elected by the General Assembly from different geographical regions and represent the principal legal systems of the world. The Commission directly reports to the General Assembly and maintains close

16 Inter-governmental regulation of legal questions may be found to have originated at the Congress of Vienna (1814–1815), where the signatory Powers of the Treaty of Paris of 1814 adopted provisions relating to the regime of international rivers, the abolition of the slave trade and the rank of diplomatic agents. Since then, codification of international law has been developed at diplomatic conferences on many subjects, such as the law of war, the regulation of maritime and aerial navigation, the pacific settlement of international disputes, the protection of intellectual property, the regulation of postal services and telecommunications. See, for example, Vec in Fassbender and Peters 2012.

17 The League of Nations created a standing organ—the Committee of Experts for the Progressive Codification of International Law—which, consisting of seventeen experts, was to prepare a list of subjects "the regulation of which by international agreement" was most "desirable and realizable" and thereafter to examine the comments of Governments on this list and report on the questions which were "sufficiently ripe", as well as on the procedure to be followed in preparing for conferences for their solution. This was the first attempt on a worldwide basis to codify and develop general international law rather than simply regulating illegal problems separately. Further information on the codification efforts by the League, see, for example, Rosenne 1972; Hudson 1930.

contact with State governments. Based on the list of subjects for codification,[18] the Commission has, to date, produced more than 50 legal instruments, some of which were subsequently adopted as international treaties. Much due to the ILC's efforts, nowadays, international treaty law covers almost every area of public international law, becoming the major source of the law for application.

Draft articles adopted by the ILC contain commentaries, which explain the terms of each article and policy considerations for State practice. The commentaries usually contain rich sources of research materials on State practice, decisions of international courts and tribunals and scholarly writings on the relevant subject matters. It is there one can find a dynamic synergy between the Court and the Commission for the development of international law. In the codification process, the Commission would consider the established jurisprudence of the Court in ascertaining the existence of customary rules and principles, while the Court frequently turns to the drafting work of the Commission to decide what constitute international rules, *lex lata*, and what is a progressive development, *lex ferenda*, the proposed (future) law.[19]

As a judicial organ, the task for the Court is to settle disputes in accordance with international law. The Court has stated on a number of occasions that the function of the Court is to state the law, but not to legislate.[20] At the same time,

18 In 1949, based on the survey of international law prepared by the Secretariat, the ILC at its first session reviewed twenty-five topics for possible inclusion in a list of topics for study and drew up a provisional list of fourteen topics selected for codification, as follows: recognition of States and Governments; succession of States and Governments; jurisdictional immunities of States and their property; jurisdiction with regard to crimes committed outside national territory; regime of the high seas; regime of territorial waters; nationality, including statelessness; treatment of aliens; right of asylum; law of treaties; diplomatic intercourse and immunities; consular intercourse and immunities; State responsibility; and arbitral procedure. The Commission has submitted a final report on all of the topics above, except for the following: recognition of States and Governments; jurisdiction with regard to crimes committed outside national territory; treatment of aliens; and right of asylum. The 1949 list of topics was further supplemented by a series of topics. Further information is available at: <https://legal.un.org/ilc/programme.shtml>.

19 For instance, in the ILC, Draft Articles on Responsibility of States for Internationally Wrongful Acts, with Commentaries (2001) UN Doc A/56/10, the Court was referred to 89 times in total, with numerous cases cited as evidence of customary rules. On ICJ's part, for example, when interpreting Article 36 of Vienna Convention on Consular Relations in a recent case, the Court studied the *travaux préparatoires* of Article 36, including the discussions of the International Law Commission in detail. *Jadhav* (*India* v. *Pakistan*), *Judgment of 17 July 2019*, *I.C.J. Reports 2019*, pp. 439–441, paras. 77–83.

20 For instance, the Court stated in *Northern Cameroons* case that "[t]he function of the Court is to state the law." *Northern Cameroons* (*Cameroon* v. *United Kingdom*), *Preliminary Objections, Judgment of 2 December 1963*, *I.C.J. Reports 1963*, p. 33. In *Fisheries Jurisdiction*, the Court indicated that "there is no incompatibility with its judicial function in making

however, no one denies that the Court positively contributes to the development of international law. How should one understand this seemingly paradoxical phenomenon?

Pursuant to Article 56 of the Statute, the Court shall in its judgment state the reasons for its decision. Moreover, the judgment shall contain the names of the judges who have taken part in adjudicating the case and voted in the decision. If the Court is not unanimous in its decision, the majority's views will be the basis for the judgment. If the Court is equally divided, the President will cast the deciding vote.[21] Judges in the minority have the right to append their individual opinions to explain the reasons for their position in the vote, which constitute part of the judgment.[22] The individual opinions may be given as a dissenting or separate opinion, or in the form of a declaration. It is this legal reasoning, either in the judgment or in the individual opinions, that exerts judicial persuasion for the resolution of the dispute. It follows, therefore, that a unanimously-adopted judgment is supposedly more persuasive than that adopted by a deeply-divided Court.

3.1 *The Tool of Legal Interpretation*

Law, by its nature, indefinitely confronts the problems of *non liquet*, and open texture, namely, the very existence of a law may be in question, or its content may be unclear and vague. A court, by its function, cannot refuse to adjudicate a case on the ground that the law is uncertain or inadequate. It must interpret the law to make it sound and applicable. At the international level, in the absence of any legislative body, an international court more often finds itself in such a situation, as the state of international law is less certain and codified than that of domestic law.[23] In clarifying the content of a rule, removing

---

a pronouncement on the rights and duties of the Parties under existing international law which would clearly be capable of having a forward reach; this does not mean that the Court should declare the law between the Parties as it might be at the date of expiration of the interim agreement, a task beyond the powers of any tribunal." *Fisheries Jurisdiction (United Kingdom* v. *Iceland), Merits, Judgment of 25 July 1974, I.C.J. Reports 1974*, p. 19, para. 40. In *Legality of the Threat or Use of Nuclear Weapons*, the Court reiterated: "[i]t is clear that the Court cannot legislate." *Legality of the Threat or Use of Nuclear Weapons, Advisory Opinion of 8 July 1996, I.C.J. Reports 1996*, p. 237, para. 18.

21 Statute of the International Court of Justice, art 55.

22 Statute of the International Court of Justice, art 57.

23 The arduousness of the work of the Court also lies in the role of the Court in the international system—the principal judicial organ of the United Nations with no compulsory jurisdiction, as discussed above. For further discussion on the role of the Court in the international system, Professor Alain Pellet pointed out, there are three elements in the Court's role as the "principal judicial organ of the United Nations"—an "organ", a "principal

ambiguity or obscurity in the law, avoiding absurdity of an interpretation, and, if necessary, laying down new rules, the Court develops the law.

3.2 *The Indirect Effect of Precedent*

It is true that according to Article 59 of the Statute, the decision of the Court has no binding force except between the parties and in respect of that particular case. The fact that the Court's decision has no binding force on third States does not mean, however, that the decision of the Court has no effect as a precedent for the Court.[24] The Court will interpret and apply the same rule in the same way in future cases.[25] This consistent legal position constitutes its jurisprudence. Unless there are compelling reasons, the Court will not deviate from its settled jurisprudence. Any State, therefore, must pay attention to the jurisprudence of the Court in its interpretation and application of the legal principles that the Court has dealt with.

---

organ", and a "judicial organ". Alain Pellet's presentation at the 50th Anniversary of the Court, in Peck and Lee 1997, 235–236: Ces tensions sont au cœur de la problématique de toute étude envisageant la Cour en tant qu' "organe judiciaire principal des Nations Unies": parce qu'elle est un "organe", un "organe principal" et un "organe judiciaire", elle bénéficie d'un statut unique qui lui confère une autorité exceptionnelle mais lui impose aussi certaines contraintes (I) qu'elle rencontre tout particulièrement dans ses relations avec les autres organes principaux des Nations Unies, essentiellement dans le domaine, si central, du maintien de la paix et de la sécurité internationales (II).

24 This was well observed by the Informal Inter-Allied Committee on the Future of the Permanent Court of International Justice in discussing Article 59 of the Statute of the PCIJ (identical to that of the ICJ Statute): The effect of this provision has, in our opinion, sometimes been misinterpreted. What it means is not that the decisions of the Court have no effect as precedents for the Court or for international law in general, but that they do not possess the binding force of particular decisions in the relations between the countries who are parties to the Statute. The provision in question in no way prevents the Court from treating its own judgments as precedents.

Report of the Informal Inter-Allied Committee on the Future of the Permanent Court of International Justice, 10 February 1944, p. 15, para. 63.

25 For instance, in its judgment on preliminary objections in the *Temple of Preah Vihear*, the Court made it clear that according to Article 59, the decision in the *Aerial Incident of 27 July 1955* case between Israel and Bulgaria is not binding on Thailand as such; nevertheless, the legal reasoning leading to that decision was relevant to the dispute at issue. *Temple of Preah Vihear (Cambodia* v. *Thailand), Preliminary Objections, Judgment of 26 May 1961, I.C.J. Reports 1961*, pp. 27–28.

4 How the Court Contributes to the Development of International Law through Judicial Law-Making

As mentioned above, when legal principles or rules are uncertain, ambiguous, or inadequate, the Court has to interpret them in such a way that it clarifies and ascertains the law so that it can apply the principles or the rules to a particular case. It is through this process that the Court contributes to the development of international law.

4.1 *When the Law Is Inadequate*

In the early days of the United Nations, the status of international organizations was not clear; whether they were, like States, a subject of international law and possessed international personality was an open question. This issue greatly affected international organizations in fulfilling their functions and interacting with member States. With a growing number of intergovernmental organizations created after the Second World War, this issue required a definite legal answer.

In 1948, when the UN Mediator and other members of the UN Mission to Palestine were assassinated in Jerusalem, the General Assembly asked the Court to address the issue, among others, whether the United Nations had the capacity to bring an international claim against the State responsible with a view to obtaining reparation for damage caused to the Organization and to the victim. In its Advisory Opinion of 11 April 1949, the Court held that the UN was intended to exercise functions and rights which could only be explained "on the basis of the possession of a large measure of international personality and the capacity to operate upon the international plane".[26] It followed that the organization had the capacity to bring a claim for reparation of damage it had suffered.[27] The Court further declared that the organization could claim reparation not only in respect of damage caused to itself, but also for the victim or persons entitled through him. The Court stated that although, according to the traditional rule, diplomatic protection has to be exercised by the national State of the victim, the organization should be regarded in international law as possessing such powers essentially for the purpose of discharging its functions, even if such powers are not expressly stated in the Charter. The Court observed that the organization may have to entrust its agents with important missions in disturbed parts of the world. In such cases, it is necessary that the

26 *Reparations for Injuries Suffered in the Service of the United Nations, Advisory Opinion of 11 April 1949, I.C.J. Reports 1949*, p. 179.

27 Ibid, p. 180.

agents should receive suitable support and protection that the organization is capable of providing.[28]

In the ensuing years, the Court gave a few more opinions with regard to different aspects of the status, functions, privileges and immunities of international organizations.[29] By these advisory opinions, the Court affirmed the international personality of international organizations, as a full subject of international law alongside States. This major development of international law greatly reinforced the role of international organizations in world affairs and accordingly the changing structure in the world legal order.[30] Nowadays no one questions that international organizations are full-fledged subjects of international law, with international personality necessary to fulfil their functions.

4.2 *When the Law Is Unclear or Uncertain*

When the law is unclear or uncertain, the Court's decisions provide legal guidance for States. After the Second World War, with the 1945 Truman Proclamation on the Continental Shelf and Latin-American countries' claims for 200 nautical miles' territorial sea, maritime rights became a focused area in international law. By the 1960s, the concept of continental shelf was generally accepted by States, but the principles for the delimitation of the continental shelf were still developing.[31]

---

28 Ibid, pp. 181–184.

29 On the legal status of international organizations, see, for example, *Interpretation of the Agreement of 25 March 1951 between the WHO and Egypt, Advisory Opinion of 20 December 1980, I.C.J. Reports 1980*, p. 73. On the privileges and immunities of international organizations and their staff, see, for example, *Applicability of Article VI, Section 22, of the Convention on the Privileges and Immunities of the United Nations*, supra note 11, p. 177; *Difference Relating to Immunity from Legal Process of a Special Rapporteur of the Commission on Human Rights, Advisory Opinion of 29 April 1999, I.C.J. Reports 1999*, p. 62. On the host State's international obligations, see, for example, *Applicability of the Obligation to Arbitrate under Section 21 of the United Nations Headquarters Agreement of 26 June 1947, Advisory opinion of 26 April 1988, I.C.J. Reports 1988*, p. 12. On the scope of the powers of international organizations, see, for example, *Certain Expenses of the United Nations (Article 17, paragraph 2, of the Charter), Advisory Opinion of 20 July 1962, I.C.J. Reports 1962*, p. 151; *Legality of the Use by a State of Nuclear Weapons in Armed Conflict, Advisory Opinion of 8 July 1996, I.C.J. Reports 1996*, p. 66.

30 For further study on status of international organizations and their role in international society, see, for example, Schermers and Blokker *2018*, 1026–1065.

31 The first UN Conference on the Law of the Sea was held in 1958 where 86 States participated. For fear of States' hesitation to join, four separate conventions were adopted instead of a comprehensive one, with their States parties varying from 39 to 63. Convention on the High Seas (adopted 29 April 1958, entered into force 3 January 1963) 450 UNTS 11, has 63 parties; Convention on the Continental Shelf (adopted 29 April 1958, entered into

In 1967, the Federal Republic of Germany with Denmark and the Netherlands respectively, by special agreements, submitted to the Court their applications concerning the delimitation of the continental shelf of the North Sea as between the Federal Republic of Germany and Denmark, and as between the Federal Republic of Germany and the Netherlands. They specifically asked the Court not to draw the maritime lines for them, but just to state the applicable principles and rules for the delimitation of the areas of the continental shelf in the North Sea which appertain to each of them.[32] They undertook thereafter to carry out the delimitations on the basis of the decisions of the Court. As the two cases presented identical issues, the Court joined the two proceedings.

In its Judgment of 20 February 1969, with regard to the contention advanced by Denmark and the Netherlands that the equidistance rule as reflected in Article 6 of the 1958 Convention on the Continental Shelf should be applicable, the Court discussed at length the legal status of the equidistance rule in international law, as the Federal Republic of Germany was not a party to the 1958 Convention and Article 6 thereof was not applicable to it. By reviewing the short history of the general legal regime of continental shelf, the Court took the view that the equitable principle, as reflecting *opinio juris* (acceptance as law), should be the applicable principle in the matter of delimitation.[33] Rejecting equidistance as an established rule, the Court stated that "no one single method of delimitation was likely to prove satisfactory in all circumstances, and that delimitation should, therefore, be carried out by agreement [...] and secondly, that it should be effected on equitable principles."[34] Under the equitable principle, the Court further established three major factors to be taken into consideration: geographical configuration of the coastlines, the

---

force 10 June 1964) 499 UNTS 311, has 58 parties; Convention on the Territorial Sea and the Contiguous Zone (adopted 29 April 1958, entered into force 22 November 1964) 516 UNTS 205, has 52 parties; Convention on Fishing and Conservation of the Living Resources of the High Seas (adopted 29 April 1958, entered into force 20 March 1966) 559 UNTS 285, has 39 parties. The régime of exclusive economic zone was yet to be adopted by then. See, for example, Jessup 1959.

32 *North Sea Continental Shelf (Federal Republic of Germany/Denmark; Federal Republic of Germany/Netherlands), Judgment of 20 February 1969, I.C.J. Reports 1969*, pp. 6–7.

33 In particular, the Court found the application of equitable principle in accordance with "the ideas which have always underlain the development of [the legal régime of continental shelf]", namely: (*a*) the parties' obligation to enter into meaningful negotiations; (*b*) the parties' obligation to take alı the circumstances into account in an equitable way; and (c) a State's continental shelf "must be the natural prolongation of its land territory and must not encroach upon what is the natural prolongation of the territory of another State." Ibid, p. 47, para. 85.

34 Ibid, p. 36, para. 55; see also pp. 46–47, para. 85, p. 50, para. 92.

unity of any deposits, and a reasonable degree of proportionality between the extent of the continental shelf appertaining to the States concerned and the lengths of their respective coastlines.[35] The jurisprudence established in the *North Sea Continental Shelf* cases was further developed in the subsequent cases, which gradually developed into a set of rules and methodologies for maritime delimitation.[36]

It is fair to say that the Court's jurisprudence on the maritime delimitation has not only contributed to the peaceful settlement of specific disputes between coastal States, adjacent or opposite, on the delimitation of maritime areas, it has also provided legal clarity and certainty to the modern law of the sea in respect of maritime delimitation.[37] Moreover, its pronouncement on the formation of customary international law in the *North Sea Continental Shelf* cases is a valuable contribution to the development of customary international law.[38]

---

35 Ibid, pp. 50–52, paras. 93–98.

36 See, for example, *Continental Shelf (Tunisia/Libyan Arab Jamahiriya), Judgment of 24 February 1982, I.C.J. Reports 1982*, p. 18; *Delimitation of the Maritime Boundary in the Gulf of Maine Area (Canada/United States of America), Judgment of 12 October 1984, I.C.J. Reports 1984*, p. 246; *Continental Shelf (Libyan Arab Jamahiriya/Malta), Judgment of 3 June 1985, I.C.J. Reports 1985*, p. 13; *Maritime Delimitation in the Area between Greenland and Jan Mayen (Denmark* v. *Norway), Judgment of 14 June 1993, I.C.J. Reports 1993*, p. 38; *Maritime Delimitation and Territorial Questions between Qatar and Bahrain (Qatar* v. *Bahrain), Merits, Judgment of 16 March 2001, I.C.J. Reports 2001*, p. 40; *Land and Maritime Boundary between Cameroon and Nigeria (Cameroon* v. *Nigeria: Equatorial Guinea intervening), Judgment of 10 October 2002, I.C.J. Reports 2002*, p. 303; *Territorial and Maritime Dispute between Nicaragua and Honduras in the Caribbean Sea (Nicaragua* v. *Honduras), Judgment of 8 October 2007, I.C.J. Reports 2007*, p. 659; *Maritime Delimitation in the Black Sea (Romania* v. *Ukraine), Judgment of 3 February 2009, I.C.J. Reports 2009*, p. 61; *Territorial and Maritime Dispute (Nicaragua* v. *Colombia), Judgment of 19 November 2012, I.C.J. Reports 2012*, p. 624; *Maritime Dispute (Peru* v. *Chile), Judgment of 27 January 2014, I.C.J. Reports 2014*, p. 3; *Maritime Delimitation in the Caribbean Sea and the Pacific Ocean (Costa Rica* v. *Nicaragua), Judgment of 2 February 2018, I.C.J. Reports 2018*, p. 139.

37 On the Court's contribution to the development of the law of the sea, see, for example, Tams and Sloan 2013.

38 *North Sea Continental Shelf*, supra note 32, p. 44, para. 77: "[n]ot only must the acts concerned amount to a settled practice, but they must also be such, or be carried out in such a way, as to be evidence of a belief that this practice is rendered obligatory by the existence of a rule of law requiring it." The influence of the *North Sea Continental Shelf* cases and further development on customary international law, see, for example, ILC, 'Draft conclusions on identification of customary international law, with commentaries' (2018) UN Doc A/73/10.

4.3 *When the Law Needs to Be Developed through Progressive Interpretation*

Although occasionally the Court has to supplement and even expand the law for application, for the most part, its task is to interpret and apply the existing law. However, in practice, when circumstances have fundamentally changed, the Court, in responding to the changes, also has to give progressive interpretation.

The cases concerning the principle of self-determination and the *Whaling* case (Australia v. Japan) serve as vivid examples in this respect.

Since the birth of the United Nations, more than 80 former colonies comprising some 750 million people have gained independence. This could not have been achieved without the persistent efforts of the United Nations in solidifying the abstract purpose of the UN Charter into a concrete legal right to self-determination in international law.[39] The principle of self-determination is enshrined in Article 1, paragraph 2 of the Charter, which addresses the purposes of the United Nations. In line with this principle, a Trusteeship Council was established as one of the six principal organs of the United Nations. The Court's deep involvement in this process and its essential role in clarifying the law are reflected in several of its judgments and advisory opinions, such as, the 1971 Opinion on *Namibia* (*South West Africa*), the 1975 Opinion on *Western Sahara*, the 1995 Judgment in *East Timor* case, and most recently, the 2019 Opinion on *Chagos Archipelago*.

In the 1950s and 1960s, many African and Asian countries overthrew colonial domination and acquired independence. During this decolonization movement, the General Assembly adopted resolution 1514 (XV) on 14 December 1960 entitled "Declaration on the Granting of Independence to Colonial Countries and Peoples". Although in the UN Charter, there is a special chapter on non-self-governing territories, the question whether and when the principle of self-determination became customary international law remained unclarified.

In 2017, by Resolution 71/292, the General Assembly requested the Court to render an advisory opinion on two legal questions: first, whether the decolonization of Mauritius was lawfully completed in 1968 when Mauritius obtained independence from the United Kingdom; and second, what consequences under international law arise from the United Kingdom's continued administration of the Chagos Archipelago. The Chagos Archipelago as part of Mauritius was under British colonial rule for many years. It was detached from Mauritius by the United Kingdom three years before its independence. By an agreement

39 See Charter of the United Nations, art 7, Chapters 12–13.

between the United Kingdom and the United States, the Chagos islands were leased to the latter for 50 years (renewed automatically in December 2016 for a further 20 years) for the purpose of establishment of a military base.[40]

In its Advisory Opinion, the Court recalled that the Charter has made respect for the principle of equal rights and self-determination of peoples one of the purposes of the UN and included provisions that would enable non-self-governing territories ultimately to govern themselves.[41] It stated, moreover, that "[t]he adoption of resolution 1514 (XV) ... represents a defining moment in the consolidation of State practice on decolonization" and that "[b]oth State practice and *opinio juris* at the relevant time confirm the customary law character of the right to territorial integrity of a non-self-governing territory as a corollary of the right to self-determination".[42] The Court in this statement clearly determined the moment when the principle of self-determination was established as a rule of customary law. More importantly, it pronounced that since respect for the right to self-determination is an obligation *erga omnes*, all States have a legal interest in protecting that right. With Chagos, the Court declared that all States must cooperate with the UN so that Mauritius' right to self-determination as to Chagos will be respected and exercised.[43]

In the decolonization movement in the early days, the Court delivered a number of opinions relating to self-determination, however, it had never been so clear and determinative as to place the principle at such a high level, which reflects the importance of human rights today. That said, it is not to be forgotten that the Court once went through a dormant period as a result of its failure to follow the discernible trend of international law on self-determination in its 1966 judgment in *South West Africa* cases, which concerned the obligations of South Africa under the mandate system towards the South West African people.[44]

In 1960, Ethiopia and Liberia, in their capacity as former States Members of the League of Nations, instituted separate proceedings against South Africa on its obligations under the mandate towards the Mandate Territory, South West

40 United Kingdom of Great Britain and Northern Ireland and Unites States of America: Exchange of Notes Constituting an Agreement concerning the Availability for Defense Purposes of the British Indian Ocean Territory (with annexes) (entered into force 30 December 1966) 603 UNTS 273.

41 *Legal Consequences of the Separation of the Chagos Archipelago from Mauritius in 1965, Advisory Opinion of 25 February 2019, I.C.J. Reports 2019*, p. 131, paras. 146–148.

42 Ibid, p. 132, para. 150, p. 134, para. 160.

43 Ibid, p. 139, para. 180.

44 For scholarly writings on South West Africa dispute, see, for example, Dugard 1973.

Africa.[45] In rejecting the applicants' claims on behalf of the South West African people, the Court gave a rather narrow reason to disqualify the applicants' standing to institute the proceedings.[46] With the votes equally divided (7–7) and the casting vote of President Spender, the majority of the Court found that the applicants had no "legal right or interest appertaining to them in the subject-matter of the present claims".[47] By taking such a mechanical positivist approach, the Court virtually let the apartheid régime "legally" continue in South West Africa, in total disregard of the overwhelming views of States against apartheid. Three months right after the delivery of the judgment, General Assembly by Resolution 2145 (XXI) on 27 October 1966, reaffirmed the inalienable right to self-determination by the people of South West Africa, declared the breach of the mandate by South Africa through the application of apartheid régime, and in due regard terminated the mandate.[48]

---

45 South West Africa was the name for the modern-day Namibia when it was under the administration of South Africa as a declared League of Nations Class C Mandate Territory under the Treaty of Versailles. With the dissolution of the League and the creation of the United Nations, General Assembly by Resolution 9(I) in 1946 invited all States administering mandate territories to place the respective territories under the UN trusteeship system. The invitation was responded by all but not South Africa. In its advisory opinion on *International Status of South West Africa* in 1950, the Court found that the dissolution of the League had not entailed the lapse of the mandate, and that South Africa was still under an obligation to give an account of its administration to the UN, which discharged the supervisory functions formerly exercised by the League. See *International Status of South West Africa, Advisory Opinion of 11 July 1950, I.C.J. Reports 1950*, p. 128. To be noted, the Court found in p. 144 that "Chapter 12 of the Charter do not impose on the Union of South Africa a legal obligation to place the Territory under the Trusteeship System;" but instead, "the provisions of Chapter 12 of the Charter are applicable to the Territory of South-West Africa in the sense that they provide a means by which the Territory may be brought under the Trusteeship System." Afterwards, the General Assembly's consistent requests that South Africa should perform its obligations were all in vain. As an extension of its domestic racial policy, South Africa administered South West Africa under the apartheid laws.

46 *South West Africa (Ethiopia* v. *South Africa; Liberia* v. *South Africa), Second Phase, Judgment of 18 July 1966, I.C.J. Reports 1966*, p. 23, para. 16. In particular, the Court emphasized that "it is necessary not to confuse the moral ideal with the legal rules intended to give it effect", and that the legal rights and obligations were those and those alone from the mandate instruments within the framework of the League. Ibid, p. 35, para. 52.

47 Ibid, p. 51, para. 99. Sir Gerald Fitzmaurice is known to have been the principal author of the majority opinion. See, for example, McWhinney 1987, 39.

48 UNGA Res 2145(XXI) (27 October 1966) UN Doc A/RES/2145(XXI). The Security Council by Resolution 276 in 1970 reaffirmed that General Assembly Resolution and declared the continued presence of and all acts taken by South Africa in Namibia illegal. UNSC Res 276 (1970) (30 January 1970) UN Doc S/RES/276 (1970).

The judgment of the Court in *South West Africa* caused a devastating damage to the Court's credibility, as a result, the Court's caseload drastically descended.[49]

In 1970, the Security Council decided to request of the Court an advisory opinion on the legal consequences for States of the continued presence of South Africa in Namibia.[50] This time when interpreting the same mandate, with the majority of the judges re-elected, the Court adopted an entirely different approach in treaty interpretation, embracing the prevailing discernable trend of State practice and opinions, reaffirming self-determination and independence of the people concerned as the ultimate objective of the sacred trust placed in the United Nations.[51] Consequently, in its advisory opinion in 1971, the Court found the continued presence of South Africa in Namibia illegal, South Africa under an obligation to withdraw forthwith its administration therefrom, and that UN Members States under an obligation to recognize the illegality of South Africa's presence and the invalidity of its acts on behalf of or concerning Namibia, and to refrain from any acts implying recognition of the legality of, or lending support or assistance to, such presence and administration.[52]

Indeed, treaty interpretation is never static; it is a living matter. This is also the situation in the environmental field. In May 2010, Australia instituted proceedings against Japan in respect of "Japan's continued pursuit of a large-scale program of whaling under the Second Phase of its Japanese Whale Research Program under Special Permit in the Antarctic ('JARPA II')". Australia accused Japan of breaching its obligations under the 1946 International Convention for the Regulation of Whaling (hereinafter "ICRW"). New Zealand intervened under Article 63 of the Statute to give its own interpretation to the provisions of the ICRW.

---

49 For years, half of its caseloads concerned maritime delimitation and fisheries matters.

50 *Legal Consequences for States of the Continued Presence of South Africa in Namibia (South West Africa) notwithstanding Security Council Resolution 276 (1970), Advisory Opinion of 21 June 1971, I.C.J. Reports 1971*, p. 17.

51 Ibid, p. 31, para. 53: "[T]he Court must take into consideration the changes which have occurred in the supervening half-century, and its interpretation cannot remain unaffected by the subsequent development of law, through the Charter of the United Nations and by way of customary law. Moreover, an international instrument has to be interpreted and applied within the framework of the entire legal system prevailing at the time of the interpretation. In the domain to which the present proceedings relate, the last fifty years, as indicated above, have brought important developments. These developments leave little doubt that the ultimate objective of the sacred trust was the self-determination and independence of the peoples concerned."

52 Ibid, p. 58, para. 133.

In this case, the key provision of the ICRW over which the Parties held opposing views is Article VIII, paragraph 1 on scientific research, which reads:

> Notwithstanding anything contained in this Convention, any Contracting Government may grant to any of its nationals *a special permit authorizing that national to kill, take and treat whales for purposes of scientific research subject to such restrictions as to number and subject to such other conditions as the Contracting Government thinks fit, and the killing, taking, and treating of whales in accordance with the provisions of this Article shall be exempt from the operation of this Convention*. Each Contracting Government shall report at once to the Commission all such authorizations which it has granted. Each Contracting Government may at any time revoke any such special permit which it has granted [emphasis added].

Clearly, this provision gives full discretion to a State party to authorize whaling for scientific research purposes. The State party itself has the right to decide the scale and the number of killing of whales, and treatment of whale meat after the use for scientific research.[53] If interpreted strictly by its ordinary meaning of the terms, Article VIII, paragraph 1, gives a free hand to Japan to grant a permit to JARPA II project. In other words, Japan followed exactly Article VIII, paragraph 1, of the ICRW. But why did the Court come to a different conclusion, deciding that Japan breached its obligation under the Convention? In the Judgment, the Court basically considered two elements: first, the reasonableness of the number of killing for the purposes of JARPA II, and secondly, the actual scientific effect and necessity of the scale of killing of the project.[54] The Court admitted that killing of non-endangered whales for scientific purposes is permitted under the Convention and the minke whales that JARPA II was to kill was not endangered species.[55] However, under JARPA II, the project permitted the killing of minke whales up to over 800 per year. Australia adduced substantial evidence to prove its claim that Japan used scientific whaling in disguise so as to circumvent the moratorium on commercial whaling. Besides, the testimony given by the Japan-appointed expert also cast doubt on the scale of the killing for scientific research purposes.

Traditionally, whaling was essential for industry and human needs. As a result of growing commercial whaling, the resources were rapidly depleted.

---

53 *Whaling in the Antarctic (Australia v. Japan: New Zealand intervening), Merits, Judgment of 31 March 2014, I.C.J. Reports 2014, Separate Opinion of Judge Xue*, pp. 421–422, paras. 5–7.

54 Ibid, *Judgment of 31 March 2014*, pp. 292–293, paras. 224–227.

55 Ibid, pp. 250–252, paras. 55–58; p. 292, para. 224.

Since early 1930s, sustainability of the whaling industry gave rise to international actions. Prior to the adoption of the ICRW, there had been two international treaties on the regulation of whaling.[56] In expressing the desire of the States parties "to secure the prosperity of the whaling industry and, for that purpose, to maintain the stock of whales",[57] these treaties prohibited the taking of certain categories of whales, designated seasons for different types of whaling, closed certain geographic areas to whaling and imposed regulations on the industry. The ICRW, adopted in 1946, was aimed at more institutionalized mechanism for whaling regulation, as was declared by the sponsor of the international whaling conference, "to provide for the co-ordination and codification of existent regulations" and to establish an "effective administrative machinery for the modification of these regulations from time to time in the future as conditions may require".[58]

As whale utilization was eventually replaced by other resources, industrial and commercial whaling were put on a permanent moratorium under the ICRW. The Convention mechanisms turned their attention to conservation and protection. However, this approach has been consistently opposed by a few whaling States, such as Japan and Norway. For many years, environmental NGOs keep attacking Japan for killing and consuming whales, prompting whaling to become a public issue in some countries.[59]

Although the reasoning of the Court's Judgment was largely based on an examination of the JARPA II programme itself, it is evident that the object and purpose of the Convention have gradually evolved from sustainable utilization to conservation, and the functions of the Scientific Committees under the ICRW have also turned to a different direction.[60] Therefore, when commercial whaling was virtually terminated, a large scale of whaling, even if for scientific research purposes as claimed by Japan, cannot be considered as falling within the sole discretion of a State party, in this case, Japan. As long as Japan remains a party to the ICRW, it should observe the treaty as it stands today, not as in

56 Geneva Convention for Regulation of Whaling (adopted 24 September 1931, entered into force 16 January 1935) 155 LNTS 349; International Agreement for the Regulation of Whaling (with Declaration) (adopted 8 June 1937, entered into force 7 May 1938) 190 LNTS 79.

57 International Agreement for the Regulation of Whaling, ibid, preamble.

58 Opening address made by Mr. Dean Acheson, then Acting Secretary of State of the United States in 1946, at the international conference on whaling convened on the initiative of the United States. *Whaling in the Antarctic*, supra note 54, p. 247, para. 44.

59 On whaling policy, politics and legislation, see, for example, Tønnessen and Johnsen 1982; Friedheim 2001; Heazle 2006; Fitzmaurice 2015.

60 *Whaling in the Antarctic*, supra note 53, p. 423, para. 11.

1946. Through treaty interpretation and application, the Court took cognizance of that change. As the Court stated before, "an international instrument has to be interpreted and applied within the framework of the entire legal system prevailing at the time of the interpretation."[61] Interpretation of the ICRW must be in line with the rising standards on environmental protection under modern international law.

After the Judgment, Japan, in its new research programme, lowered the number of killing to around 300 per year.[62] Notwithstanding that readjustment, Japan nevertheless maintains its position on sustainable whaling. For that purpose, it has taken two legal actions: one, it withdrew from the ICRW and second, it modified the scope of its optional clause declaration, specifically precluding disputes relating to living marine resources from the Court's jurisdiction.[63] That is to say, in the future Japan will not accept the jurisdiction of the Court to settle any dispute relating to whaling. This may seem unfortunate for the Court, but it in a way illustrates the limits of judicial settlement in international relations.

In conclusion, by ascertaining, clarifying and developing the law, the Court, while performing the functions of settling disputes, contributes to the development of international law.

5 Limits of Judicial Law-Making: Is Self-Restraint Necessary?

One of the inherent features of law lies in the *antinomy* of stability and evolution in view of economic and social progress. To better serve the society, the judiciary should be capable of accommodating such inherent antinomy in law and respond in a positive way. This equally applies to the ICJ. In exercising its judicial functions, the Court nevertheless is not a legislative body. As the Court is obliged "to decide [the disputes] in accordance with international law",[64] its role in law-making, therefore, is inherently limited. In this regard, two aspects need constant review.

61 *Legal Consequences for States of the Continued Presence of South Africa in Namibia (South West Africa) notwithstanding Security Council Resolution 276 (1970)*, supra note 50, p. 31, para. 53.

62 See, for example, Matsuoka, Mogoe, and Pastene 2016.

63 See, for example, Becker 2015, available at: https://www.ejiltalk.org/japans-new-optional-clause-declaration-at-the-icj-a-pre-emptive-strike/>, accessed 16 June 2022.

64 Statute of the International Court of Justice, art 38.

First, to what extent the Court may exercise judicial activism in the interpretation of the law. In settling disputes, one major aspect of the Court's function is to interpret the law, conventional or customary, as the case may be. With regard to treaty interpretation, the Court, in its early days, gave predominant effect to the wording of treaty provisions.[65] Gradually, with the development of treaty law, the Court also resorted to other elements in interpretation, emphasizing more the context of a provision, object and purpose of the treaty, the drafting history, etc.[66] As is provided for in Articles 31 and 32 of the Vienna Convention on the Law of Treaties, a treaty shall be interpreted in good faith in accordance with the ordinary meaning to be given to the terms of the treaty in their context and in the light of its object and purpose. This holistic approach has been affirmed on numerous occasions by the Court as reflecting the established customary rules on treaty interpretation.[67]

65 In the time of PCIJ, the approach of textualism dominated among others. *The Case of S.S. "Wimbledon", Judgment, P.C.I.J. Publications 1923, Series A, no. 1*, p. 22: "[t]he Court considers that the terms of article 380 are categorical and give rise to no doubt;" *The Case of S.S. "Lotus", Judgment, PCIJ Publications 1928, Series A, no. 10*, p. 16: "there is no occasion to have regard to preparatory work if the text of a convention is sufficiently clear in itself;" *Jurisdiction of the Courts of Danzig, Advisory Opinion, P.C.I.J. Publications 1928, Series B, no.* 15, p. 18: "[t]he intention of the Parties, which is to be ascertained from the contents of the Agreement, taking into consideration the manner in which the Agreement has been applied, is decisive."

66 Such an approach of textualism continued to exert its influence in the time of the ICJ, though the ICJ went through a rather zigzag path in respect of treaty interpretation over time. In *Competence of the General Assembly for the Admission of a State to the United Nations, Advisory Opinion of 3 March 1950, I.C.J. Reports 1950*, p. 8: "the first duty of a tribunal which is called upon to interpret and apply the provisions of a treaty, is to endeavour to give effect to them in their natural and ordinary meaning in the context in which they occur. If the relevant words in their natural and ordinary meaning make sense in their context, that is an end of the matter. If, on the other hand, the words in their natural and ordinary meaning are ambiguous or lead to an unreasonable result, then, and then only, must the Court, by resort to other methods of interpretation ...." The Court in *South West Africa* adopted two different approaches at preliminary phase (a more related textualism) and merits phase (strict textualism). *South West Africa (Ethiopia* v. *South Africa; Liberia* v. *South Africa), Preliminary Objections, Judgment of 21 December 1962, I.C.J. Reports 1962*, p. 336: "[the rule of natural and ordinary meaning of the words employed in the provision] is not an absolute one. Where such a method of interpretation results in a meaning incompatible with the spirit, purpose and context of the clause or instrument in which the words are contained, no reliance can be validly placed on it;" cf *South West Africa, Second Phase*, supra note 46, p. 6.

67 The Court first recognized Articles 31 and 32 of the Vienna Convention on the Law of Treaties as reflecting customary international law in 1991. *Arbitral Award of 31 July 1989 (Guinea-Bissau* v. *Senegal), Judgment of 12 November 1991, I.C.J. Reports 1991*, p. 69, para. 48: "These principles are reflected in Articles 31 and 32 of the Vienna Convention

Evidently, treaty interpretation is not purely a technical matter. The holistic approach that places less emphasis on the text of a treaty does not imply that the text is no longer determinative. On the contrary, it means that the text should continue to serve as the base of interpretation, but that base alone may not be sufficient for the purpose of interpretation. Either excessive expansion of the ordinary meaning of, or a departure from, the actual terms of treaty provisions, is contrary to the treaty law. As is pointed out by the Court, "in accordance with customary international law, reflected in Article 31 of the 1969 Vienna Convention on the Law of Treaties [...] Interpretation must be based above all upon the text of the treaty".[68] When the Court is obliged to take into account such additional and relevant elements as context, object and purpose, drafting history etc., it does not suggest that the Court has a free hand in interpreting the law. A good faith interpretation should, first and foremost, reflect what the State parties intended to undertake when they concluded the treaty in question.

In reality, difficulties often arise when the treaty practice has undergone substantial changes, as in the *Whaling* case, the ordinary meaning of the text has to be examined in the light of the object and purpose of the treaty and its subsequent practice. To what extent the Court may construe the treaty beyond its actual terms in view of the changing circumstances is not merely a theoretical question.

In the recent case instituted by Qatar against the United Arab Emirates (UAE) for the alleged violations of the International Convention on the Elimination of

---

on the Law of Treaties, which may in many respects be considered as a codification of existing customary international law on the point." Ever since *Arbitral Award of 31 July 1989*, the Court has consistently applied rules of customary international law on treaty interpretation as reflected in Articles 31 and 32 of the Vienna Convention. See, for example, *Question of the Delimitation of the Continental Shelf between Nicaragua and Colombia beyond 200 Nautical Miles from the Nicaraguan Coast (Nicaragua* v. *Colombia), Preliminary Objections, Judgment of 17 March 2016, I.C.J. Reports 2016 (I)*, p. 116, para. 33; *Application of the International Convention for the Suppression of the Financing of Terrorism and of the International Convention on the Elimination of All Forms of Racial Discrimination (Ukraine* v. *Russian Federation), Judgment of 8 November 2019, I.C.J. Reports*, p. 598, para. 106. Moreover, the Court explicitly adopted the holistic approach of treaty interpretation in *Maritime Delimitation in the Indian Ocean (Somalia* v. *Kenya), Preliminary Objections, Judgment of 2 February 2017, I.C.J. Reports 2017*, p. 29, para. 64: "Article 31, paragraph 1, of the Vienna Convention provides ... These elements of interpretation—ordinary meaning, context and object and purpose—are to be considered as a whole".

68 *Territorial Dispute (Libyan Arab Jamahiriya/Chad), Judgment of 3 February 1994, I.C.J. Reports 1994*, pp. 21–22, para. 41; cf *Oil Platforms (Islamic Republic of Iran* v. *United States of America), Preliminary Objection, Judgment of 12 December 1996, I.C.J. Reports 1996*, p. 803.

All Forms of Racial Discrimination of 21 December 1965 (CERD),[69] the Parties held opposing views on the term of Article 1, paragraph 1, of the Convention, according to which, the State parties are obliged to prohibit racial discrimination on the bases of "race, colour, descent, or national or ethnic origin".[70] Qatar contended that the measures imposed by the UAE on the Qatari nationals constituted racial discrimination, as the term "national origin" provided in CERD encompassed current nationality.[71] In this regard, it particularly referred to General Recommendation XXX adopted by the CERD Committee, an expert body established under the Convention for the treaty implementation. In that General Recommendation, the CERD Committee took the view that "differential treatment based on citizenship or immigration status will constitute discrimination if the criteria for such differentiation, judged in the light of the objectives and purposes of the Convention, are not applied pursuant to a legitimate aim, and are not proportional to the achievement of this aim".[72] The UAE, on the other hand, maintained that the term "national origin" under CERD did not encompass current nationality and therefore, its measures against Qatari nationals did not violate the Convention. In its view, the CERD Committee's general recommendations did not constitute subsequent practice or agreement of States parties to CERD regarding the interpretation of the Convention.[73]

The Court first examined the term "national origin" in the context of the Convention in the light of the object and purpose of CERD and, to confirm its conclusion, further reviewed *travaux préparatoires*, the drafting history of the Convention, the practice of the CERD Committee and the jurisprudence of the human rights bodies. Based on these considerations, the Court found that the term "national origin" in Article 1, paragraph 1, of the Convention did not encompass current nationality. With regard to the practice of the CERD

---

69 The Court delivered its Judgment on jurisdiction and admissibility on 4 February 2021.

70 Article 1, paragraph 1, of the Convention reads: In this Convention, the term "racial discrimination" shall mean any distinction, exclusion, restriction or preference based on race, colour, descent, or national or ethnic origin which has the purpose or effect of nullifying or impairing the recognition, enjoyment or exercise, on an equal footing, of human rights and fundamental freedoms in the political, economic, social, cultural or any other field of public life.

71 *Application of the International Convention on the Elimination of All Forms of Racial Discrimination* (*Qatar* v. *United Arab Emirates*), *Preliminary Objections, Judgment of 4 February 2021*, para. 74.

72 UN Committee on the Elimination of Racial Discrimination (CERD), CERD General Recommendation XXX on Discrimination Against Non Citizens (1 October 2002), para. 4.

73 *Application of the International Convention on the Elimination of All Forms of Racial Discrimination*, supra note 71, para. 74.

Committee, the Court recalled its previous statement in the *Diallo* case, that, in exercising its judicial functions, the Court was "in no way obliged [...] to model its own interpretation of the Covenant on that of the Committee", but to apply the relevant customary rules on treaty interpretation.[74] In light of these reasons, the Court upheld the preliminary objection raised by the UAE and decided that it had no jurisdiction to entertain the application filed by Qatar.[75]

Rules of treaty interpretation serve to maintain the stability, certainty and generality of contractual relations between the States parties to a treaty. A faithful interpretation that genuinely reflects what the States parties have undertaken to fulfil under international law would only strengthen the treaty regime. A State party may always choose to withdraw from a treaty if it considers that its obligations under the treaty have been unduly expanded by the Court without its consent.[76]

Another aspect of judicial limits relates to the settled jurisprudence. To render judgments on sound reasoning, the Court must follow its established jurisprudence. Unless there are compelling reasons, the Court should not deviate from that jurisprudence. To determine whether there exists any compelling reason, the Court has to assess the specific circumstances in each case. This precaution is not without merit.

In the cases filed either against or by the Federal Republic of Yugoslavia (FRY), the Court took different positions on the legal status of the State at different stages. In *Bosnia and Herzegovina* v. *Serbia and Montenegro*, the Court found that the Parties, since the entry into force on 14 December 1995 of the Dayton-Paris Agreement, recognized each other as sovereign States, and by succession, became parties to the Genocide Convention.[77] The Court did not consider that there was any legal obstacle for the FRY to be a party before the Court. In the following cases filed by Serbia and Montenegro (formerly called the FRY) against several NATO member States on *Legality of Use of Force*, the Court took a different position on the status of the State. Having recalled the historical events with the FRY, the Court came to the conclusion that Serbia and Montenegro was not a Member of the United Nations, and in that capacity a State party to the Statute of the Court, at the time of filing its application

74 Ibid, para. 101, citing *Ahmadou Sadio Diallo (Republic of Guinea* v. *Democratic Republic of the Congo), Merits, Judgment of 30 November 2010, I.C.J. Reports 2010 (II)*, p. 664, para. 66.

75 Ibid, paras. 114–115.

76 Japan's actions in the wake of the Court's Judgment in *Whaling* case illustrate this point.

77 *Application of the Convention on the Prevention and Punishment of the Crime of Genocide (Bosnia and Herzegovina* v. *Serbia and Montenegro), Preliminary Objections, Judgment of 11 July 1996, I.C.J. Reports 1996*, pp. 613–614, para. 26.

to institute the proceedings before the Court on 29 April 1999, and therefore, Serbia and Montenegro did not have access to the Court under Article 35 of the Statute. Consequently, the Court dismissed the cases for lack of jurisdiction.[78] In July 1999, Croatia instituted proceedings in the Court against Serbia for alleged violations of the Genocide Convention. This time the Court did not address the question of access, but confined its consideration to the applicability of the Genocide Convention to Serbia.[79]

Evidently, the reasons given by the Court in these cases are not consistent. If Serbia (formerly the FRY, then Serbia and Montenegro), as was confirmed by the Court in its 2004 Judgments in the cases concerning *Legality of Use of Force*, was not a Member of the United Nations until 1 November 2000 and therefore not a party to the Statute before that date, the Court could not have had jurisdiction in the subsequent case filed by Croatia against Serbia. It should be pointed out, in particular, that the 2004 Judgments were adopted by the Court in unanimity. The change of the Court's composition in the latter case cannot justify this inconsistency.[80] Predictability and certainty of the jurisprudence of the Court are imperative to maintain the trust and confidence of States in the judicial settlement. Notwithstanding its prominent position in the UN, the Court's credibility lies in its sound judgments.

78 *Legality of Use of Force (Serbia and Montenegro* v. *United Kingdom), Preliminary Objections, Judgment of 15 December 2004, I.C.J. Reports 2004*, p. 1307, pp. 1328–1341, paras. 50–89. See also *Legality of Use of Force (Serbia and Montenegro* v. *Belgium), Preliminary Objections, Judgment of 15 December 2004, I.C.J. Reports 2004*, p. 279; *Legality of Use of Force (Serbia and Montenegro* v. *Canada), Preliminary Objections, Judgment of 15 December 2004, I.C.J. Reports 2004*, p. 429; *Legality of Use of Force (Serbia and Montenegro* v. *France), Preliminary Objections, Judgment of 15 December 2004, I.C.J. Reports 2004*, p. 575; *Legality of Use of Force (Serbia and Montenegro* v. *Germany), Preliminary Objections, Judgment of 15 December 2004, I.C.J. Reports 2004*, p. 720; *Legality of Use of Force (Serbia and Montenegro* v. *Italy), Preliminary Objections, Judgment of 15 December 2004, I.C.J. Reports 2004*, p. 865; *Legality of Use of Force (Serbia and Montenegro* v. *Netherlands), Preliminary Objections, Judgment of 15 December 2004, I.C.J. Reports 2004*, p. 1011; *Legality of Use of Force (Serbia and Montenegro* v. *Portugal), Preliminary Objections, Judgment of 15 December 2004, I.C.J. Reports 2004*, p. 1160.

79 See *Application of the Convention on the Prevention and Punishment of the Crime of Genocide (Croatia* v. *Serbia), Preliminary Objections, Judgment of 18 November 2008, I.C.J. Reports 2008*, p. 412; *Application of the Convention on the Prevention and Punishment of the Crime of Genocide (Croatia* v. *Serbia), Merits, Judgment of 3 February 2015, I.C.J. Reports 2015*, p. 3.

80 For criticism of the case, see, for example, Yehuda Z. Blum, 'Consistently Inconsistent: The International Court of Justice and the Former Yugoslavia (Croatia v. Serbia)' (2009) 103(2) American Journal of International Law 264.

6 Challenges Ahead

Looking ahead, there are three major challenges facing the Court: institutional proliferation, fragmentation of the law, and credibility of third-party settlement. Since these issues, each of them, deserve a separate study, they will be briefly discussed here.

First, the post-Cold War era has witnessed a rapid growth of judicial and arbitral activities at both international and regional levels. Although the revival of the existing arbitral institutions and the creation of new courts and tribunals are generally perceived as a positive development for the peaceful settlement of international disputes, they pose challenges to the ICJ's role in the field; States may choose different forums to settle their disputes. Top talents can go and serve in other judicial institutions. More importantly, the Court must constantly improve its judicial practice so as to live up to the expectations of States.

Secondly, with multiple third-party settlement mechanisms, fragmented jurisprudence is inevitable. At the international level, there is no hierarchy among different courts and tribunals; they each act within their given competence and develop their own jurisprudence. They are not obliged to give deference to the jurisprudence of other courts and tribunals. Therefore, when a treaty clause can be interpreted differently by different tribunals, where and by whom a case is to be adjudicated becomes decisive. Consequently, "forum-shopping" and judge-selection could render the international adjudication process opportunistic. Even though for permanent courts and tribunals, such matters seldom arise, fragmented legal practice is not conducive to the development of third-party settlement.[81]

Lastly, notwithstanding the increasing workload of the Court, increasing unilateral institutions of proceedings are worth noting. In some of these cases, respondent States have either chosen not to appear,[82] or modified their

81 On proliferation of international courts and tribunals and fragmentation of international law, see, for example, ILC, 'Fragmentation of International Law: Difficulties Arising from the Diversification and Expansion of International Law', Report of the Study Group of the International Law Commission, Finalized by Martti Koskenniemi (13 April 2006) UN Doc A/CN.4/L.682; Treves, in Wolfrum and Roeben 2005; Zimmermann and Hofmann 2006.

82 Recently, in *Arbitral Award of 3 October 1899* (*Guyana* v. *Venezuela*), Venezuela did not appear before the Court during the preliminary phase. In *Relocation of the United States Embassy to Jerusalem* (*Palestine* v. *United States of America*), the Trump Administration informed the Court that the United States would not participate in the case. The basis for the Court to adjudicate in the situation of non-appearance of a party is Article 53 of its Statute. See Mangoldt and Zimmermann, in Zimmermann, Tomuschat, and

acceptance of the Court's jurisdiction afterwards. In the past eight years, six States have modified or withdrawn their acceptance of the Court's jurisdiction after they were sued in the Court. For instance, after the Marshall Islands nuclear disarmament cases against nine nuclear-weapon States,[83] the United Kingdom, India and Pakistan each amended their Optional Clause declarations under Article 36, paragraph 2, of the Statute, narrowing down the scope of their acceptance of the Court's compulsory jurisdiction.[84] As discussed before,

---

Oellers-Frahm 2006, 1141–1170. For more discussion of non-appearance, see, for example, Thirlway 1985.

83 On 24 April 2014, the Republic of the Marshall Islands filed applications against nine States (China, Democratic People's Republic of Korea, France, India, Israel, Pakistan, Russian Federation, United Kingdom and United States of America), accusing them of not fulfilling their obligations with respect to the cessation of the nuclear arms race at an early date and to nuclear disarmament. Out of the nine States, three had accepted the Court's compulsory jurisdiction (India, Pakistan and United Kingdom) while the other six had not. In accordance with Article 38, paragraph 5, of the Rules of Court, the applications filed against these six States were transmitted to them but not entered in the General List, and no action was taken in the proceedings in the absence of their consent. Later, jurisdiction was not found by the Court for the cases against the rest three States. See *Obligations concerning Negotiations relating to Cessation of the Nuclear Arms Race and to Nuclear Disarmament* (*Marshall Islands* v. *India*), *Preliminary Objections, Judgment 5 October 2016, I.C.J. Reports 2016*, p. 255; *Obligations concerning Negotiations relating to Cessation of the Nuclear Arms Race and to Nuclear Disarmament* (*Marshall Islands* v. *Pakistan*), *Preliminary Objections, Judgment 5 October 2016, I.C.J. Reports 2016*, p. 552; *Obligations concerning Negotiations relating to Cessation of the Nuclear Arms Race and to Nuclear Disarmament* (*Marshall Islands* v. *United Kingdom*), *Preliminary Objections, Judgment 5 October 2016, I.C.J. Reports 2016*, p. 833.

84 On 22 February 2017, the United Kingdom revised its declaration under Article 36(2) of the Statute of the Court dated 30 December 2014, excluding from the Court's jurisdiction, among others: "any claim or dispute that arises from or is connected with or related to nuclear disarmament and/or nuclear weapons, unless all of the other nuclear-weapon States Party to the Treaty on the Non-Proliferation of Nuclear Weapons have also consented to the jurisdiction of the Court and are party to the proceedings in question." On 29 March 2017, Pakistan revised its declaration under Article 36(2) of the Statute of the Court dated 12 September 1960, excluding from the Court's jurisdiction, among others: "disputes relating to or connected with any aspect of hostilities, armed conflicts, individual or collective self-defence or the discharge of any functions pursuant to any decision or recommendation of international bodies, the deployment of armed forces abroad, as well as action relating and ancillary thereto in which Pakistan is, has been or may in future be involved;" and "all matters related to the national security of the Islamic Republic of Pakistan." On 27 September 2019, India also revised its declaration under Article 36(2) of the Statute of the Court dated 18 September 1974, further excluding from the Court's jurisdiction, among others: "disputes relating to ... measures taken for protection of national security and ensuring national defence." See "Declarations recognizing as compulsory the jurisdiction of the International Court of Justice under Article 36, paragraph 2, of the

Japan modified its declaration of acceptance after the *Whaling* case. Colombia withdrew from the Pact of Bogotá, a treaty on which the Court founded its jurisdiction in the case instituted by Nicaragua against Colombia.[85] Recently, after Iran, on the basis of the 1955 Treaty of Amity, Economic Relations and Consular Rights between Iran and the United States, sued the United States in the Court in two cases, the United States terminated the said treaty.[86]

These cases show that jurisdiction of the Court bears heavily on the national interests of States. Whether a dispute should be submitted to a third-party for a binding settlement, whether a dispute should be subject to judicial scrutiny, and whether a dispute should be examined as a separate legal issue detached from the overall political context: all these are not purely legal issues. They are political questions, first and foremost, for political decisions.[87] Undoubtedly, the Court cannot dictate how States should submit their disputes to the Court for settlement, unilaterally or otherwise by agreement. The Court can only act in accordance with the Statute and Rules of the Court to settle the disputes in question. What is at stake is the credibility of the Court if judicial decisions fail to bring about effective resolutions to the disputes.

References

Becker M, Japan's New Optional Clause Declaration at the ICJ: A Pre-Emptive Strike? (2015), available at: <https://www.ejiltalk.org/japans-new-optional-clause-declaration-at-the-icj-a-pre-emptive-strike/.>, accessed 12 May 2022.

Statute of the Court", available at: <https://treaties.un.org/pages/ViewDetails.aspx?src=TREATY&mtdsg_no=I-4&chapter=1&clang=_en> accessed 16 June 2022.

85 See *Territorial and Maritime Dispute* (*Nicaragua* v. *Colombia*), supra note 36, p. 624.

86 The two pending cases based on the 1955 Treaty are: *Certain Iranian Assets* (*Islamic Republic of Iran* v. *United States of America*), *Preliminary Objections, Judgment of 13 February 2019, I.C.J. Reports 2019*, p. 7; *Alleged Violations of the 1955 Treaty of Amity, Economic Relations, and Consular Rights* (*Islamic Republic of Iran* v. *United States of America*), *Preliminary Objections, Judgment of 3 February 2021*. (In the past, Iran also brought three other cases based on the 1955 Treaty (and on other bases): *United States Diplomatic and Consular Staff in Tehran* (*United States of America* v. *Iran*), *Judgment of 24 May 1980, I.C.J. Reports 1980*, p. 3; *Aerial Incident of 3 July 1988* (*Islamic Republic of Iran* v. *United States of America*), *Memorial of the Islamic Republic of Iran, 24 July 1990*; *Oil Platforms*, supra note 68, p. 803).

87 For example, Rosenne 2006, Vol. II, 803 observes: "The question whether and to what extent the Court has jurisdiction is frequently of political importance no less than the decision on the merits, if not more. When a respondent raises a matter of jurisdiction […] it frequently indicates the absence of political agreement that the Court should entertain the case. These are not mere technical issues."

Blum Y Z, Consistently Inconsistent: The International Court of Justice and the Former Yugoslavia (Croatia v. Serbia), (2009) 103(2) American Journal of International Law 264.

Brownlie I, International Law and the Use of Force by States (Clarendon Press 1963).

Dugard J (ed), The South West Africa/Namibia Dispute: Documents and Scholarly Writings on the Controversy Between South Africa and the United Nations (University of California Press 1973).

Friedheim R L (ed), Toward a Sustainable Whaling Regime (University of Washington Press 2001).

Fitzmaurice M, Whaling and International Law (Cambridge University Press 2015).

Hague Convention, Pacific Settlement of International Disputes (1899)/1899 Convention/ The Hague Convention 1899/Hague (I) 1899, 1 Bevans 230, 1 AJIL 103 (1907).

Hague Convention, 1907 Convention for the Pacific Settlement of International Disputes (Hague Convention I), UKTS 6 (1971) Cmnd. 4575, 1 Bevans 577, 2 AJIL Supp. 43 (1908).

Heazle M, Scientific Uncertainty and the Politics of Whaling (Washington University Press 2006).

Hobér K, Essays on International Arbitration (JurisNet 2006).

Hudson M O, The First Conference for the Codification of International Law (1930) 24(3) American Journal of International Law 447.

Hudson M O, International Tribunals: Past and Future (Carnegie Endowment for International Peace 1944).

International Court of Justice (ICJ),Reparations for Injuries Suffered in the Service of the United Nations, Advisory Opinion of 11 April 1949, I.C.J. Reports 1949.

International Court of Justice (ICJ), International Status of South West Africa, Advisory Opinion of 11 July 1950, I.C.J. Reports 1950.

International Court of Justice (ICJ),Preliminary Question, Judgment of 15 June 1954, I.C.J. Reports 1954.

International Court of Justice (ICJ), Monetary Gold Removed from Rome in 1943, Italy v. France et al., Judgment, I.C.J. Reports 1954.

International Court of Justice (ICJ), Temple of Preah Vihear (Cambodia v. Thailand), Preliminary Objections, Judgment of 26 May 1961, I.C.J. Reports 1961.

International Court of Justice (ICJ), Certain Expenses of the United Nations (Article 17, paragraph 2, of the Charter), Advisory Opinion of 20 July 1962, I.C.J. Reports 1962.

International Court of Justice (ICJ), South West Africa (Ethiopia v. South Africa; Liberia v. South Africa), Preliminary Objections, Judgment of 21 December 1962, I.C.J. Reports 1962.

International Court of Justice (ICJ), Northern Cameroons (Cameroon v. United Kingdom), Preliminary Objections, Judgment of 2 December 1963, I.C.J. Reports 1963.

International Court of Justice (ICJ), South West Africa (Ethiopia v. South Africa; Liberia v. South Africa), Second Phase, Judgment of 18 July 1966, I.C.J. Reports 1966.

International Court of Justice (ICJ), North Sea Continental Shelf (Federal Republic of Germany/Denmark; Federal Republic of Germany/Netherlands), Judgment of 20 February 1969, I.C.J. Reports 1969.

International Court of Justice (ICJ), Legal Consequences for States of the Continued Presence of South Africa in Namibia (South West Africa) Notwithstanding Security Council Resolution 276 (1970), Advisory Opinion, I.C.J. Reports 1971.

International Court of Justice (ICJ), Fisheries Jurisdiction (United Kingdom v. Iceland), Merits, Judgment of 25 July 1974, I.C.J. Reports 1974.

International Court of Justice (ICJ), Western Sahara, Advisory Opinion of 16 October 1975, I.C.J. Reports 1975.

International Court of Justice (ICJ), Judgment of 24 May 1980, I.C.J. Reports 1980 (I).

International Court of Justice (ICJ), Interpretation of the Agreement of 25 March 1951 between the WHO and Egypt, Advisory Opinion of 20 December 1980, I.C.J. Reports 1980 (II).

International Court of Justice (ICJ), Continental Shelf (Tunisia/Libyan Arab Jamahiriya), Judgment of 24 February 1982, I.C.J. Reports 1982.

International Court of Justice (ICJ), Continental Shelf (Libyan Arab Jamahiriya/Malta), Application to Intervene, Judgment of 21 March 1984, I.C.J. Reports 1984.

International Court of Justice (ICJ), Delimitation of the Maritime Boundary in the Gulf of Maine Area (Canada/United States of America), Judgment of 12 October 1984, I.C.J. Reports 1984.

International Court of Justice (ICJ), Continental Shelf (Libyan Arab Jamahiriya/Malta), Judgment of 3 June 1985, I.C.J. Reports 1985.

International Court of Justice (ICJ), Applicability of Article VI, Section 22, of the Convention on the Privileges and Immunities of the United Nations, Advisory Opinion of 15 December 1989, I.C.J. Reports 1989.

International Court of Justice (ICJ), Land, Island and Maritime Frontier Dispute (El Salvador/Honduras: Nicaragua intervening), Application to Intervene, Judgment of 13 September 1990, I.C.J. Report 1990.

International Court of Justice (ICJ), Arbitral Award of 31 July 1989 (Guinea-Bissau v. Senegal), Judgment of 12 November 1991, I.C.J. Reports 1991.

International Court of Justice (ICJ), Certain Phosphate Lands in Nauru (Nauru v. Australia), Preliminary Objections, Judgment of 26 June 1992, I.C.J. Reports 1992.

International Court of Justice (ICJ), Maritime Delimitation in the Area between Greenland and Jan Mayen (Denmark v. Norway), Judgment of 14 June 1993, I.C.J. Reports 1993.

International Court of Justice (ICJ), Territorial Dispute (Libyan Arab Jamahiriya/Chad), Judgment of 3 February 1994, I.C.J. Reports 1994.

International Court of Justice (ICJ), Legality of the Threat or Use of Nuclear Weapons, Advisory Opinion of 8 July 1996, I.C.J. Reports 1996.

International Court of Justice (ICJ), Application of the Convention on the Prevention and Punishment of the Crime of Genocide (Bosnia and Herzegovina v. Serbia and Montenegro), Preliminary Objections, Judgment of 11 July 1996, I.C.J. Reports 1996.

International Court of Justice (ICJ), Oil Platforms (Islamic Republic of Iran v. United States of America), Preliminary Objection, Judgment of 12 December 1996, I.C.J. Reports 1996.

International Court of Justice (ICJ), Difference Relating to Immunity from Legal Process of a Special Rapporteur of the Commission on Human Rights, Advisory Opinion of 29 April 1999, I.C.J. Reports 1999.

International Court of Justice (ICJ), Maritime Delimitation and Territorial Questions between Qatar and Bahrain (Qatar v. Bahrain), Merits, Judgment of 16 March 2001, I.C.J. Reports 2001.

International Court of Justice (ICJ), Land and Maritime Boundary between Cameroon and Nigeria (Cameroon v. Nigeria: Equatorial Guinea intervening), Judgment of 10 October 2002, I.C.J. Reports 2002.

International Court of Justice (ICJ), Preliminary Objections, Judgment of 15 December 2004, I.C.J. Reports 2004.

International Court of Justice (ICJ), Territorial and Maritime Dispute between Nicaragua and Honduras in the Caribbean Sea (Nicaragua v. Honduras), Judgment of 8 October 2007, I.C.J. Reports 2007.

International Court of Justice (ICJ), Preliminary Objections, Judgment of 18 November 2008, I.C.J. Reports 2008.

International Court of Justice (ICJ), Maritime Delimitation in the Black Sea (Romania v. Ukraine), Judgment of 3 February 2009, I.C.J. Reports 2009.

International Court of Justice (ICJ), Ahmadou Sadio Diallo (Republic of Guinea v. Democratic Republic of the Congo), Merits, Judgment of 30 November 2010, I.C.J. Reports 2010 (II).

International Court of Justice (ICJ), Territorial and Maritime Dispute (Nicaragua v. Colombia), Judgment of 19 November 2012, I.C.J. Reports 2012.

International Court of Justice (ICJ), Maritime Dispute (Peru v. Chile), Judgment of 27 January 2014, I.C.J. Reports 2014.

International Court of Justice, Whaling in the Antarctic (Australia v. Japan: New Zealand intervening), Merits, Judgment of 31 March 2014, I.C.J. Reports 2014.

International Court of Justice (ICJ), Application of the Convention on the Prevention and Punishment of the Crime of Genocide (Croatia v. Serbia), Merits, Judgment of 3 February 2015, I.C.J. Reports 2015.

International Court of Justice (ICJ), Preliminary Objections, Judgment of 17 March 2016, I.C.J. Reports 2016 (I).

International Court of Justice (ICJ), Preliminary Objections, Judgment 5 October 2016, I.C.J. Reports 2016 (II).

International Court of Justice (ICJ), Maritime Delimitation in the Caribbean Sea and the Pacific Ocean (Costa Rica v. Nicaragua), Judgment of 2 February 2018, I.C.J. Reports 2018.

International Court of Justice (ICJ), Maritime Delimitation in the Indian Ocean (Somalia v. Kenya), Preliminary Objections, Judgment of 2 February 2017, I.C.J. Reports 2017.

International Court of Justice (ICJ), Draft conclusions on identification of customary international law, with commentaries (2018) UN Doc A/73/10.

International Court of Justice (ICJ), Preliminary Objections, Judgment of 13 February 2019, I.C.J. Reports 2019 (I).

International Court of Justice (ICJ), Legal Consequences of the Separation of the Chagos Archipelago from Mauritius in 1965, Advisory Opinion of 25 February 2019, I.C.J. Reports 2019 (II).

International Court of Justice (ICJ), Jadhav (India v. Pakistan), Judgment of 17 July 2019, I.C.J. Reports 2019 (III).

International Court of Justice (ICJ), Application of the International Convention for the Suppression of the Financing of Terrorism and of the International Convention on the Elimination of All Forms of Racial Discrimination (Ukraine v. Russian Federation), Judgment of 8 November 2019, I.C.J. Reports 2019 (IV).

International Court of Justice (ICJ), Application of the International Convention on the Elimination of All Forms of Racial Discrimination (Qatar v. United Arab Emirates), Preliminary Objections, Judgment of 4 February 2021. I.C.J. Reports 2021.

International Law Commission (ILC), Draft Articles on Responsibility of States for Internationally Wrongful Acts, with Commentaries (2001) UN Doc A/56/10.

International Law Commission (ILC), Fragmentation of International Law: Difficulties Arising from the Diversification and Expansion of International Law, Report of the Study Group of the International Law Commission, Finalized by Martti Koskenniemi (13 April 2006) UN Doc A/CN.4/L.682.

Jessup P C, United Nations Conference on the Law of the Sea, (1959) 59 Columbia Law Review 234.

Mangoldt H v and Zimmermann A, Article 53, in: Zimmermann A, Tomuschat C and Oellers-Frahm K (eds), The Statute of the International Court of Justice (Oxford University Press 2006), 1141–1170.

Matsuoka K, Mogoe T and Pastene L A, Overview of the first field survey of the New Scientific Whale Research Program in the Antarctic Ocean (NEWREP-A) in 2015/16. SC/66b/SP/05 (International Whaling Commission, Cambridge, UK, 2016).

McWhinney E, The International Court of Justice and the Western Tradition of International Law (Martinus Nijhoff 1987).

Miller D H, The Peace Pact of Paris: A Study of the Briand-Kellogg Treaty (Putnam's Sons 1928).

Peck C and Lee R L (eds), Increasing the Effectiveness of the International Court of Justice: Proceedings of the ICJ/UNITAR Colloquium to Celebrate the 50th Anniversary of the Court (Martinus Nijhoff 1997).

Permanent Court of International Justice (PCIJ), The Case of S.S. "Wimbledon", Judgment, P.C.I.J. Publications 1923, Series A, no. 1.

Permanent Court of International Justice (P.C.I.J.), The Case of S.S. "Lotus", Judgment, PCIJ Publications 1928, Series A, no. 10.

Permanent Court of International Justice (P.C.I.J.), Jurisdiction of the Courts of Danzig, Advisory Opinion, P.C.I.J. Publications 1928, Series B, no. 15.

Permanent Court of International Justice (P.C.I.J.), Competence of the General Assembly for the Admission of a State to the United Nations, Advisory Opinion of 3 March 1950, I.C.J. Reports 1950.

Rosenne S, League of Nations Committee of Experts for the Progressive Codification of International Law (1925–1928) (Dobbs Ferry, Oceana Publications 1972).

Rosenne S, The Law and Practice of the International Court, 1920–2005, Vol. I, The Court and the United Nations (Martinus Nijhoff 2006).

Shotwell J T, War as an Instrument of National Policy and its Renunciation in the Pact of Paris (Harcourt, Brace and Company 1929).

Schermers H G and Blokker N M, International Institutional Law (6th edn, Brill Nijhoff 2018).

Spiermann O, International Legal Argument in the Permanent Court of International Justice: The Rise of the International Judiciary (Cambridge University Press 2005).

Tams C J and Sloan J (eds), The Development of International Law by the International Court of Justice (Oxford University Press 2013).

Thirlway H W A, Non-Appearance before the International Court of Justice (Cambridge University Press 1985).

Tønnessen J N and Johnsen A O, The History of Modern Whaling (R. I. Christophersen trans, University of California Press 1982).

Treves T, Judicial Lawmaking in an Era of "Proliferation" of International Courts and Tribunals: Development or Fragmentation of International Law?, in: Wolfrum R and Roeben V (eds), Developments of International Law in Treaty Making (Springer 2005).

United Nations, Charter of the United Nations, 24 October 1945, 1 UNTS XVI, available at: <https://www.refworld.org/docid/3ae6b3930.html>, accessed 12 May 2022.

United Nations, Headquarters Agreement, Applicability of the Obligation to Arbitrate under Section 21 of the United Nations, Headquarters Agreement of 26 June 1947, Advisory opinion of 26 April 1988, I.C.J. Reports 1988.

United Nations, Report of the Informal Inter-Allied Committee on the Future of the Permanent Court of International Justice, 10 February 1944.

United Nations, Statute of the International Court of Justice, 18 April 1946, available at: <https://www.refworld.org/docid/3deb4b9c0.html>, accessed 12 May 2022.

United Nations Committee on the Elimination of Racial Discrimination (CERD), CERD General Recommendation XXX on Discrimination Against Non Citizens (1 October 2002), para. 4.

United Nations General Assembly (UNGA), Res 2145(XXI) (27 October 1966) UN Doc A/RES/2145(XXI).

United Nations Security Council (UNSC), UNSC Res 276 (1970) (30 January 1970) UN Doc S/RES/276 (1970).

United Nations Treaty Series (UNTS), Convention on the High Seas (adopted 29 April 1958, entered into force 3 January 1963) 450 UNTS 11.

United Nations Treaty Series (UNTS), Convention on the Continental Shelf (adopted 29 April 1958, entered into force 10 June 1964) 499 UNTS 311.

United Nations Treaty Series (UNTS), Convention on the Territorial Sea and the Contiguous Zone (adopted 29 April 1958, entered into force 22 November 1964) 516 UNTS 205.

United Nations Treaty Series (UNTS), Convention on Fishing and Conservation of the Living Resources of the High Seas (adopted 29 April 1958, entered into force 20 March 1966) 559 UNTS 285.

Vec M, From the Congress of Vienna To the Paris Peace Treaties of 1919, in: Bardo Fassbender and Anne Peters (eds), The Oxford Handbook of the History of International Law (Oxford University Press 2012).

Wolfrum R and Roeben V (eds), Developments of International Law in Treaty Making (Springer 2005).

Zimmermann A and Hofmann R (eds), Unity and Diversity of International Law (Duncker & Humblot 2006).

Zimmermann A, Tomuschat C and Oellers-Frahm K (eds), The Statute of the International Court of Justice (Oxford University Press 2006), 1141–1170.

CHAPTER 15

2020 AIIB Legal Conference Report

*Georgia Papalexiou**

1 Introduction – Funding International Organizations: Innovations of Law and Practice

On 3 and 4 December 2020, the Asian Infrastructure Investment Bank (AIIB) held its fourth annual Legal Conference, the first one to be held virtually. The Legal Conference consisted of four webinars which helped participants gain a greater understanding of the legal challenges and opportunities that international development organizations (IDOs) encounter in the course of their funding operations by examining the law and practice governing their funding mobilization. The Legal Conference assembled a very accomplished set of speakers with a diverse array of experiences: experts representing other international financial institutions (IFIs), experts from governments or agencies, leading practitioners from global law firms and distinguished representatives from academia. The audience itself also consisted of a highly accomplished group of individuals, well represented across different sectors.

Over two days, four panels, each chaired by a member of AIIB's legal department, addressed the following topics: (I) the role of international organizations (IOs) in the development of local capital markets; (II) the legal status of IOs; (III) innovations in resource mobilization; and (IV) innovations in structure and development.

2 The Role of International Organizations in the Development of Local Capital Markets

The first panel discussed a number of critical matters with respect to the role of IOs in the development of domestic capital markets.

The rapid growth of debt capital markets in emerging economies shows the great potential of these markets and reflects the growing domestic liquidity. However, the economic challenges presented by the COVID-19 pandemic and

* Counsel, Asian Infrastructure Investment Bank, georgia.papalexiou@aiib.org.

the resulting increase in currency risks underline the need for further development of liquid and self-sustaining local capital markets. It was highlighted that debt markets are crucial sources of capital funds, especially for the purpose of closing the financing gap in sectors like infrastructure. One of the key functions of IFIs is to stimulate and encourage the development of domestic capital markets. There are several ways in which IFIs contribute to the development of domestic capital markets: through the credit enhancement of bonds, IFIs enable first time issuers to access capital markets by offering credit enhancement to their issuances, whereas by issuing onshore local currency denominated bonds themselves, IFIs diversify their funding sources of local currency which they can further deploy in investment operations by offering local currency loans to their clients.

The benefits of IFI presence in local capital markets were discussed at length by the panel. First, the important demonstration and signaling effect: IFI borrowing in local currency stimulates the development of local capital markets as the bonds of a triple A issuer serve as an alternative pricing benchmark to the local government bond market. Second, the reform of the local regulatory framework: IFIs, as trend setters, work closely with local authorities and regulators with a view to establishing functioning and more transparent securities markets with improved issuer and investor friendly processes which include, among others, favorable issuance and disclosure rules, credible money market indexes, functional settlements systems that can guarantee sound delivery versus payment procedures in order to mitigate any risks in the settlement of local currency transactions, flexible account opening processes with local banks, registrars and custodians, properly functioning depositories, an appropriate investor base, clear rules for admission to trading, specifically adapted to cater for IFIs' status, and comprehensive use of proceeds requirements. Third, IFI lending in local currency has become an important tool in mitigating currency exposures of borrowers who seek to manage their foreign currency risks. It has also contributed to the expansion of the investor base by introducing new investors to several local capital markets, including those seeking exposure to a specific currency who were previously excluded due to regulatory restrictions, as well as those who seek to gain exposure to a certain currency without being exposed to local credit risks. With respect to local currency projects, their financing through onshore local currency issuances allows for longer maturities, while IFI participation improves their creditworthiness.

The discussion, finally, shifted to the contribution of IFIs to the development of China's debt capital markets, with a brief reference to Panda Bonds, which are Ren Min Bi (RMB) denominated bonds issued by international issuers in China's domestic capital markets. It was noted that a lot of foreign exchange controls that China has had in place for a long time were eased thanks to the presence of IFIs, allowing therefore other international investors to finally access Chinese debt capital markets. Among other benefits, those of particular importance are product innovation, more transparent regulatory frameworks and more robust disclosure regimes for issuers. A number of key developments from the recent past of China's debt capital markets were mentioned. In 2015, the regulatory framework was reformed allowing three new types of foreign investors to access China's domestic capital markets, the Interbank Bond Market: IOs, foreign central banks and sovereign wealth funds, while in 2016, the scope of permitted international investors expanded further to include foreign institutional investors, mainly commercial banks, insurance companies, securities firms, fund management companies, asset management companies and their investment funds products. In 2015, China's Interbank Foreign Exchange Market allowed IOs to become members of the foreign exchange trading system and introduced simplified procedures for foreign institutional investors in relation to foreign exchange registration procedures, currency conversion, funds remittance and repatriation. Finally, in November 2020, the restrictions for qualified financial institutions to invest in the Interbank Bond Market, as well as the futures market were also eased. IOs have also been a driving force in product innovation in China's debt capital markets. The International Bank for Reconstruction and Development was the first IFI to issue a Singapore dollar (SDR) denominated bond in 2016, which was also the first ever SDR denominated bond offering in China and the first SDR denominated bond which settled in RMB. It was finally also noted that Chinese regulators take a more pragmatic approach to introducing new rules by testing a new approach first through oral guidance to issuers, which is then transformed into a draft on which market participants are invited to provide comments before a rule, accompanied by guidance in the form of Q&As and operational manuals, is finally crystalized in writing and released.

3 The Legal Status of International Organizations

The second session focused on the legal status of IOs. Distinguished legal practitioners shared their views on issues related to IDOs' privileges and immunities, as well as economic sanctions, focusing on the approach of certain jurisdictions in relation to IDO capital raising and IDO legal capacity and authority to enter into derivatives transactions.

One panelist elaborated on the privileges and immunities of IOs in light of a recent U.S. Supreme Court decision where it was considered whether immunity from suit granted to IOs is analogous to the immunity from suit granted to foreign governments in the United States (U.S.). It was noted that the concept of immunity for IOs is not rooted in equality, as is the case for state immunity, but rather in operational necessity, including the desire to avoid state interference and undue litigation costs. The immunities provided to IOs, and in particular immunity from suit and legal process, protect IOs from unilateral control by a member nation over the activities of the IO within its territory. Because IO immunity is rooted in operational necessity, it is often referred to as functional immunity, and in practice it resembles restrictive immunity, which is confined to suits involving foreign states' public assets and does not extend to cases arising out of foreign states' strictly commercial acts.

The question was raised as to how a particular IO assesses its possible exposure to be sued in the U.S. It was noted that, as a first step, the source of the IO's immunity should be determined. Once the source of the immunity has been determined, the next inquiry is about the scope of such immunity and whether a potential waiver exists. It was noted that, in fact, many IOs expressly waive immunity from suit in connection with their fundraising activities. However, the prevailing practice is that waiver language is narrowly construed to allow only the type of suit by the type of plaintiff that would benefit the IO over the long term. This means in practice that courts will typically infer a waiver in the context of commercial transactions, including suits brought by debtors, creditors and bondholders, on the theory that otherwise private parties would be hesitant to transact with IOs.

The discussion then shifted to the analysis of U.S. regulations regarding capital raising by IDOs. It was noted that one of the principal challenges that need to be addressed for financings in the U.S. relate to IDO compliance with the various securities laws administered by the U.S. Securities and Exchange Commission (the SEC). The two main pieces of legislation were adopted in the aftermath of the Great Depression as a result of what appeared to be abuses in offerings of securities during the late 1920s and are the following: the Securities Act of 1933 (the Securities Act), which addresses mainly offerings of securities by corporations, trusts or other types of organizations, and the Securities Exchange Act of 1934 that addresses a broad range of matters, such as regulation of stock exchanges, financial intermediaries, like broker dealers, and information provided by issuers after their issuance of securities. The Securities Act provides a comprehensive regulatory scheme for capital raising in the U.S. through a broad and overarching requirement that every public offer and sale of a security must be registered with the SEC unless there's an exemption. The SEC registration process is quite rigorous and can be difficult to complete, both for corporate issuers and for foreign governments. To allow for fewer delays, the SEC has created an innovative system known as shelf registration, under which issuers can register a large amount of securities and have the SEC clear a generic prospectus, allowing issuers to sell securities whenever they see a market window. This approach provides issuers with immense flexibility in deciding when to sell securities, but also reduces the need for a long form prospectus containing a great detail of information about issuers by allowing short form prospectuses that cleverly incorporate by reference annual and other interim reports that have already been filed with the SEC. It should be noted, though, that the SEC has never actually issued generally applicable rules for these issuers, requiring in effect each issuer to ask for permission to set up a debt shelf registration statement for ongoing and continuous offerings of debt securities. However, over the years, the SEC has improved and introduced enhanced features of shelf registration for corporate issuers, by allowing them, for example, to register securities with the SEC virtually on demand – a streamlined filing process under which there is no delay between filing a registration statement and the ability to use it to sell securities (the Automatic Shelf Registration). The Automatic Shelf Registration allows eligible issuers to avoid delays, which further provides a large measure of certainty to corporate issuers in hitting market windows not available to IDOs under the schedule B shelf registration route. Another enhancement is the ability to pay the SEC registration filing fee on a "pay as you go" (with each offering) basis, rather than all up-front. The "pay as you go" system is currently not available for foreign governments or IDOs, but is a feature which would certainly be good to have and could facilitate registered offerings by the SEC. One last challenge which was discussed was the SEC registration process itself and the amount of time it often requires to complete. Although a number of IDOs are exempt from SEC registration by the U.S. Congress, since 1996 the SEC has crafted new exemptions to facilitate capital raising and also expand investment opportunities for other U.S. investors. It was highlighted that this is an area which could be further explored and expanded, especially in order to include new IDOs that are well supported by numerous countries and carry out an important mission.

The panel then discussed issues relating to the legal status and immunities applicable to IFIs from a Chinese (PRC) law perspective, with a particular focus on how a PRC court will look at the jurisdictional and capacity/authority issues relating to IDOs. It was noted that unlike other jurisdictions such as the United Kingdom or the U.S., where the legal personality of certain IDOs is recognized by specific legislation, under PRC law there is no domestic regulation which specifically applies to or regulates IDOs or their establishment. In this case, PRC courts will usually start from the principle of IDO immunity, looking to first assess whether the IDO has waived such immunity. PRC courts have always adopted absolute immunity, which means that only if there is a clear waiver of immunity by the relevant IDO, the PRC court will further proceed with its assessment of the legal capacity of the IDO. If there is no express waiver of immunity, the PRC court will not be able to assert jurisdiction over a claim against an IDO. In case of a clear waiver of immunity, if the PRC court identifies a foreign element in the relevant transaction, it will apply international treaties which have been acceded to by China. The PRC court will also look at the constitutional documents of the IDO in order to determine whether it has the legal personality and capacity to enter into a transaction.

Finally, the panel discussed the issue of economic sanctions in IDO funding and operations. Economic sanctions can be imposed by the United Nations (U.N.) under chapter 7 of the U.N. Charter. Most IOs abide by U.N. economic sanctions as they feel that this is incumbent on them as a member of the U.N. system. Some IOs are part of the U.N. system, having an agreement with the U.N. system in place to give them enough autonomy, however when it comes to issues like U.N. economic sanctions, they would observe them. Most IDOs observe U.N. economic sanctions as a matter of due deference to the fact that they have as shareholders U.N. members. Alongside U.N. economic sanctions, most IDOs observe also national economic sanctions, in particular the U.S. economic sanctions system, which is probably the largest and most robust, the European Union economic sanctions system and the economic sanctions imposed by the U.K. Treasury. It was explained that U.S. sanctions essentially work because they govern access to the U.S. financial system. If there is a sanctions consideration, the U.S. banking system cannot be used for purposes of making funds transfers, whether on the fundraising side or on the lending side. Any transaction in U.S. dollars is quite likely to involve the U.S. financial system. U.S. sanctions apply to U.S. persons, which in general encompass U.S. citizens, U.S. permanent residents, and any person who is physically located in the U.S. In case an IDO has a member which is on U.S. sanctions list, U.S. sanctions considerations should be analyzed with respect to the capital of such IDO. Capital structures at IDOs involve paid in capital and callable capital. The question then becomes how an IDO could receive capital from a shareholder that is on a sanctions list, what precautions does one need to take in order to make sure that that transaction or transfer is not frozen or otherwise interfered with, or what is the situation with IDOs which might be asked by a shareholder to return capital.

U.S. sanctions are also relevant in the funding process itself because underwriters have high standards with respect to their counterparties. The underwriting agreement for a bond issue includes a series of representations and warranties to be provided by the issuer, a few of which relate to U.S. economic sanctions: Is the issuer doing business with any sanctioned entity (be it a sovereign, an individual or a corporation)? Or how are the issuance proceeds going to be used? Then, of course, due consideration is given to the swaps that are entered into in the context of a bond issuance, as swap counterparties have their own standards with respect to economic sanctions. And when it comes to project operations, economic sanctions considerations have practical implications on a variety of aspects starting with project design missions and the ability of IDO personnel to travel and spend money in the country that the IDO staff are being sent to.

4 Innovations in Resource Mobilization

The discussion then shifted to innovations in resource mobilization for IDO funding, focusing on a few paradigms of organizational structures, such as the Global Fund to Fight AIDS, Tuberculosis and Malaria, as well as the GAVI alliance. The examples of treaty-based organizations without equity base and with a relatively narrow scope of activities and the examples of entities established pursuant to a resolution of a conference or organizations established in the form of trust funds were highlighted to give prominence to the fact that new business models are adopted for the implementation of new funding modalities.

The case of the Green Climate Fund (GCF) as a unique funding vehicle was then examined. GCF is the world's largest climate change fund. It was established in 1992 under the U.N. Framework Convention on Climate Change (the Convention). Based on its business model, developed countries shall contribute financial resources to meet the costs incurred by developing countries in complying with their obligations under the Convention. GCF has 24 member countries, 50% of which are developed countries. The mandate of GCF is set out in its governing instrument and consists of the following pillars: a shift towards low emissions by providing support to developing countries to limit or reduce greenhouse gas emissions and further adapt to the impact of climate change; the provision of adequate financing to catalyze climate investment in the public and private sector; and the promotion of environmental, social and economic country-driven programs in full transparency and accountability. The Board of GCF is entrusted with the full responsibility and authority to manage resources and govern GCF. In terms of capital raising, GCF functions on a contributions-based system, with voluntary contributions from developed countries in accordance with their obligations under the Convention but has also the authority to raise additional funding from other sources, as financial contributions can also be received from countries which have not acceded to the Convention, and other public or private entities. Contributions are not earmarked for specific purposes. Another interesting feature is that contributions in the form of loans should be accompanied by a grant contribution to GCF to cover administrative costs, and a grant contribution to be used as cushion for non-performing loans. In order to raise funds, GCF usually holds a series of consultation meetings with various donors, which is followed by a formal pledging conference where countries pledge to contribute funds to GCF. These commitments, which are purely political, are then crystalized into contribution agreements which are negotiated and executed with the support of GCF's Secretariat so that compliance with GCF's policies can be ensured. Any special conditions imposed by donors must be approved by the Board. Contribution agreements are backed by actual cash resources under the form of promissory notes, and once a minimum level of contributions has been received, GCF is able to commit those resources to fund projects and programs, known as the GCF Commitment Authority. The above explain the uniqueness of GCF's funding modalities. Of course, it was noted, GCF resources are supplemented by more conventional income sources, such us returns on equity investments, investment income earned from trust funds, as well as reflows from outgoing loans through interest and principal payments.

Most IDOs finance their activities through bond issuances in the international capital markets, as donations from member countries are mostly deployed through the establishment of trust funds. Thanks to IDO activity, bond markets have developed considerably over the last years allowing for a wider variety of products and specialized forms of themed bonds, a recent example of which are bonds that have been launched to finance the fight against the COVID-19 pandemic. Climate awareness bonds were an innovative product 15 years ago and their development was rather slow during the first few years. Nowadays, a variety of themed bonds are available to investors. Main types of themed bonds are green bonds, social bonds and sustainability-linked bonds, where financial and structural characteristics can vary depending on whether the issuer achieves predefined sustainability or ESG (environmental social governance) objectives. The International Capital Markets Association (ICMA) plays a key role in the development of these frameworks by creating principles and guidelines. The main topic of discussion is whether a market driven entity like ICMA should be in the driving seat of developing new ways of structuring bonds, or whether more robust legislation should be put in place to regulate such investment activities and ensure the credibility of new structures.

Finally, the panel briefly elaborated on initiatives taking place in the context of smart infrastructure, the idea of using corporate funds and venture capital to develop integrated smart city projects to manage energy consumption, building use and traffic control. The role of IDOs in the deployment of new technologies that are being implemented globally in infrastructure projects was highlighted by one of the speakers. As new technologies become more embedded into projects, IDOs should safeguard policies which protect affected people against environmental, social and health risks by discussing policy initiatives with governments and the people that they serve, as the choices made regarding regulation have a significant impact on the technology and vice versa. The panel concluded by agreeing that effective policy and smart regulation will help achieve the necessary balance between the implementation of new technologies in smart city projects and the protection of citizens' privacy, freedom of expression and national security.

5 Innovations in Structure and Development

The last session focused on innovations in funding structures. The example of the U.S. Agency for International Development (USAID) was analyzed first. USAID has been providing U.S. foreign development assistance, mainly through contracts and grants, for the last 60 years. During that time, due to the dramatic shift in the world economy and the world stage, new ways of channeling financial flows into sectors in need have been developed. Solicitation and stepping into the world of private sector by creating synergies and alliance models through co-investing are some of these examples. The reality of operating within the confines of government restrictions pushes government agencies like USAID to find creative ways to use such limitations in the right way, such as by promoting more inclusive and sustainable business practices in corporations, or by catalyzing investment and mobilizing financing. Engaging with communities, with non-governmental organizations (NGOs) as well as with local companies has allowed USAID to detect financing gaps which it tries to fill by providing funding in exchange for projects which meet certain development goals, even when such projects are not going to be profitable. Traditional methods are also used side by side with innovative structures: the provision of technical assistance to projects in order to reduce barriers to entry, de-risk investments, investments in a value or supply chain, pooling government funding with private sector funding for different small and medium sized enterprises and multistakeholder alliances, the so called *co-creation*, by bringing stakeholders together for research and development agreements with the private sector, or even the *gift authority*, which allows USAID to pull money from various donors like the Gates Foundation and create a bigger pool of funding that is slightly less restrictive to do things with.

The panel then moved on discussing other funding structures by using as an example the financial instruments deployed by the European Investment Bank (EIB), which mainly invests funds coming from a third party or takes a guarantee from third parties to support its activities with a particular focus on the European Union (EU). The budget of the EU has its plans and five-year cycles, the *budgetary periods*, and is implemented either at member state level, under a shared management model, or through the European Commission (EC) which can further entrust some of the budget to other entities, EIB being one of them. The EC has created a guarantee instrument called the European Fund for Sustainable Development, focusing, among others, on the following thematic investment windows: sustainable energy and connectivity; micro, small and medium-size enterprises financing; sustainable agriculture; rural development and agribusiness; sustainable cities; and digital for development. The innovative feature of this structure is that instead of using funded instruments, the main instrument used is guarantees, which means that the funding doesn't have to come up-front. There is normally a funding of some kind of a provisioning race, depending on the riskiness of the operations that would be covered by the guarantee. Another innovative feature of the above financing structure, and interesting from an accounting point of view in terms of balance sheet treatment, is the requirement for a co-investment by the implementing partner, requiring the latter to put in own resources each time the EC provides a budgetary guarantee in order to align the interests of the implementing partner though a skin in the game requirement.

The question of how does an entity access funds under these instruments was then discussed. The process was described as fairly complicated and includes the following: the first step is an assessment of the ability of the entity to manage EU funds – a fairly sophisticated piece of legislation called the Financial Regulation comes into play, which comprises the financial rules applicable to the budget of the EU, the basic principle of which is the following: if the EC intends to allow an entity to implement part of the budget under this indirect management, it must be sure that that entity can offer the same level of protection as applies when the EC implements the budget directly. The entity needs to go through a pillar assessment of a deep dive into procedures and contractual standards, even further complicated by the fact that some of the rules that sit behind these elements are not actually in place very long.

The focus on implementation of the EU budget has shifted over the last few years to cover not only the cost of *what* the EU invests in, but also *how* should the EU invest. And this policy is really evident now throughout the applicable legislation and the governance structures, and it goes beyond the more obvious policy areas such as quality or sustainable development into areas that have not been foreseen before. When implementing the EU budget, entities which find themselves in a long list of dishonorable situations varying from bankruptcy to breach of tax obligations, professional misconduct, fraud, child labor, or having committed an irregularity, which is a very wide concept in EU law, introducing an additional complexity, are excluded.

6 Conclusion

The contribution of IOs in the development of domestic capital markets is undisputable. IFIs stimulate and encourage the development of domestic capital markets through the credit enhancement of local currency denominated bonds which are issued by third parties, or by issuing onshore local currency denominated bonds themselves. In most cases such onshore issuances are accompanied by a reform of the local regulatory framework to make it issuer friendly for foreign issuers. Usually, the process is long but rewarding as it leads to an enlarged investor base and better functioning as well as more transparent securities markets.

Privileges and immunities as well as economic sanctions are relevant issues with respect to IO capital raising. Immunity from suit granted to IOs in the U.S. is analogous to the immunity from suit granted to foreign governments in the U.S., but the concept of immunity for IOs is not rooted in equality, as is the case for state immunity, but rather in operational necessity, including the desire to avoid state interference and undue litigation costs. Many IOs expressly waive immunity from suit in connection with their fundraising activities, but the waiver language is narrowly construed to allow only the type of suit by the type of plaintiff that would benefit the IO over the long term. From a U.S. regulatory perspective, the Securities Act is mostly relevant for IO capital raising in the U.S. Every public offer and sale of a security must be registered with the SEC unless there's an exemption. To allow for fewer delays, the SEC has created an innovative system known as shelf registration. Most IOs issue securities in the U.S. via the Schedule B Shelf Registration route. Economic sanctions are another important topic in the context of IDO funding. Most IOs abide by U.N. economic sanctions, alongside a number of national economic sanctions, in particular the U.S. economic sanctions system, the EU economic sanctions system and the economic sanctions imposed by the U.K. Treasury.

Innovations in resource mobilization for IDO funding show the demand for greater flexibility in order to meet the growing capital raising needs of IOs.

There are more and more examples of treaty-based organizations without equity base and with a relatively narrow scope of activities, or cases of entities established pursuant to a resolution of a conference, or even organizations established in the form of trust funds. Product innovation is another element which underlines IOs' need for new funding modalities. Themed bonds are a developing area with room for market creativity and very adaptable to the surrounding circumstances – the recent case of COVID-19 pandemic bonds being a prime example.

Innovations in funding structures also include solicitation and stepping into the world of private sector by creating synergies and alliance models through co-investing. Engaging with communities, NGOs and local companies allows IOs to detect financing gaps which they then try to fill by using innovative structures alongside traditional methods: the provision of technical assistance, de-risking investments, pooling government funding with private sector funding or even pooling money from various donors. The financial instruments deployed by EIB constitute another innovative funding structure. EIB mainly invests funds coming from a third party or takes a guarantee from third parties to support its activities. The European Fund for Sustainable Development, which is an instrument deployed by the EC, uses guarantees instead of funded products. Another innovative feature is the requirement for a co-investment by the implementing partner, requiring the latter to put in own resources each time the EC provides a budgetary guarantee. However, in some cases, the process of deploying such innovative products is described as complicated as these instruments are usually established through detailed and sophisticated pieces of legislation which may prove that their theoretical conception is easier than their application in practice.

www.ingramcontent.com/pod-product-compliance
Lightning Source LLC
LaVergne TN
LVHW020632300926
849161LV00004B/681